January 14, 1990

Jenny —

Sometimes our lives are filled with too many words.
...Feast your eyes.

I love you like a sister.

Beth —

LEGACY OF LIGHT

LEGACY OF LIGHT

EDITED BY CONSTANCE SULLIVAN

INTRODUCTION BY PETER SCHJELDAHL

ESSAYS BY GRETEL EHRLICH, ROBERT STONE,

RICHARD HOWARD, AND DIANE JOHNSON

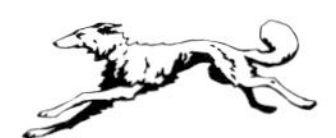

A POLAROID BOOK ALFRED A. KNOPF NEW YORK 1987

THIS IS A BORZOI BOOK
PUBLISHED BY ALFRED A. KNOPF, INC.

Prepared and produced by the Publications Department of Polaroid Corporation.
Published in the United States by Alfred A. Knopf, Inc., New York,
and simultaneously in Canada by Random House of Canada Limited, Toronto.
Distributed by Random House, Inc., New York.

Library of Congress Cataloging-in-Publication Data

Legacy of light.

1. Photography, Artistic. 2. Instant photography.
I. Sullivan, Constance. II. Ehrlich, Gretel.
TR654.L443 1987 779'.0973'074013 87-45496
ISBN 0-394-56365-4

Manufactured in the United States of America

First Edition

Front cover: Jan Groover, Untitled, 1986
Back cover: Michael Spano, *Flower Bed*, 1984

CONTENTS

PREFACE

The Polaroid photographs in *Legacy of Light* were assembled from hundreds produced over the last thirty years by some of the finest American photographers and artists. They have brought to the materials of instant photography the insight, expressiveness, and strong individual vision that characterize all good photography.

The book is organized thematically in order to provide a clear approach to a broad survey. Evocative essays addressing the subjects of landscape, portraiture, the nude, and still life precede each section of pictures. In these, noted novelists and poets Gretel Ehrlich, Robert Stone, Richard Howard, and Diane Johnson consider ideas and concerns essential to the photographs rather than offer critical commentary. Their writing conveys views that although not related to specific photographs are very relevant to them—to their imagery as well as to the concepts that inform them. The two forms of expression thus enhance one another, enlarging our understanding and appreciation of each. In his lively introduction, art critic and poet Peter Schjeldahl places the invention of the instant photograph in a cultural context, offering his responses to and perceptions about the work in these pages.

This collection brings together classic Polaroid photographs by such renowned photographers as Ansel Adams, Paul Caponigro, Marie Cosindas, Imogen Cunningham, Walker Evans, and Minor White with new work by contemporary masters like Robert Frank, Lucas Samaras, Chuck Close, and David Hockney. Approximately a third of the anthology is devoted to work by younger, less well known picture-makers including Bill Burke, Jan Groover, Nancy Hellebrand, Barbara Kasten, and Michael Spano. Each is represented by several examples in order to give a sense of the photographer's larger body of work. The limitations of space made it impossible to include more than a sampling of experimental work and images by emerging artists.

These photographs were made with a wide variety of cameras, from the earliest Polaroid Land cameras to the more recent SX-70 and Spectra System cameras, to 4 × 5, 5 × 7, and 8 × 10 view cameras modified with Polaroid backs, to the Polaroid 20 × 24 studio camera and the room-sized camera at the Museum of Fine Arts in Boston. The selection includes prints from instant negatives made in silver and platinum, and by the Fresson process, as well as unique positive prints.

These images were chosen principally because they express authentic and particular visions. In addition to being pleasing to look at, the photographs expand our awareness of the experience of seeing in ways both subtle and dramatic. It is hoped the reader will share in the pleasure of that experience.

CONSTANCE SULLIVAN

THE INSTANT AGE

They rage against materialism, as they call it, forgetting that there has been no material improvement that has not spiritualized the world.

—OSCAR WILDE

An invention starts as a curiosity, extra to what seems necessary. We may regard it at first from a mental distance of amusement or amazement, as something bizarre or exotic. Then, if successful, the invention moves in, bringing pandemonium. Like a rearrangement of our furniture, it treacherously alters familiar terrain. It disrupts habits, roughs up values, and generally remolds us—dramatically, like the automobile; subtly, like the microchip—into different people in a different kind of world. The human spirit is stunned by this presumption on the part of *things*: inanimate devices insolently changing everything, ready or not, like it or not. But the spirit darkly adjusts, with mixed feelings of gain and loss and, almost always, with some quantum of released, surprising creative energy. Finally, the invention blends into our shared sense of what humans want, need, and are.

The many devices that comprise photography do more than exemplify this cycle: they illuminate it to the imagination. Because vision is the strongest human sense, because images are the lingua franca of an international century, because eyes are the windows of the soul—make your own list of reasons—photography, considered as the tree of which film, television, and mechanical reproduction are branches, is *the* modern invention for materializing spirit and spiritualizing matter. Photography has filled, filtered, and to some extent replaced reality in the epoch that began with its inception. We are the great-great-great-grandchildren of Daguerre.

This volume documents and celebrates the climax of the invention cycle for one of photography's most extraordinary advances: the so-called "instant photograph." The news is that this particular technological marvel is, suddenly, no longer new. Nor is its triumph any longer confined to its popular appeal. What in 1948 immediately captivated the amateur snapshooter, and today remains, in social use, emblematic of a culture of instant gratification, has quietly attained at least an equal footing with other serious types and techniques of camera art. I wonder if many photography professionals, even, are completely prepared for the assembled evidence of how far and how fast this improbable invention has come, spawning a host of exceedingly various accomplishments mature to the point of seeming quite classical.

I was astonished. "But these," I thought on first seeing the pictures, "are . . . *beautiful photographs*!" I had, I realized, an outdated sense of instant photography as a field still tentative, miscellaneous, experimental—or problematic, to name a condition we intellectuals sink into with sighs of contentment. Instead of problems, mainly solutions confronted me. Despite a few raw, quirky, and risky works (most from the late 1960s and early 1970s, a wildly experimental period in all the arts), it struck me that the instant-photography system has become just another tool in the photographer's kit: an instrument with a certain liability (lack of control over the developing process) offset by a distinct advantage (immediate checking of results). On further reflection, however, I decided that this is an instrument all the stranger for having won ostensible parity with other means of making photographs. Because it is a means with a difference.

As an aesthetic phenomenon, instant photography has a poetic—almost a metaphysic—all its own. Its hallmark is the unique, automatic, on-the-spot print. On the simplest material level—the level on which spirit, as Wilde suggests, is most profoundly galvanized—unique-print film is a coup of photographic technology at odds with that technology's famously reproductive, *multiple* logic. Although some of its processes do deliver negatives, instant photography is mainly an idiom of singularities—an aspect to stress because physical uniqueness is, of course, impossible to convey in a book. The unique print has a fine-art aura, a commonality with painting and sculpture, that helps to explain the medium's appeal to fine artists.

This fact of singularity informs any unique-print photograph at all, imparting a mental aroma to anybody's drawerful of SX-70 or Spectra snapshots. The medium's capacity to memorialize an occasion, in an image that is also a *thing*, makes for a species of folk magic that has permeated our culture. A laboratory in a wafer, a genie in a flat lamp, a hermetic light trap, the self-developing "instant" picture is as much a piece of reality as a document of it. Not truly instantaneous at all, this picture entails a duration that enhances its spell: the faintly suspenseful long moment of watching the image appear, a definitively contemporary experience of time that, if Proust were alive, would be good for some dozens of pages of the most angelic prose.

The universality and automatic wizardry of instant photography have two main consequences for artistic use of the medium. First, such use will engage a peculiarly sophisticated mass audience. In the nineteenth century, when properly educated middle-class persons could draw you a passing likeness and then tinkle you some Chopin on the family upright, technical (though perhaps not aesthetic) appreciation of painting and music was relatively quick and keen. So it is today with instant photography, in which most of us enjoy a certain competence that sharpens, though perhaps also prejudices, our eye. Second, the medium's facility erects a high hurdle for creativity. The very hardest thing about instant photography as a serious mode is probably how easy it is. Where so much effect comes so effortlessly, the narrow range of choice that remains must be brought to white heat. Like abstraction in painting and "free verse" in poetry, instant photography is so simple that only those with a certain genius can really master it.

Ansel Adams had genius if anyone ever does, of a sort very nineteenth-century in both style and appeal. I used to resist his work as old-fashioned, until the man's sheer, radiant *aptitude* beat me into admiration. While looking at originals from Adams's early foray into instant photography, it became clear that, beginning in the 1950s, he took charge of the Polaroid Land camera like an animal trainer making a tiger roll over to have its tummy rubbed. The incredible harmonies of tone and value (white/black, warm/cool) he managed with that earliest, peel-apart film are startling in the original. Turning the prints slightly sideways, it was possible to make out their relief of gummy emulsion. Full-face again, the pressed goo resolved into Adamsian atmospheric deep space, singing with light. The object in my hand—sole relic of a moment when Adams peered at a landscape and decided that God had arranged it acceptably—seemed to me pure alchemy: lead into gold.

Now compare Adams's approach with the later, antithetical, utterly twentieth-century one of another great photographer, Walker Evans. No less than that of Adams, Evans's use of the medium was a kind of star turn or cameo performance; but where Adams, making a rudimentary technique approximate high-quality conventional photography, suppressed its idiosyncrasies, Evans exalted them. He took an SX-70 camera on the road in search of examples of an accustomed subject matter—forlorn small-town America—that would interact with such peculiarities of the medium as its affinity for hypersaturated color and its generally glossy, artificial look. Thus the livid russet and electric blue of a decrepit theater ignite a scene of loss, and an exceedingly low-tech ice-cream sign takes on special poignance in the high-tech picture.

Like a poet writing in slang, Evans makes us feel that he is doing something we can do, too—or could do, if we had the maddeningly elusive knack of the poet (always somehow more a measure of what is left out than of what is shown). He makes it look as easy as, for him, it was. Adams, on the contrary, makes pictures that look all but impossible, convincing us that we could rival such results, if ever, only after years of training and practice. These two tones—the democratic vernacular of Evans, the aristocratic formality of Adams—have parallels in any art, of course. But they gain a specific timbre in and from instant photography, with its definitive features of universality and ease. Observe, accordingly, how Adams succeeds by making all thought of the medium dissolve into contemplation of his mastery, and how Evans succeeds by apparently surrendering to the medium, as if the picture more or less took itself.

Between these two poles—the medium subsumed, the medium in charge—stretches the whole possible spectrum of serious instant photography. No other pictures reproduced here strike me as being so purely at one or the other extreme as those of Evans and Adams. Every other photographer, including even the very formal Jan Groover, for instance, or the very demotic Mary Ellen Mark, engages in some complicated give-and-take with the medium. Groover's poetic formalism is masterful, all right—what Adams is to mountains she is to silverware, able to make knives and forks sing the visual equivalent of the "Hallelujah Chorus"—but she softens the edge of her own power by highlighting the artificiality of the process. Where Adams's formalism was foursquare and romantic, hers is exquisite and classicist. Working from the other extreme, Mark qualifies the shaggy spontaneity of Spectra sharpshooting by nonchalantly nailing, again and again, finesses of light and color that you or I might get by accident every hundred or so shots.

Besides formalism versus populism, the short history of instant photography offers another, even more dramatic opposition: between professional photographers of all kinds, on the one hand, and moonlighting fine artists, on the other. The latter, of whom the most notable here are Lucas Samaras, David Hockney, Chuck Close, William Wegman, and Andy Warhol, may be few in number, but theirs has been a disproportionate share of the most inventive and powerful instant photography. If their feats seem like beginner's luck, I think that is rather exactly what they are: the inspired clarity of the tyro for whom ignorance is, if not bliss, a state of open-mindedness. Hare to professionalism's tortoise, artistic sensibility jumps out to a big, although temporary, lead by responding speedily and freshly to anomalies of the new technology.

Lucas Samaras, the Greek-American artist who has set his provocative stamp on many visual mediums, is surely the most original practitioner of instant photography so far, especially in his hand-manipulated "Autopolaroids" and "Photo-transformations" of the late 1960s and early 1970s. Samaras fully capitalized on the objectness of the unique print, treating pictures of his own body as, in themselves, bodies of a kind. Caressing and punishing the prints into icons as beautiful as jewelry and as crude as wounds, he made a perversely brilliant art that exists simultaneously on a level of high technique and a level of feelings straight from the backbrain magma. Although flat and still, his self-portraits become a sort of kinetic sculpture in the mind. They are as much creatures as creations.

David Hockney, instant photography's other instant master, found in the new medium a new way of drawing. The essence of his devilishly clever SX-70 collages—which evoke Cubism, that most cerebral of realisms, in a spirit that partly parodies and partly rivals—is to describe a complex visual experience by assembling photographed fragments of it in an order approved by the seeing mind. An almost physical sense of *being there*, engrossed in the subject, is lyrically heightened, pointing up a tone of "presence" that is endemic to all instant photography. Hockney's way of framing his life-size Double Portraits underlines this tone. The frame is like a booth the two young men briefly inhabit, not so much posing for a picture as presenting themselves so that a picture can be made. This razor-thin distinction tilts our sense of the medium, which suddenly seems less a means of representation than a mode—occasion, protocol—of social appearance, a theater of manners.

Not only Hockney but most artists who have used instant photography show a characteristic matter-of-factness about the pictorial framing edge, perhaps conditioned by lifetimes of facing blank canvases. In the head shots by Close, Wegman, and Warhol (as in none by any professional), the frame feels like a preexisting zone, a box into which faces have been fitted. The crackling success of this approach strikes me as sheer serendipity, a happy accident of instant photography's aesthetic chemistry. Experienced photographers could never treat the frame so rigidly. For them, framing happens in the viewfinder as a decisive event, perhaps the most expressive demanded and permitted by photography; they regard format not as an arbitrary container but as a virtual philosophy of seeing, thinking, and feeling. It just so happens that the objectness of the process pays an aesthetic dividend—cheap, perhaps, but effective—when bolstered by objective, passive framing.

At the slow and steady pace recommended for victorious tortoises, meanwhile, professionals develop instant photography's expressive identity and potential on a sounder basis. A result of patient practice rather than flashy intuition, their progress is subtle. It may be useful, in gauging it, to ask how work that might have been done with any equipment is decisively altered by the employment of an "instant" process. I think the telltale signs, no less strong for being often unconscious, are usually a particular intentness, a congested warmth, a hanging on the moment, above all an intimacy—effects caused, I believe, by the medium's elimination of distance in time between choosing a subject and approving a picture of it. The result is a collapsed emotional distance between photographer and viewer. I am reminded of poet Frank O'Hara's seriocomic announcement in 1959 of a new literary movement he called "Personism": "The poem is at last between two persons instead of two pages." Many an instant photograph, of even the most seemingly neutral subject, gives me a similar feeling of tender, itchy, erotic closeness.

Given the premium that instant photography sets on effects of "presence," it is not surprising that the medium's two strongest genres should be, I am convinced, landscape and portraiture: the first entails maximum presence of viewer to subject (you are put into a place), the second maximum presence of subject to viewer (a person is brought to you). So insistent is this genre affinity that instant photographs of nudes and still lifes tend to be experienced as landscape-like or portrait-like. The two master genres even tend to magnetize each other, as in the facial topographies of Nancy Hellebrand and the place-portraiture of Philip Trager's Palladian villas, the latter as beautiful, it seems to me, as any photographs I have ever seen. In terms of erotic charge, instant photographs show a low potential for titillation (not generating enough distance for voyeurism) and a high potential for various kinds of embarrassment (self-consciousness is built in). Photographers using the medium are automatically alert to the comedy or the obscenity of subjects who are not what they think they are—observe Bill Burke's sickening shot of a Khmer Rouge Rambo. It is photography's preeminent medium for home truths.

The creative future of instant photography resides in these intrinsic aesthetic and emotional quirks, and in the extrinsic happy circumstance of mass familiarity with the medium. It is a fascinating fact that this most intimate of today's visual technologies is also the most widely practiced. No longer an alien object, instant photography is now all but second nature to us—an organic extension of our seeing, and thus of our thinking and feeling, knowing and becoming. As I have noted, such vast commonality tends to daunt merely individual artistry, unless that artistry is of a very high order. I have little doubt that the next true genius of photography will do his or her signal work in some instant process, and that he or she will draw as much on the medium's burgeoning vernacular tradition as on such elevated achievements as those here arrayed. This collection's imposing look of encyclopedic completeness is, finally and fortunately, a bit misleading, indicating the end only of a beginning. The Instant Age is just under way.

PETER SCHJELDAHL

LANDSCAPE

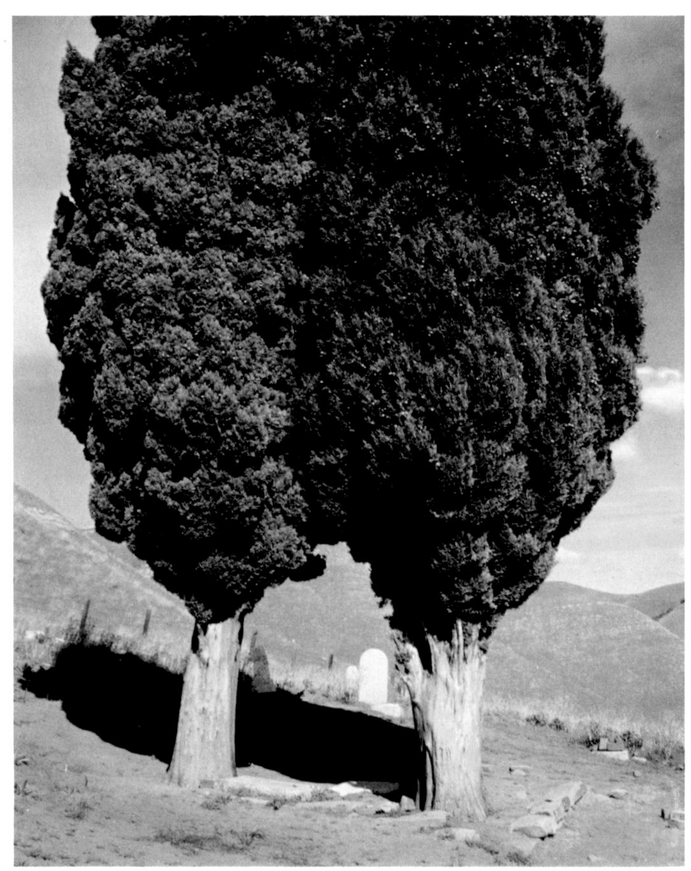

Ansel Adams · *Poplars, Cemetery near Mount Diablo, California* · 1960

Landscape does not exist without an observer, without a human presence. The land exists, but the "scape" is a projection of human consciousness, an image received. It is a frame we put around a single view and the ways in which we see and describe this spectacle represent our "frame of mind," what we know and what we seek to know.

Last year I spent a week on top of Mauna Kea, a Hawaiian mountain that rises sharply from sea level to nearly 14,000 feet. It is a dormant shield volcano with long slopes of reddish-black lava, hardened tides that have pooled on the outskirts of Hilo. Mauna Kea is sacred to native Hawaiians. It is the domain of Pali, a goddess whom legend describes as "beautiful, with a back as straight as a cliff and breasts rounded like moons." Mauna Kea's peak is also the site of five world-class observatories. There I joined several astronomers who were recording the last passes of Halley's Comet.

Their huge telescope lenses were trained on single views that gave back a "cometscape," a "galaxyscape"—exotic aperçus. From these physical details the astronomers were attempting to piece together an understanding of what might be the tiniest landscape: the universe at the moment of creation.

To think in such infinite and microscopic terms simultaneously had a disassembling effect. Every vista I viewed from my high perch seemed suddenly random and chancy—nothing more than a temporary arrangement of galactic dust. On the other hand, there was a sacred feeling about the peak. The cratered top was austere, snow-covered, barren, wind-whipped. A full moon rose behind the great domed observatories that themselves resembled moons. When the actual moon went into eclipse and the shadows the domes cast on the snow vanished, the sky darkened and I could see stars. I felt as if Pali, this snowbound Polynesian goddess, were watching me.

Native Hawaiians say that if you take a piece of rock from Mauna Kea, bad things will happen in your life until the rock is returned. The rock is all lava, and one piece looks like another. What the Hawaiians are saying is that a rock is a rock and at the same time it is a holy thing, it has its powers. Sacred or secular, what is the difference? If every atom inside our bodies was once a star, then it is all sacred and all secular at the same time.

One of the reigning notions of our culture is that the land is our adversary, that nature is a dirty thing (think of the double meaning of the word "soil") and that God put human beings here to dominate it, to make Edenic gardens out of the wasteland. We are the great-great-grandchildren of Cortés, the children of Emerson.

Cortés's missions to the New World had more to do with finding gold than with religious conversion. When he and his sailors were victorious over Montezuma, Cortés took possession of the land and its peoples. He branded his captives with hot irons and gave them to his sailors as slaves. As inheritors of this legacy, we have learned to make imperialistic gestures toward the earth. We wear as a badge of honor our ability to conquer, dominate, change, and tame, to bring to the ugly face of the "wasteland" a civilized appearance. Too late we have realized that in order to "possess" we have first dispossessed; that in order to "tame" we have committed many violations.

Emerson and the Transcendentalists were gentle and well-intentioned. By the time his essay *Nature* was published, in 1836, the terms "God" and "Nature" were being used interchangeably; and in at least some American minds God was to be found everywhere and sermons could, indeed, be found in stones. The American dream was once an agrarian dream. It inspired two approaches to nature in the nineteenth century: one was that of the human as romanticizer of wilderness; the other, based on the Jeffersonian idea, was that of the human as cultivator, gardener of the world.

But did the idea of landscape-as-garden arise from a fear of nature, or from a love of wild things? Either way, in the wrong hands this "civilizing" process in effect blinded us. It reduced the wildness, diversity, and transience of nature to a formula that said: this is a flower and this is a weed; this is sublime and this is ugly. As conquerors and as gardeners we came to a landscape with serious intentions: not simply to know, but to change; not just to visit, but to possess. Much that was done was good, much was bad. We presumed too much. We imposed on what we found; we could not cherish without embellishing or altering what was simply there.

I live on a ranch in Wyoming. We raise beef cattle and crops of grain and hay, but all around us is wildness. At night the mountain lions come down from their rock caves and kill fawns out of the herd. Black bears emerge from their dens hungry. We see their tracks overprinted by the cubs' smaller ones, coming and going from den to creek, den to winterkills. In June the elk bring their calves to a sage-covered bench to play. Directly below are our hayfields. Where our fences stop, their game trails begin. The native grasses we irrigate are for them too. At worst our two landscapes clash; at best, they blend.

Our ranch is an "end-of-the-road place," isolated by the ten-thousand-foot mountains that rise behind us. If I rode a horse north, I would not reach a fence or a town for three days. In the other direction there is no one view—it is all view, a hundred miles in three directions. The mountains behind us rose seventy million years ago. They're young and steep and still rising. The shallow seas that had covered Wyoming receded, leaving a colorful carpet of mudstones and sandstones: red, orange, green, gray, and white. The mountains rose and the basins fell, and the commotion of upthrusts, faults, and folds resulted in sheer rock faces of limestone, granite, and dolomite. Dinosaurs came and went.

On our lower meadow, a quarry worked by the American Museum of Natural History offered up twenty-five complete skeletons. The fossil record of the area is replete with early organisms: hundred-million-year-old sponges as well as the remains of saber-tooth tigers and mastodons who arrived much later. Some landscapes are surface—what we see out our back doors—while others start farther down in the earth.

On the other hand, a Wyoming landscape can be almost all sky. I try to catalogue the names for all the blues—Prussian, French, and Italian; indigo, periwinkle, powder, beryl, and cobalt; robin's egg, peacock, and eggshell; lapis and azure—and still there aren't enough words to describe the aerial landscape above.

Blues dominate, and in winter so does darkness. And because of the big sky and the long nights I notice stars and birds. There is a place below our ranch where two small creeks meet. Something is always happening there. A big culvert goes under the road, leading one stream to the other. One night a friend and I lay in the bed of my pickup and watched meteors shower the sky. Sprays of cosmic sparks bloomed and faded. In the morning a blue heron stood where the waters join: one leg in South Beaver Creek, one in North Beaver. Overhead a sparrow hawk rose out of a tree and cried as it followed one of the streams north. Then it circled back and near a cliff snatched a darting mud swallow out of the air. A belted kingfisher, perched on the edge of the big culvert, peered into the waters where they mixed, then dove. I thought of the meteor showers the night before. Had the stars become birds? When night fell, would the birds become meteors? I look to see, not to make sense of things.

Another day the landscape was a screen of bugs. A hatch of mayflies blackened the air, then vanished, replaced by bumblebees catapulting from currant bush to thistle. The screen of bugs became a front moving in. Tattered black clouds headed for me. All across the state the wind carried tree branches, dust from plowed fields, debris of all sorts, and transient winged seeds. When the storm centered over the ranch, the wind stopped. The clouds picked themselves apart and fell to the ground in wisps. The mist thickened and hung in the sagebrush. It carried the landscape away, or rather, the landscape became mist only, a blindness that was not black but blank. Then the ceiling rose as quickly as it had come down and slid against the granite face of the mountain behind me, rising and dropping as if taking part in the old geological tumult of landforms.

That night the clouds returned with rain. Branched lightning gave the landscape a ghostly hue: the greens, blues, and browns looked tarnished. Somehow the colors were all wrong and the landscape appeared false. But it was just another version of the same, changing thing.

I like to think of landscape not as a fixed place but as a path that is unwinding before my eyes, under my feet. John Muir, the botanist, writer, and conservationist, walked when he wanted to see things. He left his house in Wisconsin one day, walked to New York, north to Canada, south to Florida, and later walked from the Oakland ferry dock in California to the top of the Sierras. He walked thousands of miles in his life, bending down to examine a plant, digging into "treasuries of snow," climbing trees to experience a gale-force wind, teetering on a precipice to feel the thunder and spray of Yosemite Falls on his skin. There was nothing he did not find holy except, perhaps, sheep. He walked and walked, and the earth and the holiness of the earth came up through the soles of his feet.

To see means to stop, to breathe in and out. John Muir considered studying the history of a single raindrop for the rest of his life. To see and to know a place is a contemplative act. It means emptying our minds and letting what is there, in all its multiplicity and endless variety, come in. We talk about looking into someone's eyes as "seeing into" them. Why not look "into" the earth? If John Muir had pursued his study of the raindrop, he would have discovered the entire natural world.

Lilla, my eighty-year-old Hungarian friend, said, "I'm too religious to believe in religion. You don't have to believe in a sacred world. It slaps you in the face. It's everywhere." The root word in "religion" means "to bind." It is no mere coincidence that our feelings about a place take on spiritual dimensions. An old rancher once told me he thought the lines in his hand had come directly up from the earth, that the land had carved them there after so many years of work. We are bound to place. The Japanese poet and priest Ikkyu referred to any passionate connection as "red threads." Perhaps it is red thread that holds me here in Wyoming.

The ways in which we come to know a landscape are preliterate. "A sense of place" implies a sensory knowledge. It mounts up in our minds: empires of smells and sounds, textures and sights held fast by memory, flooding back again and again in such urgent, pungent ways as to let us reenter those places. A river slits its neck for us; the eerie sound a sandhill crane makes comes into our human throats as song; in the mountain fastness of granite cracks a pine tree grows, and we humans dive backward and forward in time, beginning seventy million years ago, when the mountains came into being. We rise with the landforms. We feel the upper altitudes of thin air, sharp stings of snow and ultraviolet on our flesh.

I have lived on Wyoming ranches for eleven years but was born in the Mediterranean climate of a coastal California town. No matter where we live as adults, the landscape or cityscape in which we grew up stains us with its indelible ink, as if the umbilical cord by which we were tethered to life carried not only nutrient liquids but also minerals, seawater, soil, and sun.

The first earthquake I experienced shook my sister, who was paralyzed with polio, out of bed. I grabbed my parakeet, Willy, ran outside, and lay down. To feel the ground move in this way was to learn what "ground" means in all senses of the word: ground as primary place, as movement, as the foundation of what is knowable—according to Webster's, "the surface which limits the downward extent of something."

Other California disasters taught me how to see. During one raging brushfire in which my sister and I had to move a herd of horses to the beach for safety, I saw a whole lemon grove go up in flames, and forever after I thought of lemons as orbs of fire, and recalled the smell of fire as sour.

There were quiet nights too—so quiet we could hear the seals barking on the channel islands. Their cries bounced against the mountains directly behind us and fell down on the roof of my head, poured into my ears so that when I woke I thought I was a seal floating.

All during our lives, in any and every place we live or visit, the sacramental landscape unrolls before us. It is our text. It is public and private, social and wild, political and aesthetic. To see—that is, to discover—is not an act of interpretation, of transfixing with preconceived ideas what is before us; rather, it is an act of surrender.

The writer and naturalist Barry Lopez talks about bowing to the earth. Too often we have confused bowing with kowtowing; bowing is a gesture of respect, of dignity, of mutuality. If the earth could stand up and bow back, perhaps it would. Maybe that is what an earthquake is all about.

Sometimes when I am walking or riding in heavy weather I imagine that it is leaving stains on me, and that if I were able to see the inside of my skin, I would see its marks: snow, rain, hail, frostbite, sun. Surrendering means stripping down, taking away every veil, every obstacle between ourselves and the earth. It means losing ourselves in the otherness of a place, delighting in its strangeness. To bend down and kiss a rock, as poet William Butler Yeats claimed to have done, is to seek equality, not dominance; it is to open ourselves to every small and ordinary thing for the larger purpose of knowing its truth. It is to become drenched, to be, in the words of Henry James, "one on whom nothing is lost"; it is to allow ourselves to be touched from above and below and within, to let a place leave its watermark on us. If we go out in order to find, not to impose, the landscape touches us and we it. Only then is a sense of place born.

GRETEL EHRLICH

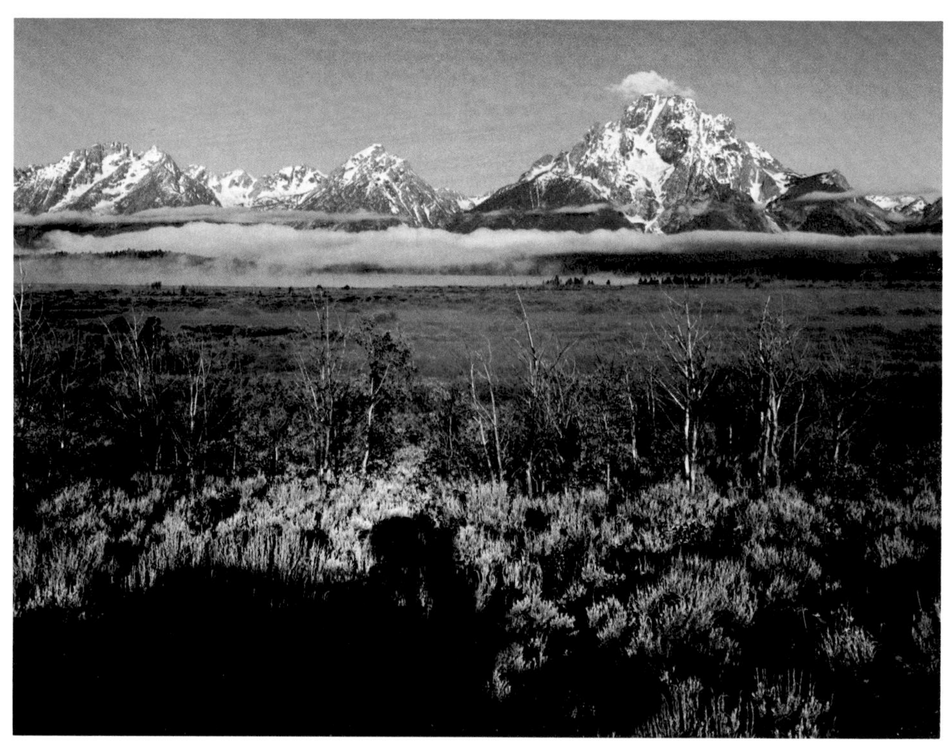

Ansel Adams · *The Tetons, Meadow and Fog* · c. 1965

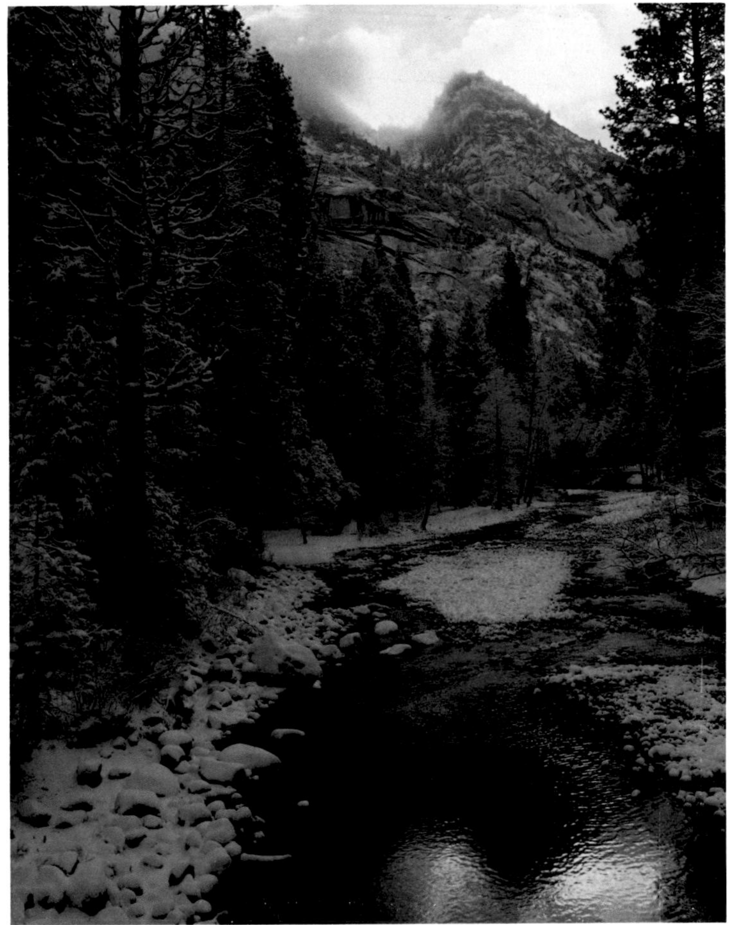

Ansel Adams · *Merced River, Winter, Yosemite National Park* · c. 1959

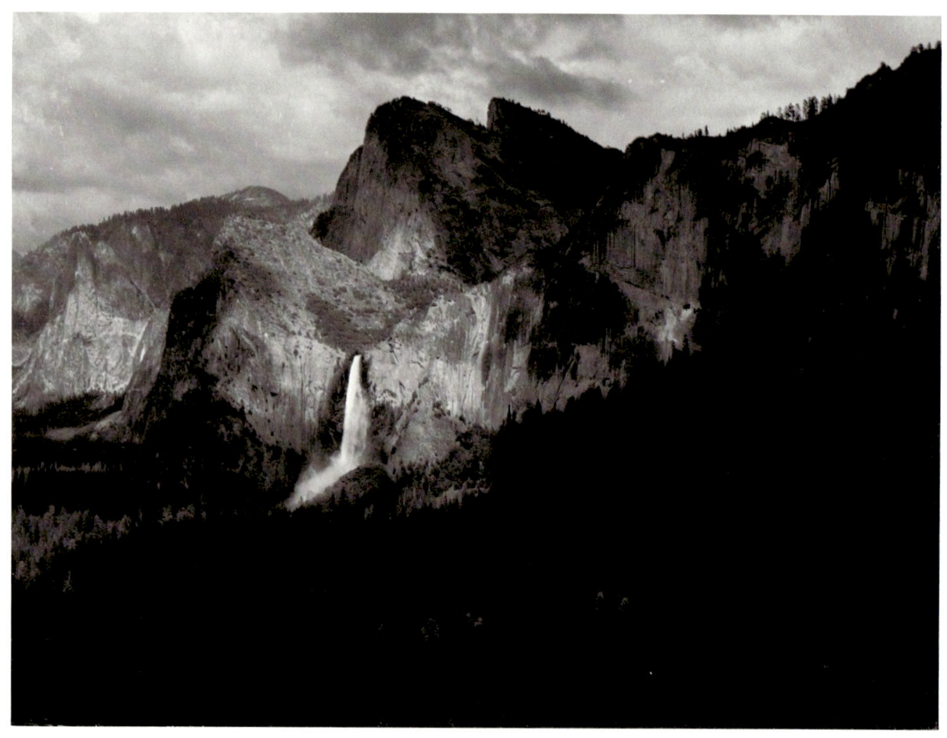

Ansel Adams · *Bridal Veil Fall and Cathedral Peaks, Yosemite National Park* · 1968

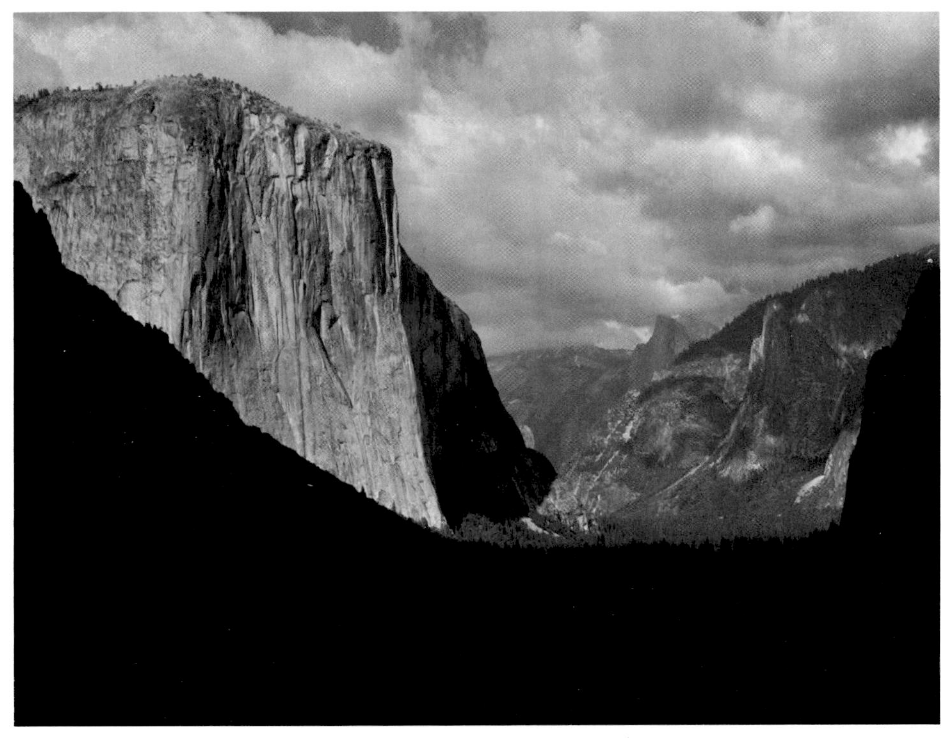

Ansel Adams · *El Capitan and Valley View to Half Dome, Yosemite National Park* · 1968

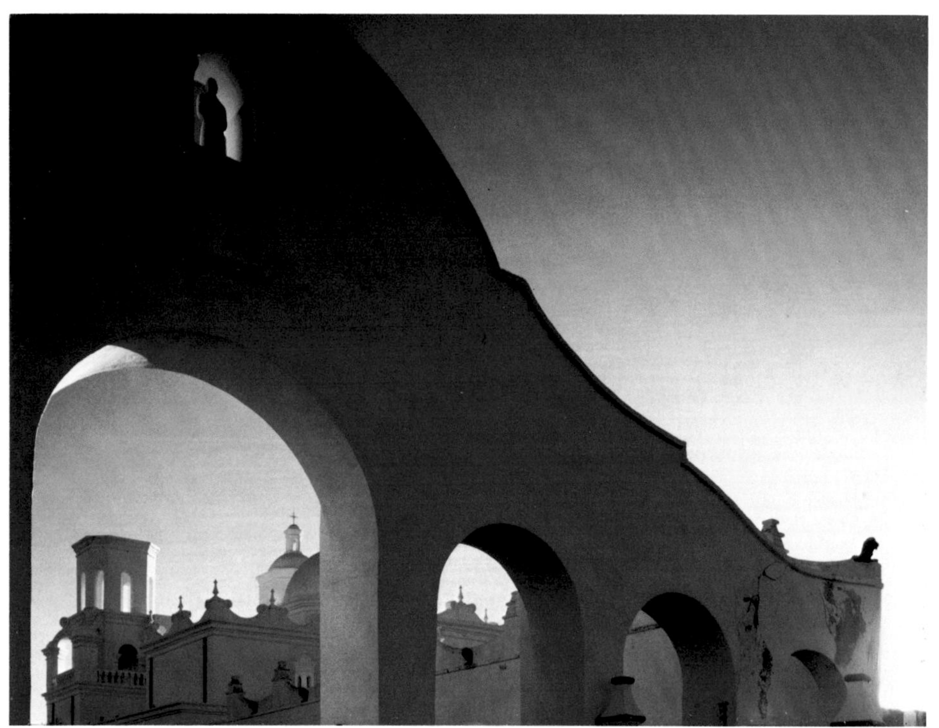

Ansel Adams · *Arches, Mission San Xavier del Bac, Tucson, Arizona* · 1968

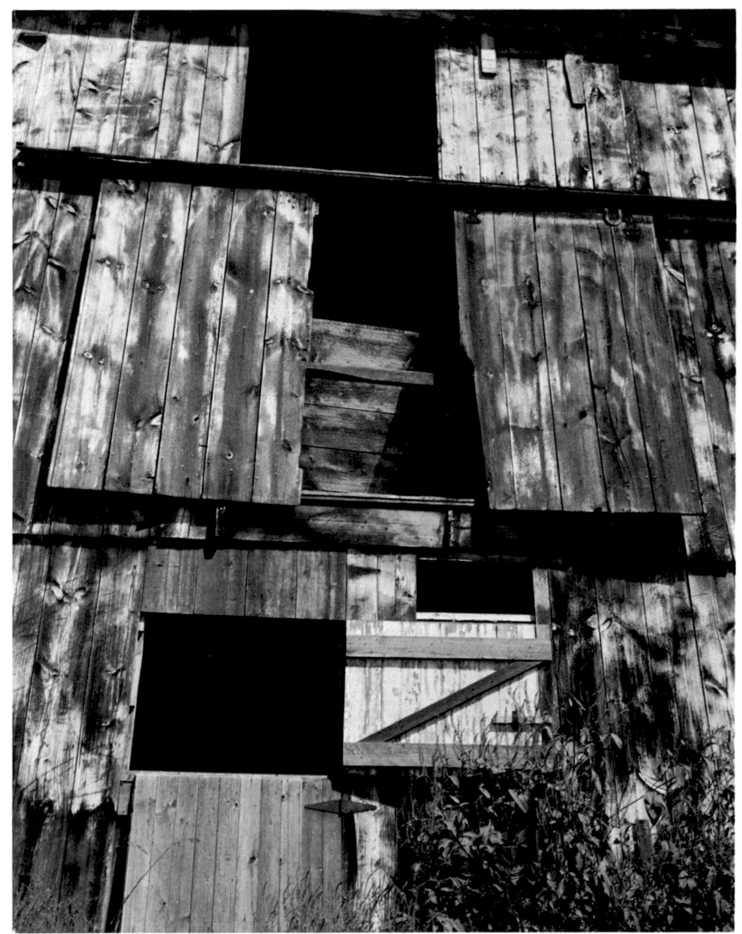

Ansel Adams · *New England Barn, Peterborough, New Hampshire* · c. 1960

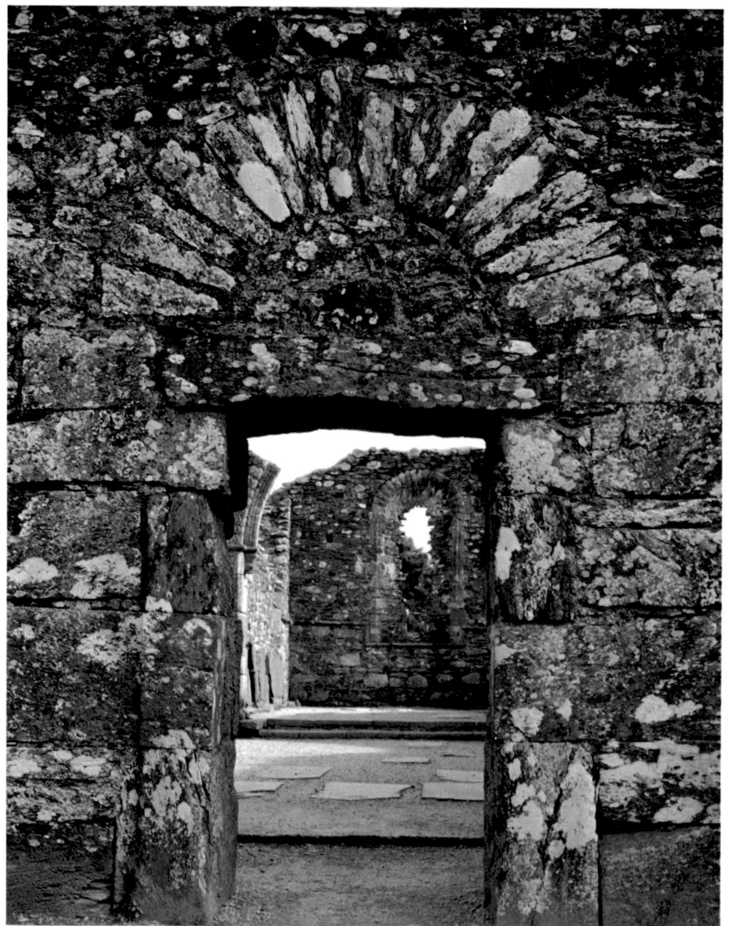

Paul Caponigro · *Detail of Ruined Church, Glendalough, County Wicklow, Ireland* · 1966

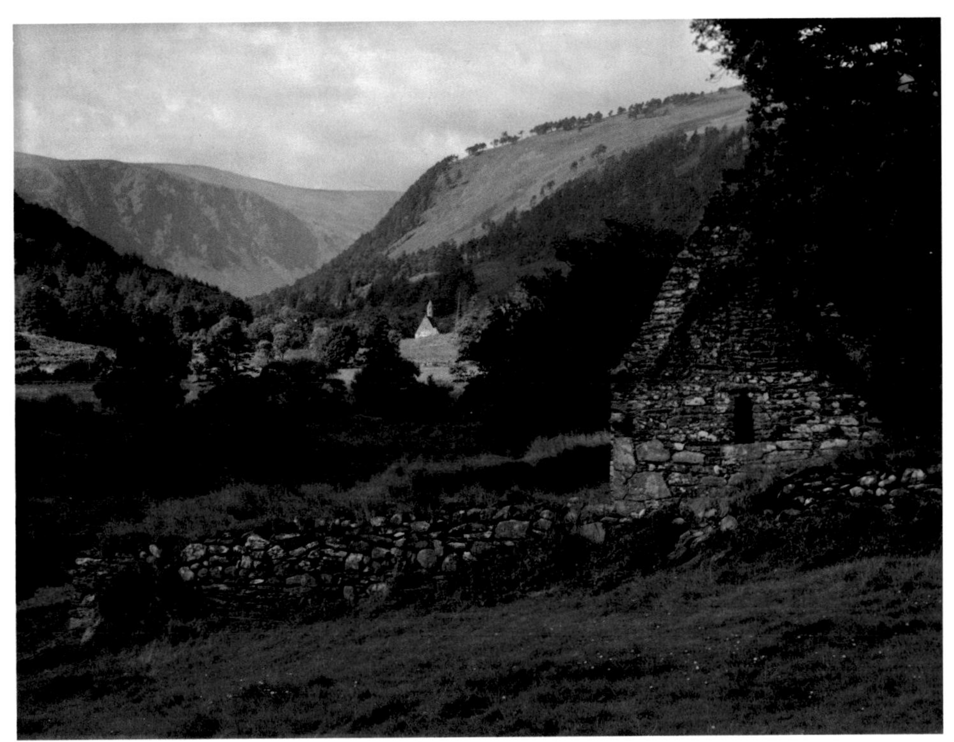

Paul Caponigro · *Monastic Site, Glendalough, County Wicklow, Ireland* · 1966

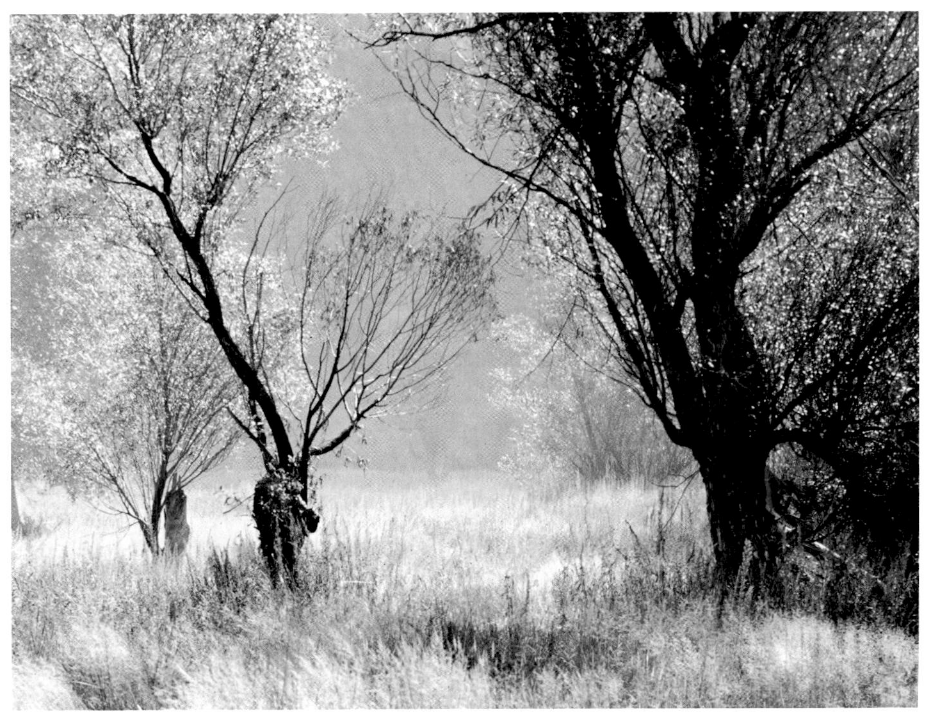

Paul Caponigro · *Yosemite Valley, Yosemite National Park* · 1974

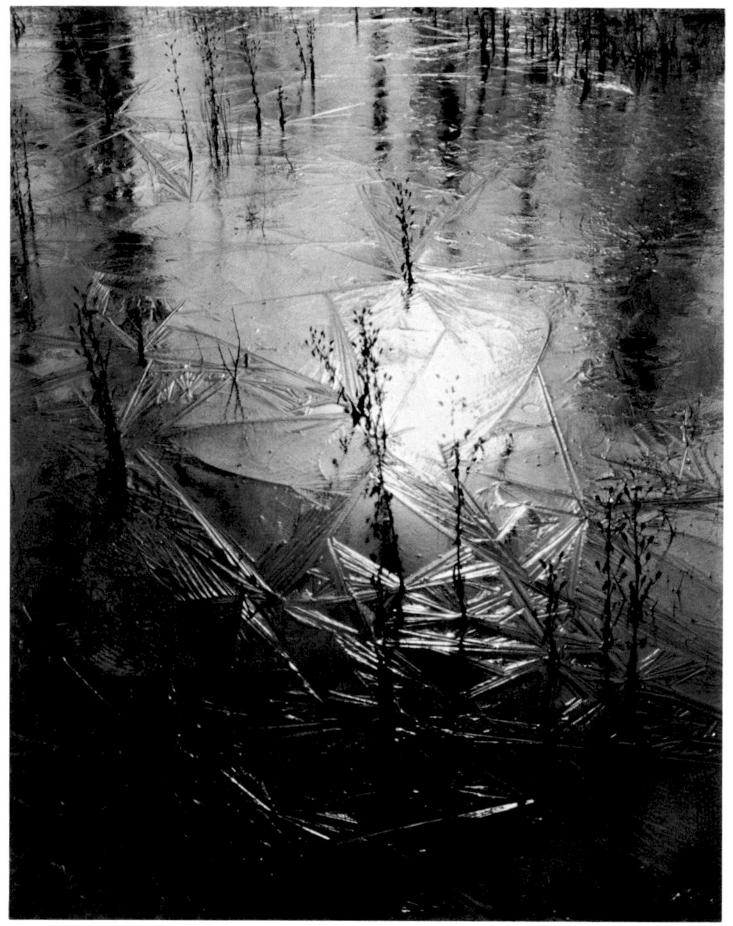

Paul Caponigro · *Frozen Pond, Coventry, Connecticut* · c. 1962

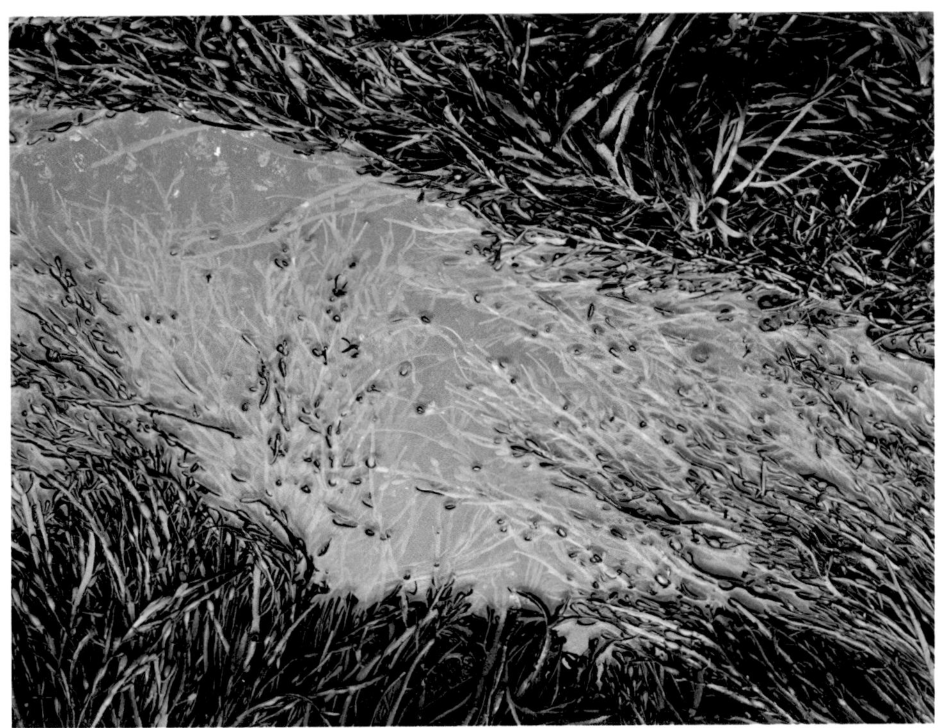

Paul Caponigro · *Tide Pool, Nahant, Massachusetts* · c. 1965

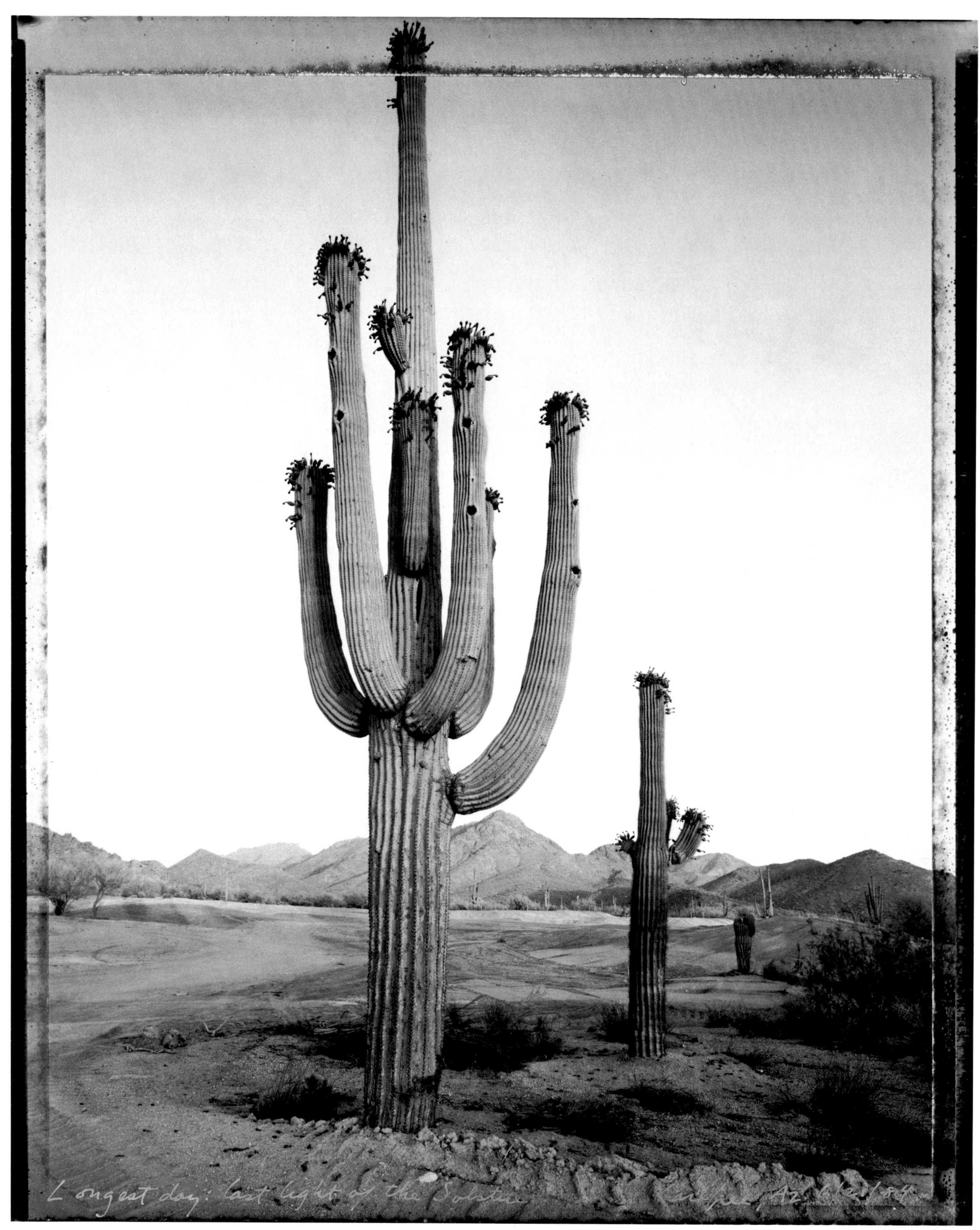

Mark Klett · *Longest Day: Last Light of the Solstice, Carefree, Arizona, 6/21/84*

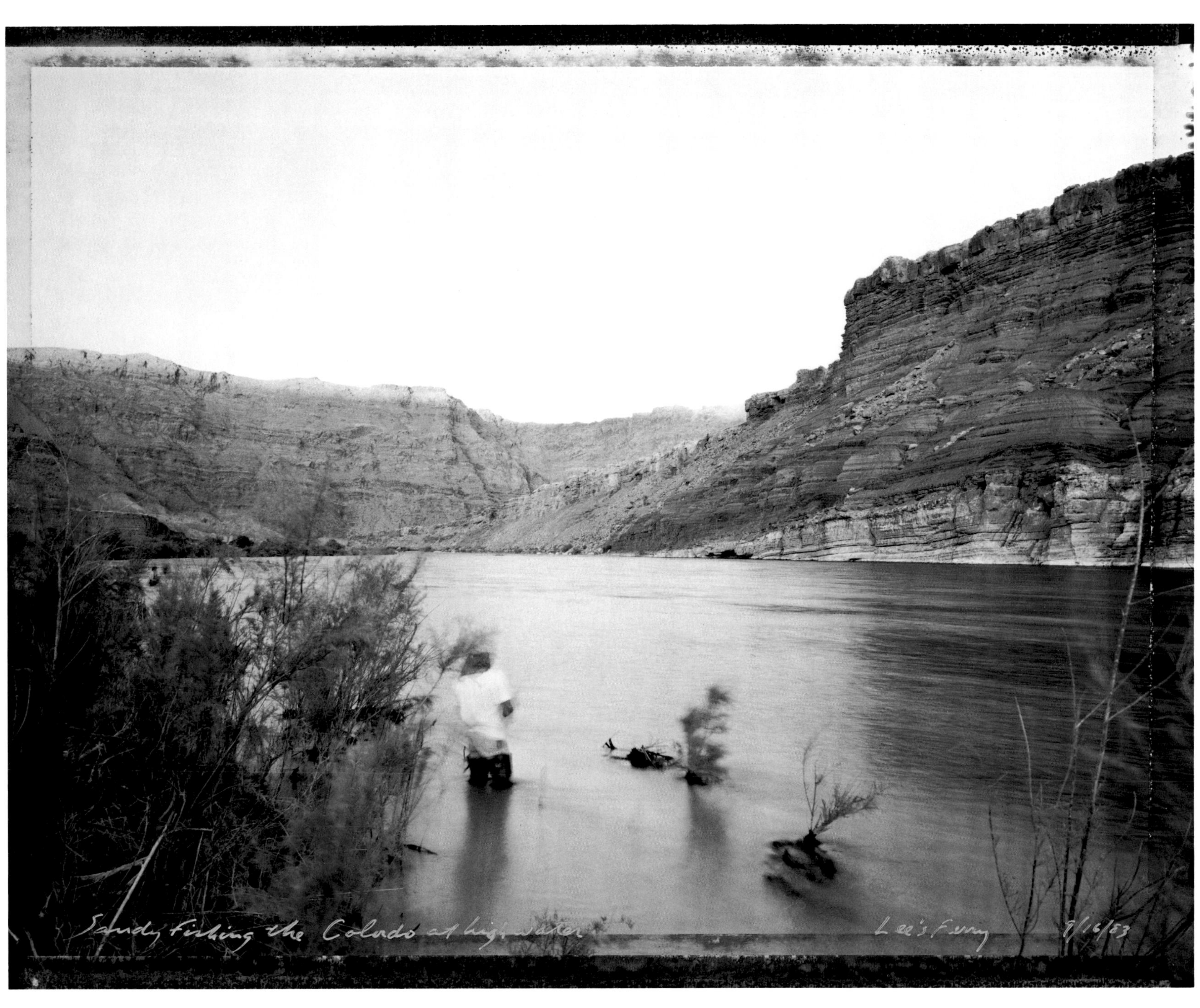

Mark Klett · *Sandy Fishing the Colorado at High Water, Lee's Ferry, 9/16/83*

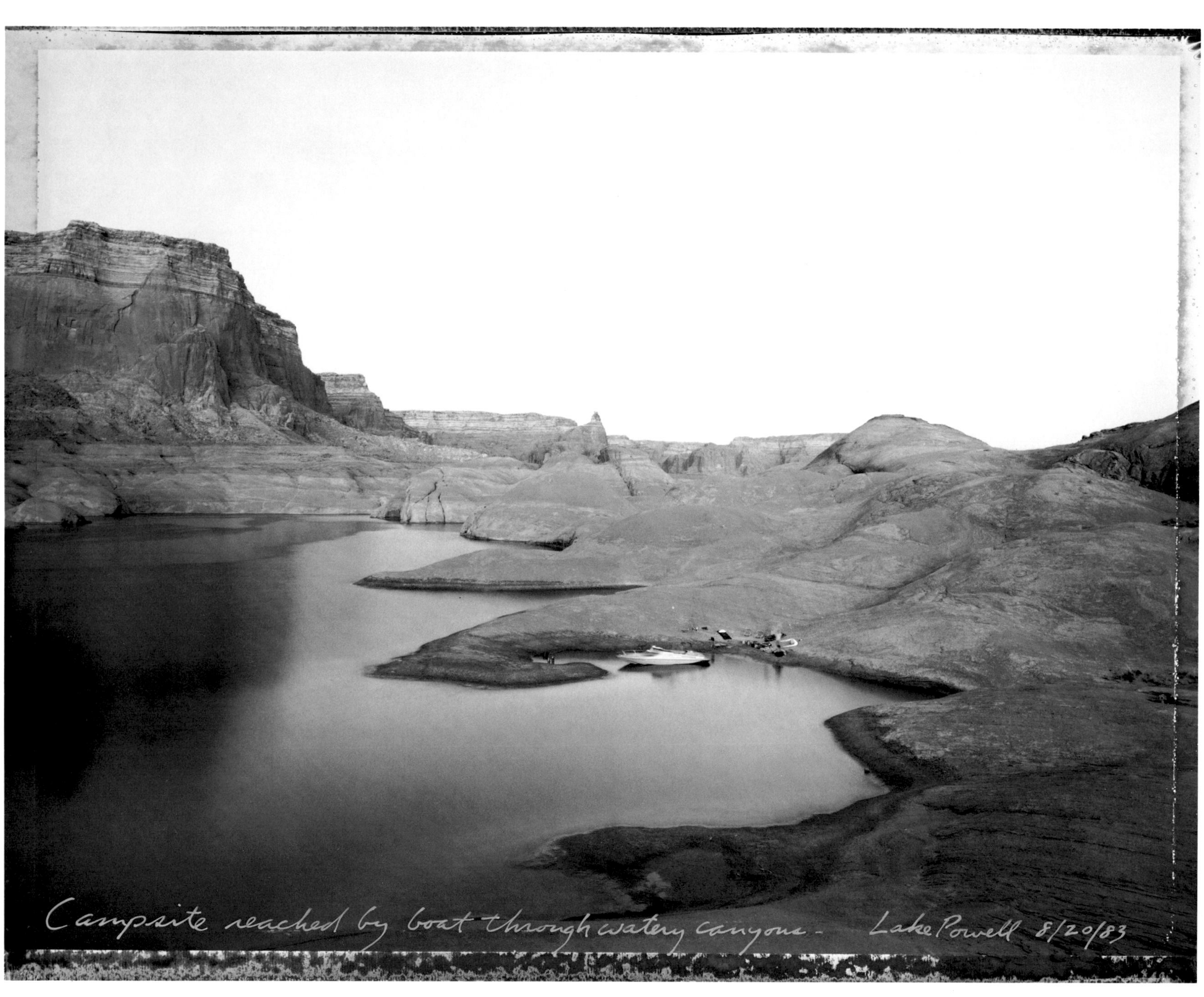

Mark Klett · *Campsite Reached by Boat through Watery Canyons, Lake Powell, 8/20/83*

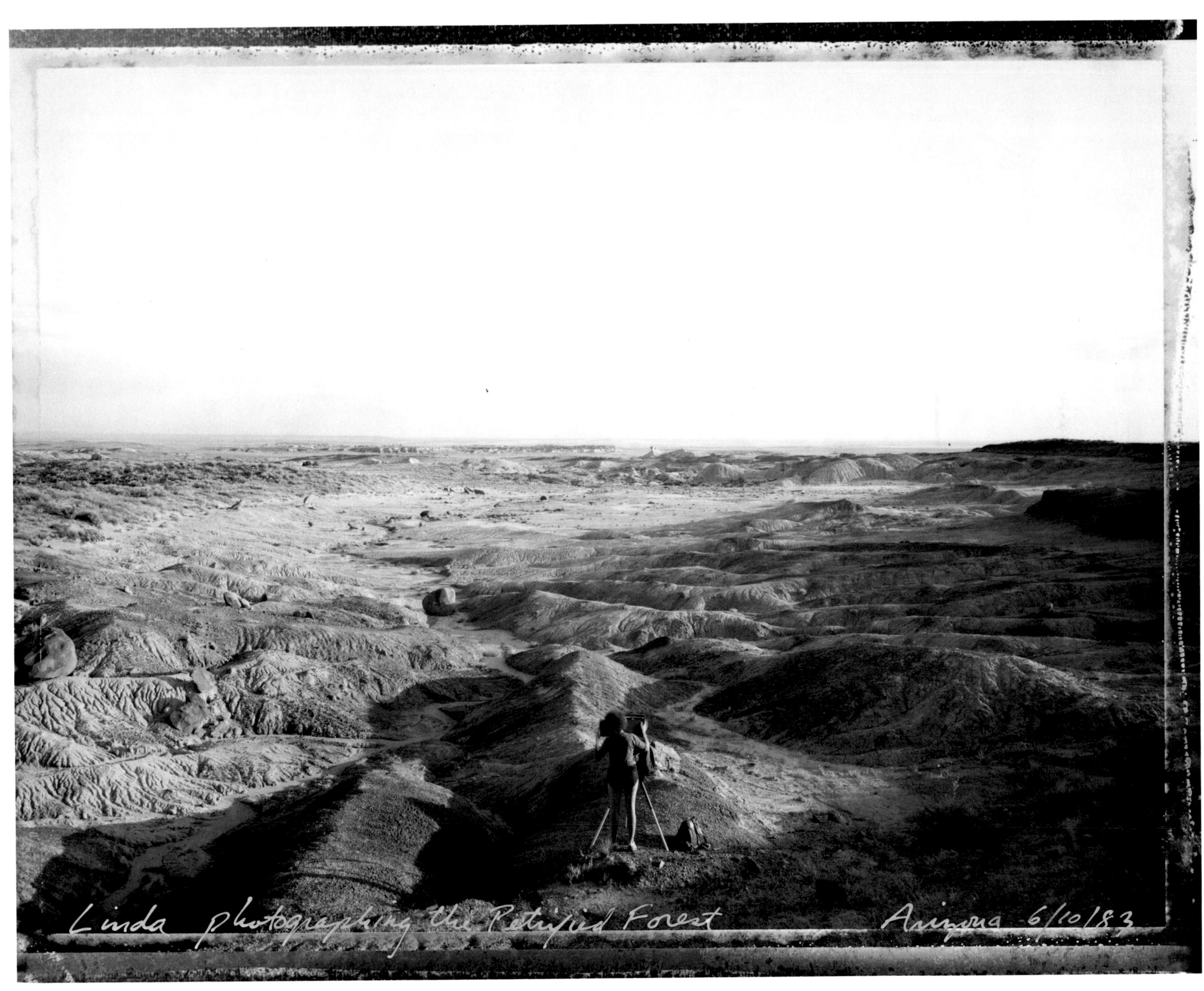

Mark Klett · *Linda Photographing the Petrified Forest, Arizona, 6/10/83*

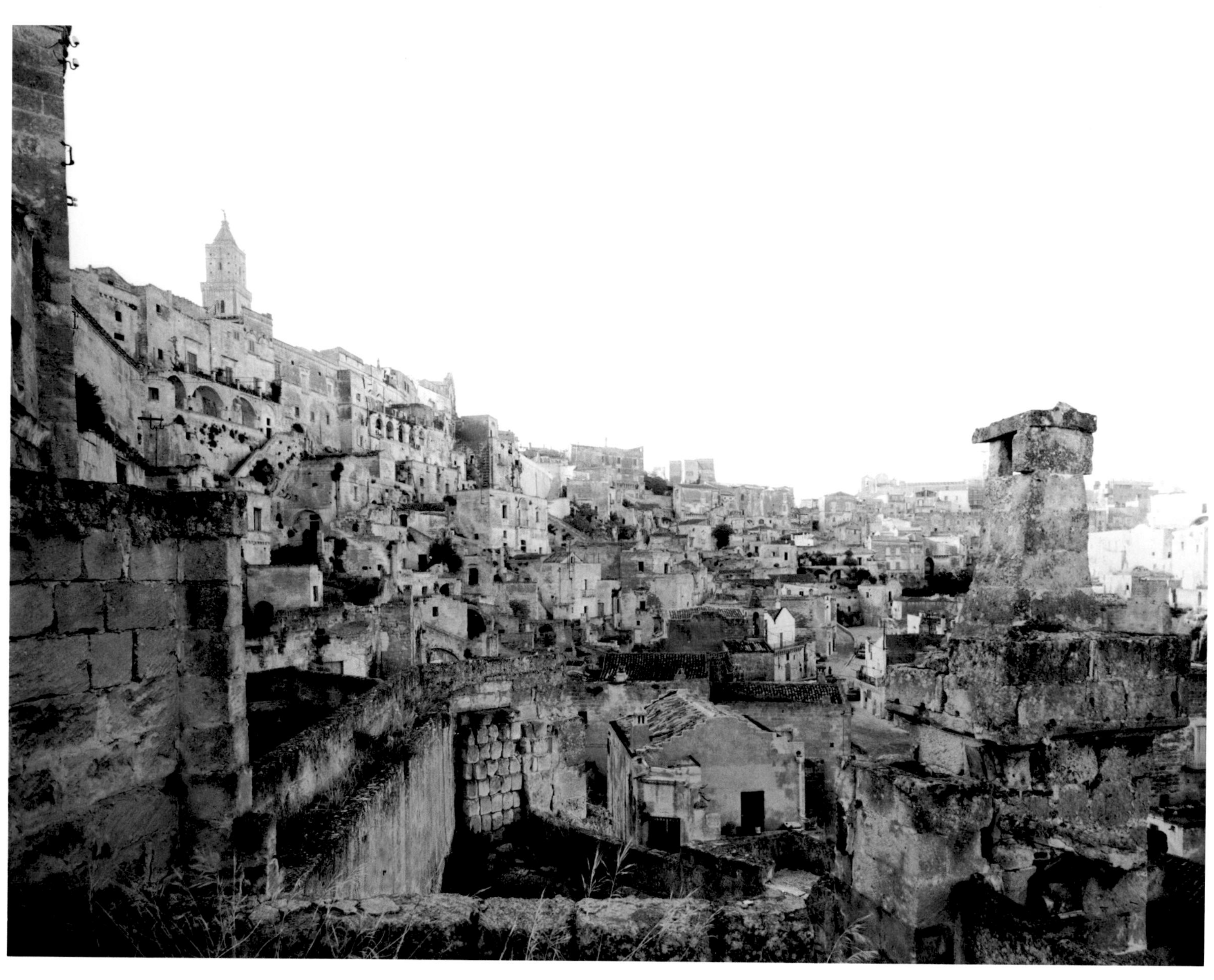

Emmet Gowin · *Matera, Italy* · 1983

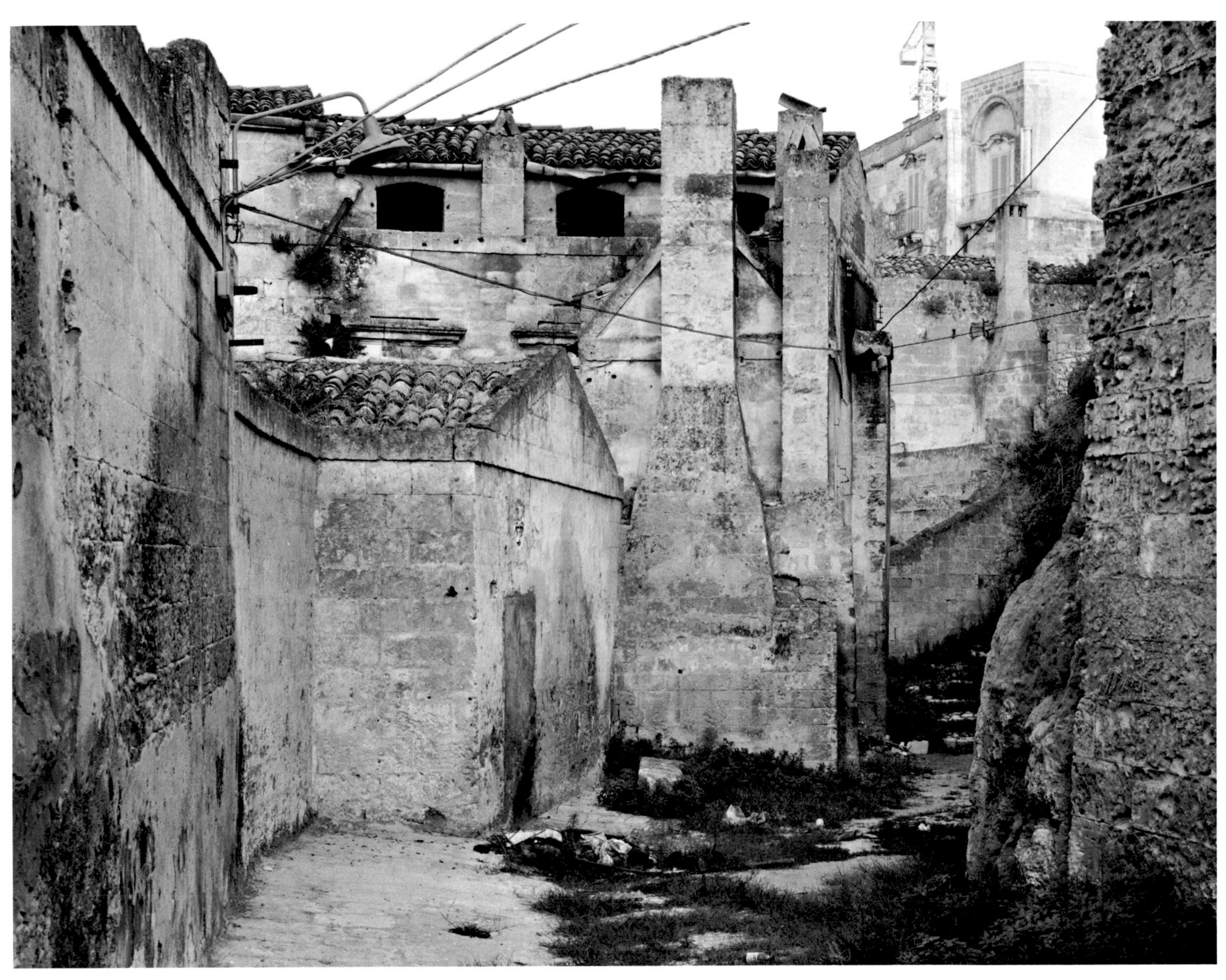

Emmet Gowin · *Matera, Italy* · 1983

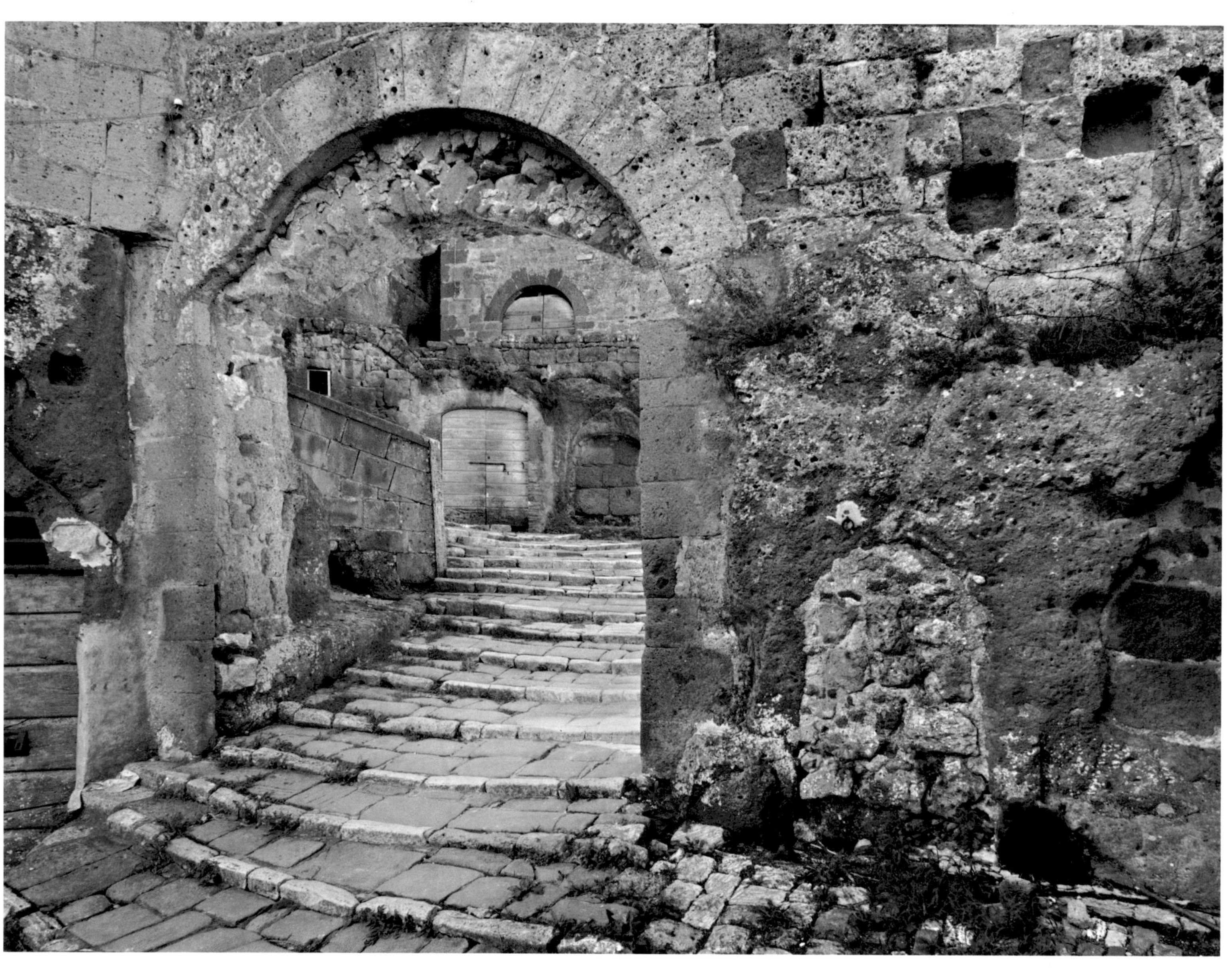

Emmet Gowin · *Pitigliano, Italy* · 1983

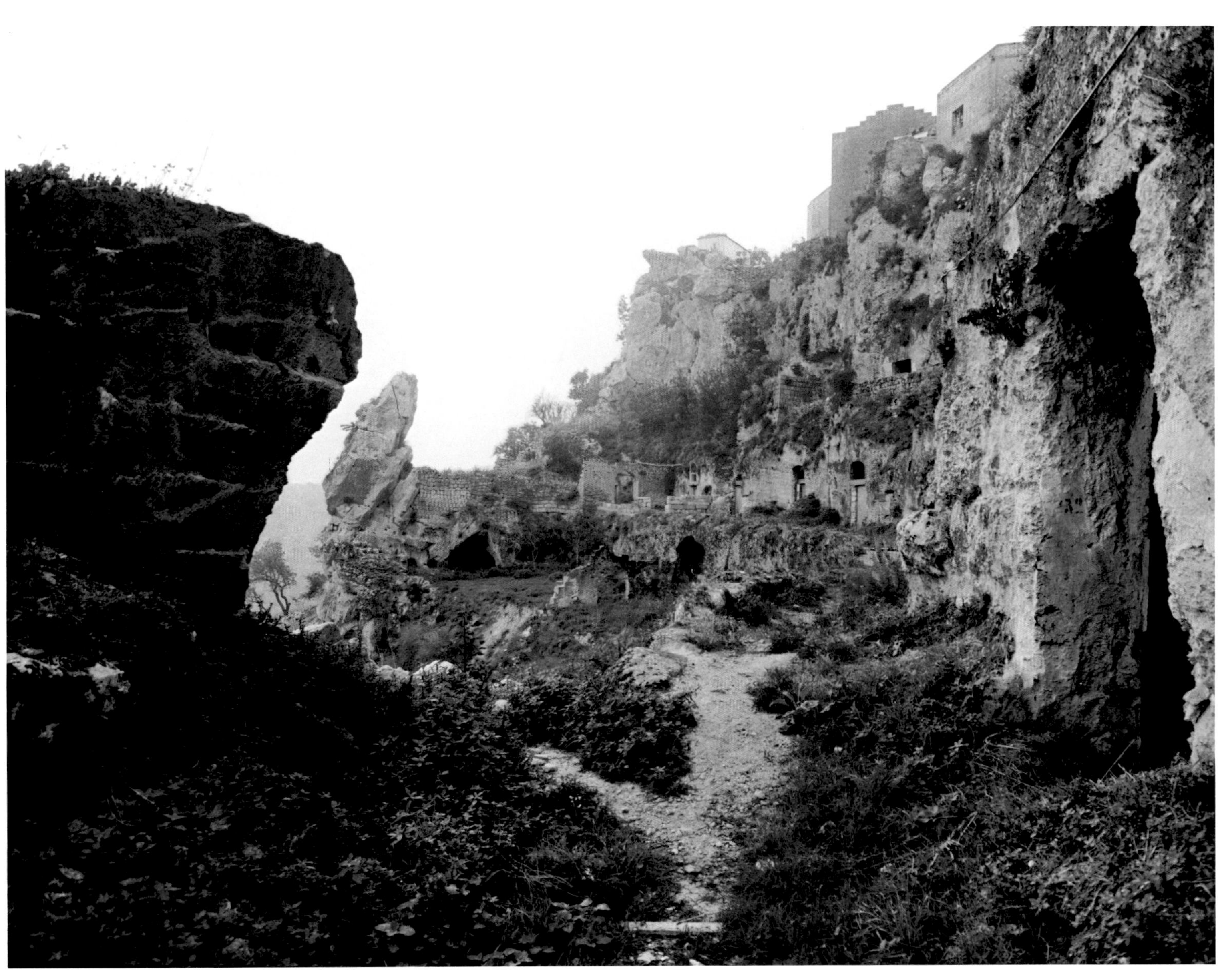

Emmet Gowin · *Matera, Italy* · 1983

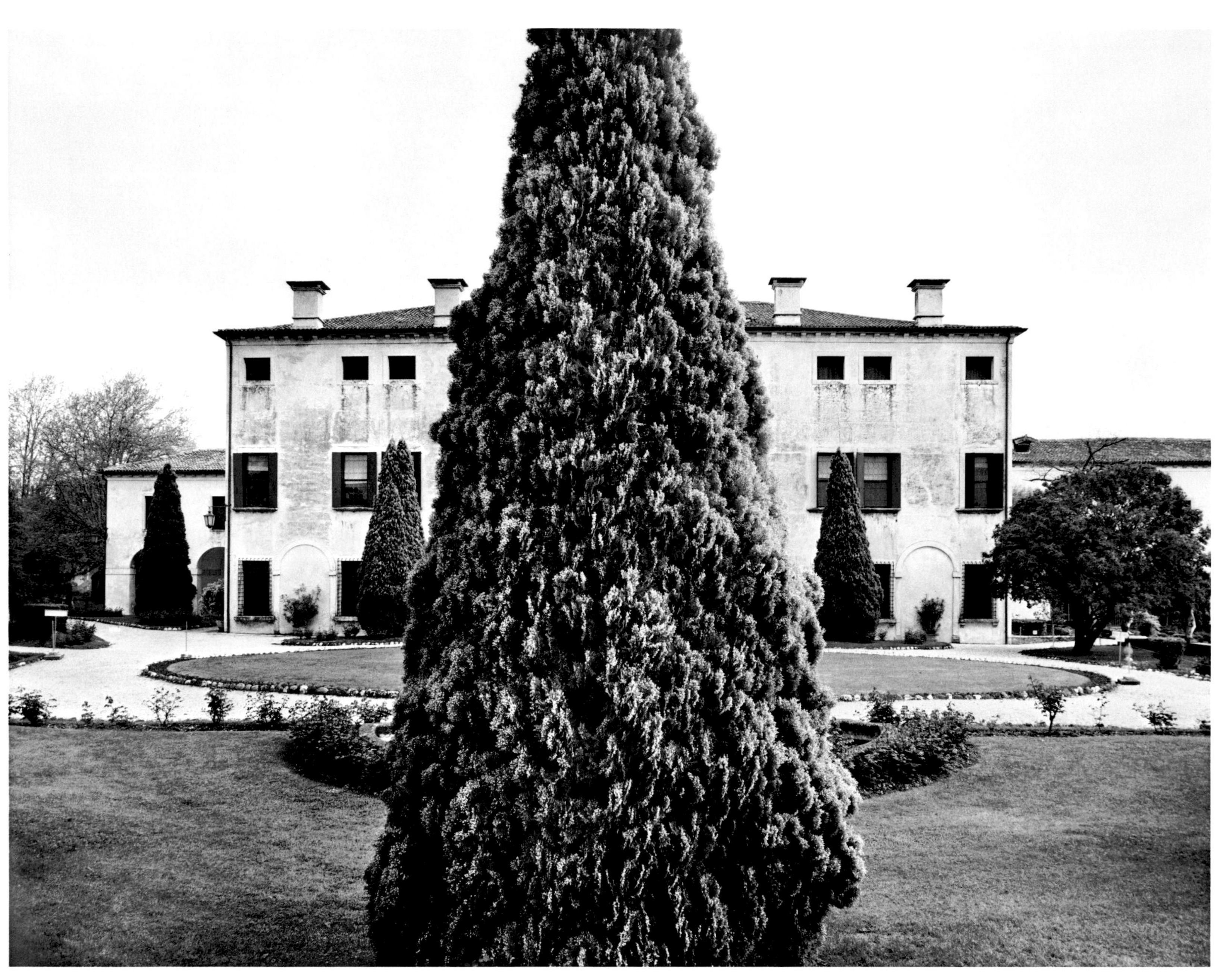

Philip Trager · *Villa Godi* · 1984

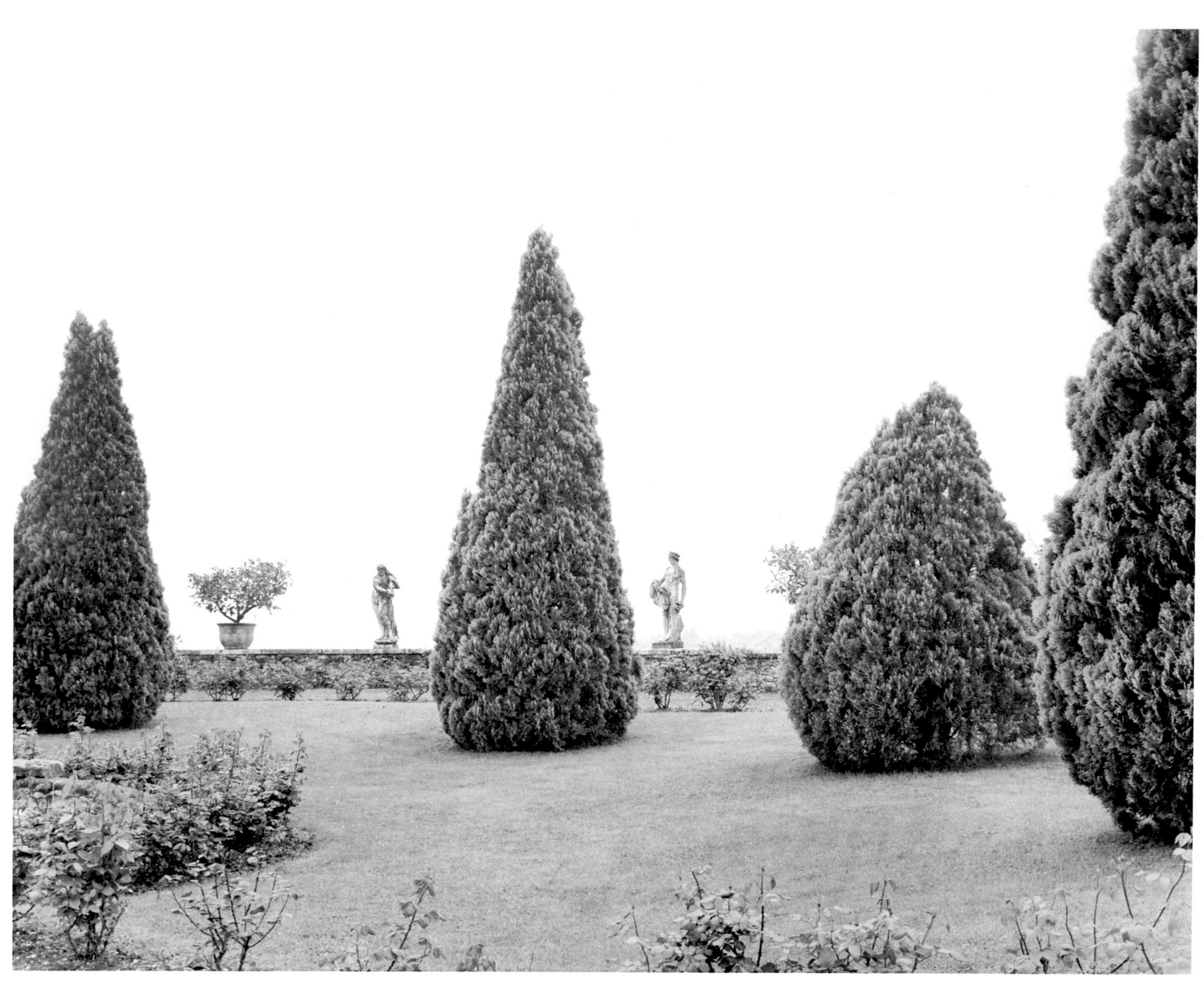

Philip Trager · *Villa Godi* · 1984

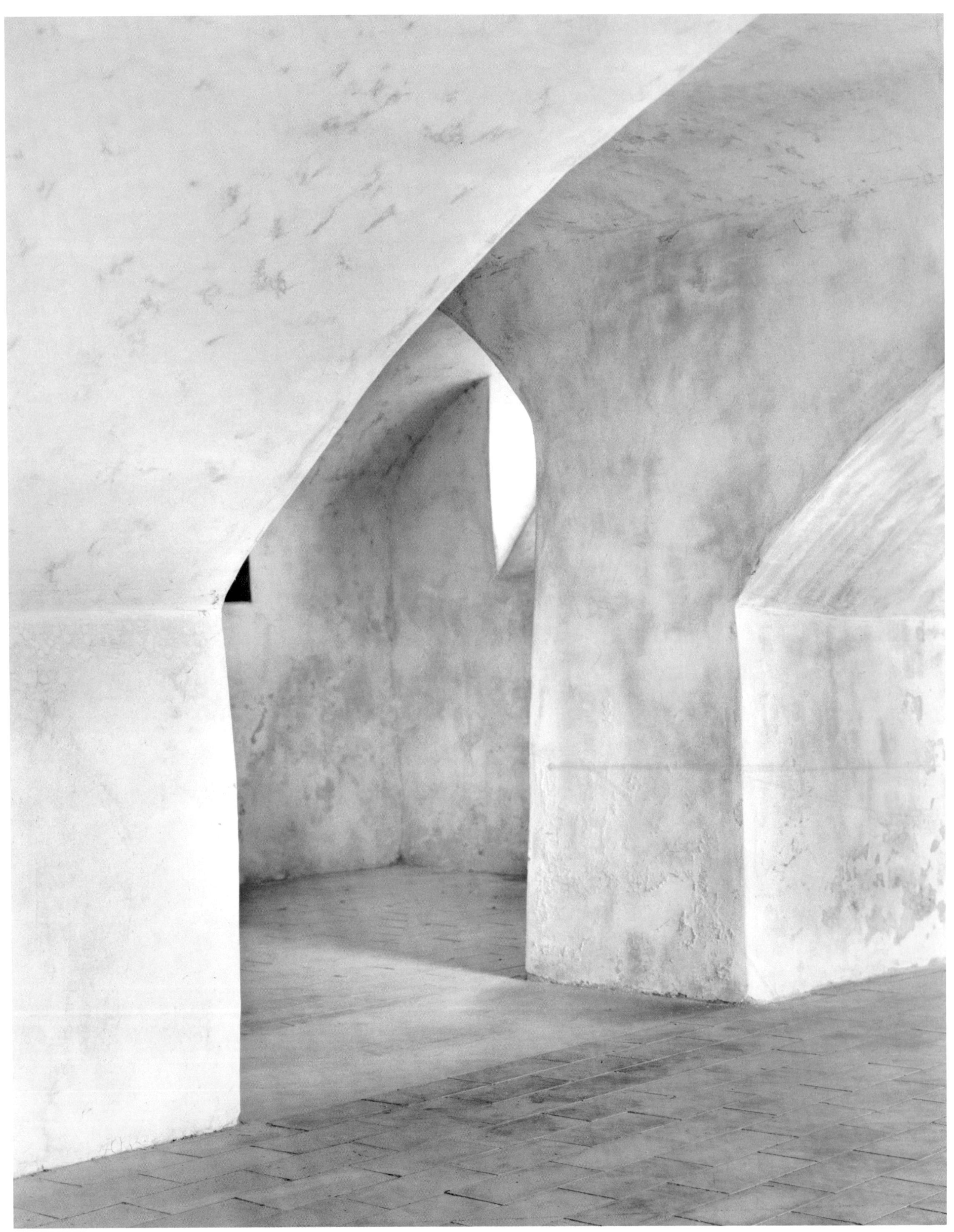

Philip Trager · *Villa Pojana* · 1984

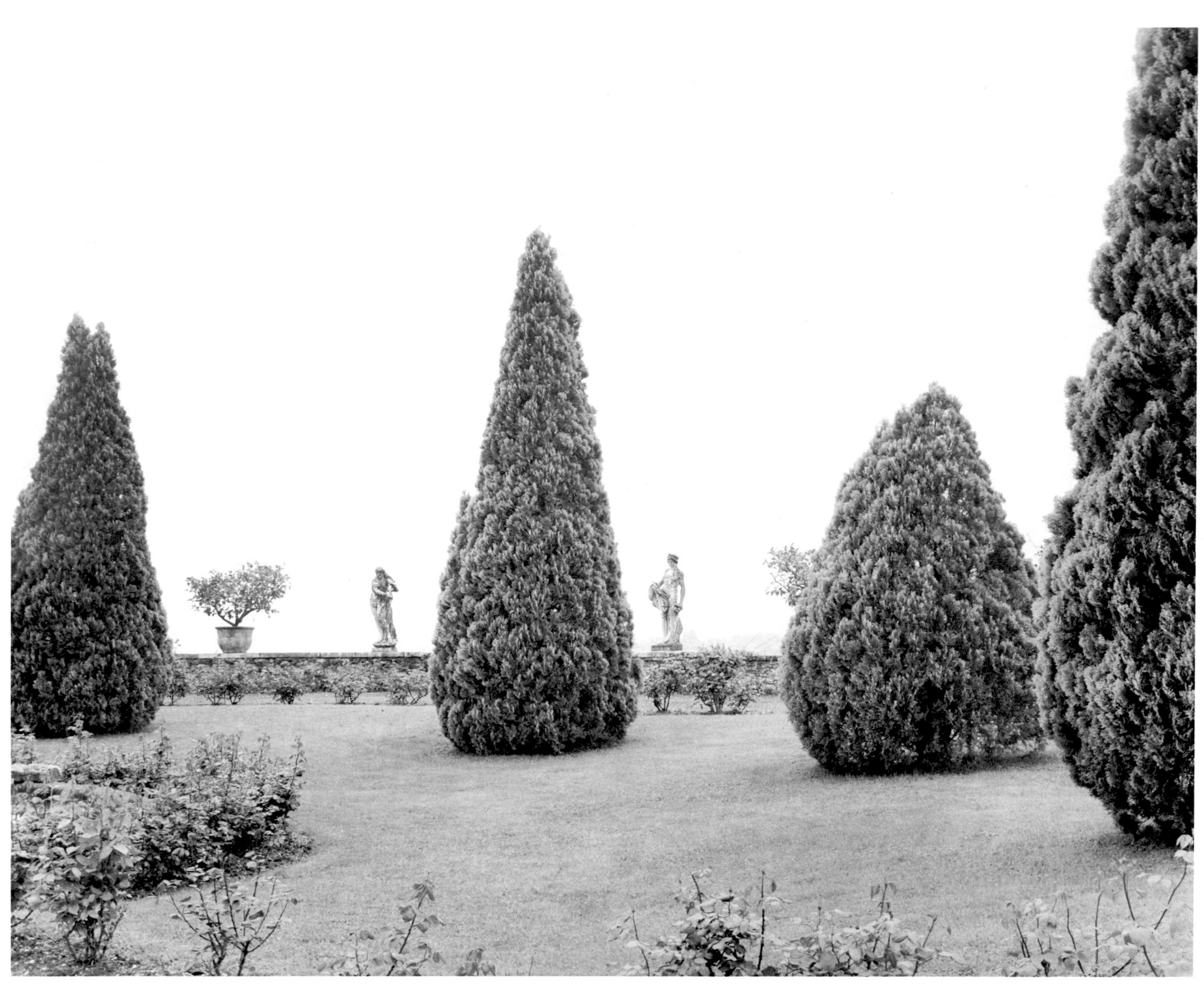

Philip Trager · *Villa Godi* · 1984

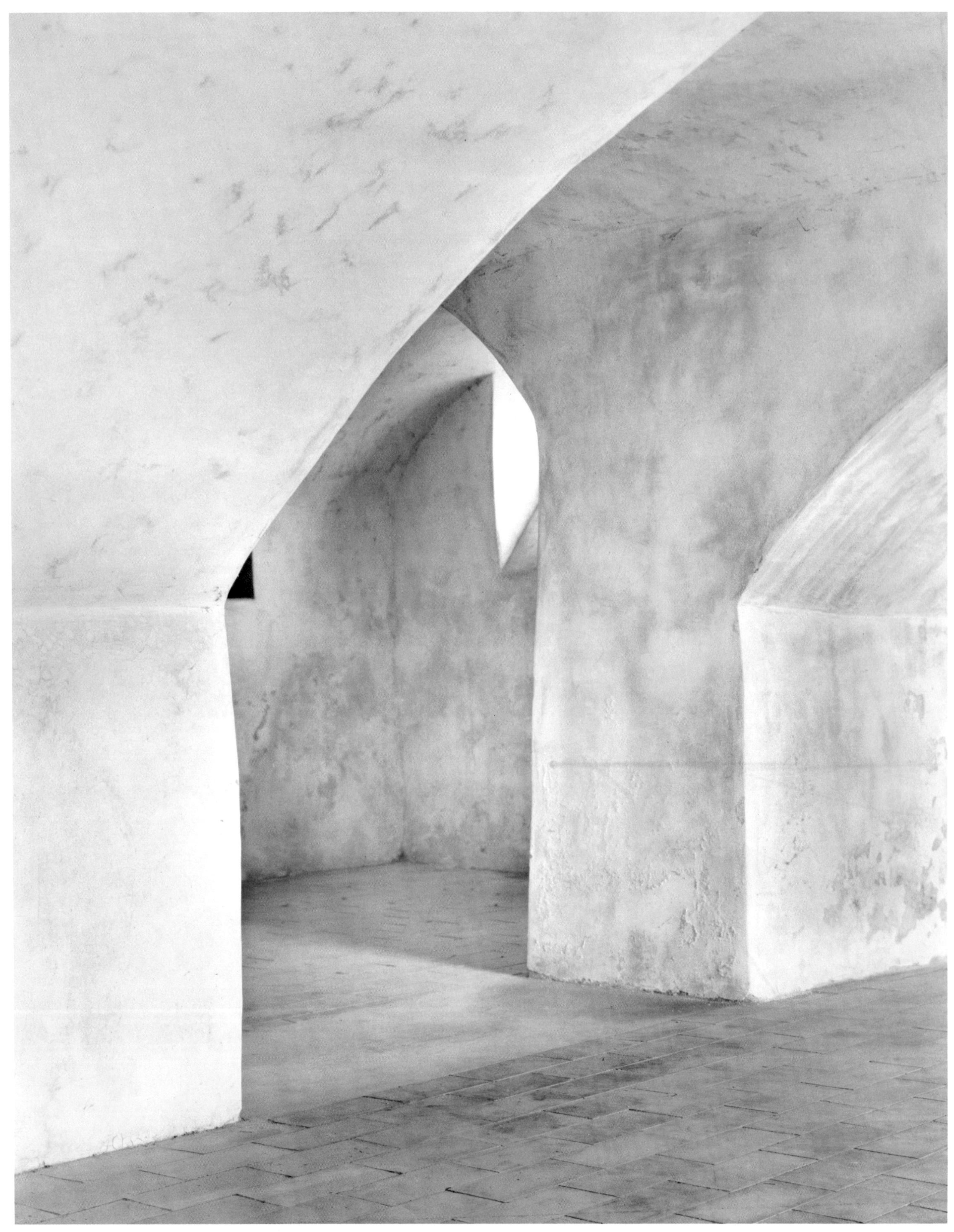

Philip Trager · *Villa Pojana* · 1984

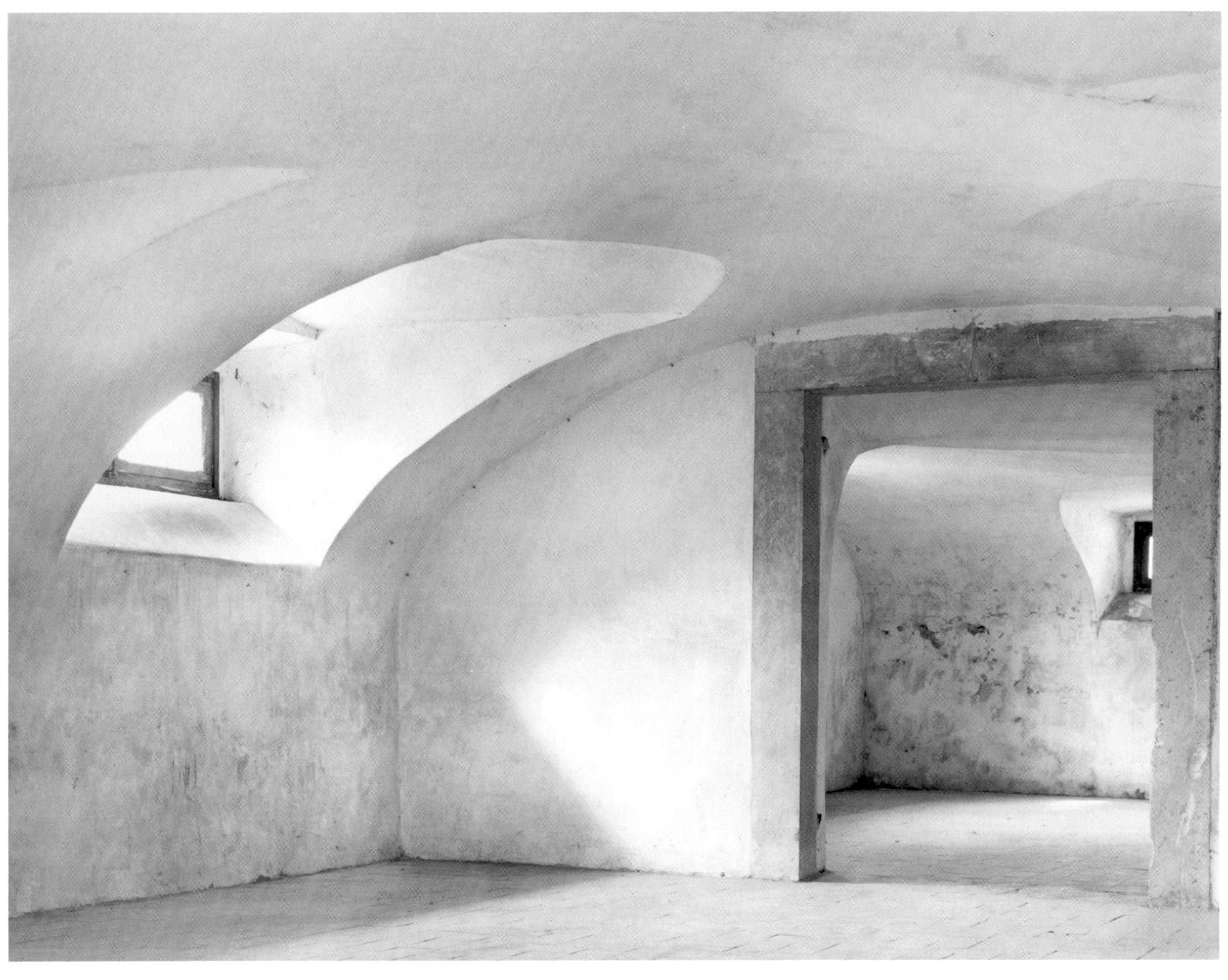

Philip Trager · *Villa Pojana* · 1984

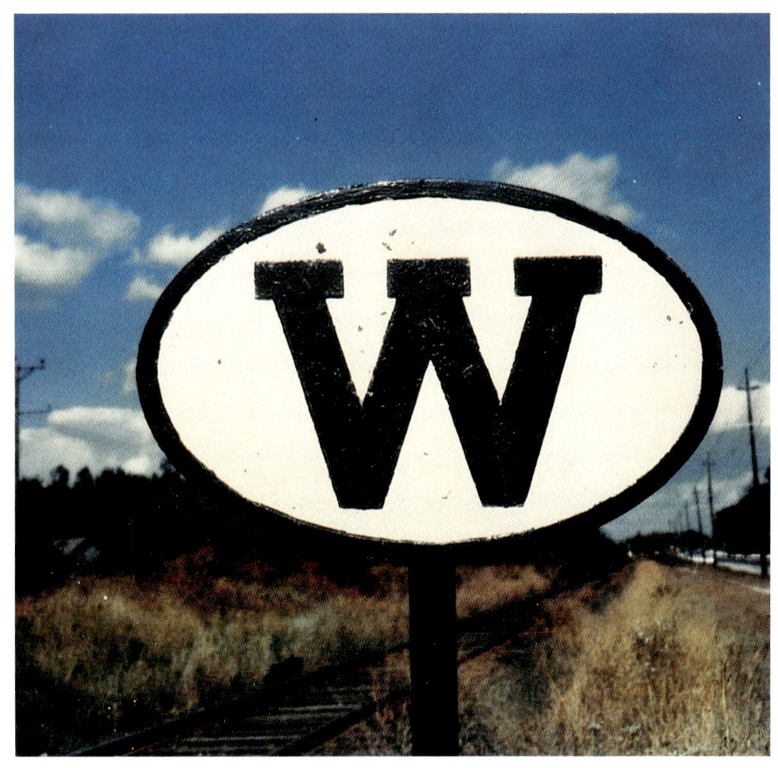

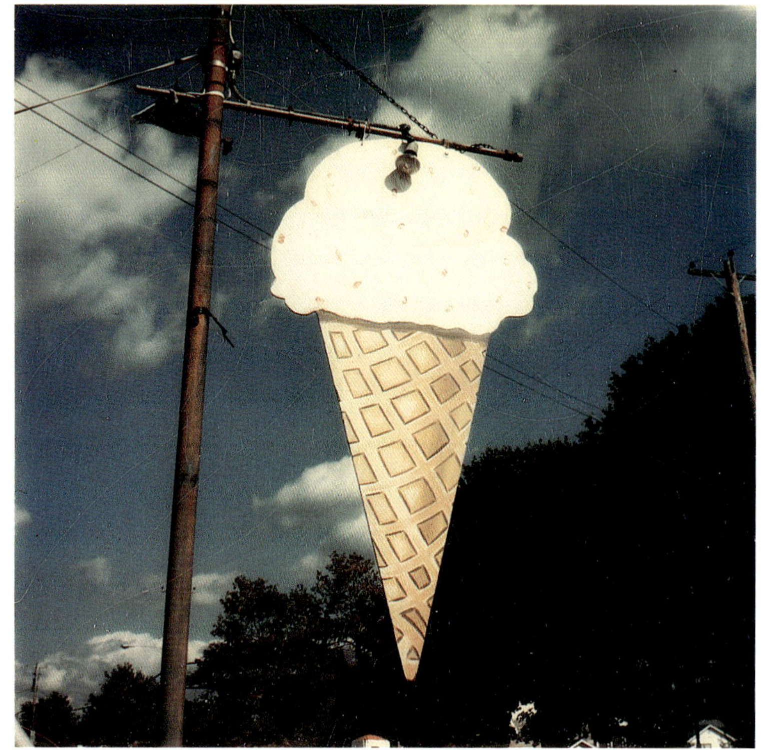

Walker Evans · Untitled · c. 1973

Walker Evans · Untitled (Connecticut) · c. 1973

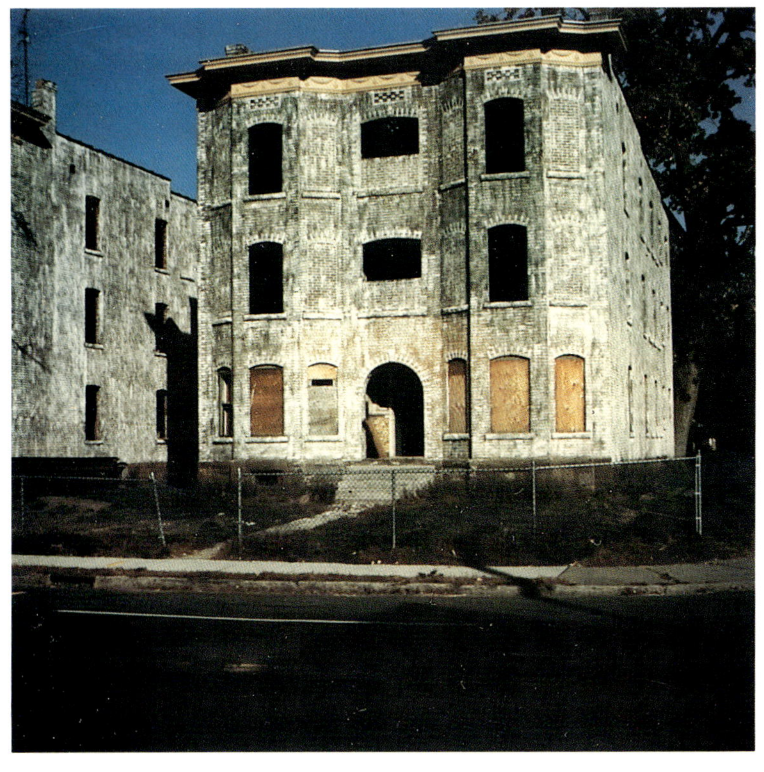

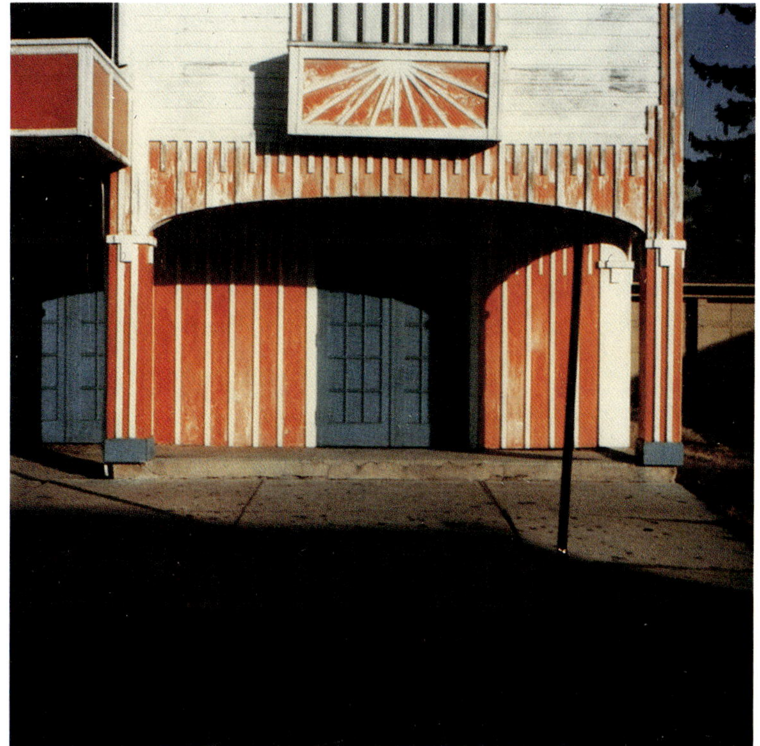

Walker Evans · Untitled · c. 1973

Walker Evans · *Strand Theater, Old Saybrook, Connecticut* · c. 1973

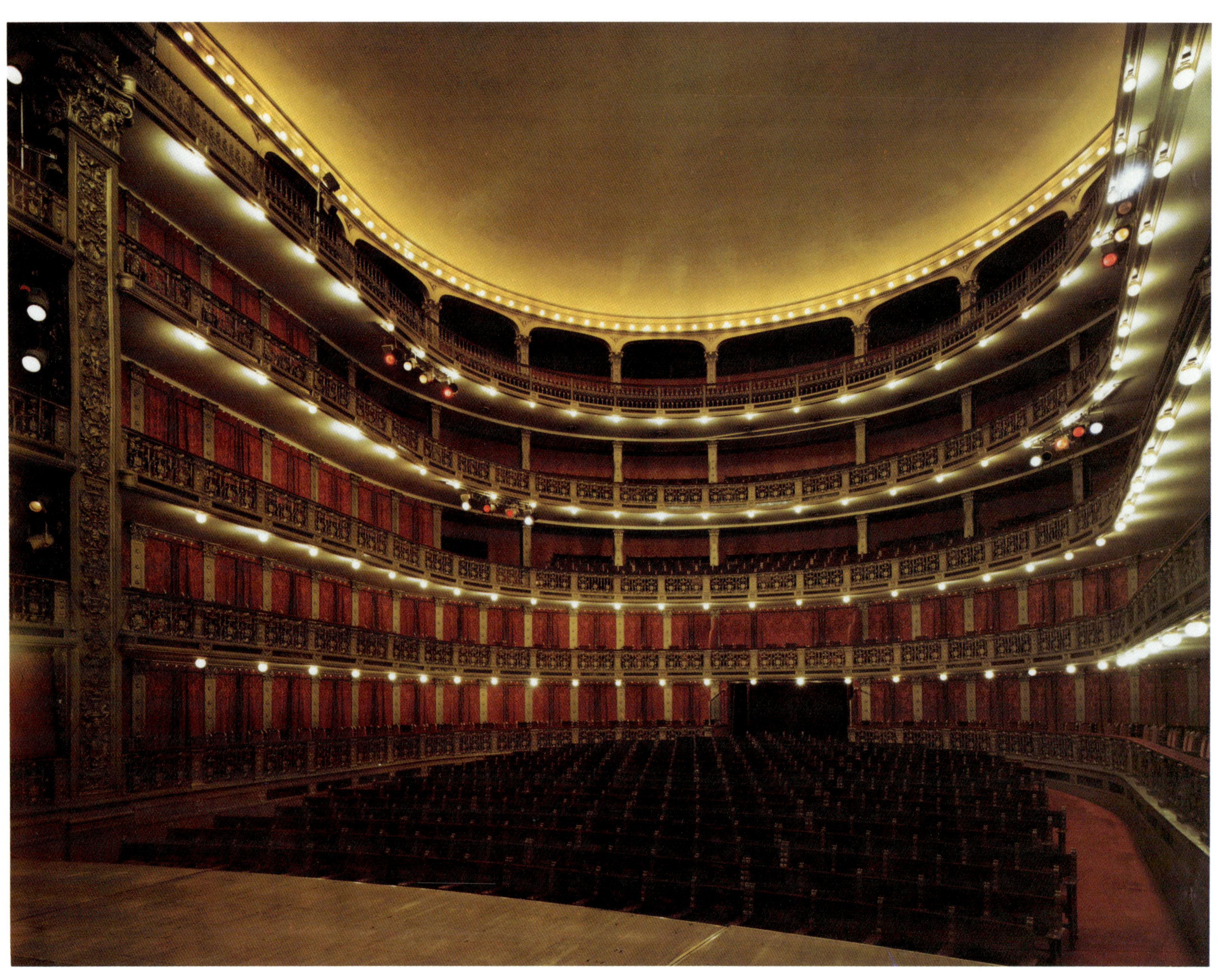

Jim Dow · *Cervantes Theatre, from the Stage, Buenos Aires* · 1986

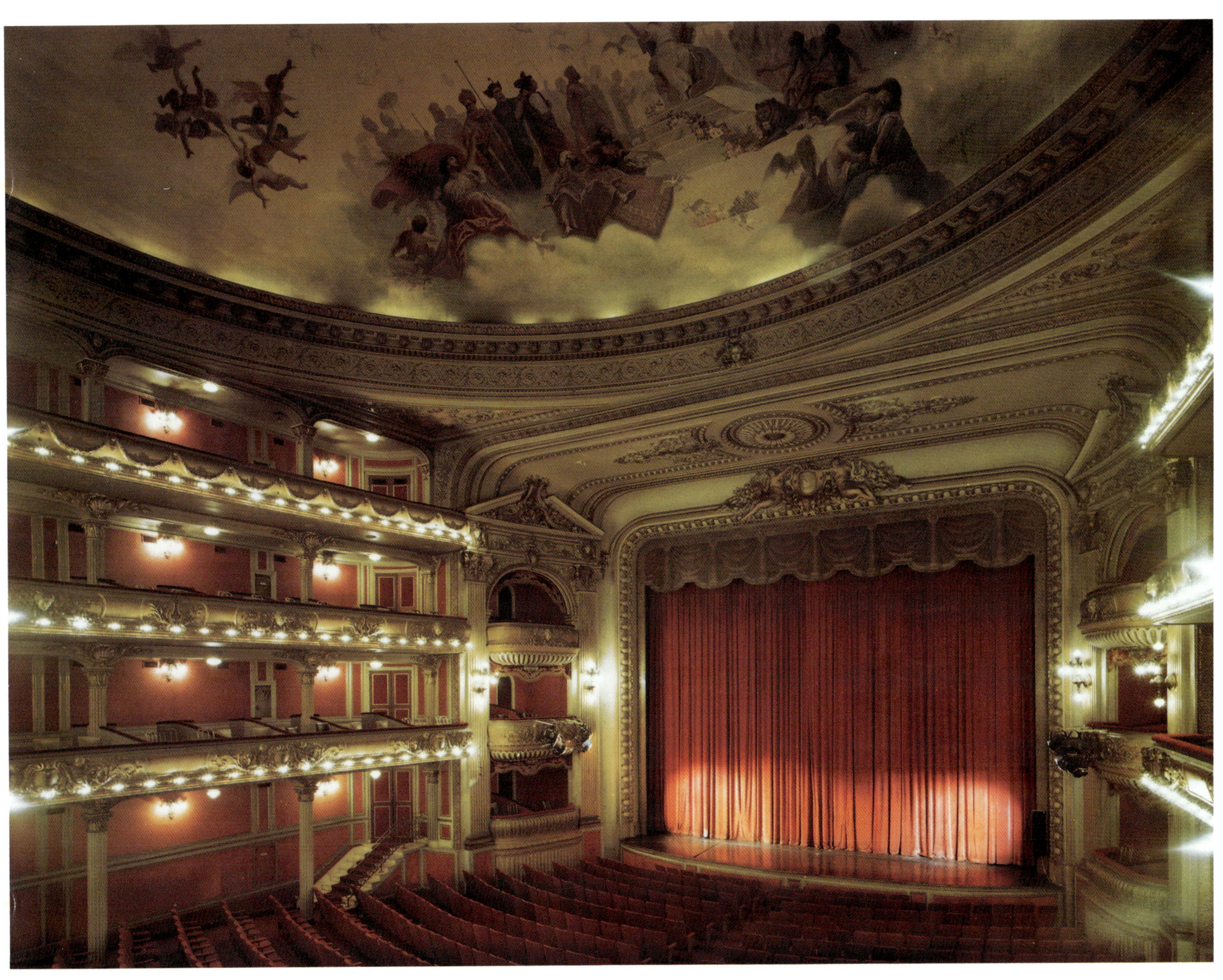

Jim Dow · *The Grand Splendid Theatre, Buenos Aires* · 1986

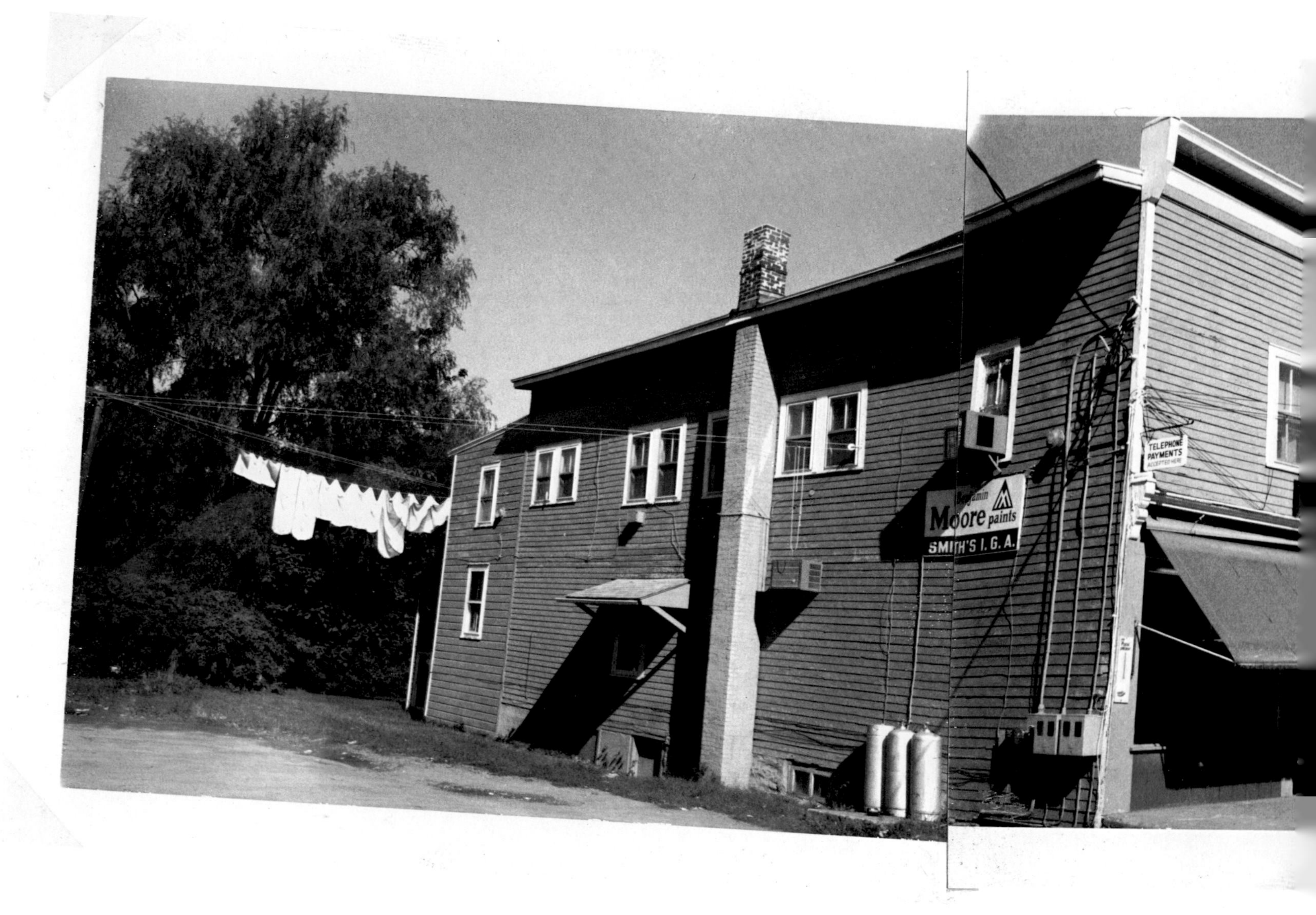

Danny Lyon · *IGA, Clintondale* · 1986

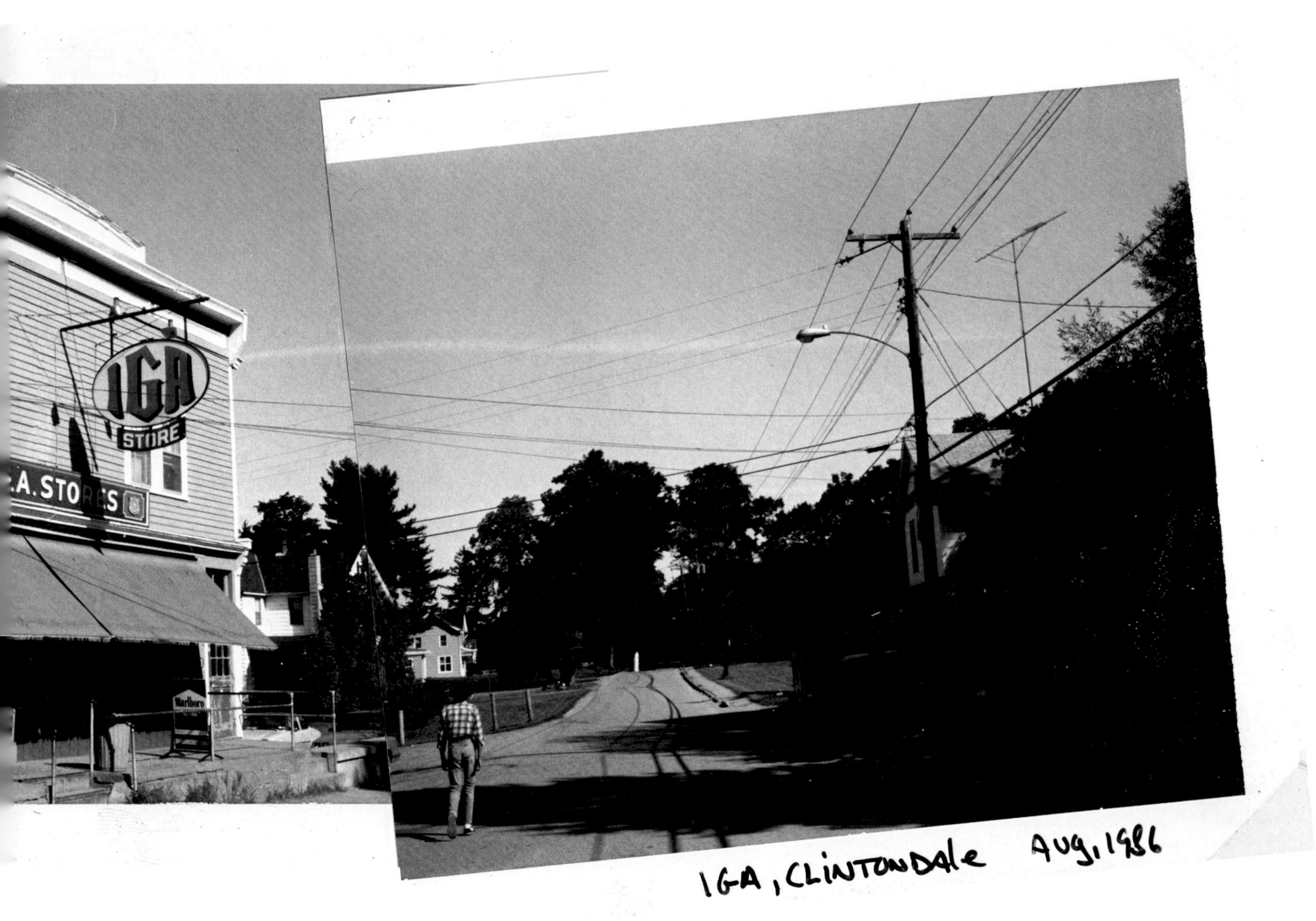

IGA, CLINTONDALE AUG, 1986

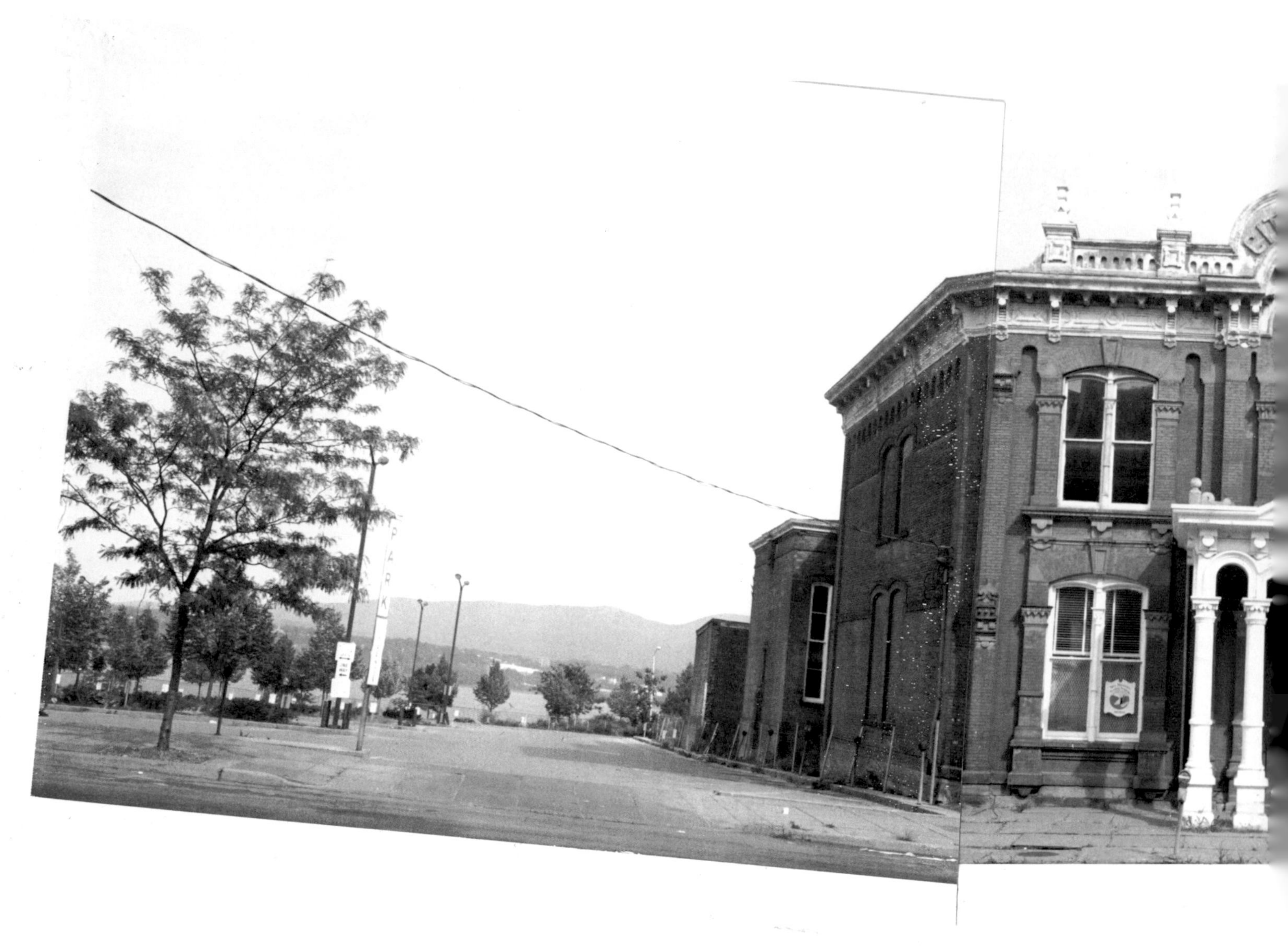

Danny Lyon · *Newburg City Library* · 1986

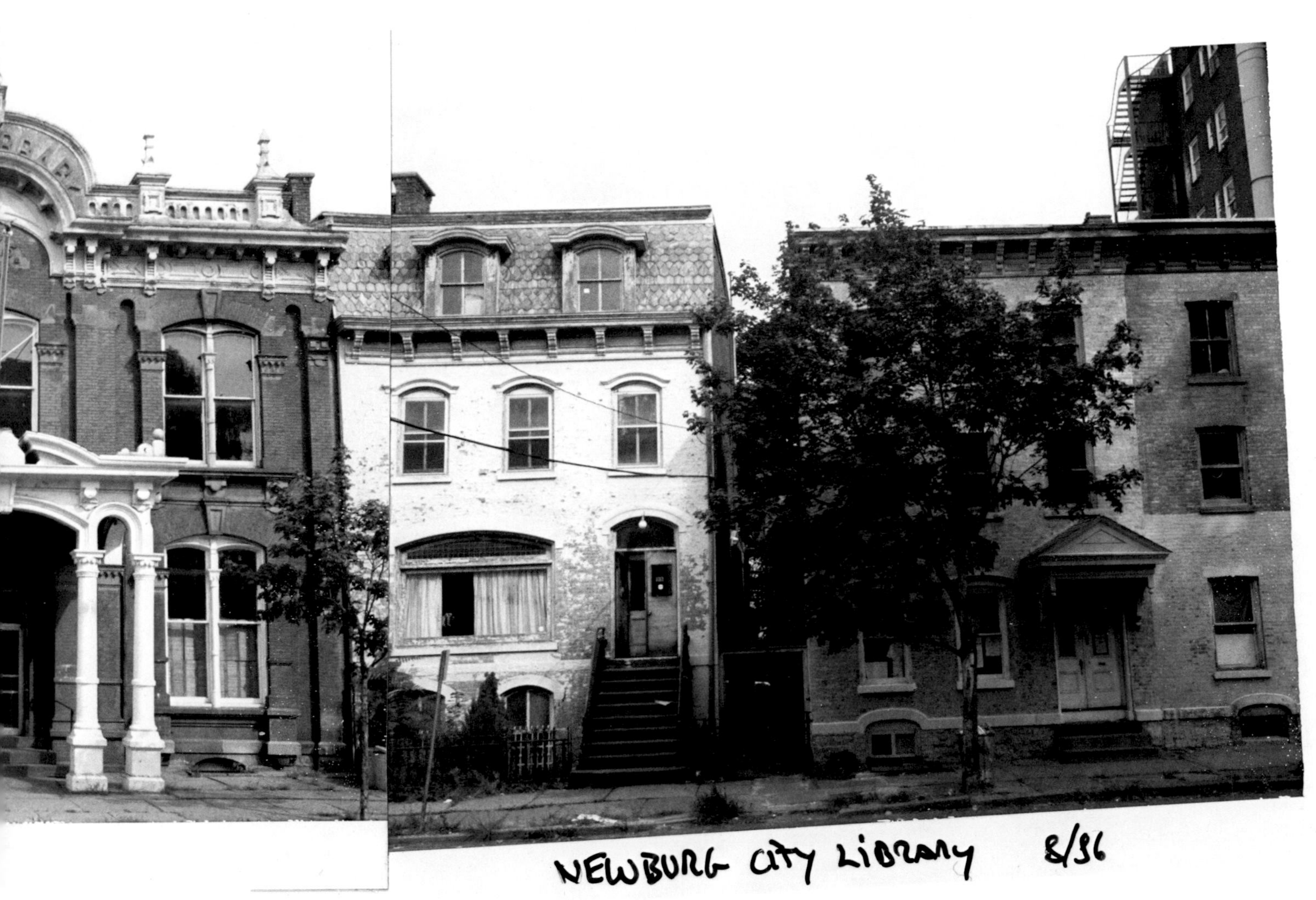
NEWBURG CITY LIBRARY 8/86

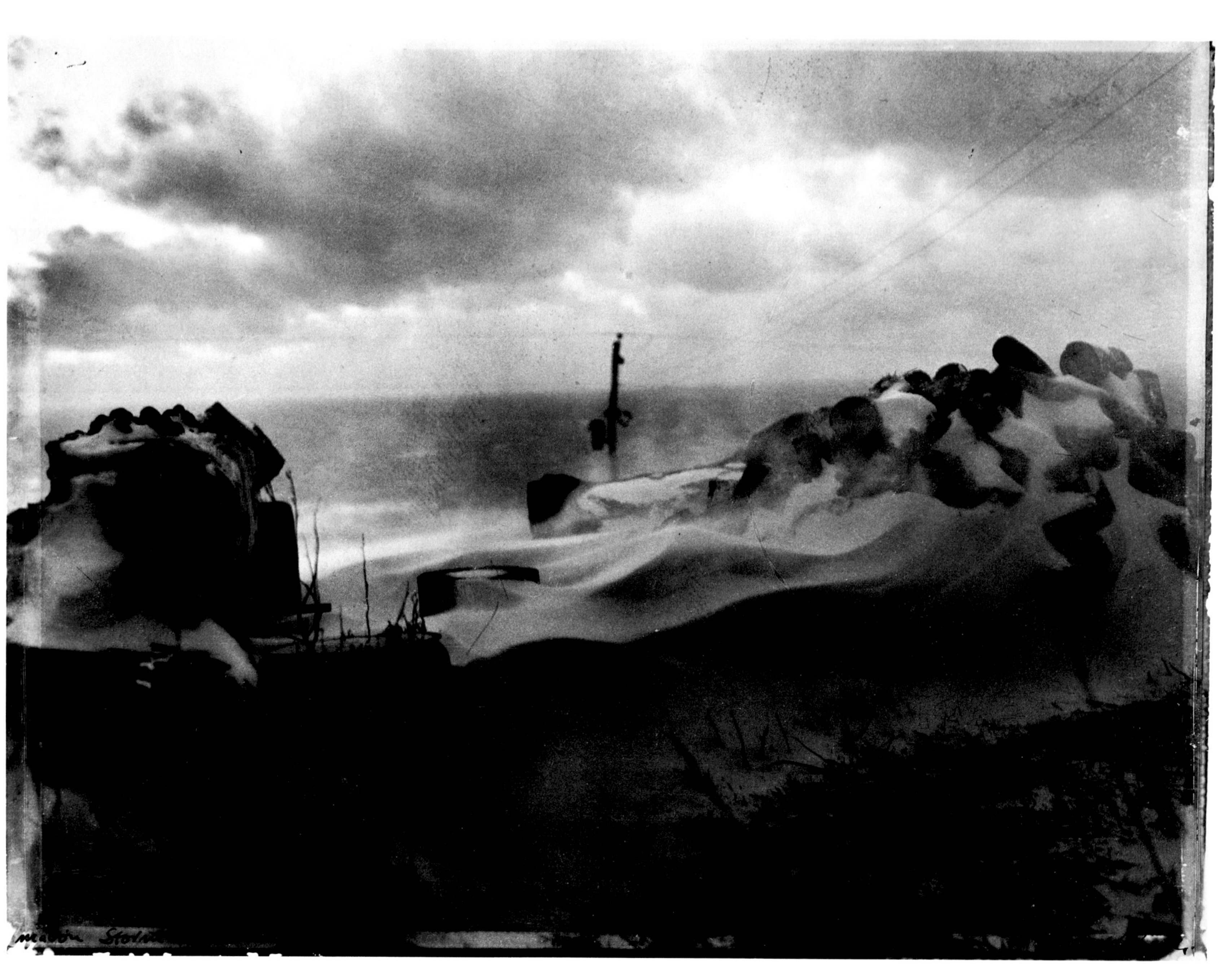

Robert Frank · *Mabou Storm, New Year's Day* · 1981

Robert Frank · *Pour la Fille* · 1980

PORTRAIT

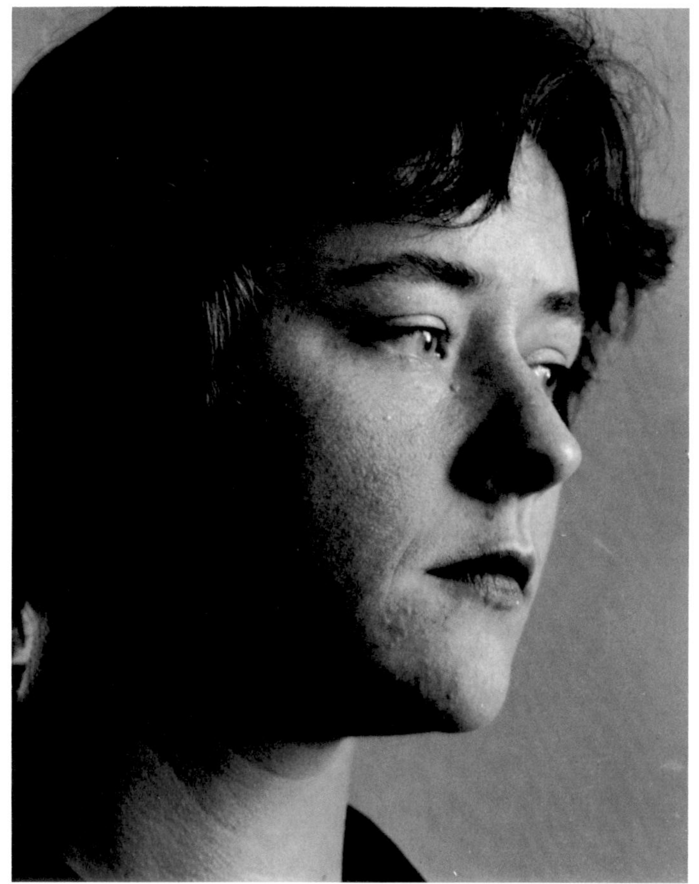

Ansel Adams · *Gerry Sharpe, San Francisco, California* · 1960

In this teeming world, each of us is condemned to a fundamental solitude. We live much of our lives in the isolation of the self.

A primal mystery separates one human being from another and in the end we can only imagine our way across this gulf. The earliest and most important lessons we learn concern how to make ourselves at home in a world whose most significant quality is the presence of other people.

What is human in the world is what is most familiar, yet human nature and human motivation and action remain the things we argue and ponder most and by which we are most often bewildered. Our moral systems tell us to identify ourselves with our neighbors, but we quickly recognize others as an ambiguous presence, sometimes even as a threat to life and safety rather than a source of fellowship and support. Human nature, it is finally agreed, is very enigmatic. "Know thyself," we say, the implication being that this helps. We say "the heart has its reasons."

In our struggle to resolve the perplexities of identity, selfhood, otherness, we are forever contemplating ourselves physically. Hamlet stares into the eyeless skull of Yorick, looking for the meaning of his own impending death. Broken kings call for a looking glass. Readers of modern history turn to the photographic sections that now accompany most books and stare into the impassive faces of victims, failed dreamers, and mass murderers. What are the readers looking for there? What's going to be in a picture? This Gauleiter has a cruel mouth or else he looks surprisingly benign. That general has a haunted look. A diplomat smiles super-serviceably. Most of the photographs displayed are banal commercial shots intended to depersonalize and hence conventionalize their subjects within a limited repertory of acceptable poses: brave soldier, man of affairs, happy bride.

The human image has had profound associations since the beginning of time. It was widely held that it reflected the image of the gods. In the Hebrew tradition the belief that the divine likeness had been stamped upon man made human life sacred. All images were forbidden to be reproduced as a guard against idolatry, but the prohibition against rendering the human form was designed to prevent this holiest of images from being debased. The Lord was mighty beyond measure. The earth was his footstool. He was not to be "captured."

The idea of portraiture as "capture" is not gratuitous. An aversion to being photographed is not confined to tribal people outside Western culture. It is an instinctive reaction of many people walking our city streets, not all of whom are on the lam. All the socialization in the world cannot remove completely the partly threatening nature of the Other. The possession or contemplation of another person's image really does provide us with a degree of power over that person; it is the power that our insight can bring to bear, our opportunity to try to understand the personality depicted. What we understand is always a little less threatening, a dread presence is more manageable, if we have the chance to penetrate its mystery. So our fascination with portraits can be seen as yet another way of confronting the old problem of Otherness.

The compulsion to portray, like so many other impulses that are humanistic and life-affirming, may thus be shown to have some root in the ground of primordial combat. And it is strange how much of art has something about it that is vaguely suggestive of conflict—the very word "art" and words associated with it can be quickly construed into synonyms for guile, deception, and trickery. Illusion is understandably suspect, and art is nothing if not illusion: it involves pretending, substituting a likeness for the thing itself.

Art might also be defined as the reduction of the things of life to the comprehensible. As an expression of the human soul, it forever obsesses over the human problem of self and other. Even at its most transcendental—during the ages of faith in the West—it never ceased its relentless examination of the human condition. The great religious paintings of Christianity were as much concerned with the mysteries of human salvation as with those of divinity for its own sake. The contemplation of a crucifixion scene isn't likely to remove us psychically from the plane of human suffering, human cruelty, and human self-sacrifice. It will spiritualize those things, help us to share them, invite us to believe that the very universe involves itself in them, but such a work of art will still have as its ultimate subject the destiny of human souls.

One of the things we will always require of art is an element of recognition. To succeed in its purpose a painting, a photograph, a poem, or a piece of music must elicit from the observer a certain complicity. As an example of this principle let's examine an extremely modest, not to say vulgar, art form: the joke. Jokes aren't often sublime, but it's usually quite easy to tell whether they're any good or not. If they're good they're funny and we laugh at them. Otherwise they're not and we don't.

Why is a good joke funny? Why should it produce that curious simian spasm called laughter? What makes it work? A good joke calls forth from us a certain recognition of the conditions of our existence. The implicit punch line to every joke is: That's how it is! All jokes work the same way, on the principle of recognition. And all art works the same way.

From the oldest jazz records available to the frostiest postmodernist jazz on the digital discs of today, if the performance was recorded live and the audience is on the track, the same one-word response keeps resounding, greeting a solo, or an ingenious piece of collective improvisation: "Yeah." That's how it is. That's life, trouble, good times, or love. Recognition is everything.

To say so much is to say that all art has truth as its object. That part of art which takes humanity as its subject will be bound to pursue truths about the nature of humankind and to compel recognition of these truths. It will not be enough to state the obvious. The observer, reader, listener must be led to the necessary recognition of truth through the mediation of the work and led, moreover, to discover it for himself or herself, as something fresh and new, as an insight. If Narcissus had been able to look at himself every day for a month, instead of only once in a pool, he might have found himself with a lot to think about. He might have saved himself with a few second thoughts.

Definitions of truth vary. During the long history of art, artists' attempts to depict, describe, define humankind have been guided by different philosophies. In some periods the individual mattered less than in others. The classical world's way of approaching the truth about humanity was to render the ideal; the ideal human form was *truer* than the bodies people walked around with because it was the "original" beside which ordinary bodies could be seen to display flaws. To the classical world perfection was truth, and truth was available to mortals only through art.

Two thousand years later, Imperial court painters like David might render the unprepossessing Bonaparte as a physically beautiful, dynamic youth. David's flattery also had philosophical support because it could be held that the "true" Napoleon was not the small, sallow man in the unadorned uniform but the radiant, godlike genius whom it was the painter's business to discern.

Regardless of philosophy, the enterprise was the same: to display to humankind an element of truth about its nature. This was to be done by rendering the artificial impression of a human presence, to make people seeing only paint or stone or mere words believe that they were experiencing a person.

Certain artists have always excelled at this and it is interesting, although difficult, to consider why. It has to do, I think, with a certain way of looking at the world. The artist who deals in recapitulating what is human has to be a good listener and a good watcher. He must command the facility to identify and examine all the elements, large and small—all the contradictions and passions that together make up the most ordinary person. In a way, he must deny the existence of such a thing as an ordinary person. He must understand that clichés do not exist in nature, not even in human nature, but only in art. No matter how embittered he may be, he must finally be in sympathy with humankind.

All this, of course, is the easy part. His skill as an observer has now to be equaled by his skill in execution. Knowing the dynamics of an arm in motion and the revelations in a complacent glance, he has to get them down. Just as he understands that a human personality is made up of many disparate elements, he must understand that portrayals are also composed in multiples. There are all the questions to be resolved and all the decisions to be made. What to put in? What to leave out?

The portraitist must also know his enemies. He has to relentlessly fight conventionalization, that eternal enemy of portraiture, the breeder of kitsch and lies. Even if he works in a country where the conventionalization of human nature is demanded by the authorities, he must fight against it secretly or transcend it.

Above all he must know the difference between sympathy for his subject and sentimentality. Sentimentality kills in art; it destroys everything dignified and honorable about humanity. It insults and degrades sentiment.

The artist who represents the human must realize that only vigilance and discipline will keep him away from things like conventionalization and sentimentality. Modestly, he must also realize the tremendous importance of the work he does and the service he provides.

The humanist artist is indeed a hunter, out to capture. Like a tribesman snatching a salmon from a creek, he needs to be quick and deft, able to lay hands on a moment. Taking hold of it, he lifts it up against the sky. It is beautiful, all colors, sinuous, virtually perfect. We recognize the beauty of it and the hunter's skill.

There is nothing like the capture of a human moment. Going to some of the oldest literature still available, consider Genesis 4:9, when God accuses Cain.

"Where is Abel, thy brother?" the Lord demands.

"And he said: I know not. Am I my brother's keeper?"

The moment of this discourse stays with us. Its authenticity reaches us across time and myth and all of human history. Cain's voice—sullen, sarcastic, and bitter—is a voice that compels us to recognition. We recognize a lonely, self-pitying, guilty adolescent faced with the consequences of a bloody big mistake. Through the verisimilitude of Cain's voice we are put in mind of all such adolescents. Beyond that we are made to recognize ourselves: we, the tribe of actual and potential Cains.

Among all the tricks of art there is none greater than the mediation of human identity, the illusion of life being lived in time. All those captured moments become part of our personal history. All great portrayals combine theater and meditation; around them hang the richest silences in the world. They place before our insight a wealth of recognitions. Peasants, gentlemen and ladies, doges and Grand Inquisitors are there for us, commanded to perform the drama of their personalities.

At the core of human portraiture lies a great irony. Looking at Titian's portrait of Aretino, we learn so much about the man. At the same time we are learning how little we can ever know about anyone. In the greatest art, questions and answers are suspended units, connected but never meant to be resolved, in an ongoing process like that chase on the Grecian urn. Titian tells us more about human nature than we can absorb and leaves us the more questioning. The sixteenth-century Florentine painter Bronzino's *Portrait of a Young Man* seems to be explaining its subject while in a sense it mocks both him and us. Who does the young man, smooth and arrogant, think he is? What does he know about anything? And we who examine Bronzino's picture, what do we think we are looking at? What assurance can we bring to bear to match the youth's hauteur? The painting seems to suggest that we and this insolent young courtier somehow deserve each other.

In Albrecht Dürer's self-portrait the process of the artist capturing life is itself depicted. Dürer doesn't actually show himself painting, but he faces the world beyond his picture like a man looking into a mirror. He is a young, confident artist; a sly, observing aspect to his features makes the work appear to lack the gravity of the aging Rembrandt's self-portrait. At the same time there is a suggestion of wonder, and even timidity, as though he could not continue this bold confrontation with himself or face his own steady gaze for very long. It appears he has decided to be pleased with himself, but his expression is questioning. He has reversed the game and rendered Self as Other. Before him lie all the arcana of humanity. Like Rembrandt's self-portrait, the Dürer painting might well bear the inscription that, centuries later, Paul Gauguin was to write on one of his own examinations of the human condition: "Who are we? Where do we come from? Where are we going?"

At the end we get the mystery back. What can people know about people? How much is out there to see? After all the haunted canvases of the great painters, and all the living prose of the great writers and poets, after the Titians, the Botticellis, the Dickenses and Shakespeares, after Balzac, Brady, Vermeer, the most significant element of humanity remains what is unknowable.

Art will forever remain, as André Malraux said it was, the voice of silence. It is what we oppose to the silence around us. It is the order that we dare to impose on things, finding ourselves, as we do, just *out here*—out here in this vast, apparently indifferent chain of phenomenology.

As dreams are to the waking mind, art is to human history. It is something vital and irreplaceable. Humanity must always be the principal subject of art. Our selves are the units through which the conscious universe perceives itself.

ROBERT STONE

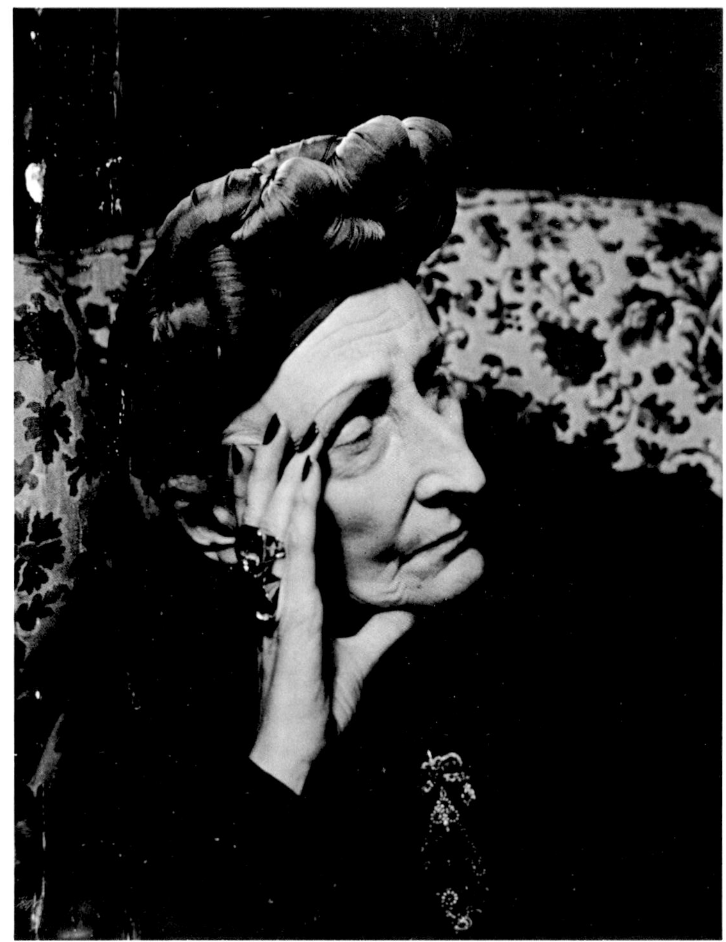

Philippe Halsman · *Edith Sitwell* · 1958

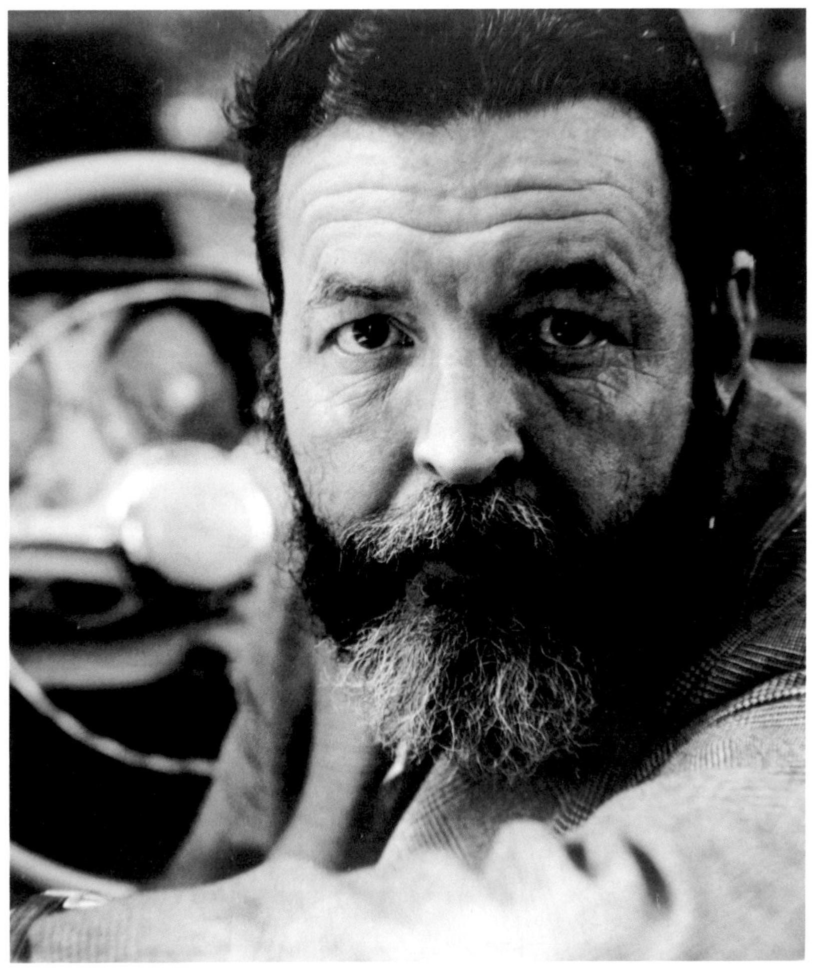

Philippe Halsman · *Randall Jarrell* · 1958

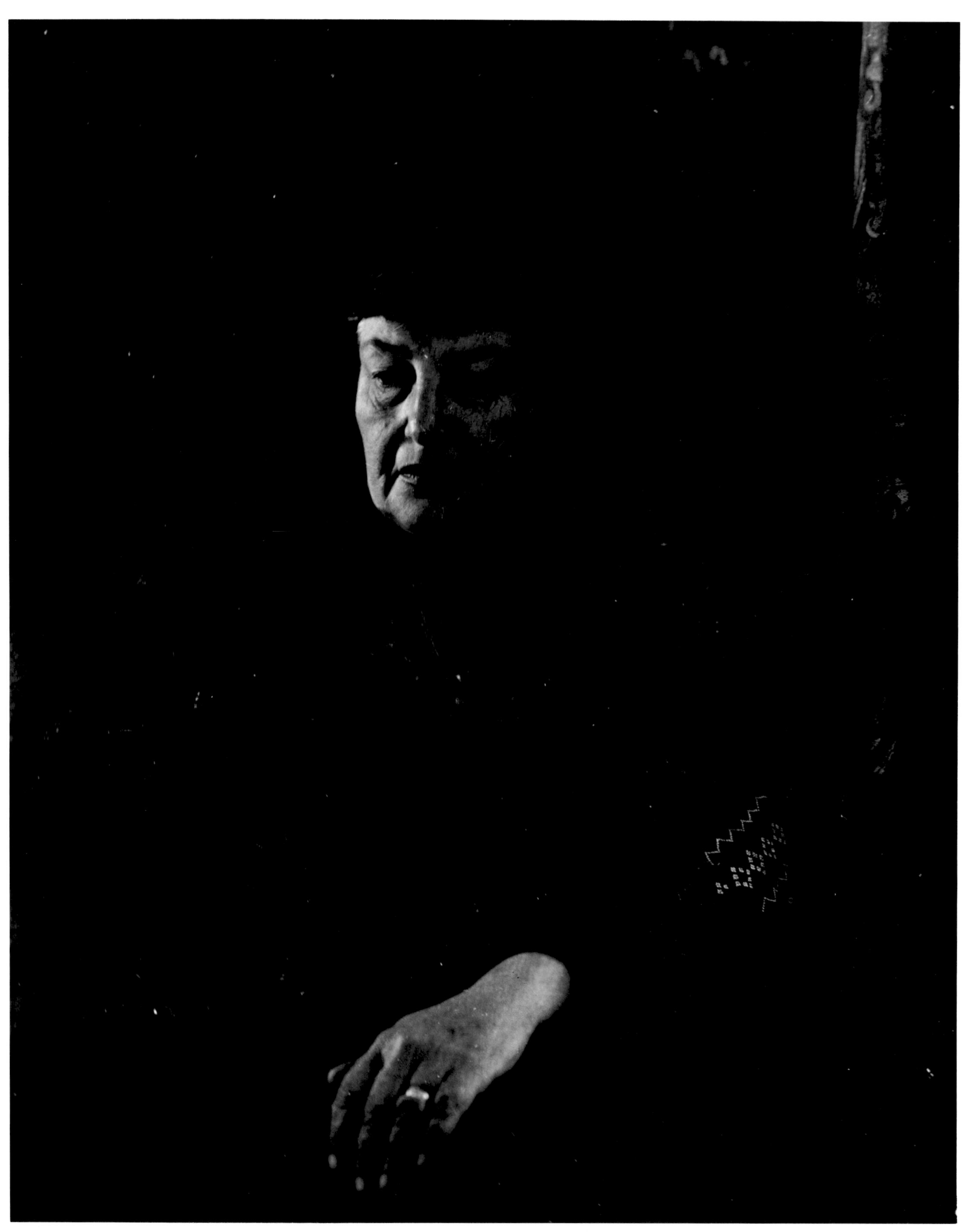

Imogen Cunningham · *Portrait of a Woman* · n.d.

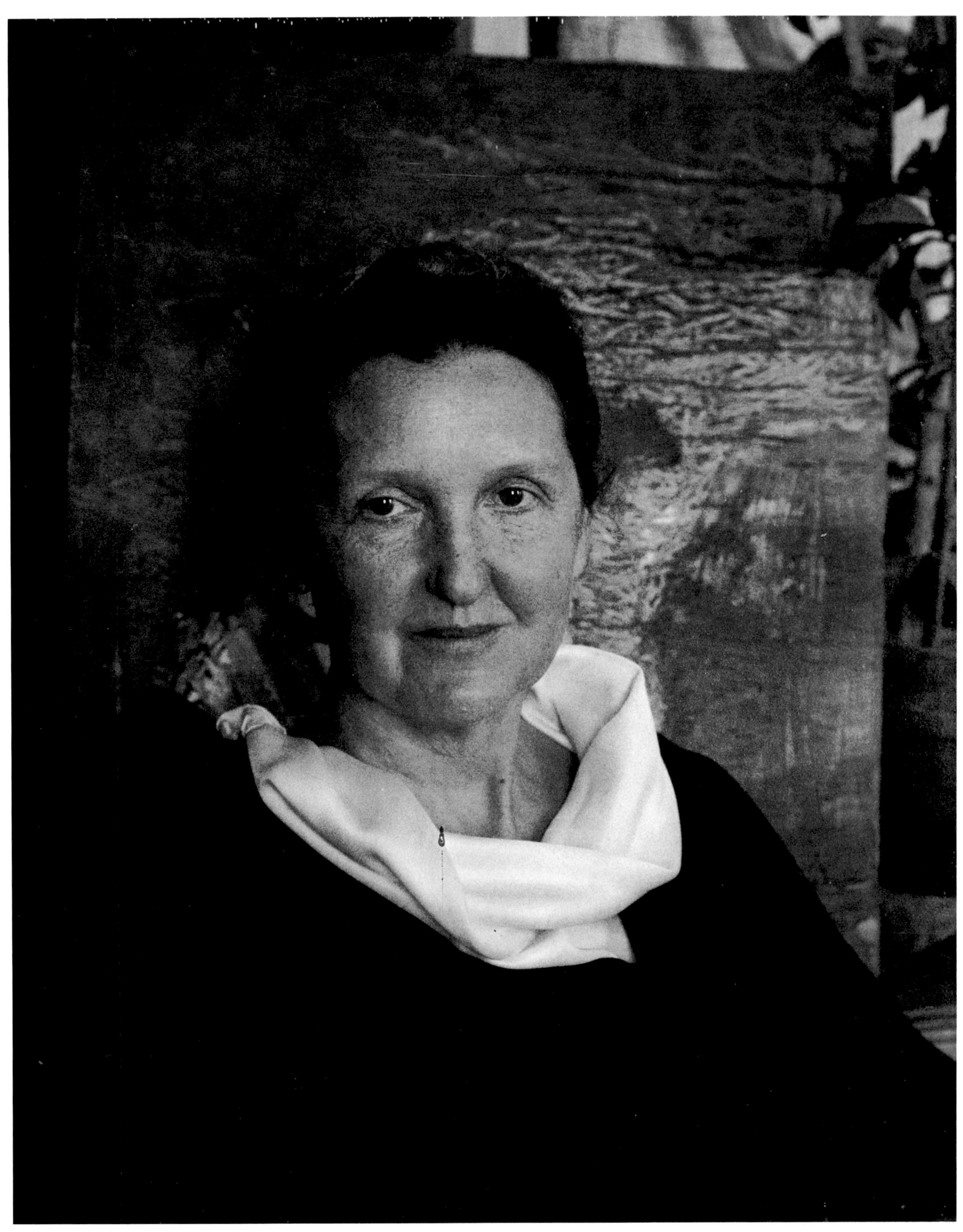

Imogen Cunningham · *Portrait of a Woman 2* · n.d.

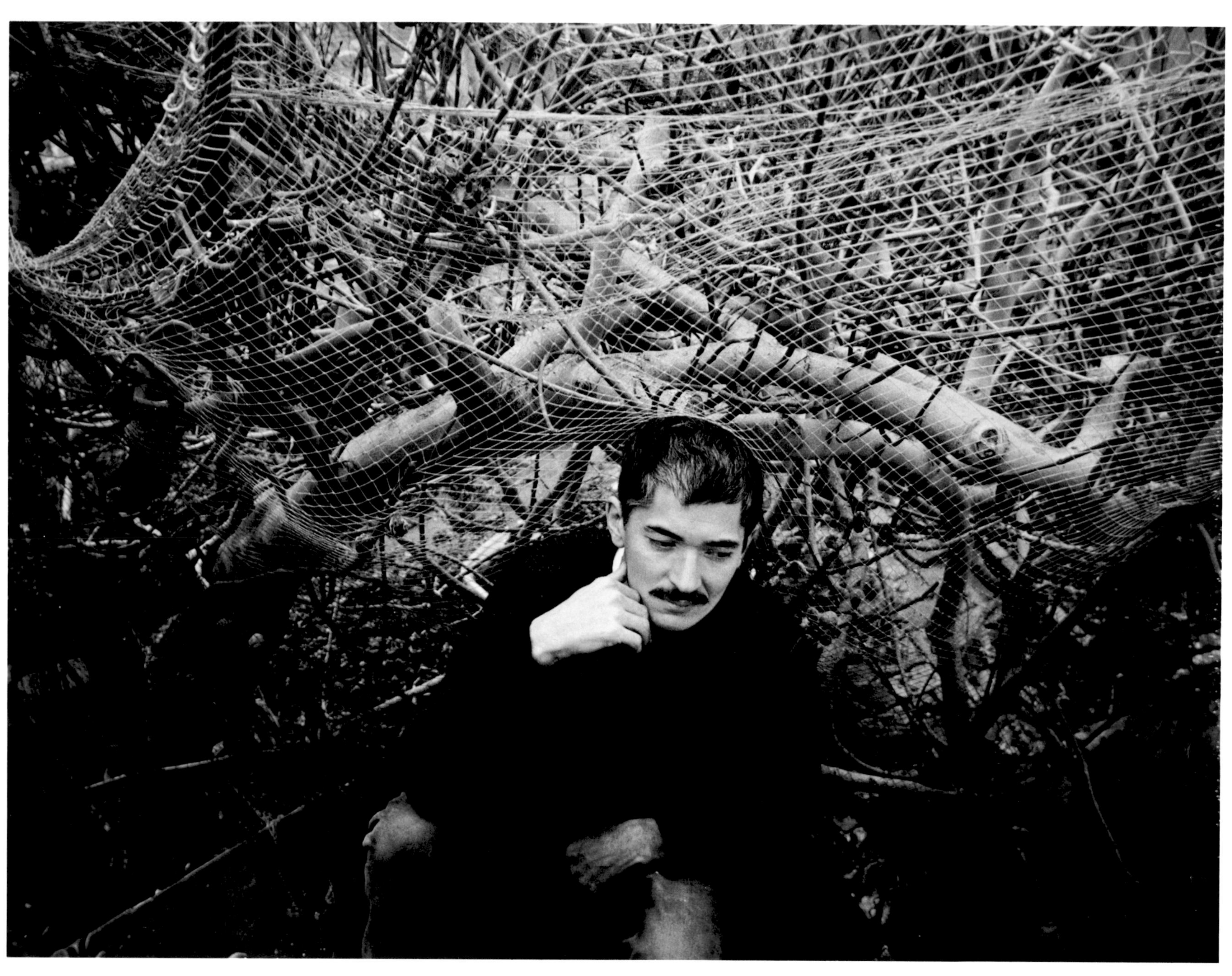

Imogen Cunningham · *Under my Fig Tree* · n.d.

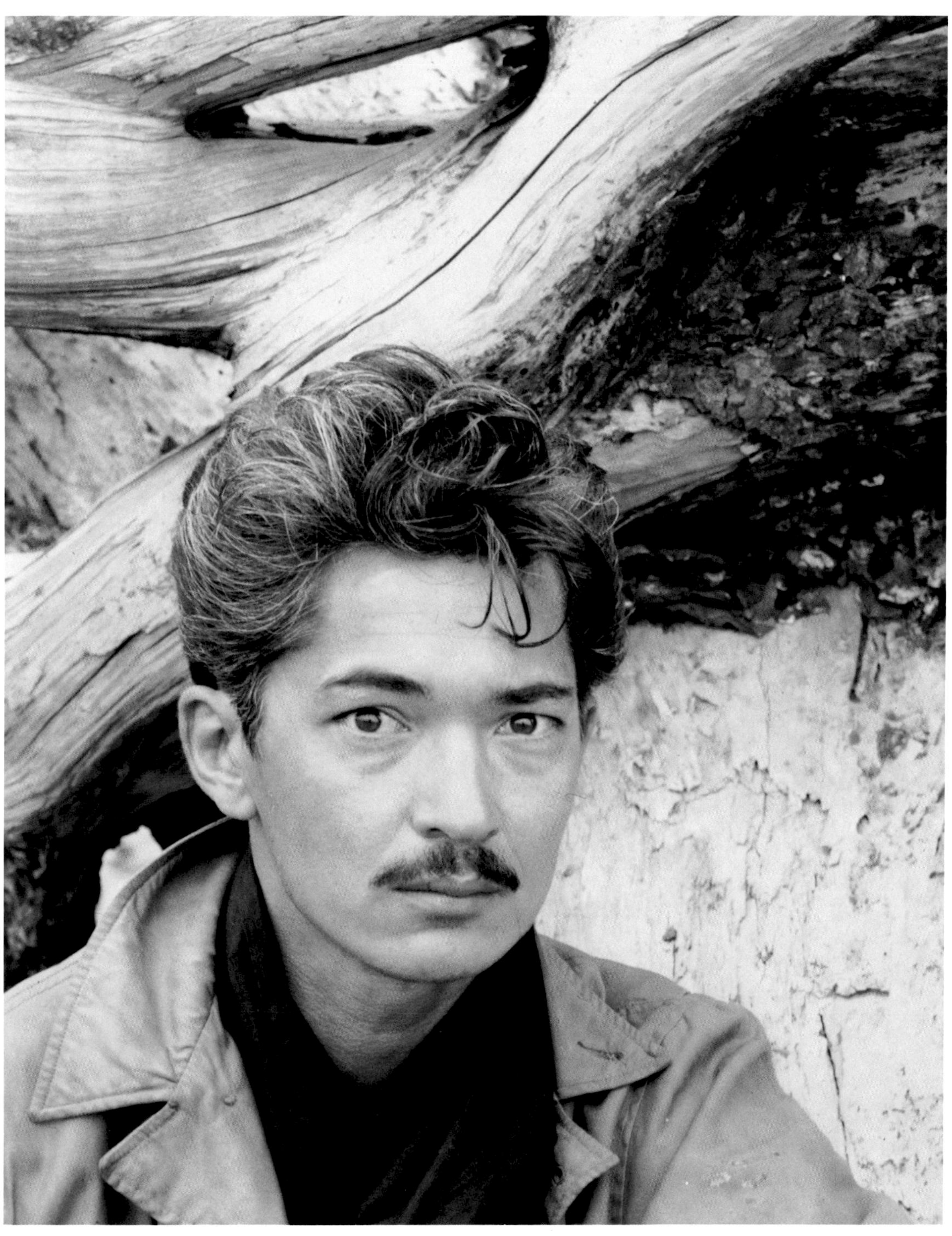

Minor White · [Bill] *LaRue and Tree Root, Cape Meares, Oregon* · 1961

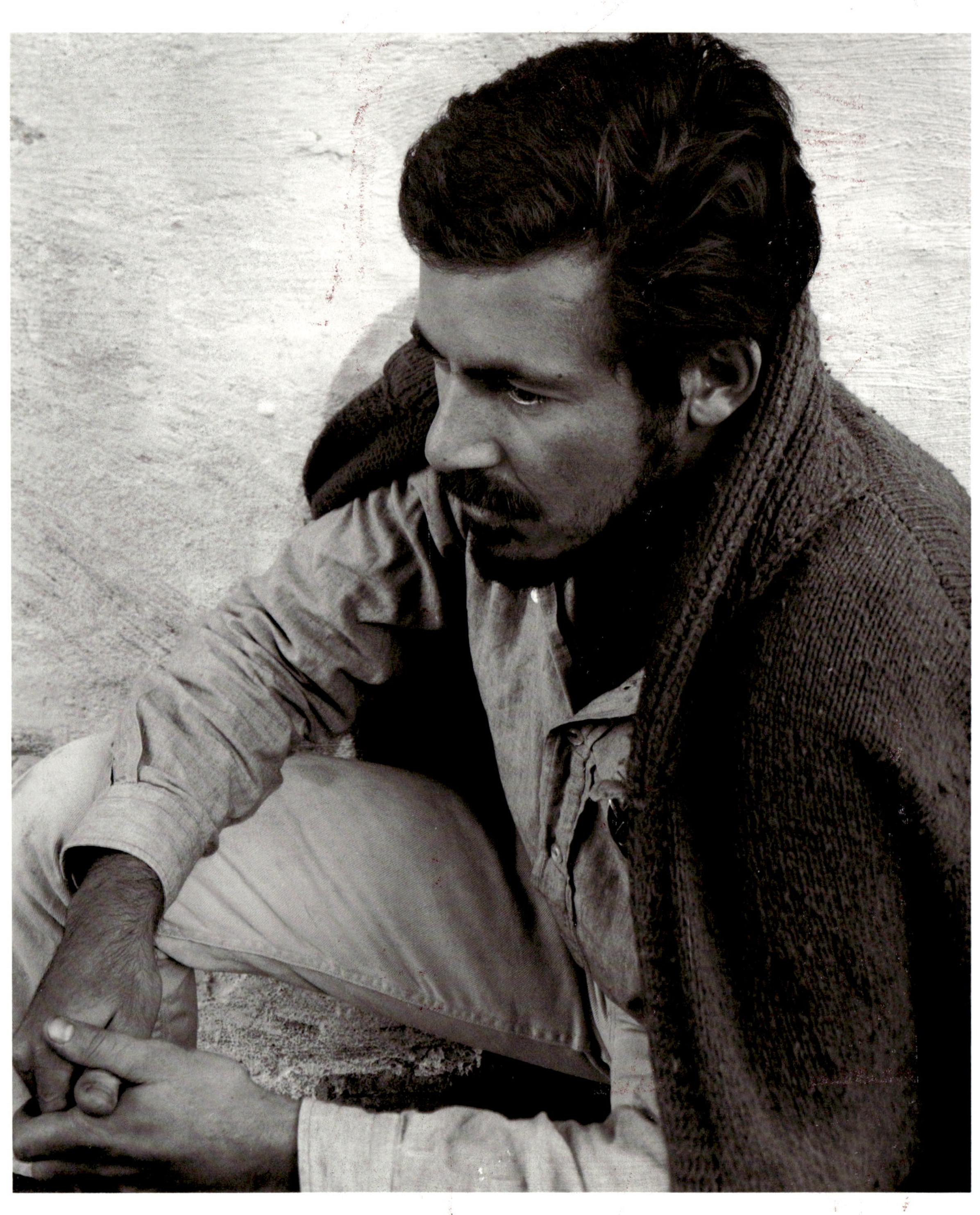

Paul Caponigro · *Don Harrison, Brewster, New York* · c. 1963

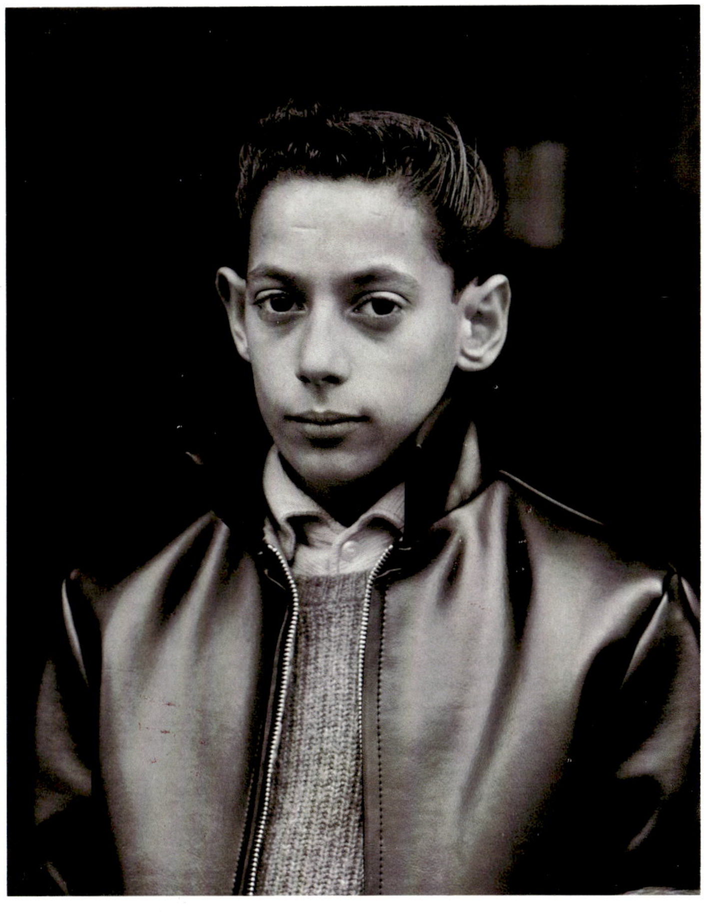

Paul Caponigro · *Italian Boy, North End, Boston, Massachusetts* · c. 1961

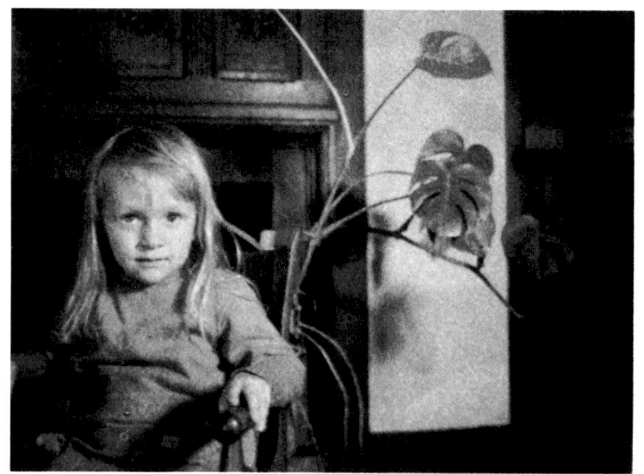

William Clift · *Wendy, Boston, Massachusetts* · 1956

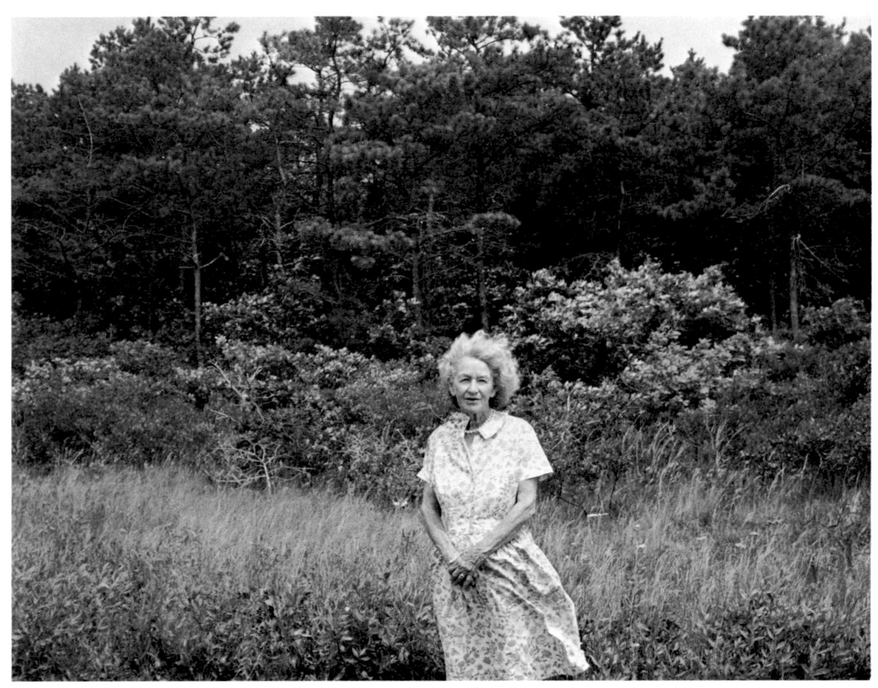

William Clift · *Barbara Pearmain, Cape Cod, Massachusetts* · 1967

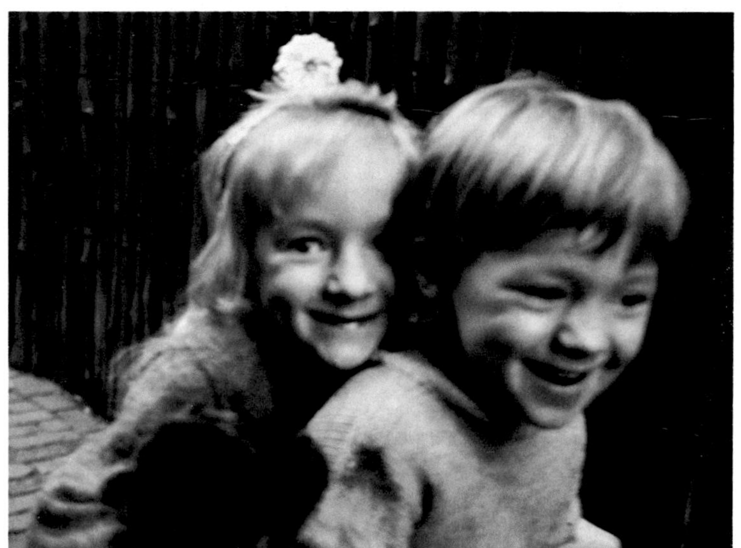

William Clift · *Sandy and Jody, Boston, Massachusetts* · 1962

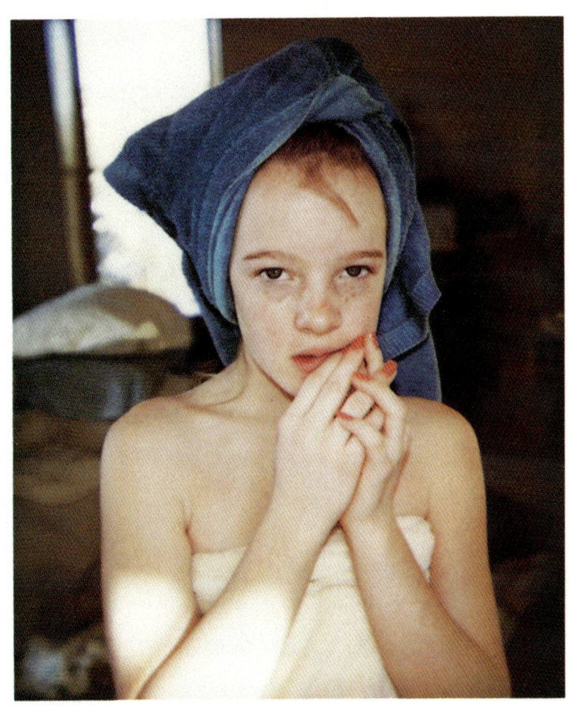

William Clift · *Carola, Santa Fe, New Mexico* · 1987

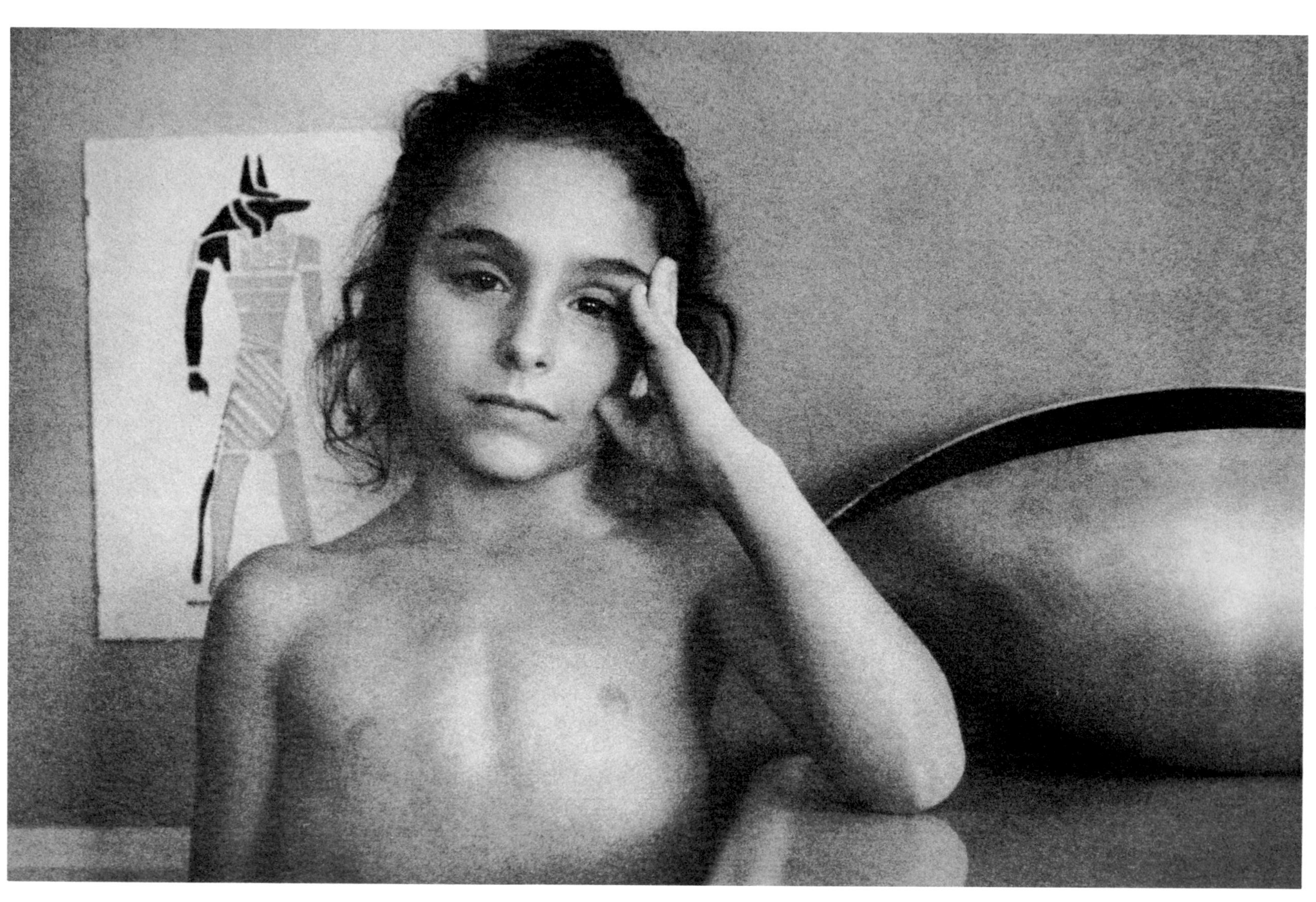

Sheila Metzner · *Stella, Mouillé Shapes* · 1986

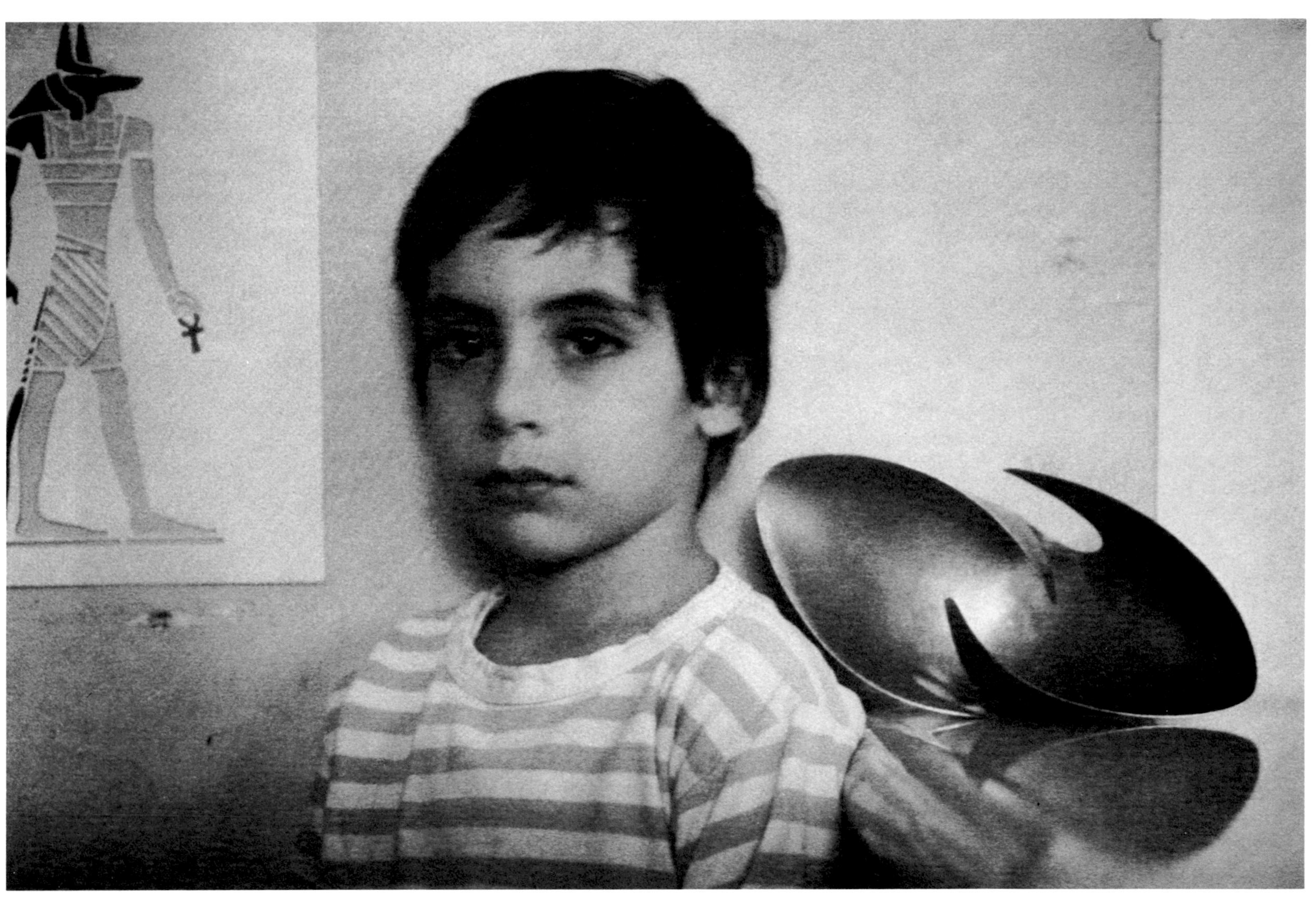

Sheila Metzner · *Louie, Mouillé Shapes* · 1986

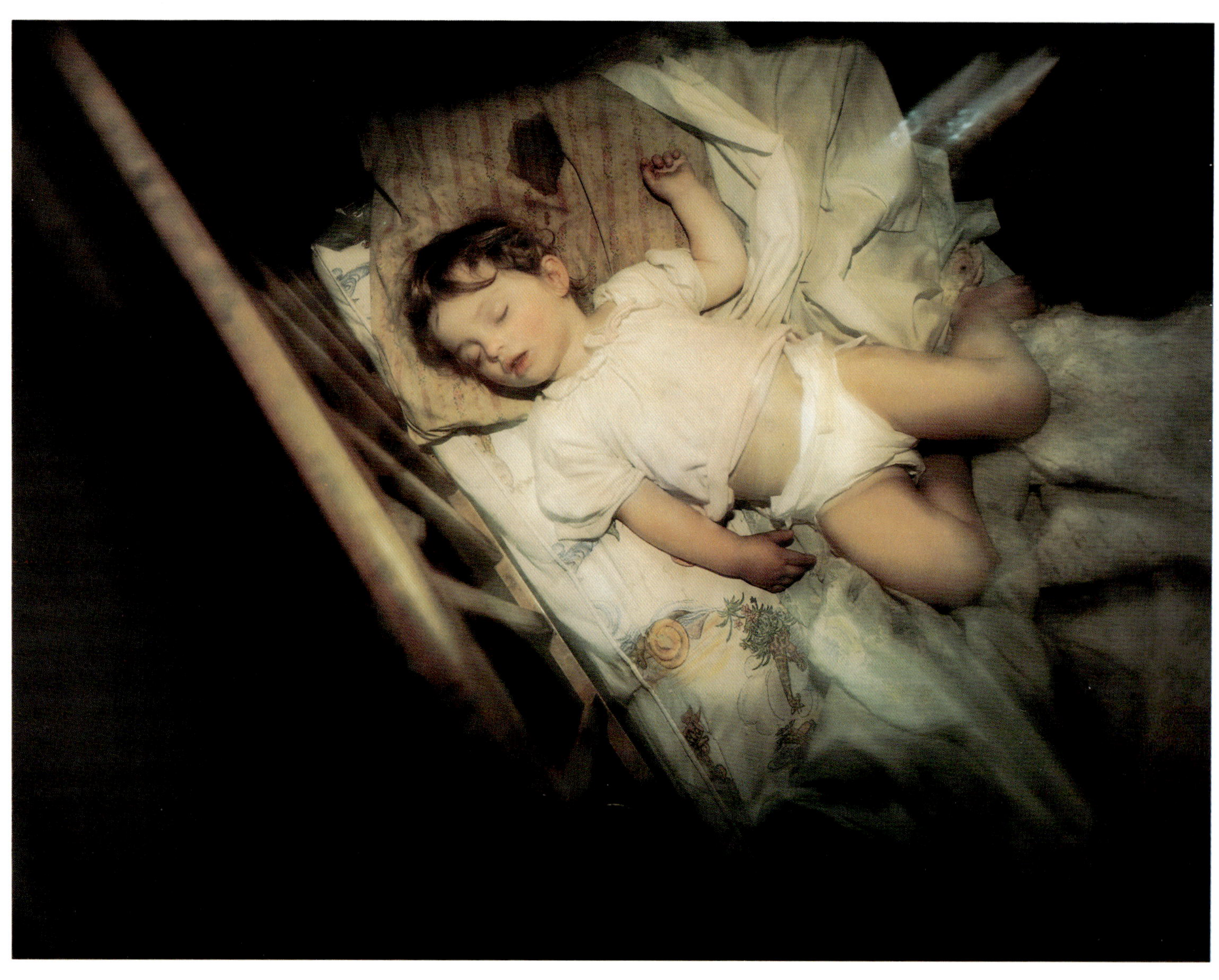

Sally Mann · *Virginia in Bed* · 1987

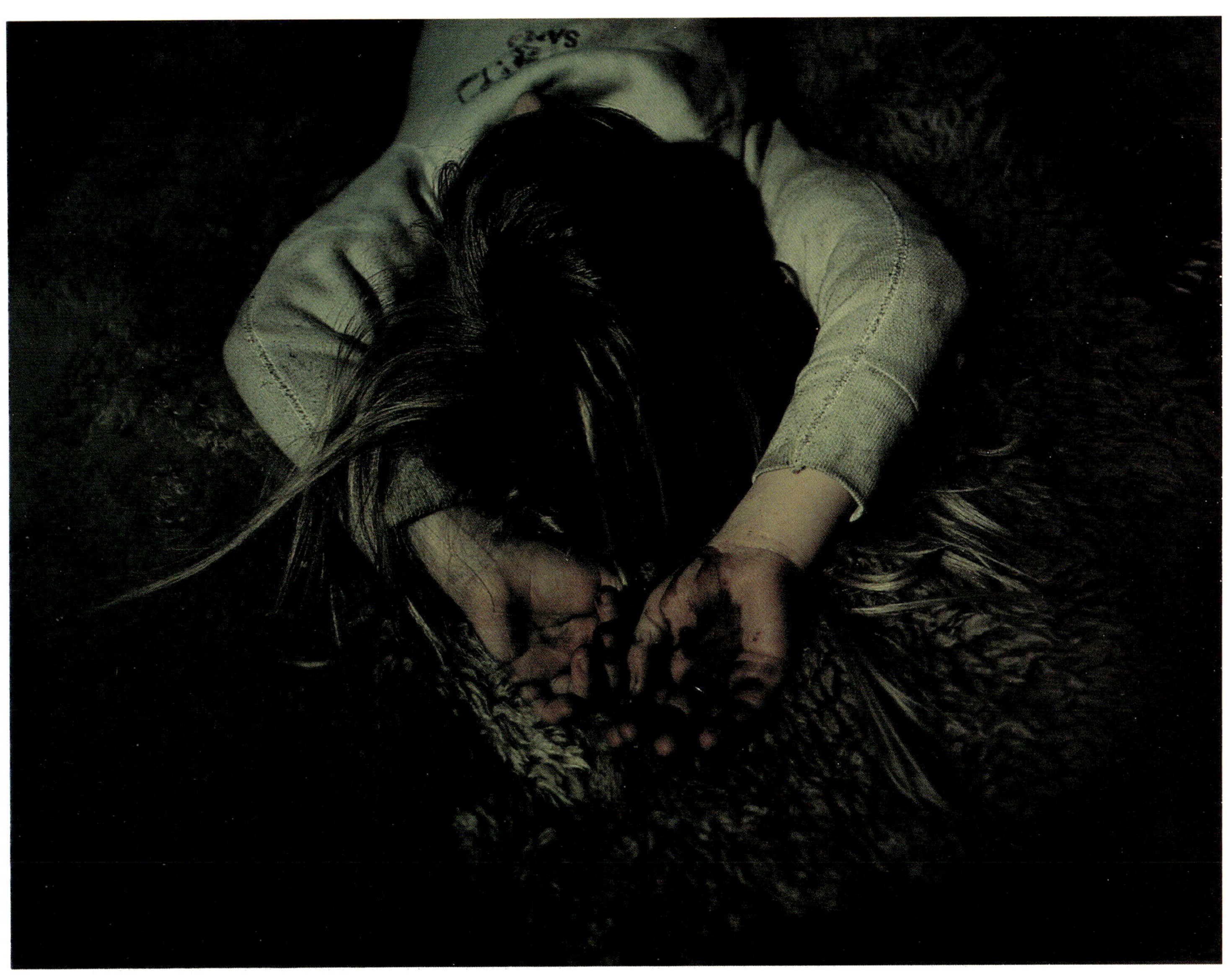

Sally Mann · *Jessie's Hands* · 1987

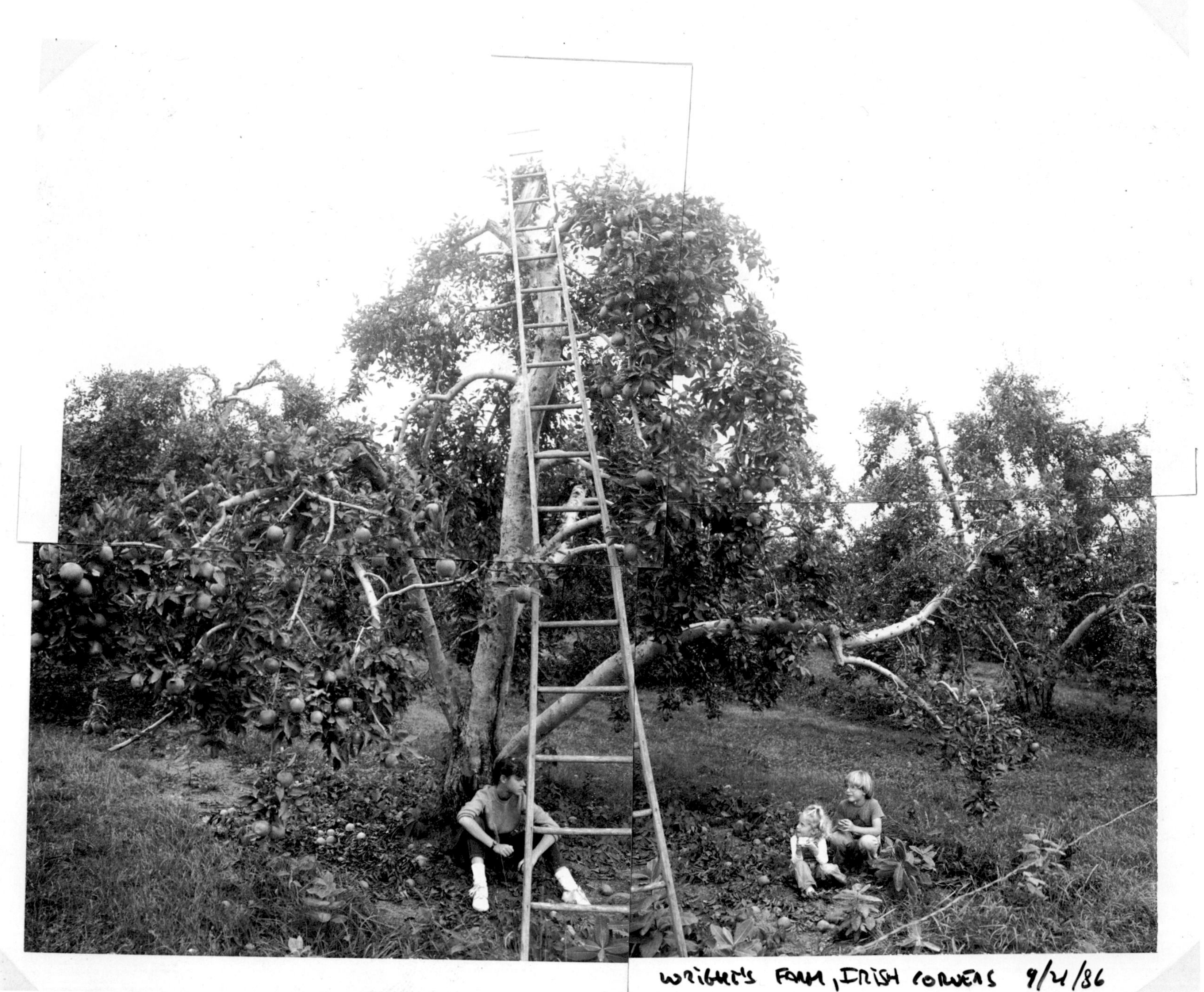

Danny Lyon · *Wright's Farm, Ireland Corners* · 1986

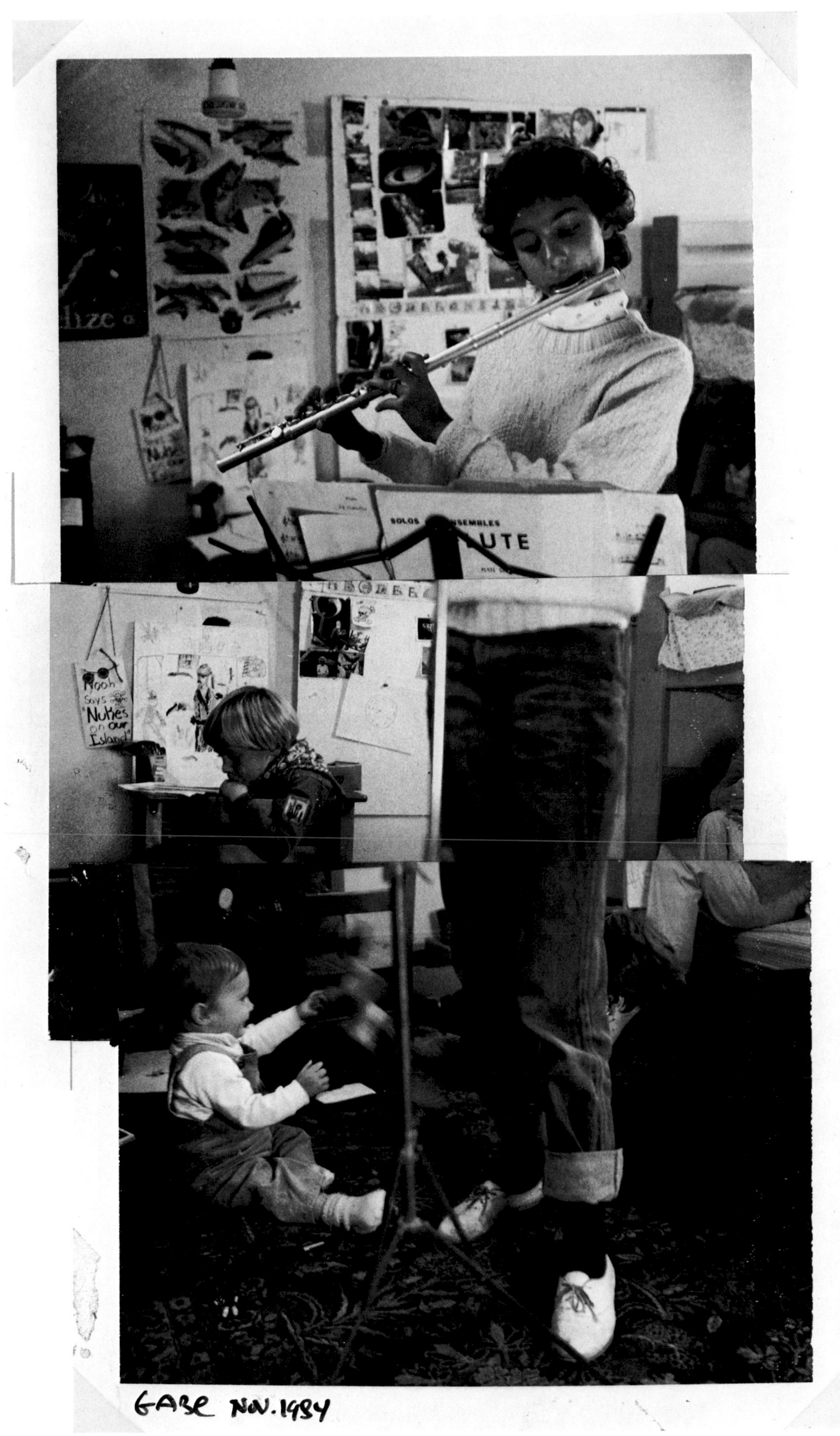

Danny Lyon · *Gabe* · 1984

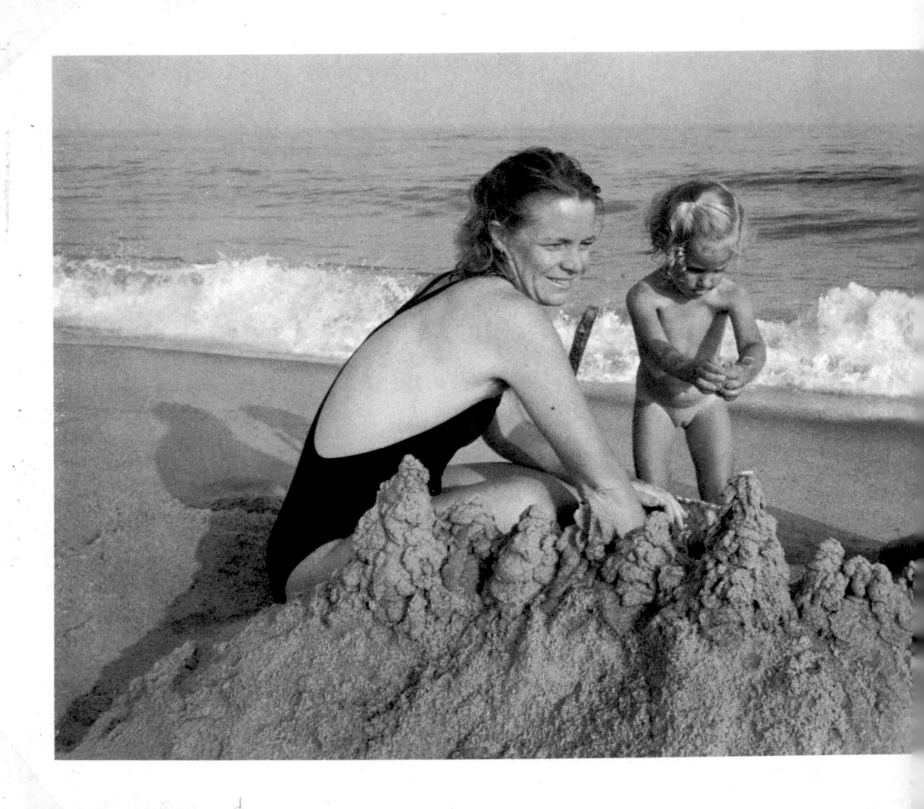

Danny Lyon · *At Addie's Beach* · 1986

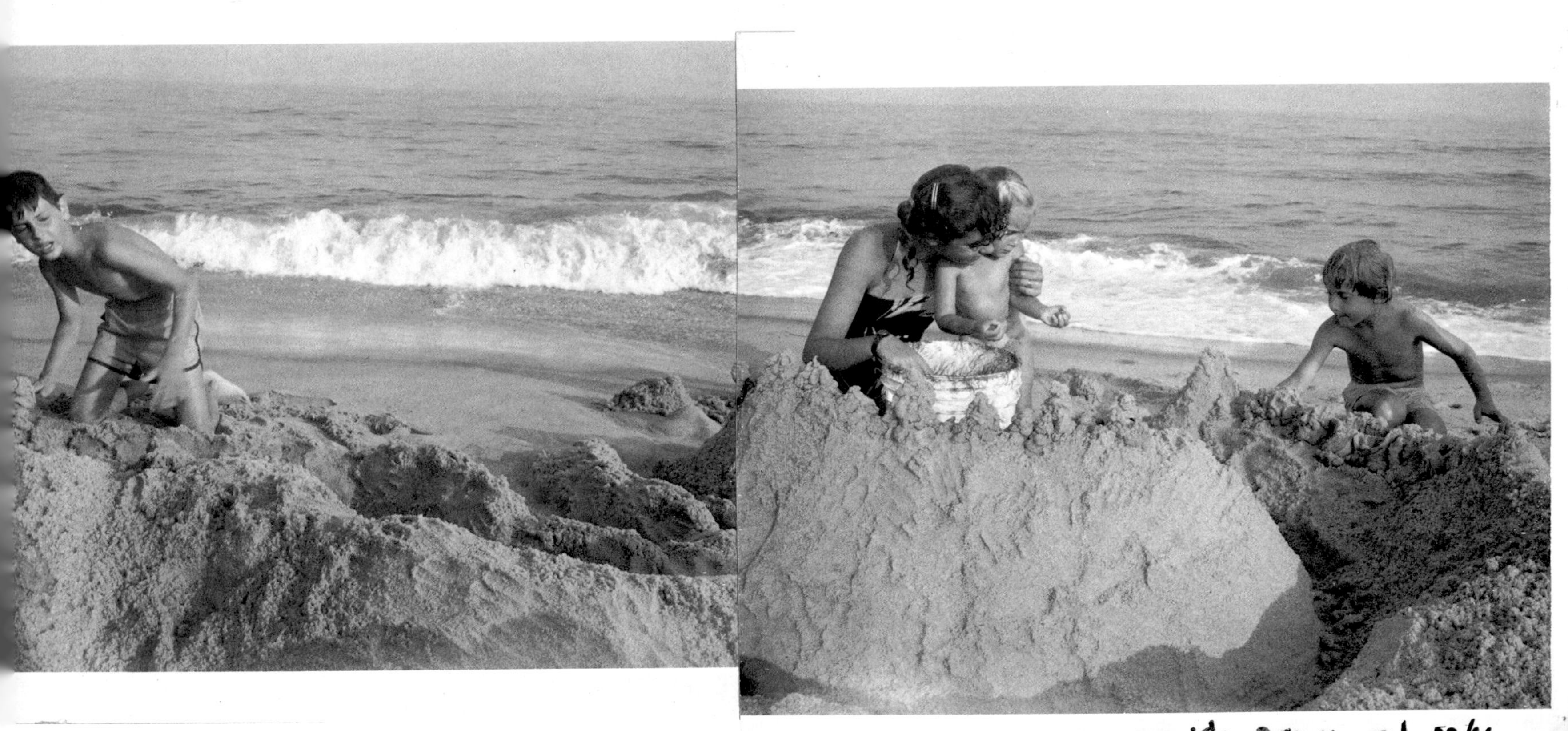
AT ADDIE'S BEACH July 23/86

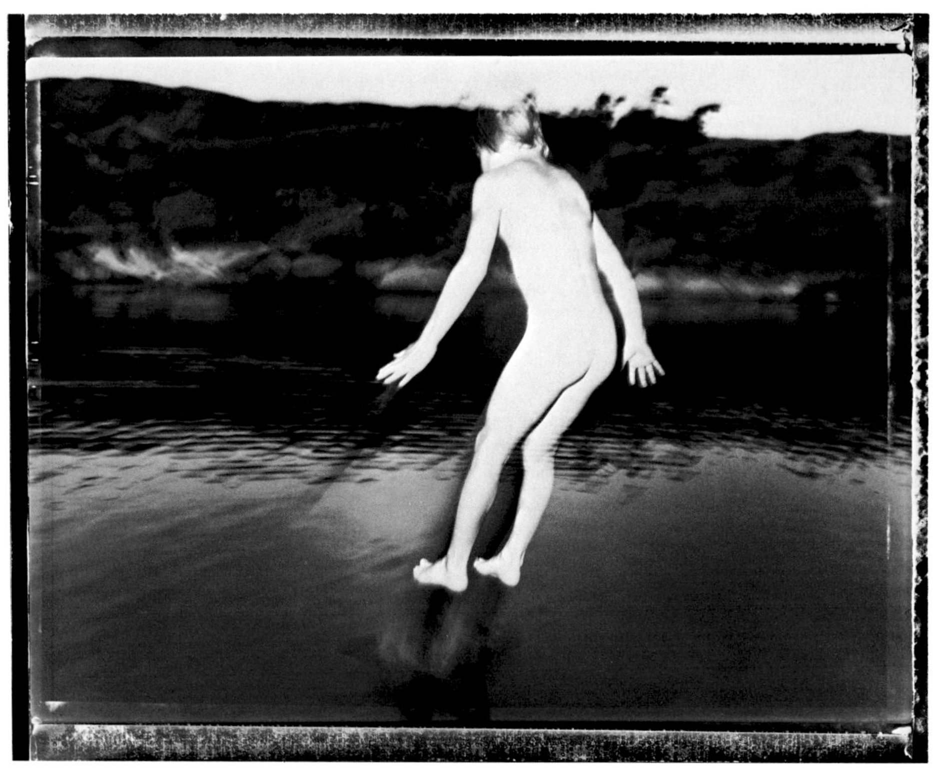

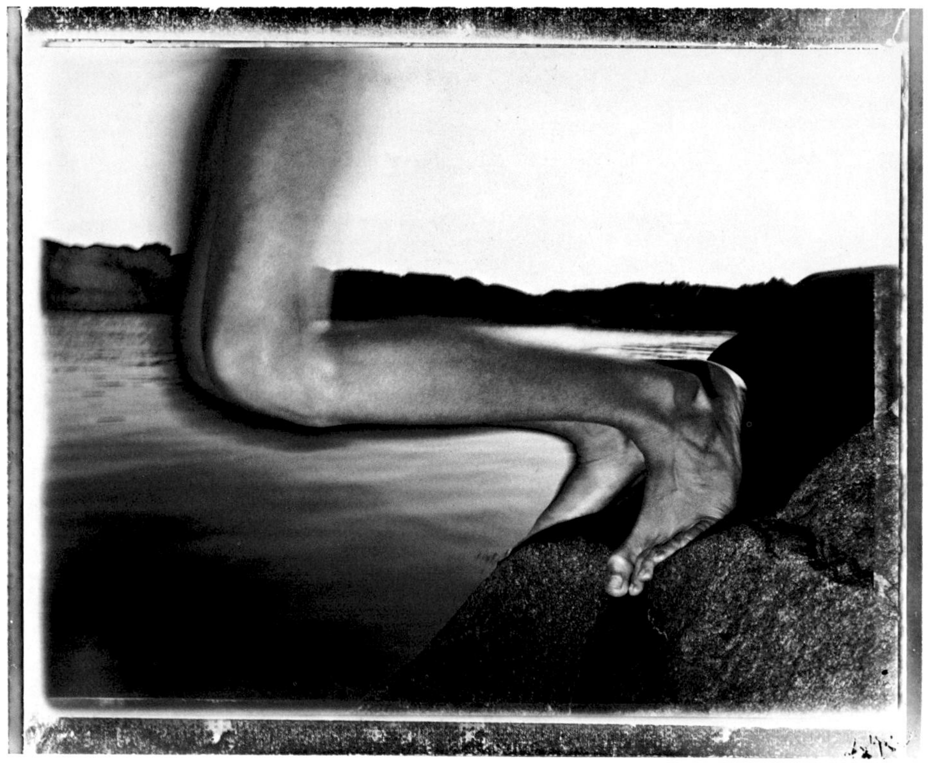

Jim Bengston · Untitled, Slow Motion Series · 1978

Jim Bengston · Untitled, Slow Motion Series · 1977

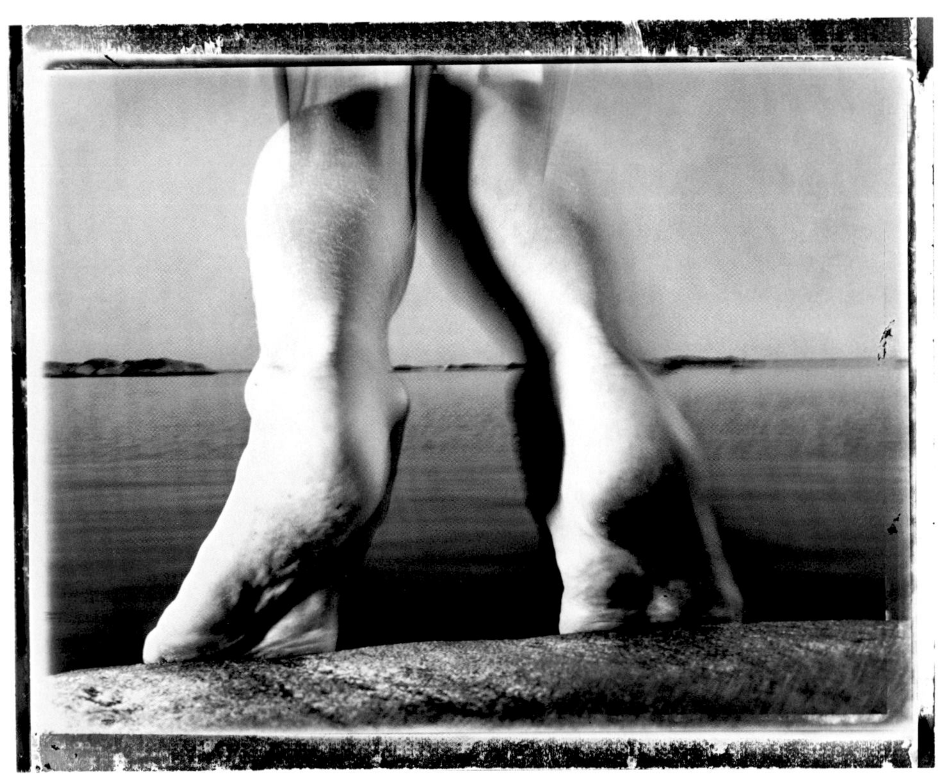

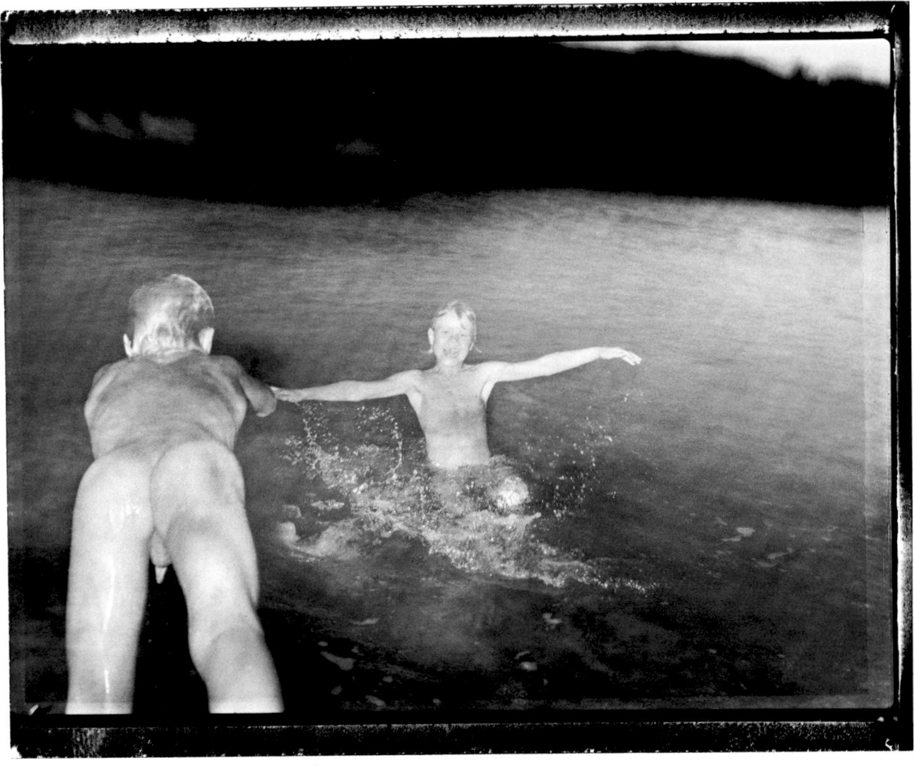

Jim Bengston · Untitled, Slow Motion Series · 1977

Jim Bengston · Untitled, Slow Motion Series · 1979

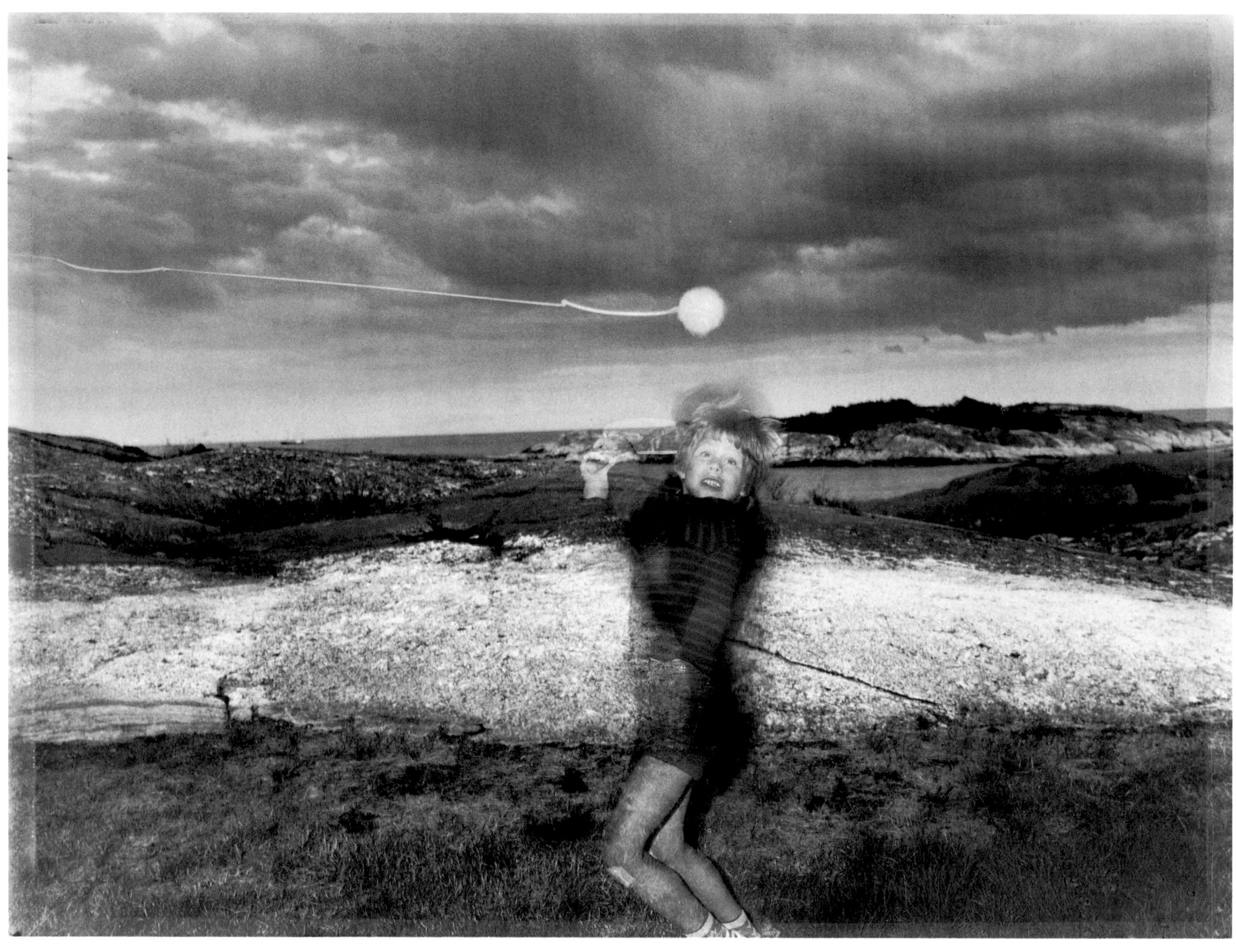

Jim Bengston · Untitled, Slow Motion Series · 1977

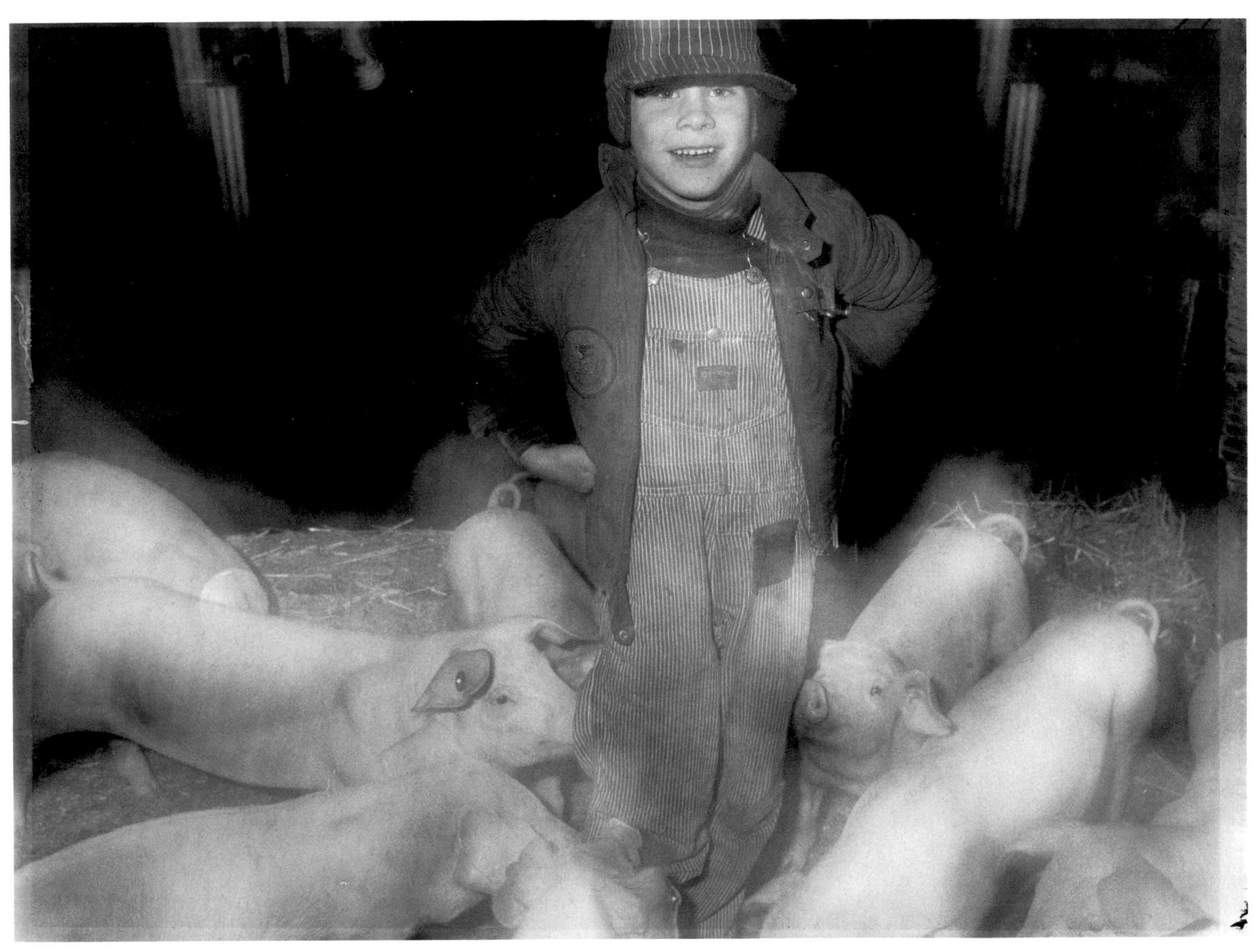

Jim Bengston · Untitled, Slow Motion Series · 1979

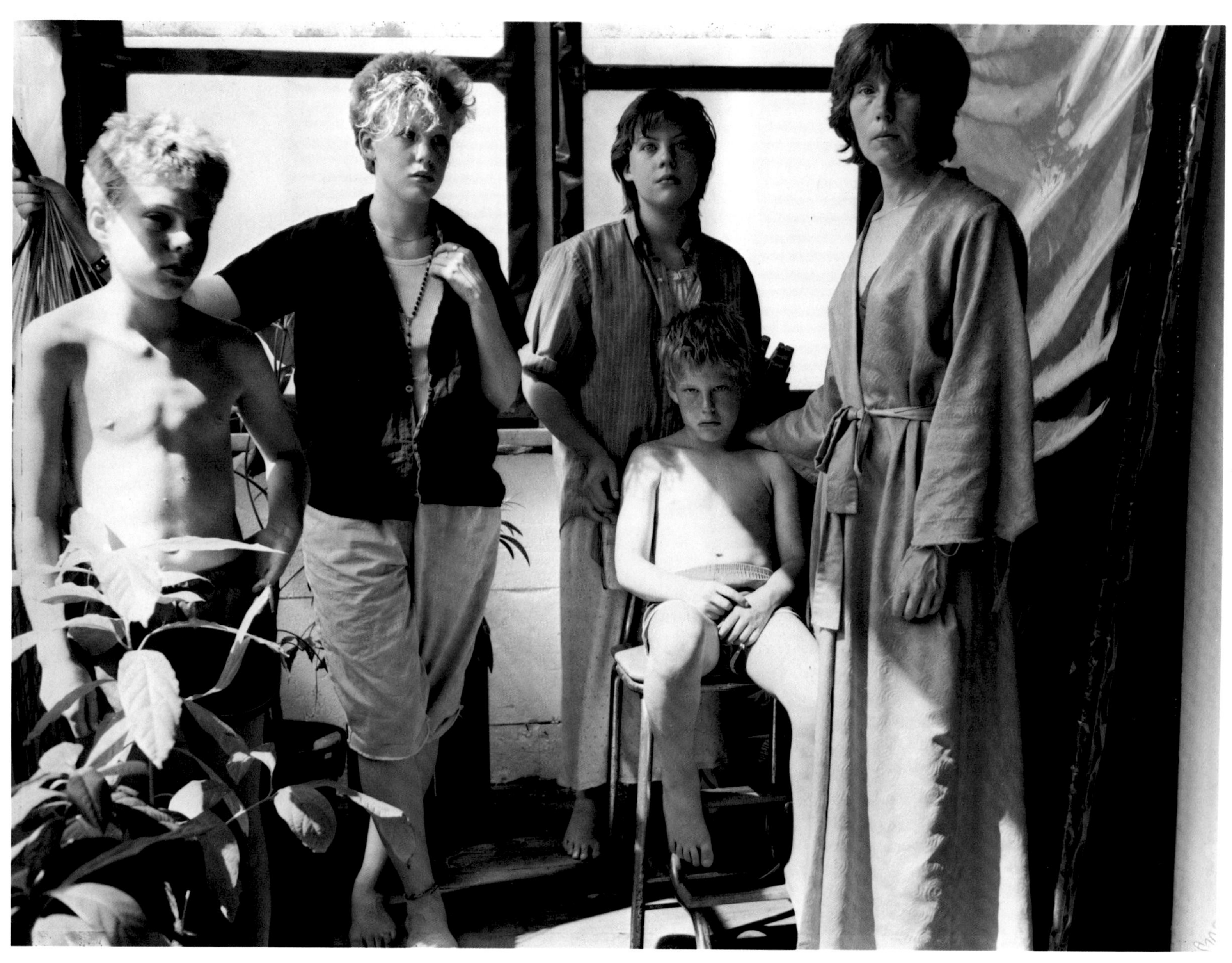

Judith Black · *Self with Children* · 1984

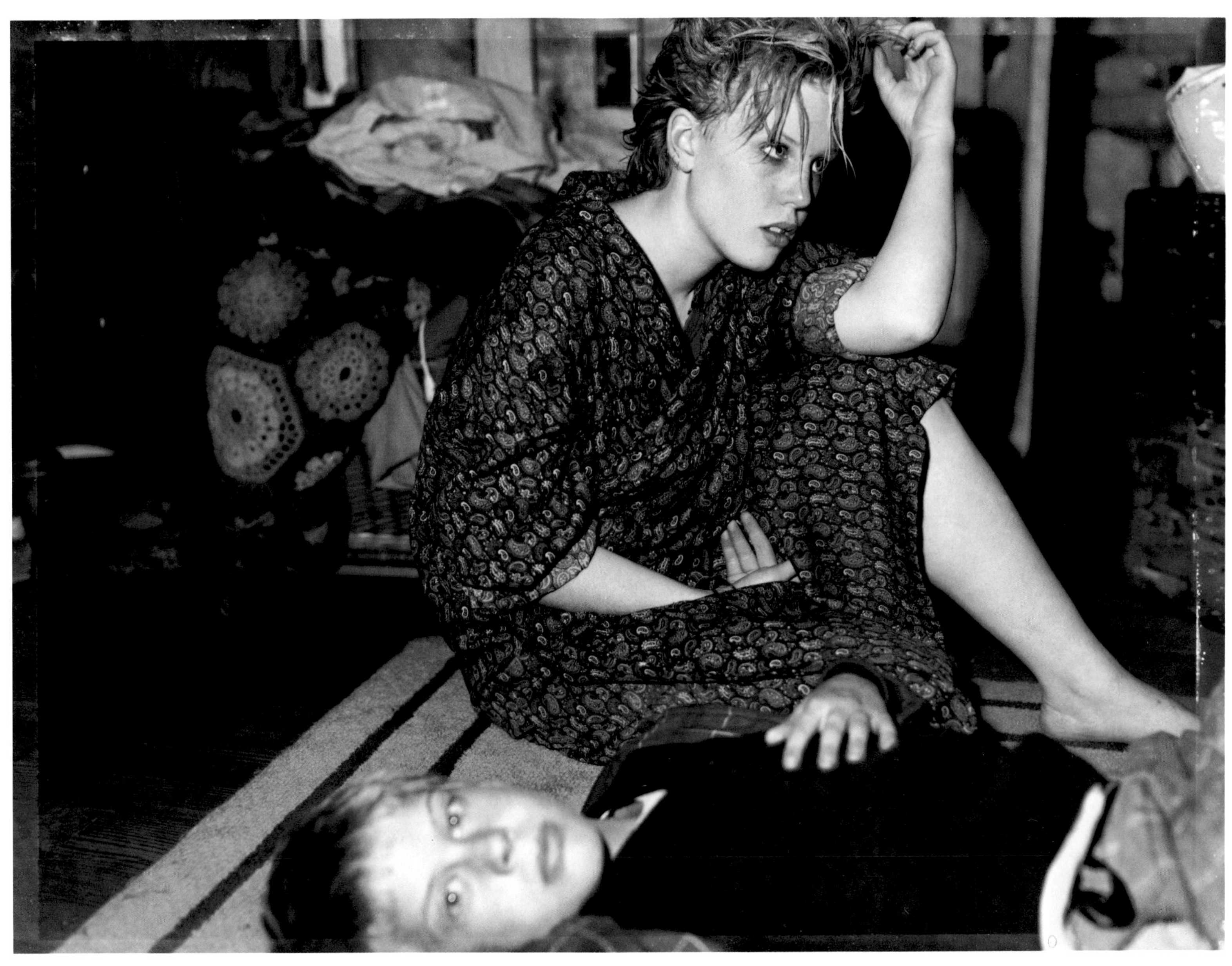

Judith Black · *Laura and Dylan* · 1984

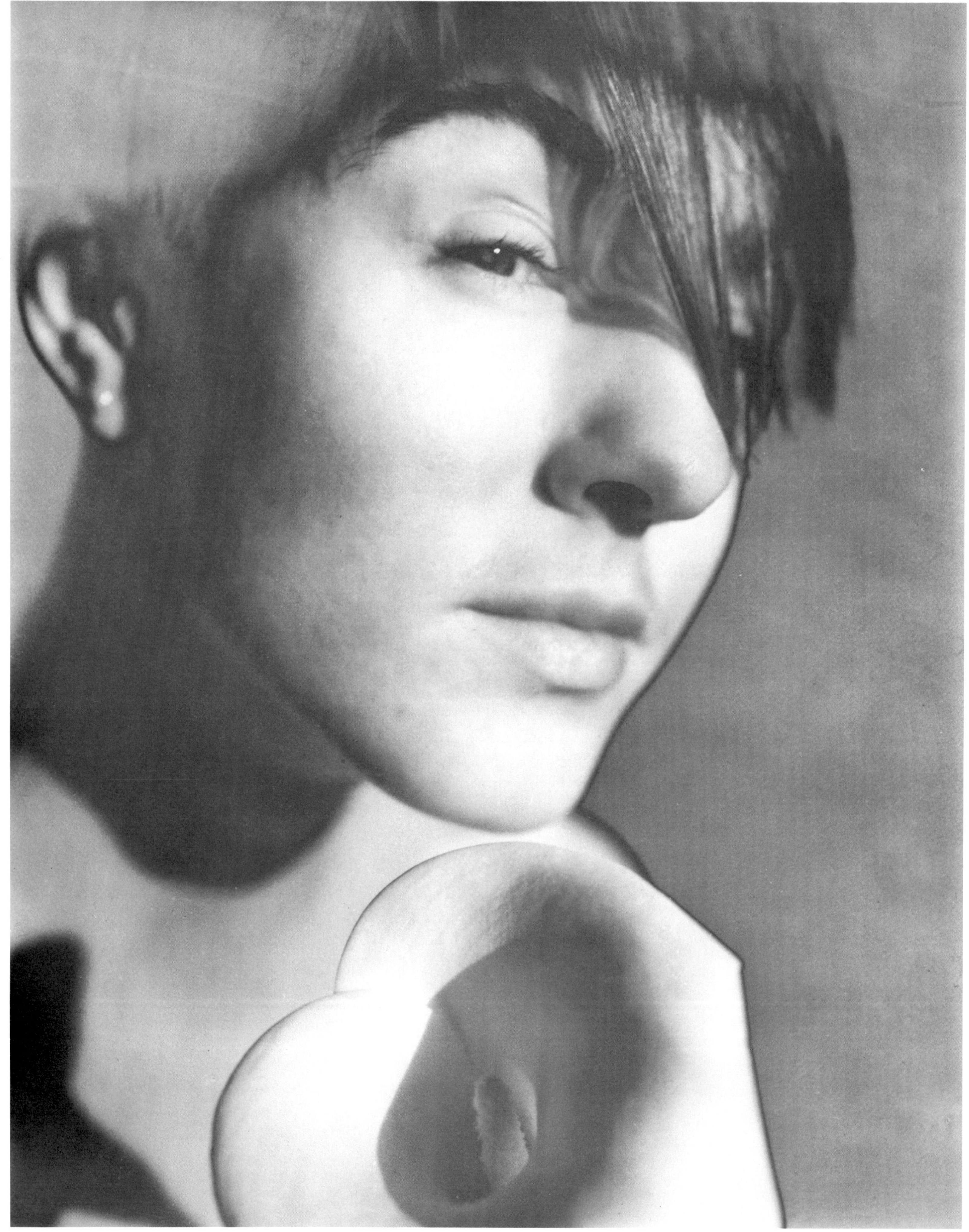

Michael Spano · *With Lily* · 1986

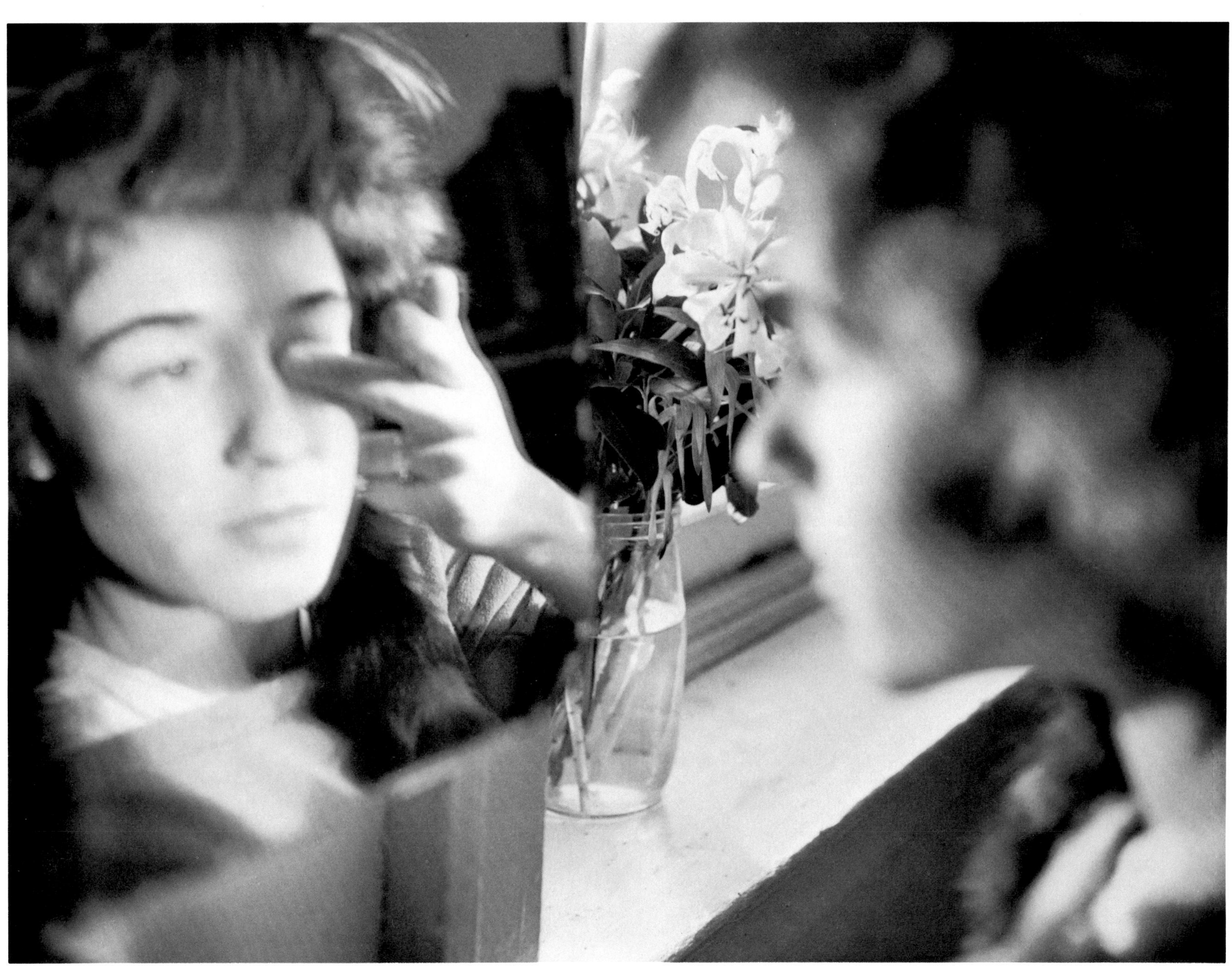

Michael Spano · *Portrait* · 1984

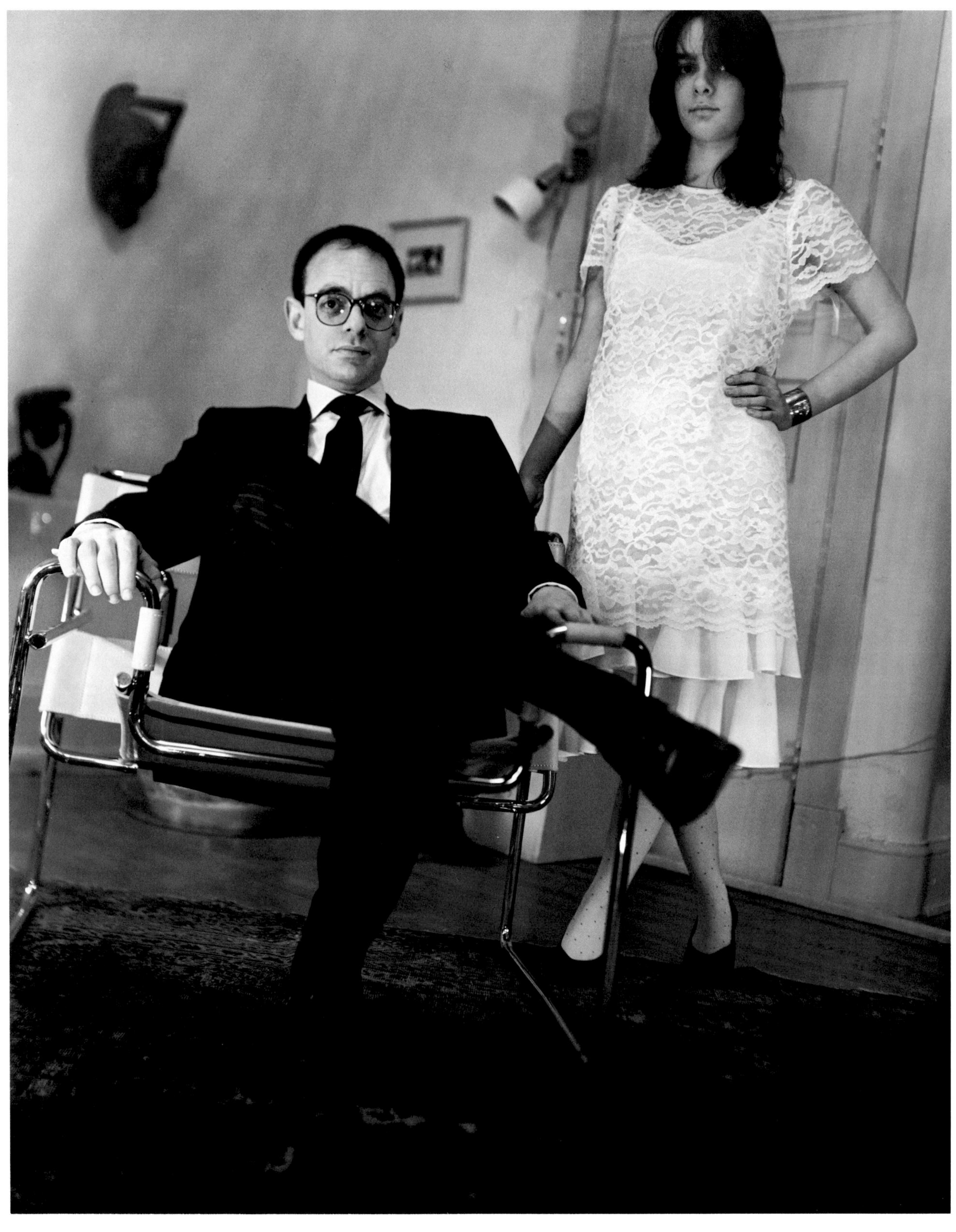

Ann Zelle · *Father and Daughter* · 1983

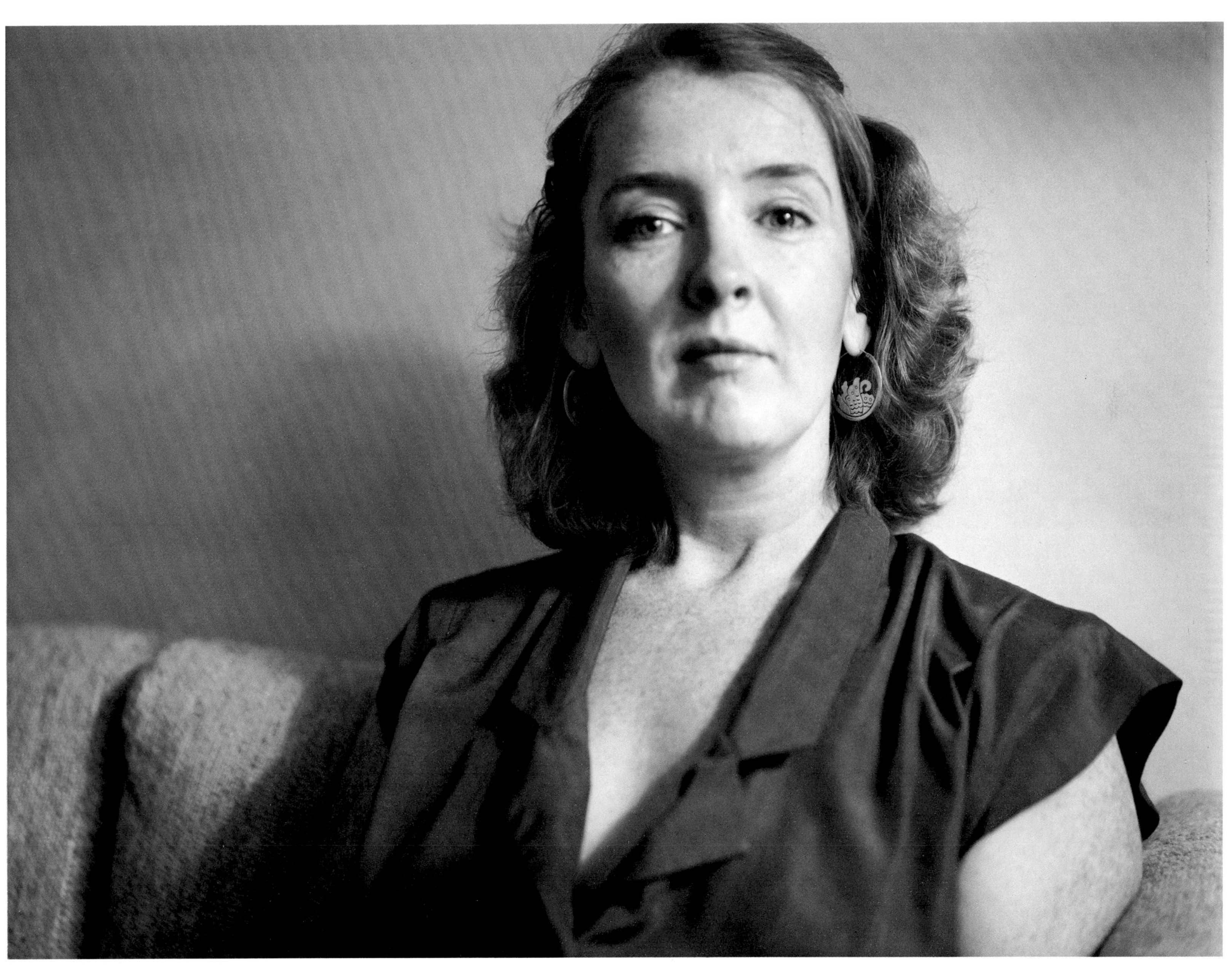

Ann Zelle · *Writer* · 1982

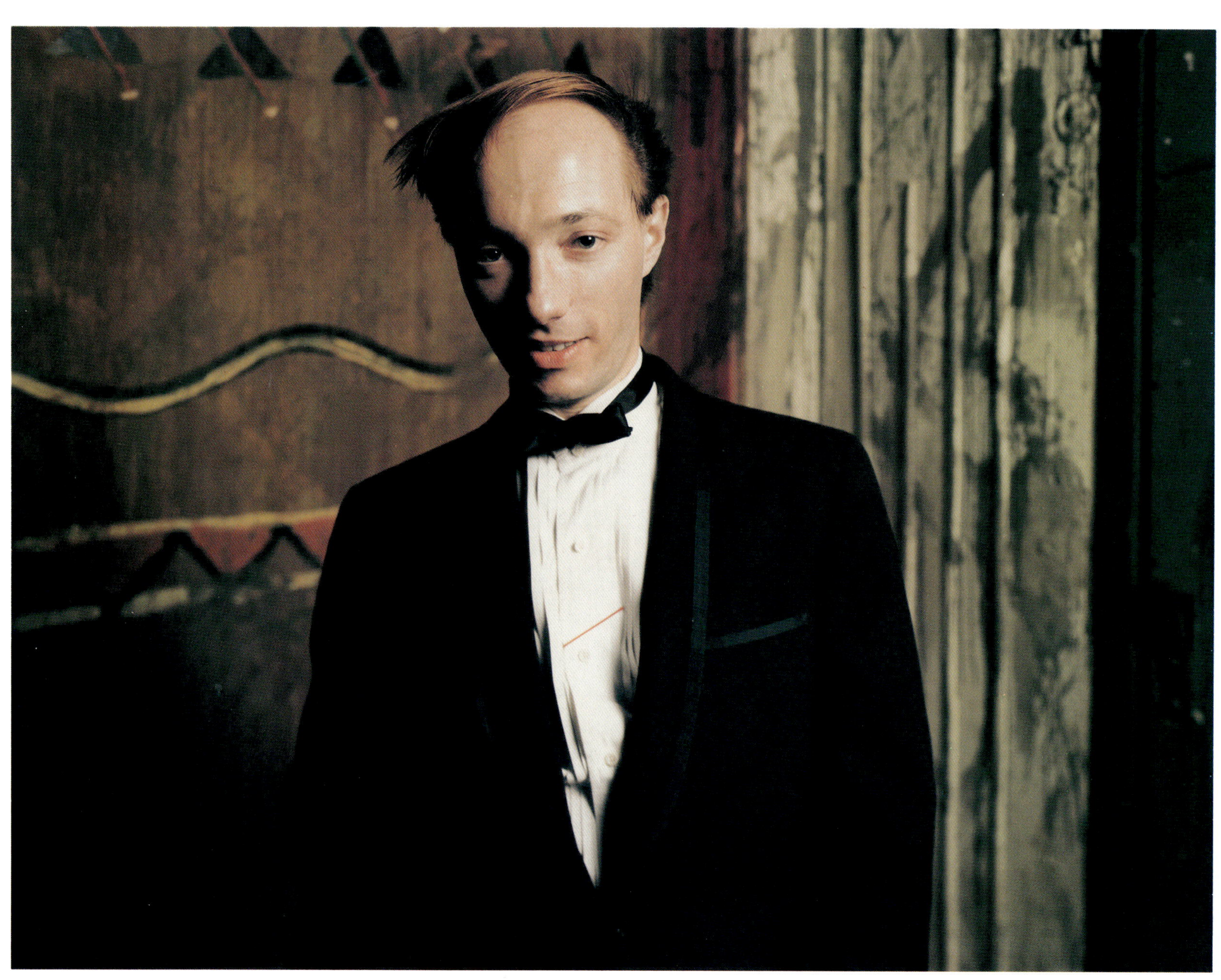

Joel Meyerowitz · *Dean Rolston* · 1983

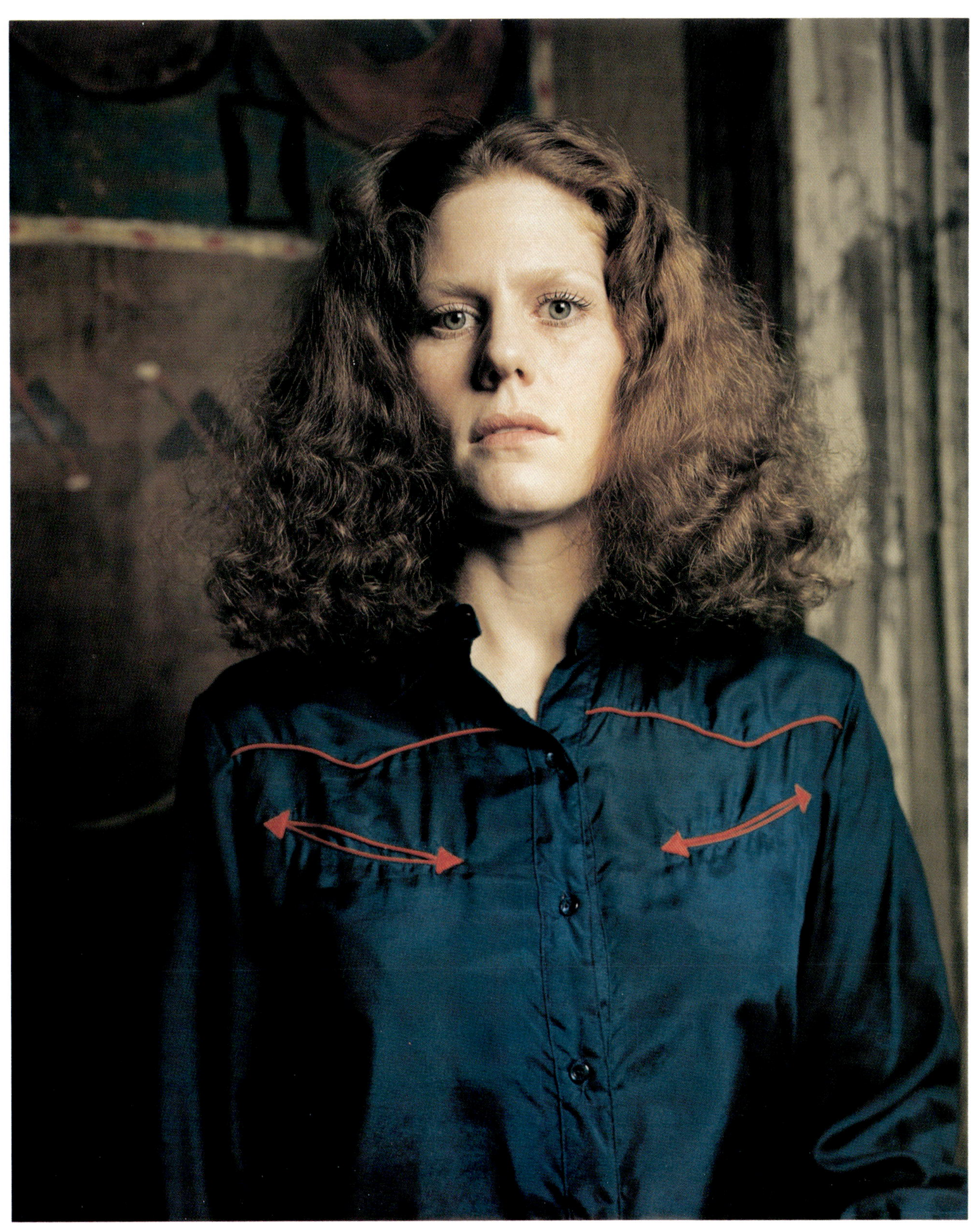

Joel Meyerowitz · *Victoria Brown* · 1983

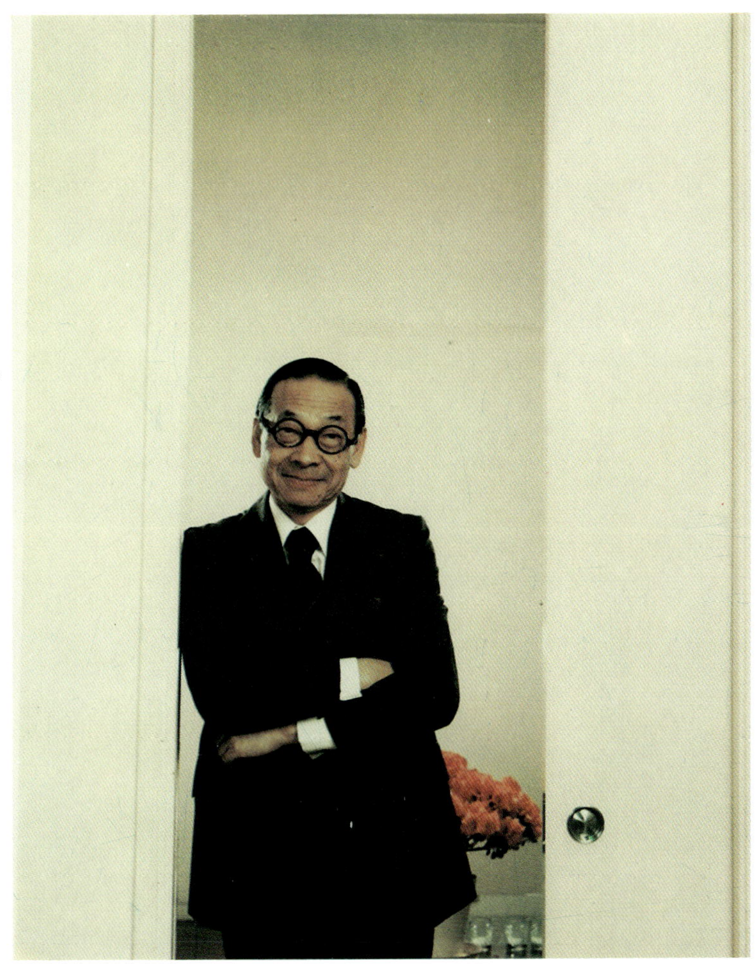

Yousuf Karsh · *I.M. Pei* · 1979

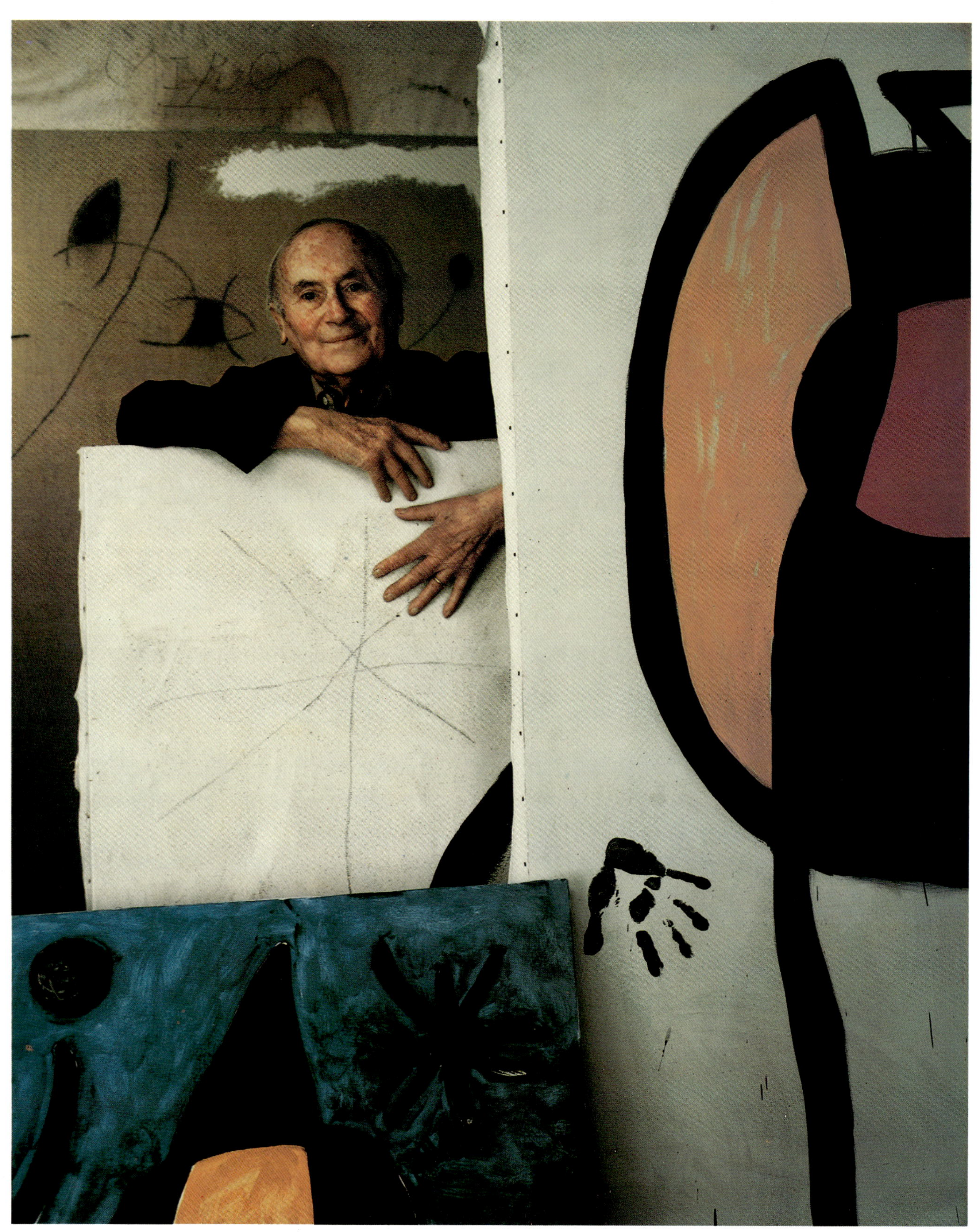

Arnold Newman · *Joan Miró, Palma, Mallorca* · 1979

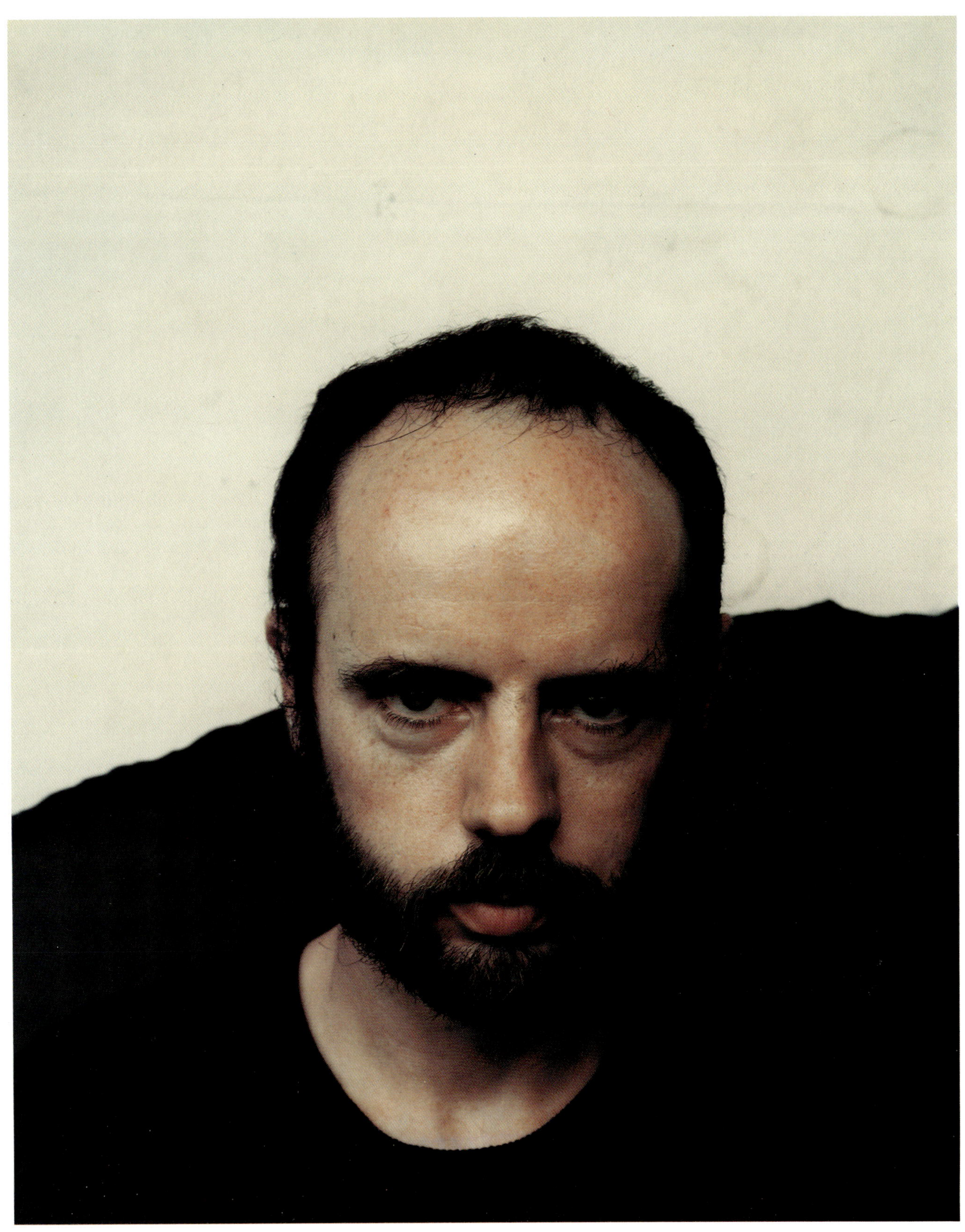

Arnold Newman · *Eugene Richards, New York* · 1977

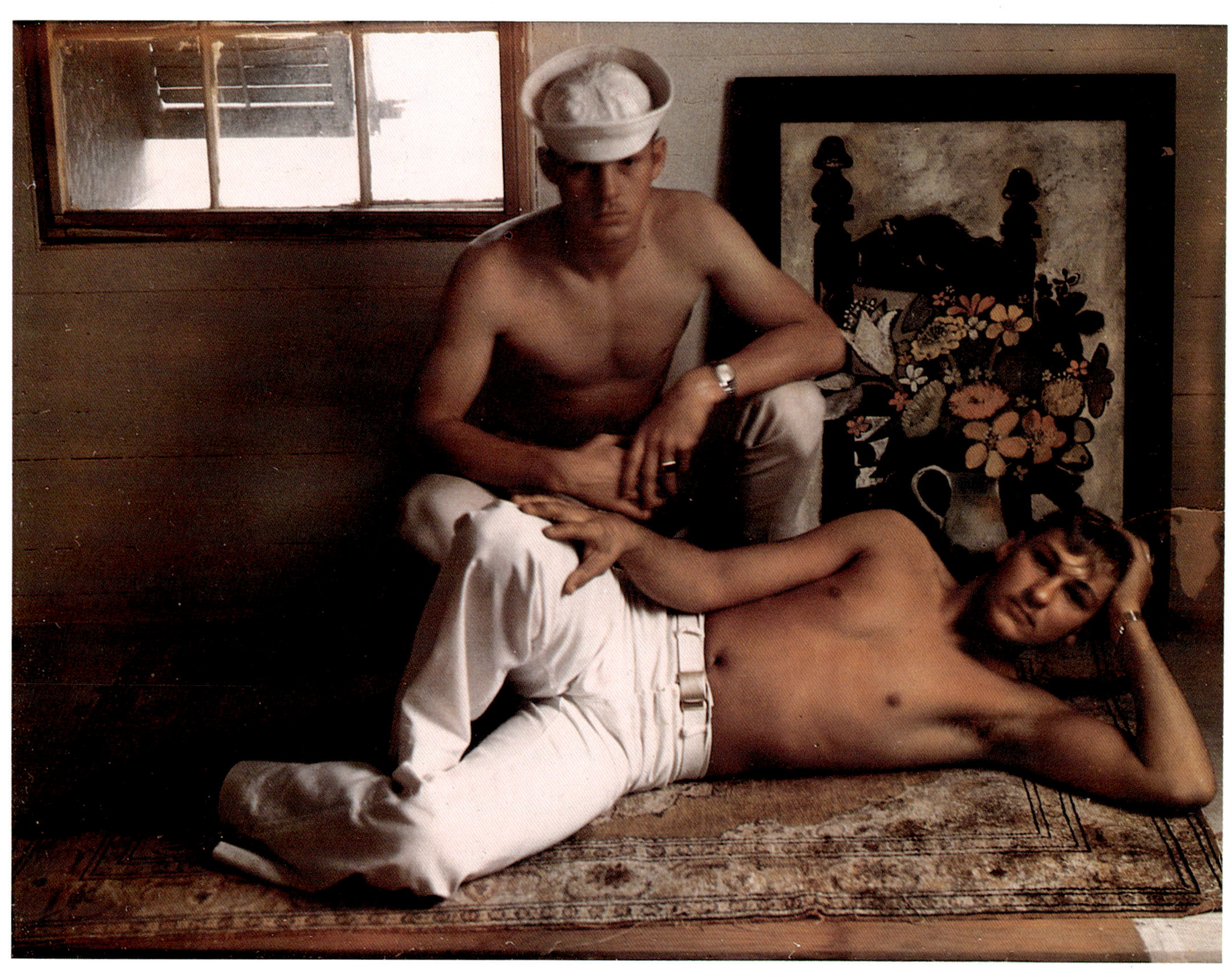

Marie Cosindas · *Sailors, Key West* · 1966

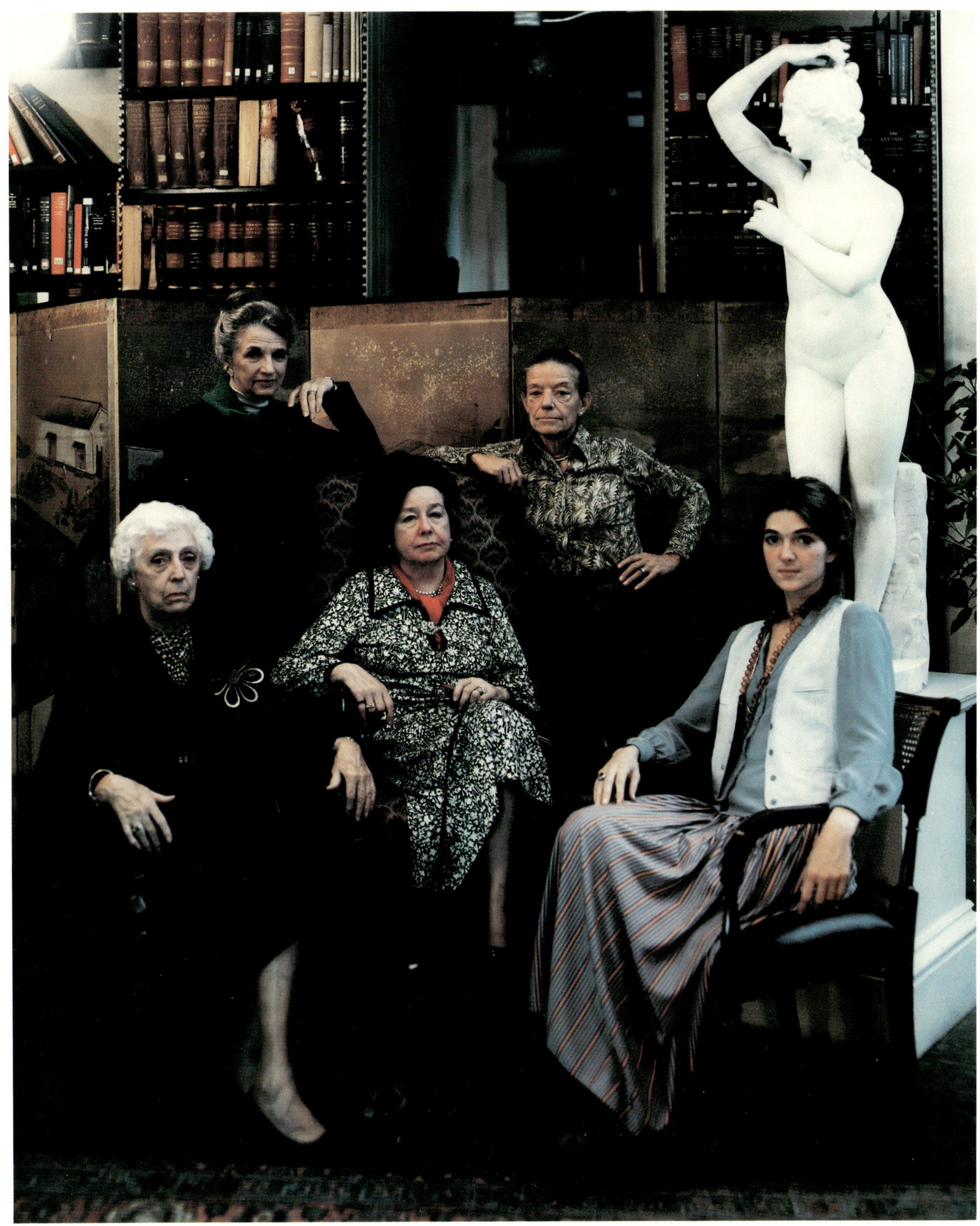

Marie Cosindas · *Boston Ladies* · 1982

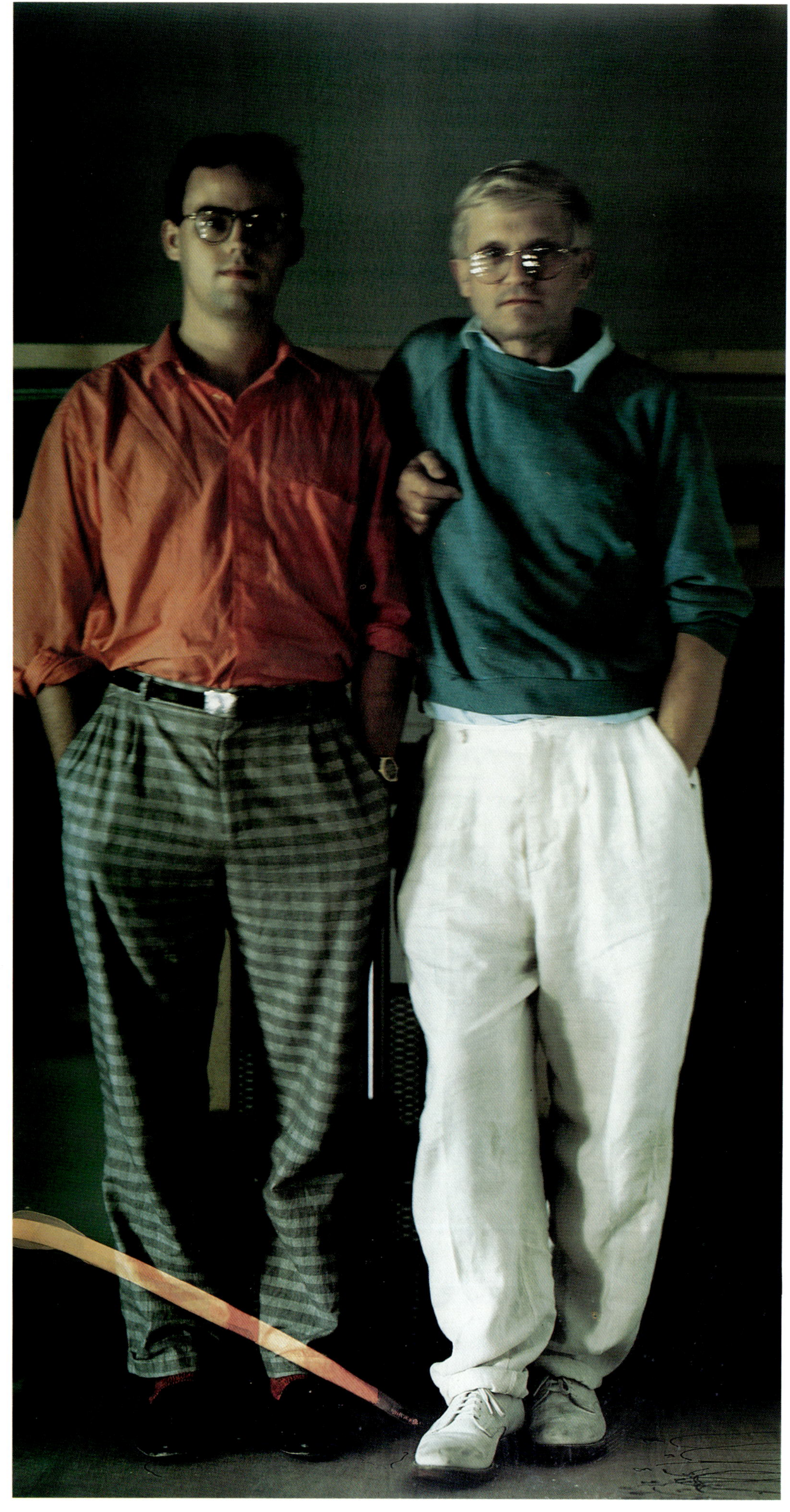

David Hockney · *Double Portrait, One Minute* · 1986

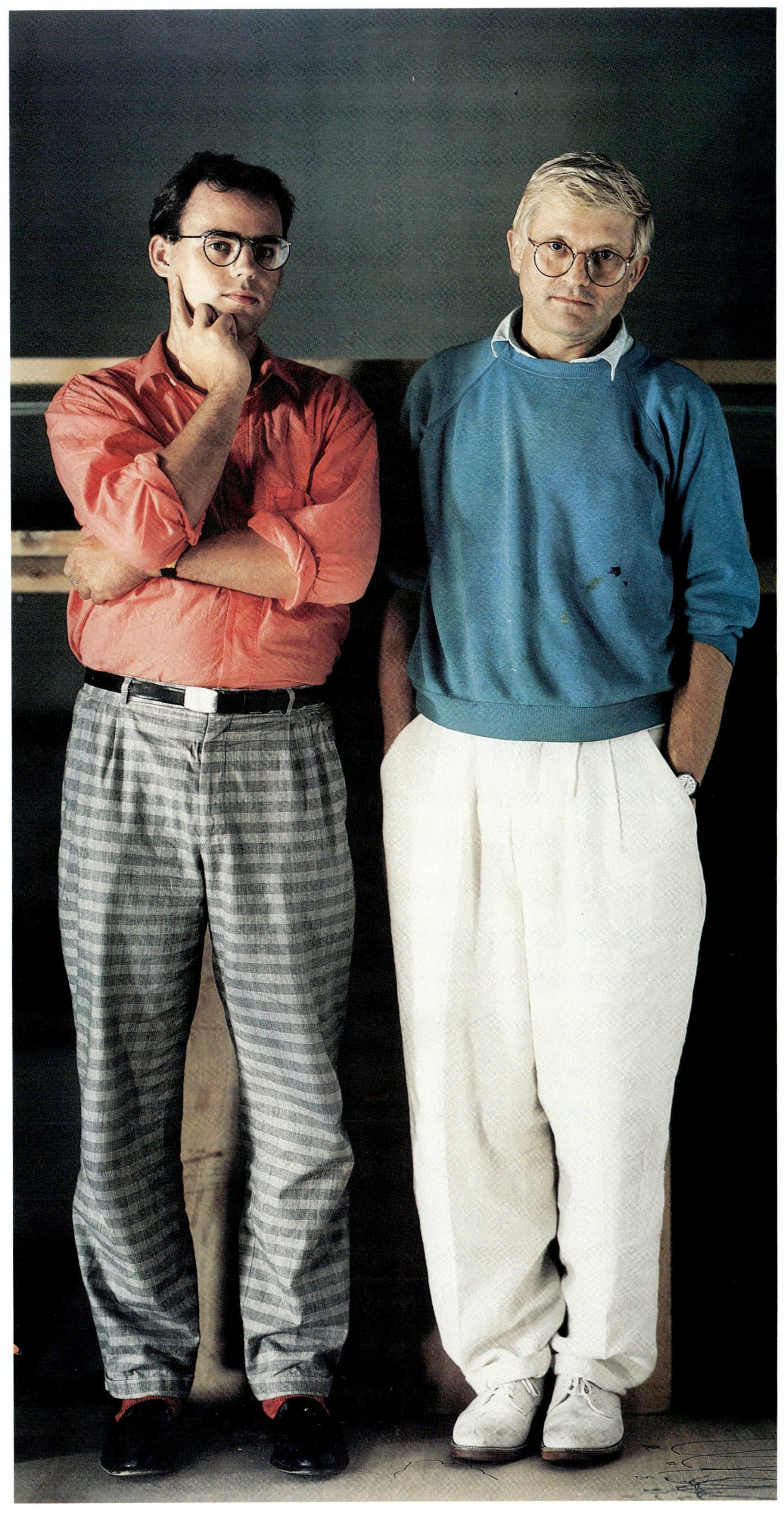

David Hockney · *Double Portrait, 125th of a Second* · 1986

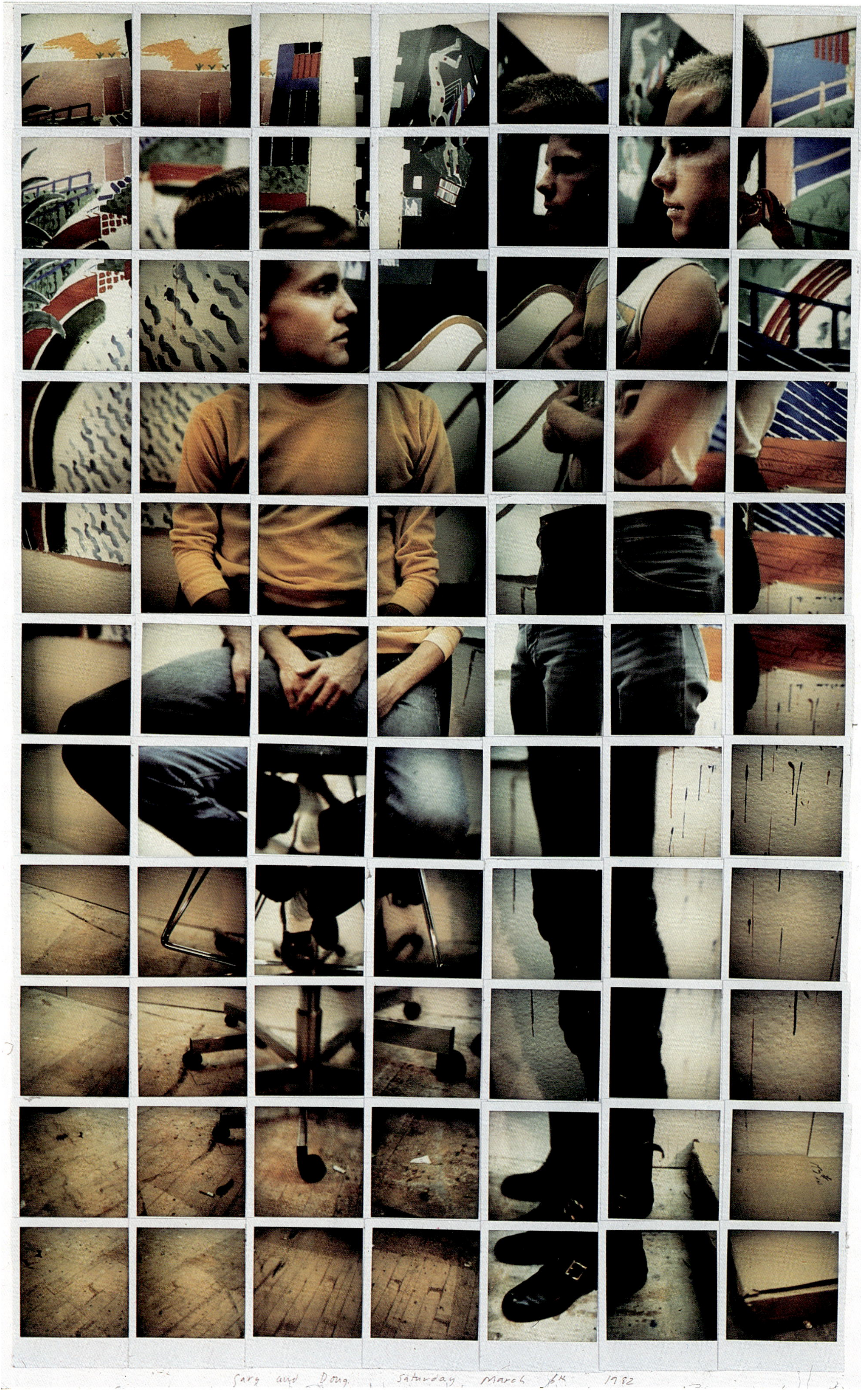

David Hockney · *Gary and Doug, L.A., March 6, 1982*

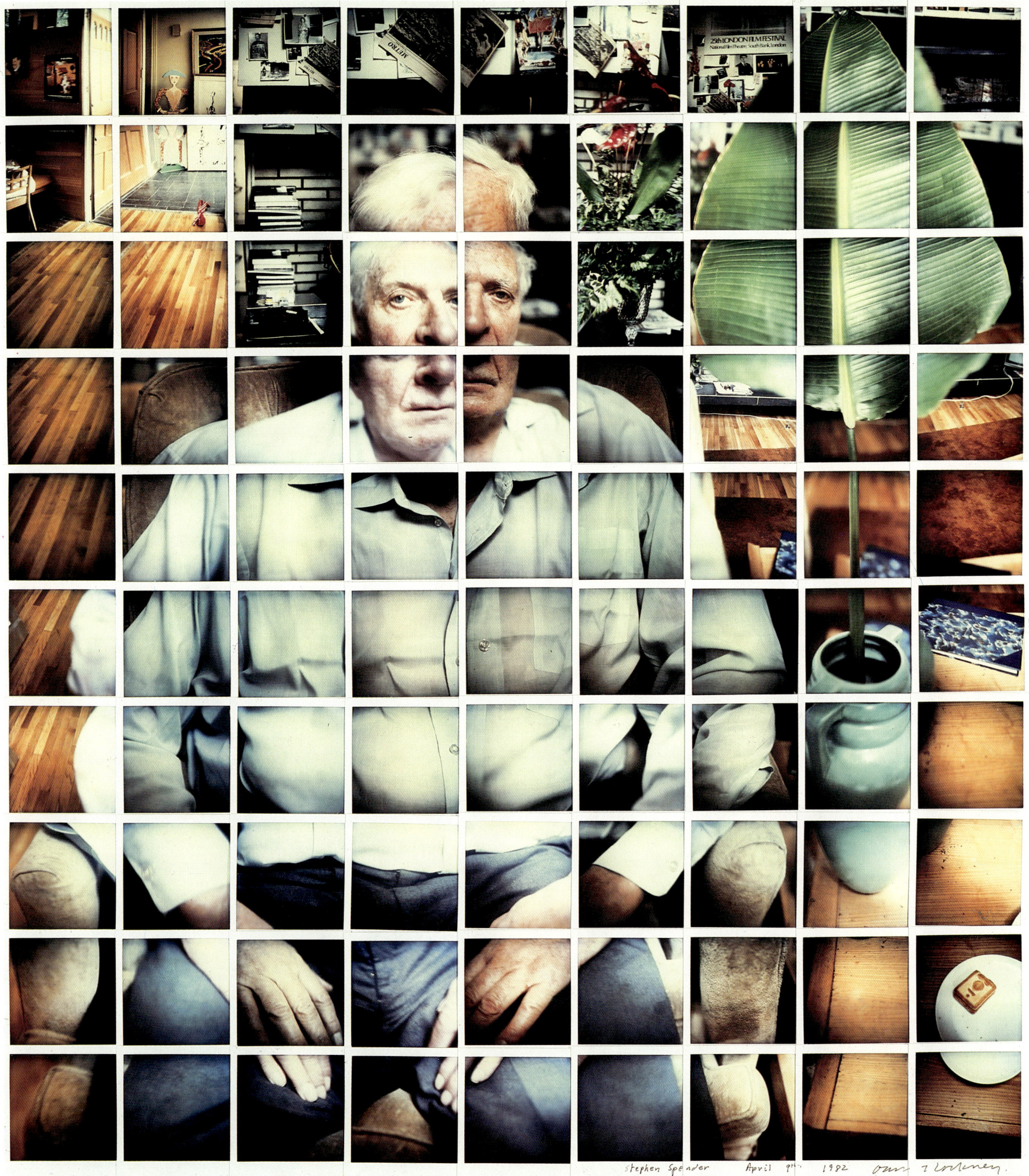

David Hockney · *Stephen Spender, L.A., 9th April 1982*

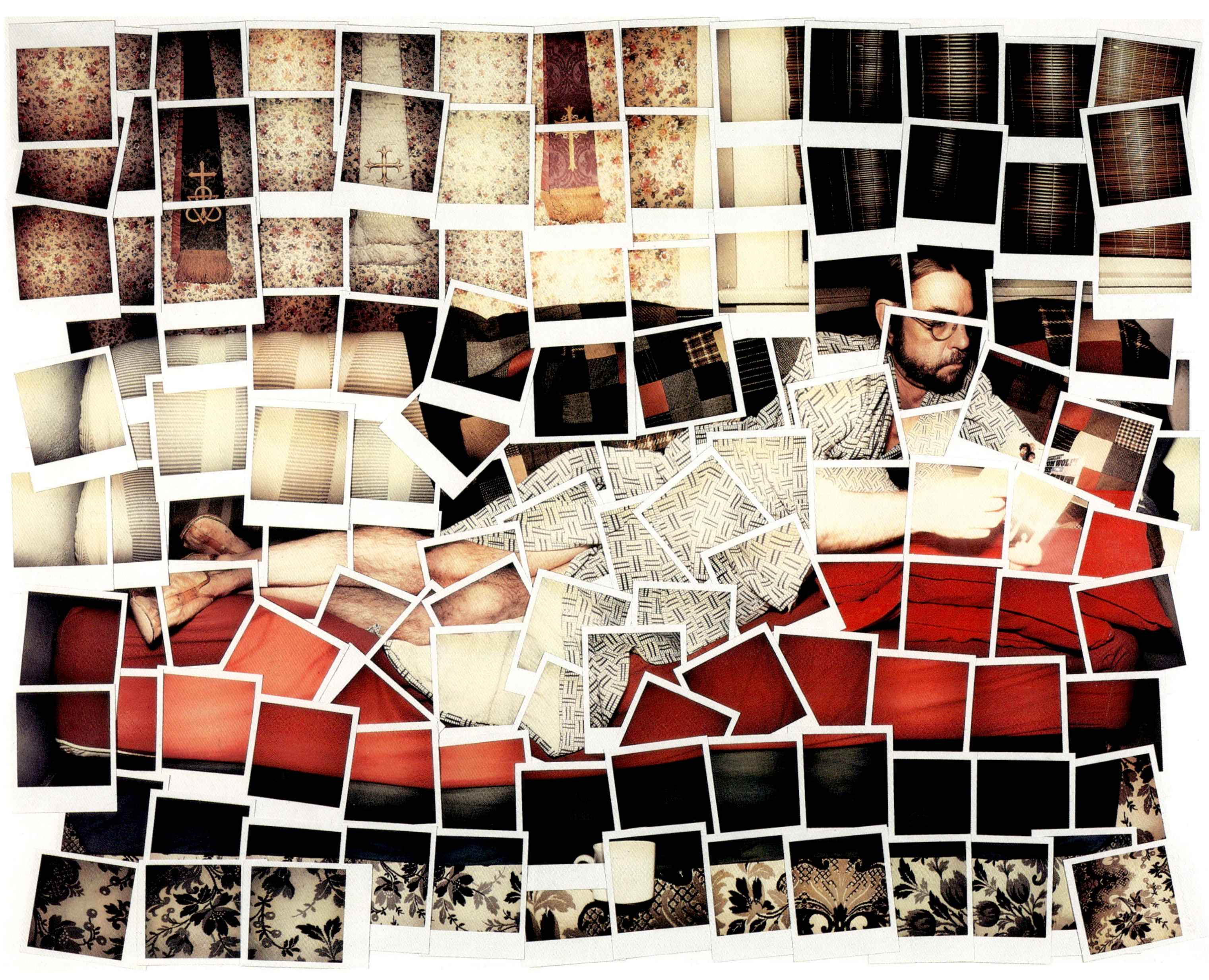

Joyce Neimanas · Untitled #3 · 1980

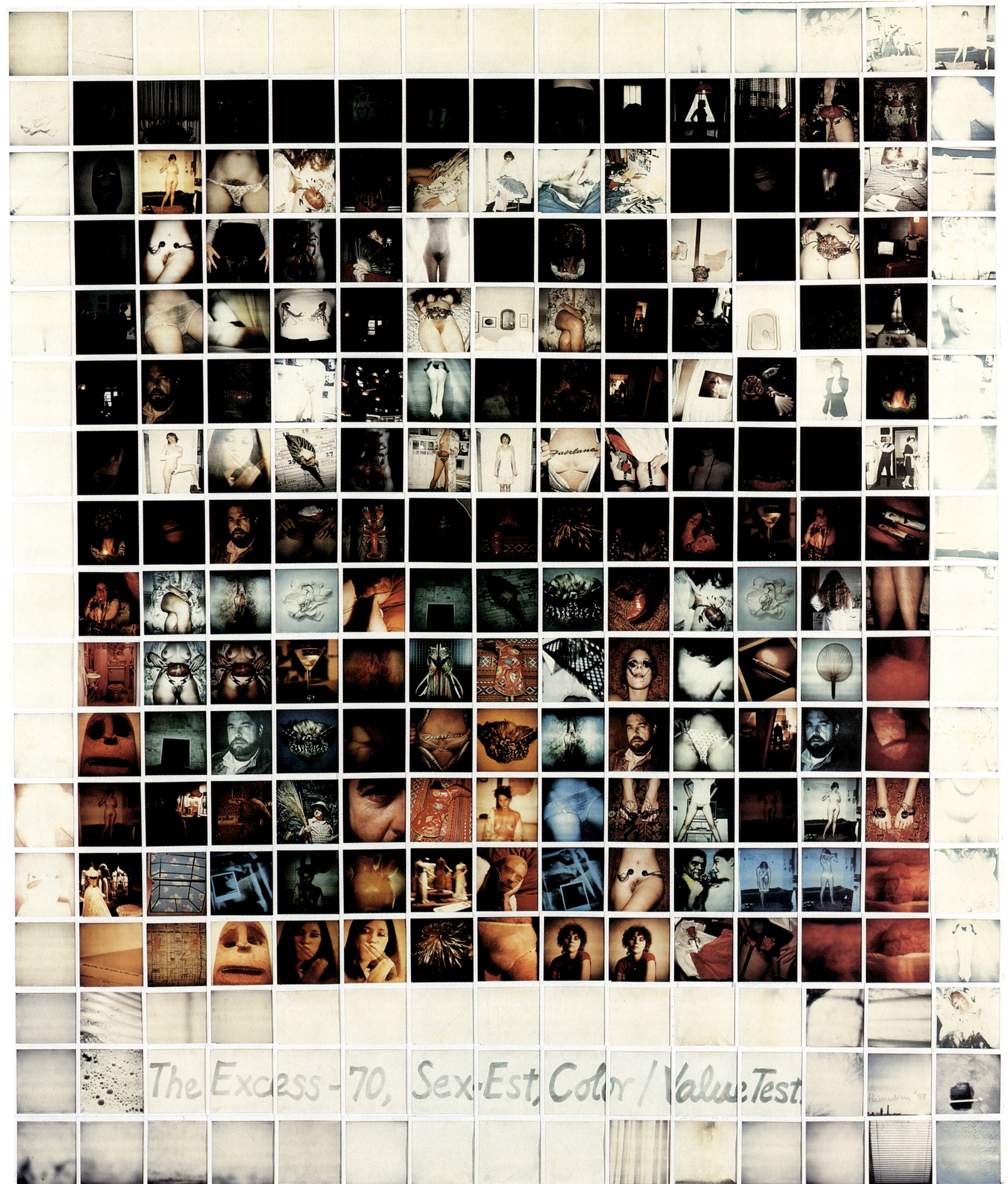

Robert Heinecken · *The Excess-70, Sex-Est, Color/Value Test* · 1978

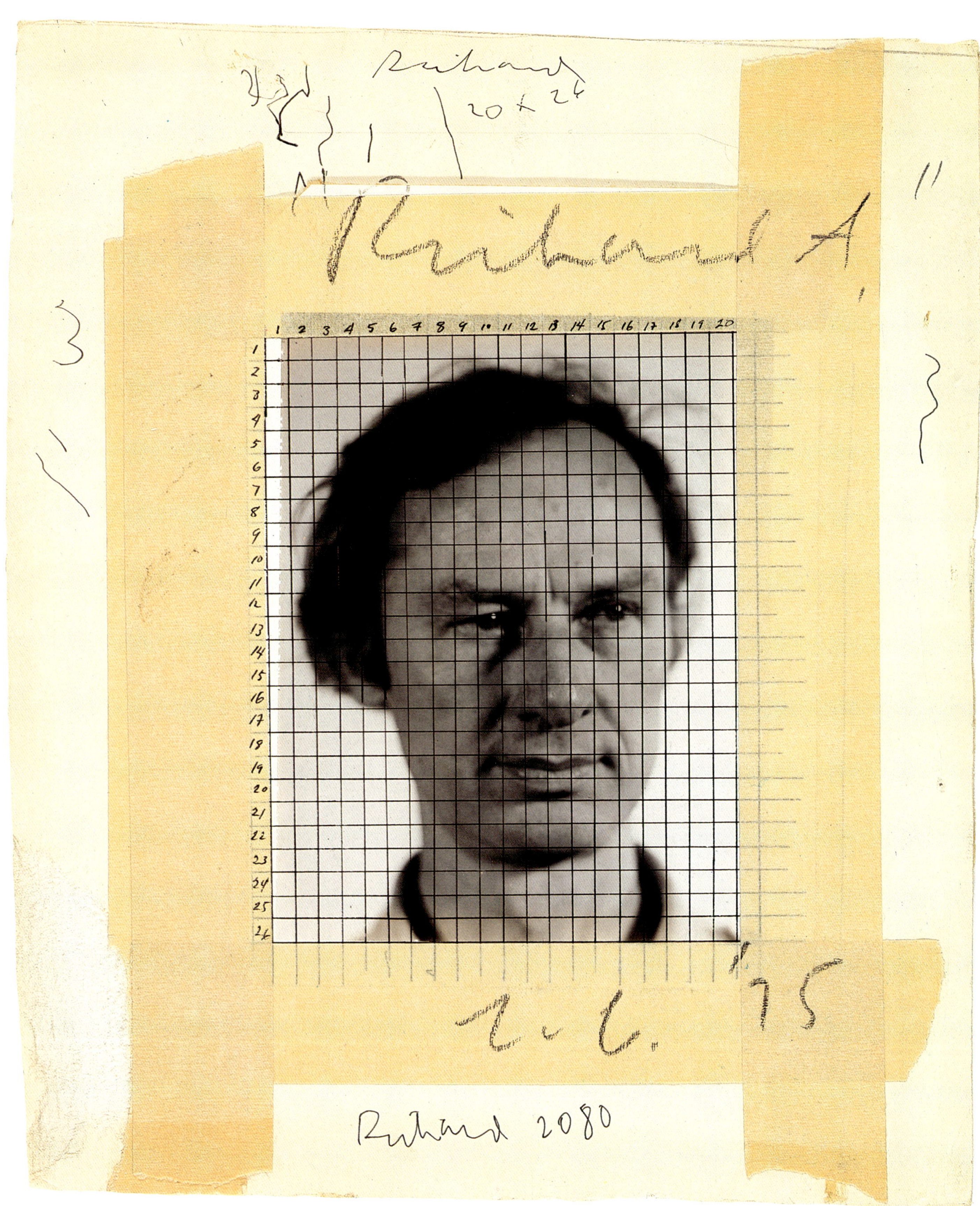

Chuck Close · *Richard A.* · 1975

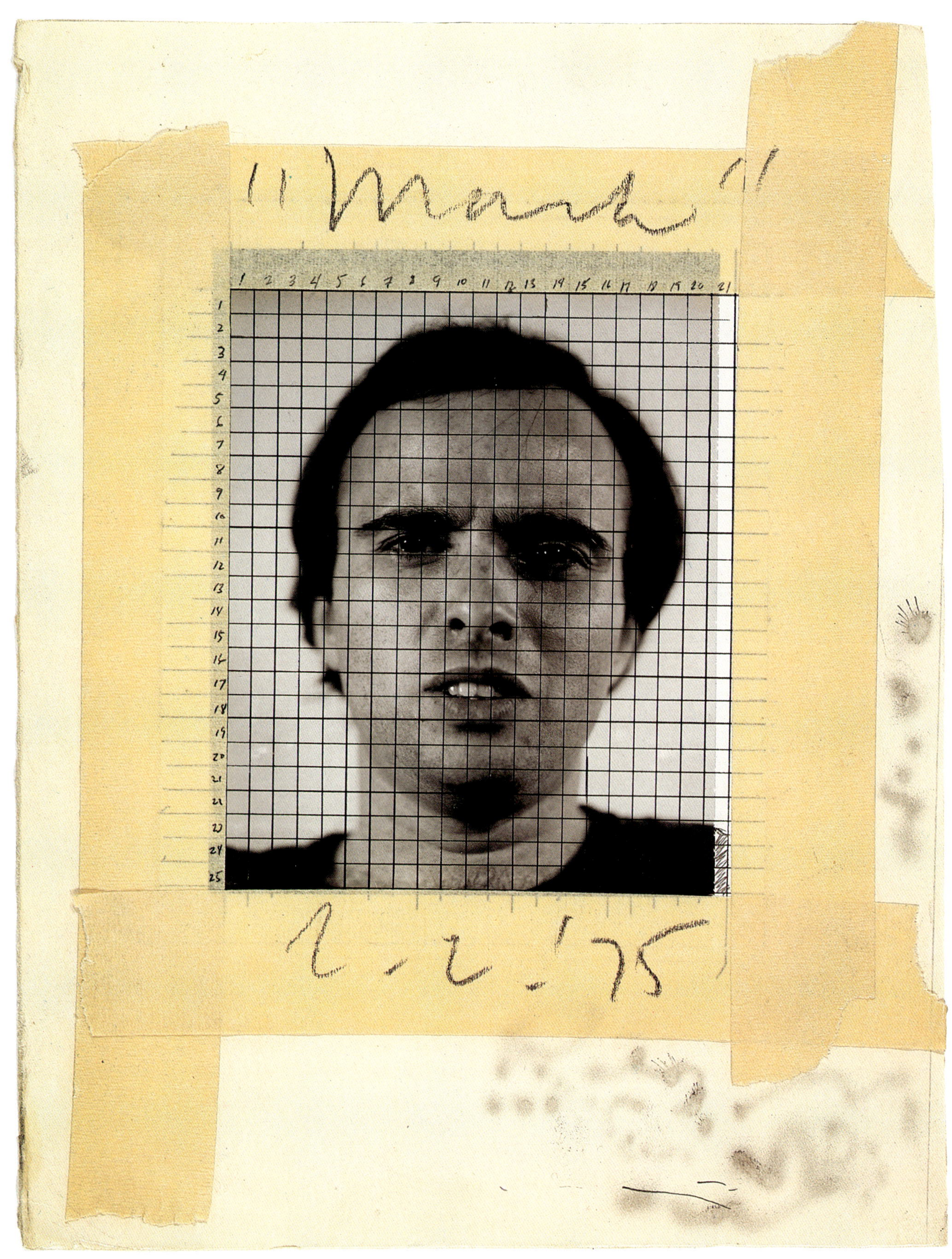

Chuck Close · *Mark* · 1975

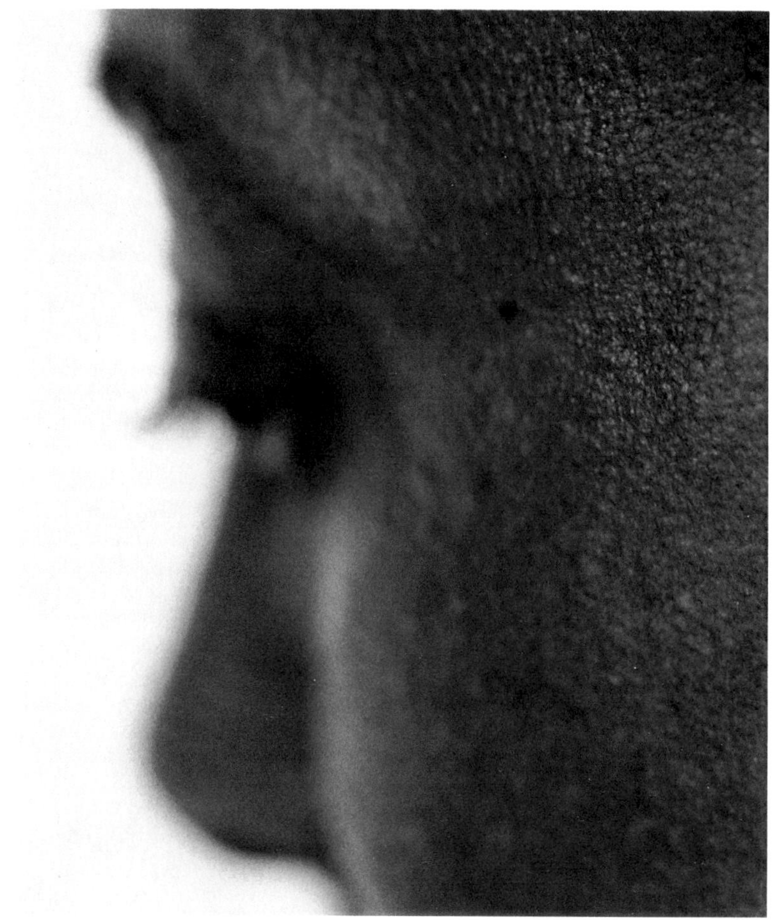

Nancy Hellebrand · Untitled · 1985

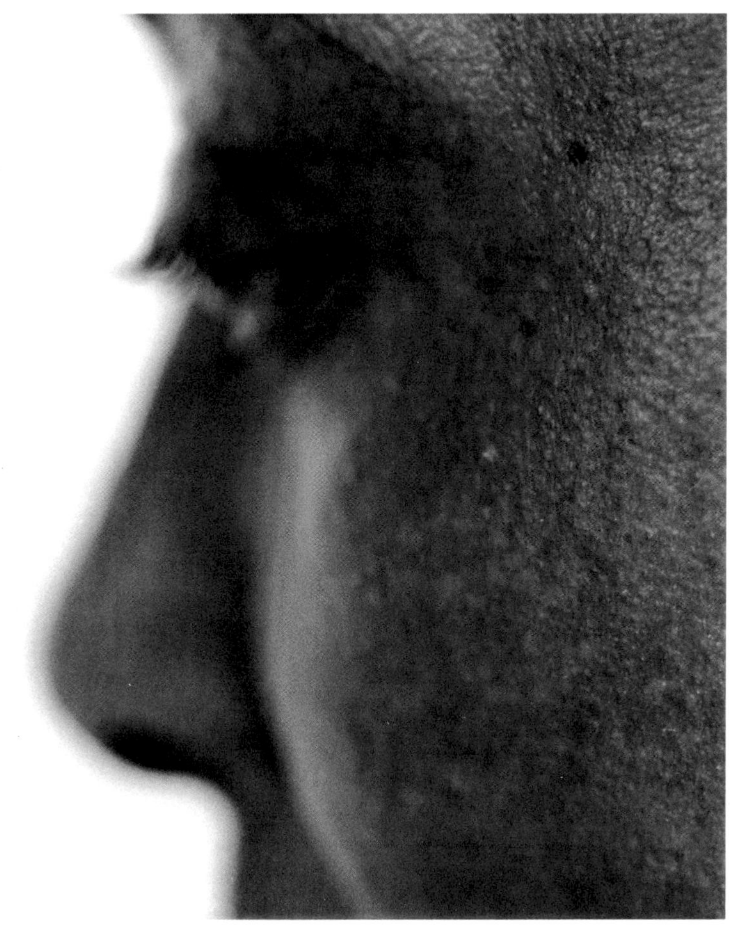

Nancy Hellebrand · Untitled · 1985

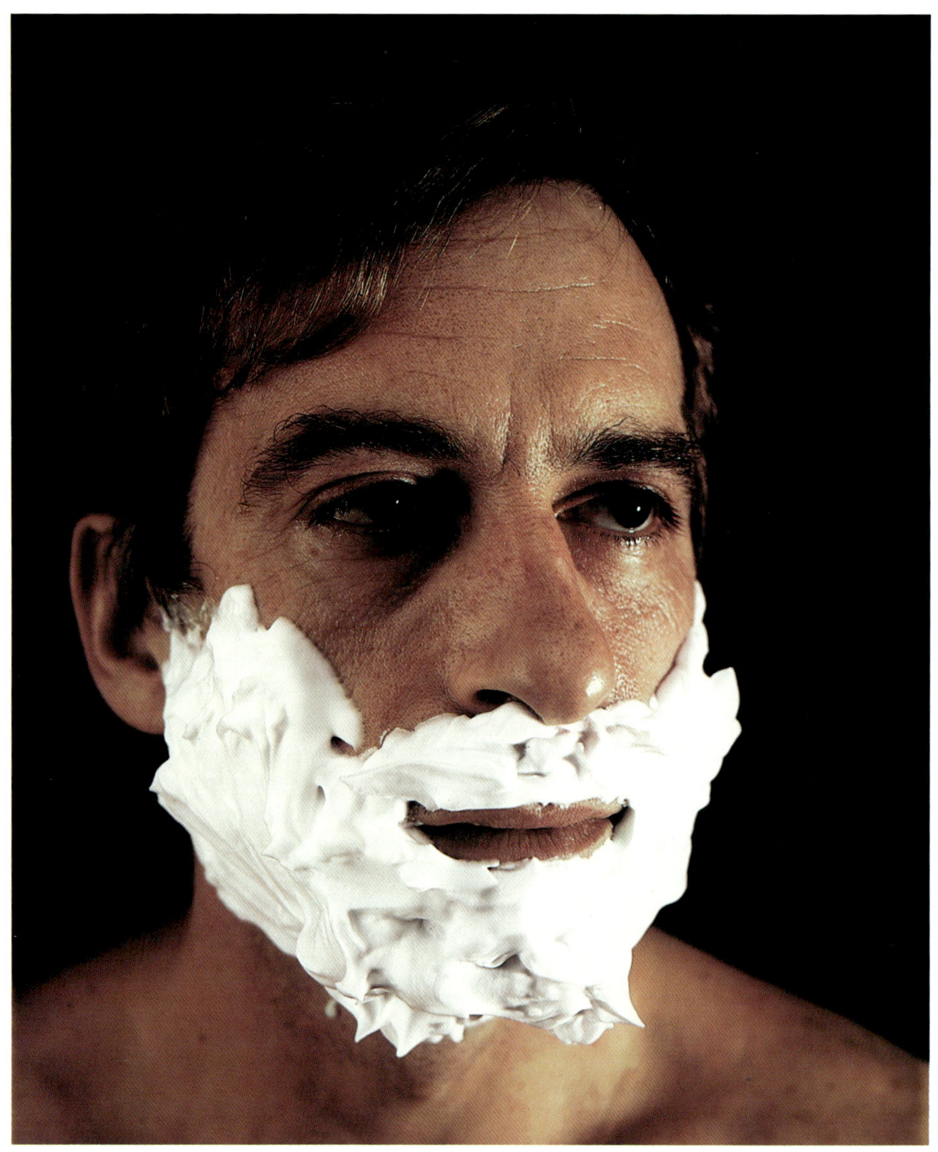

William Wegman · *Foamy, Aftershave* (diptych) · 1983

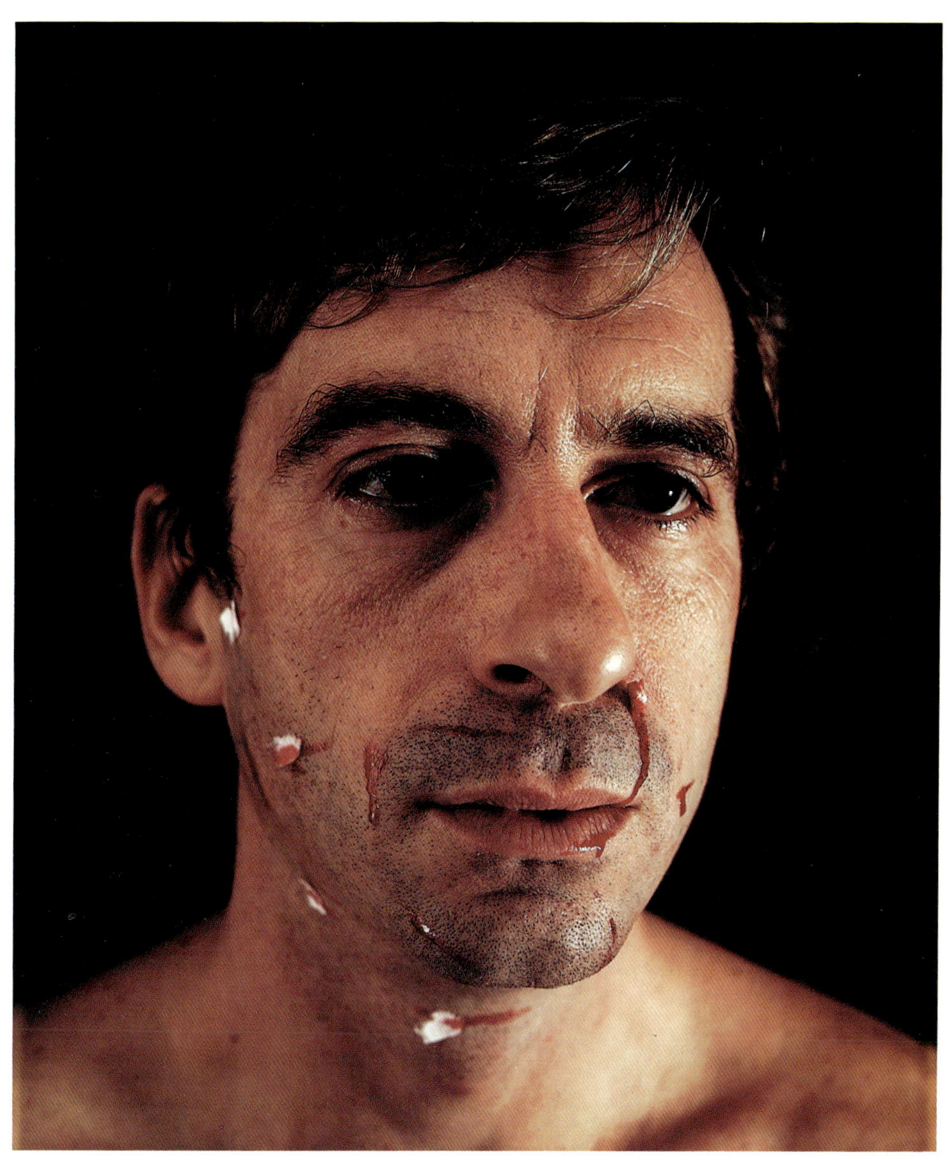

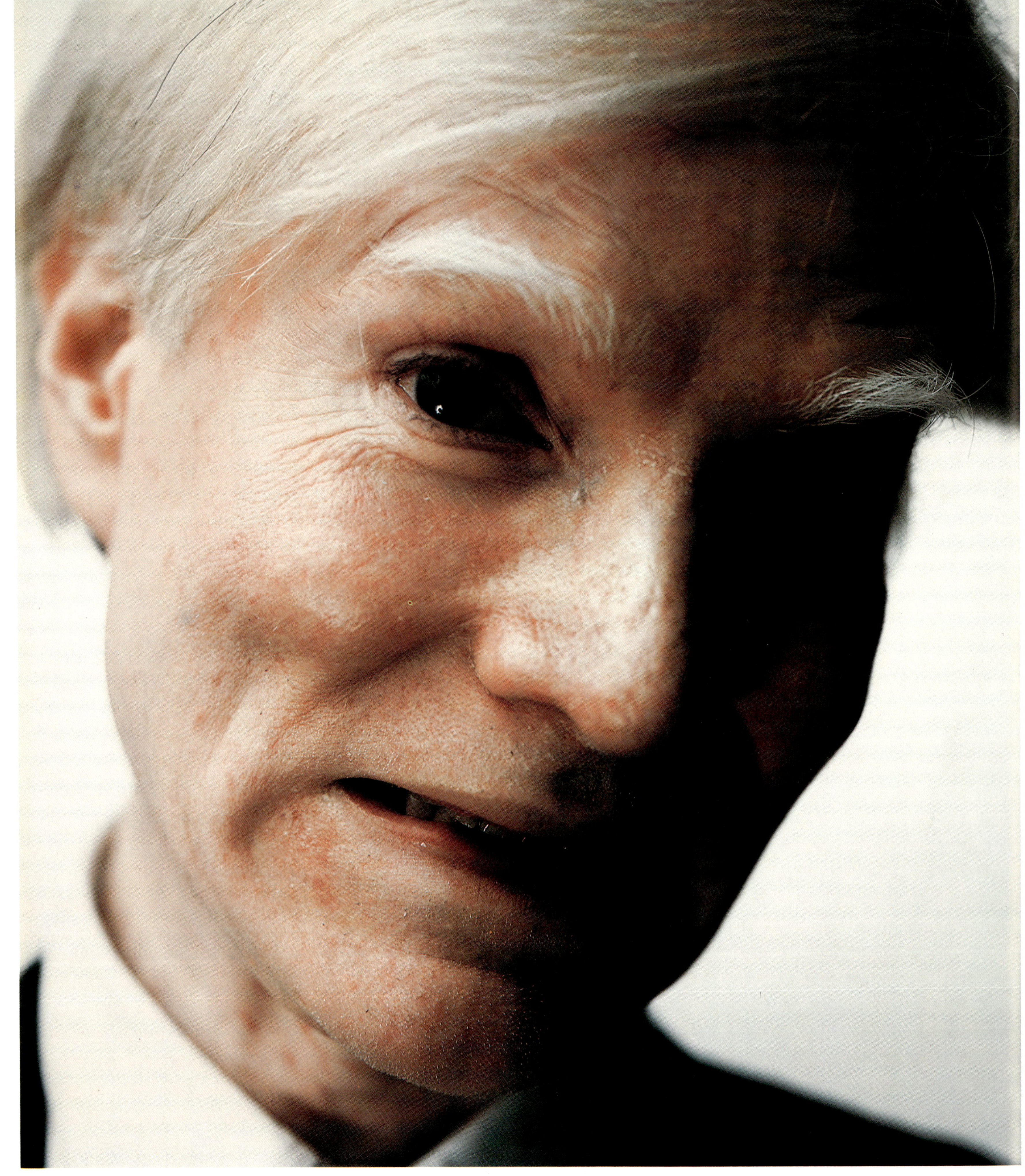

Andy Warhol · *Self-Portrait* · 1979

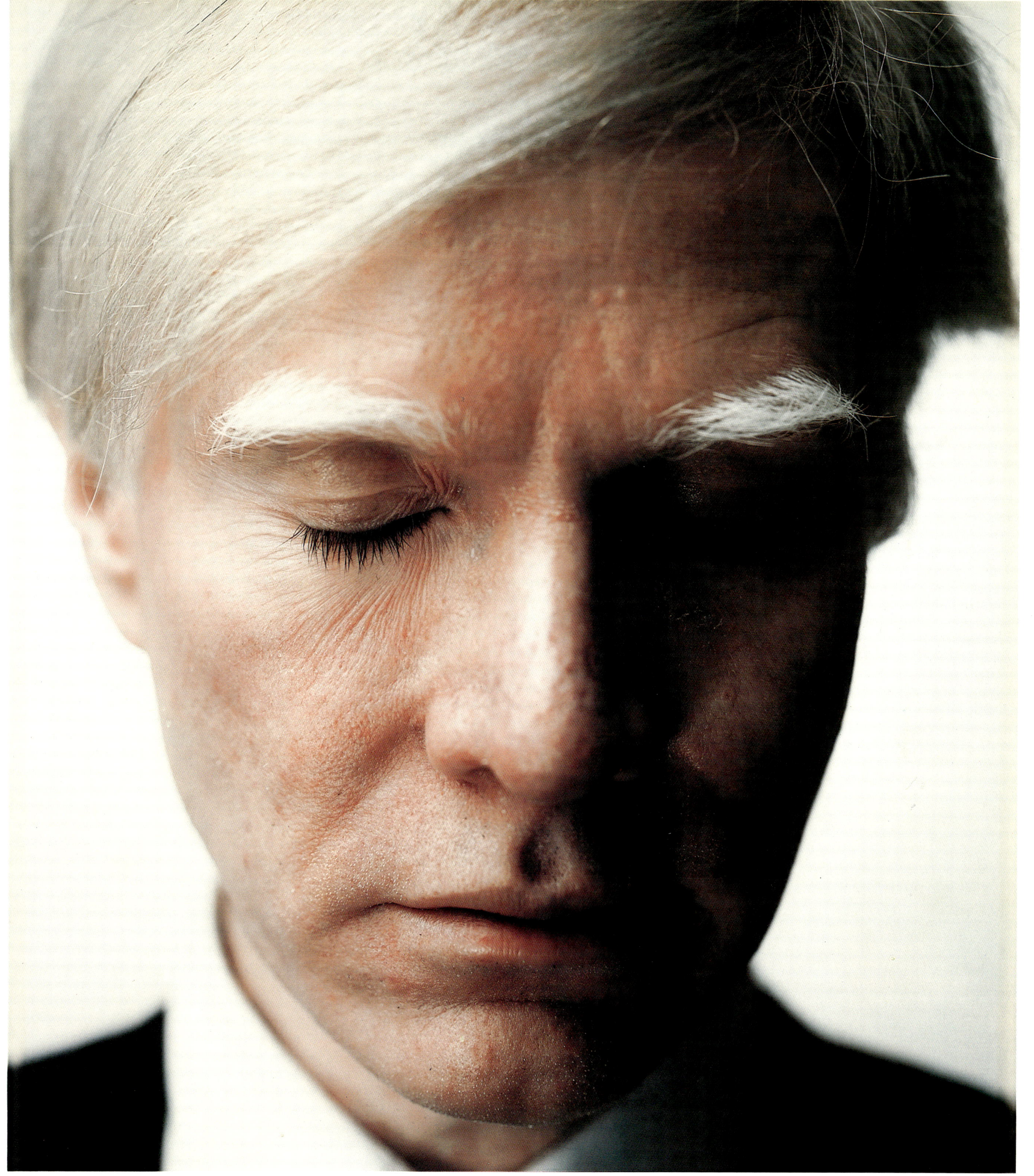

Andy Warhol · *Self-Portrait* · 1979

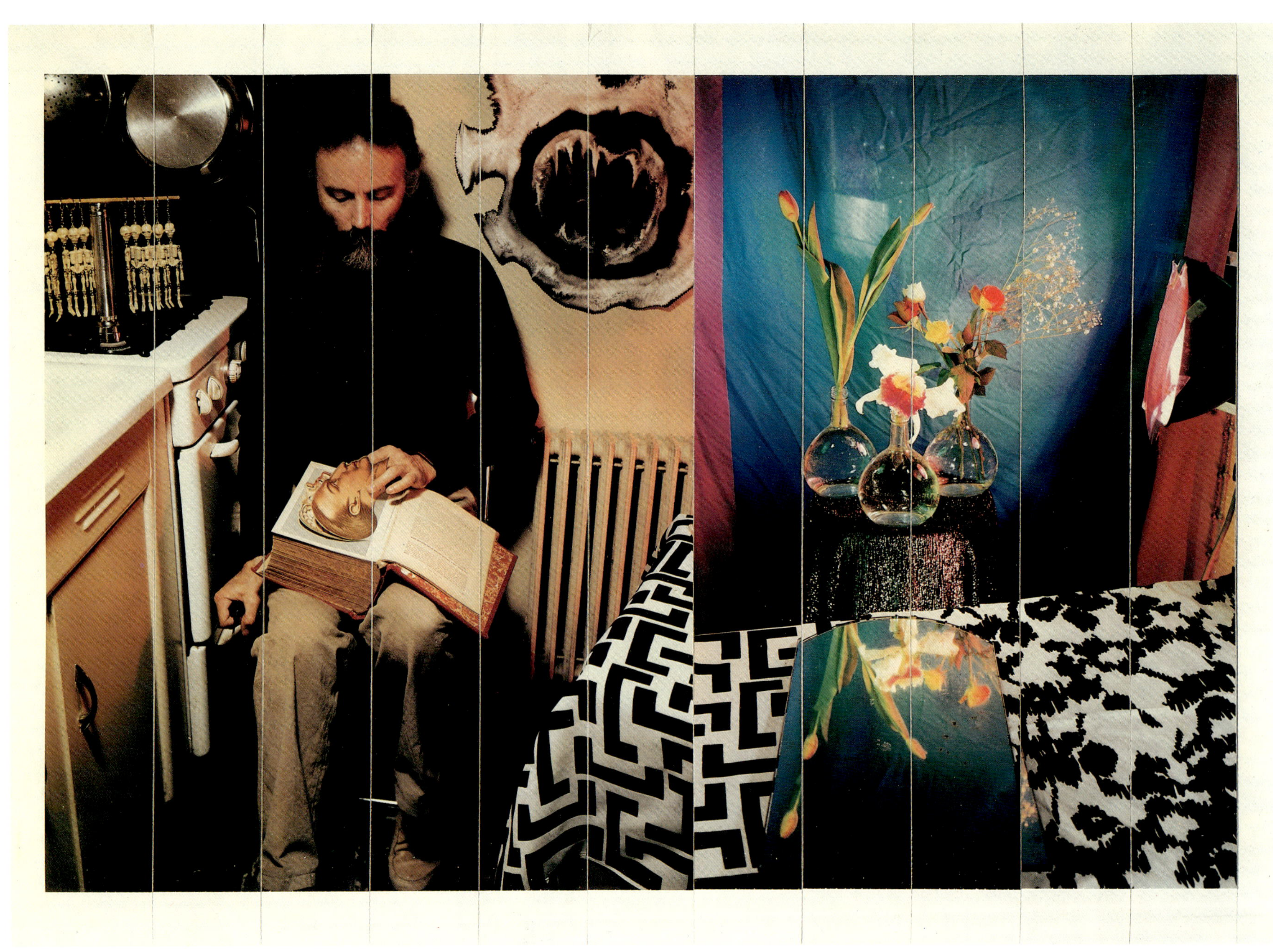

Lucas Samaras · *Panorama, 11/30/84*

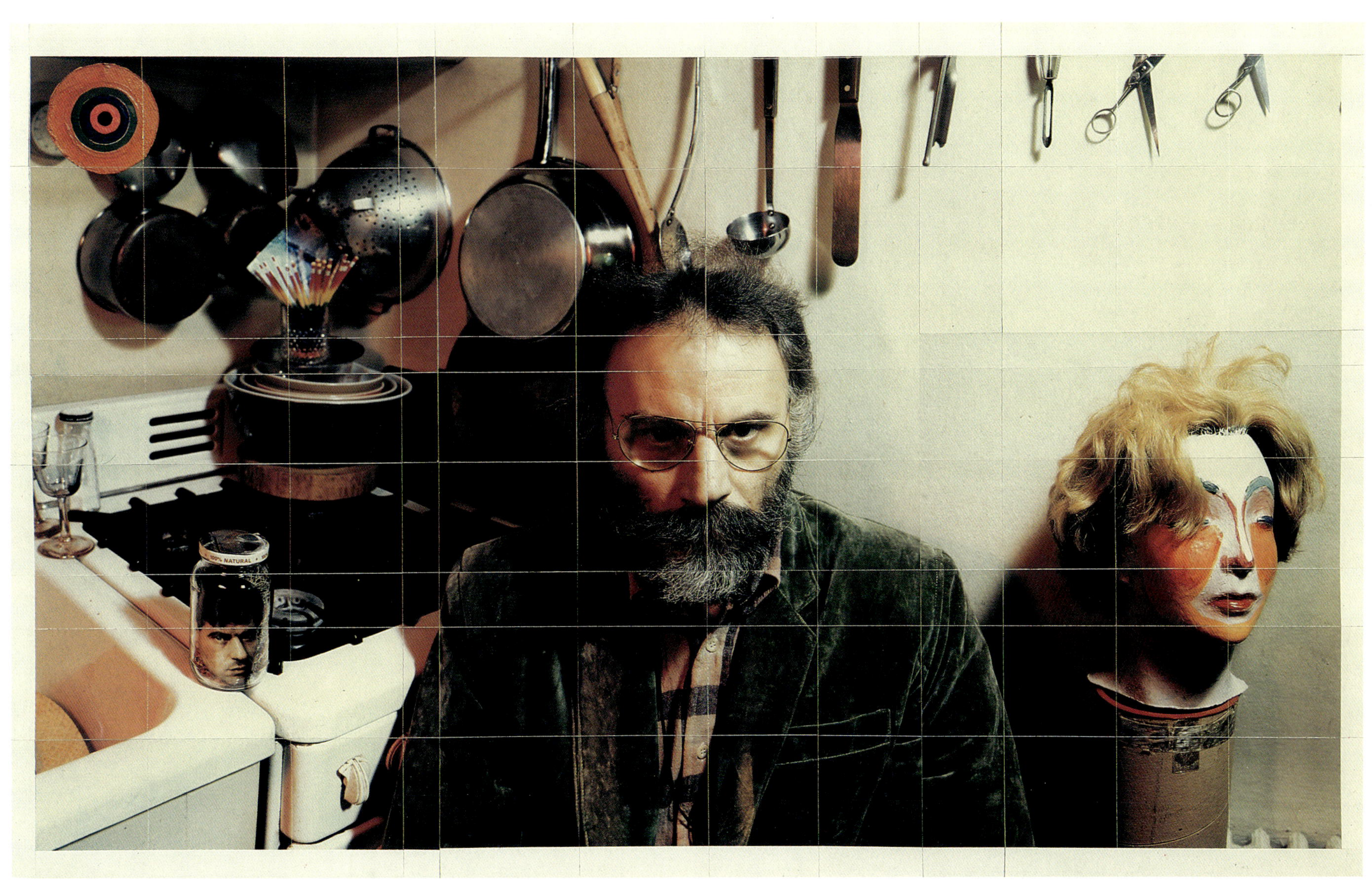

Lucas Samaras · *Adjustment, 1/13/86*

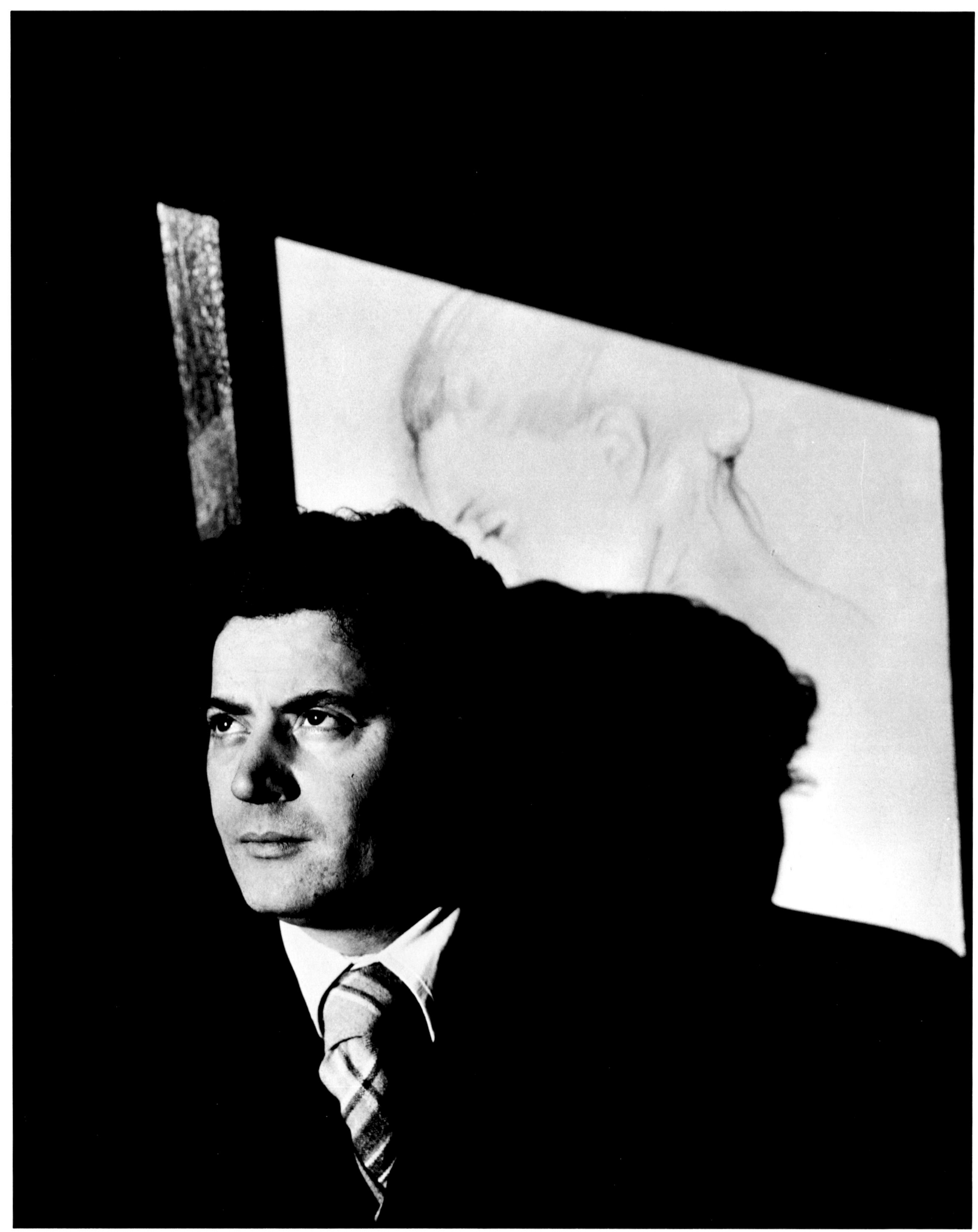

Ralph Gibson · Untitled (Piazza Navonna, Rome) · 1978

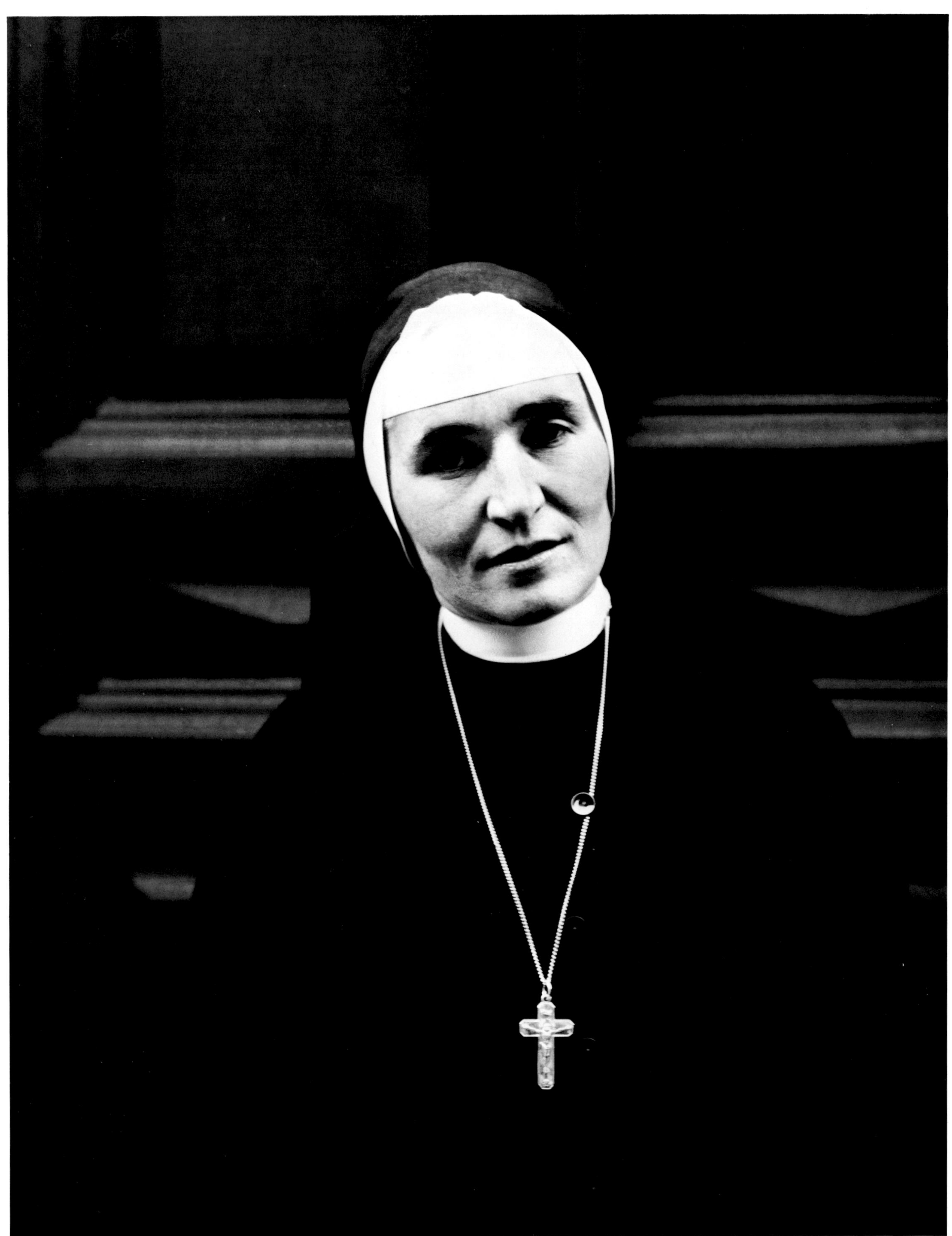

Ralph Gibson · Untitled (Piazza Navonna, Rome) · 1978

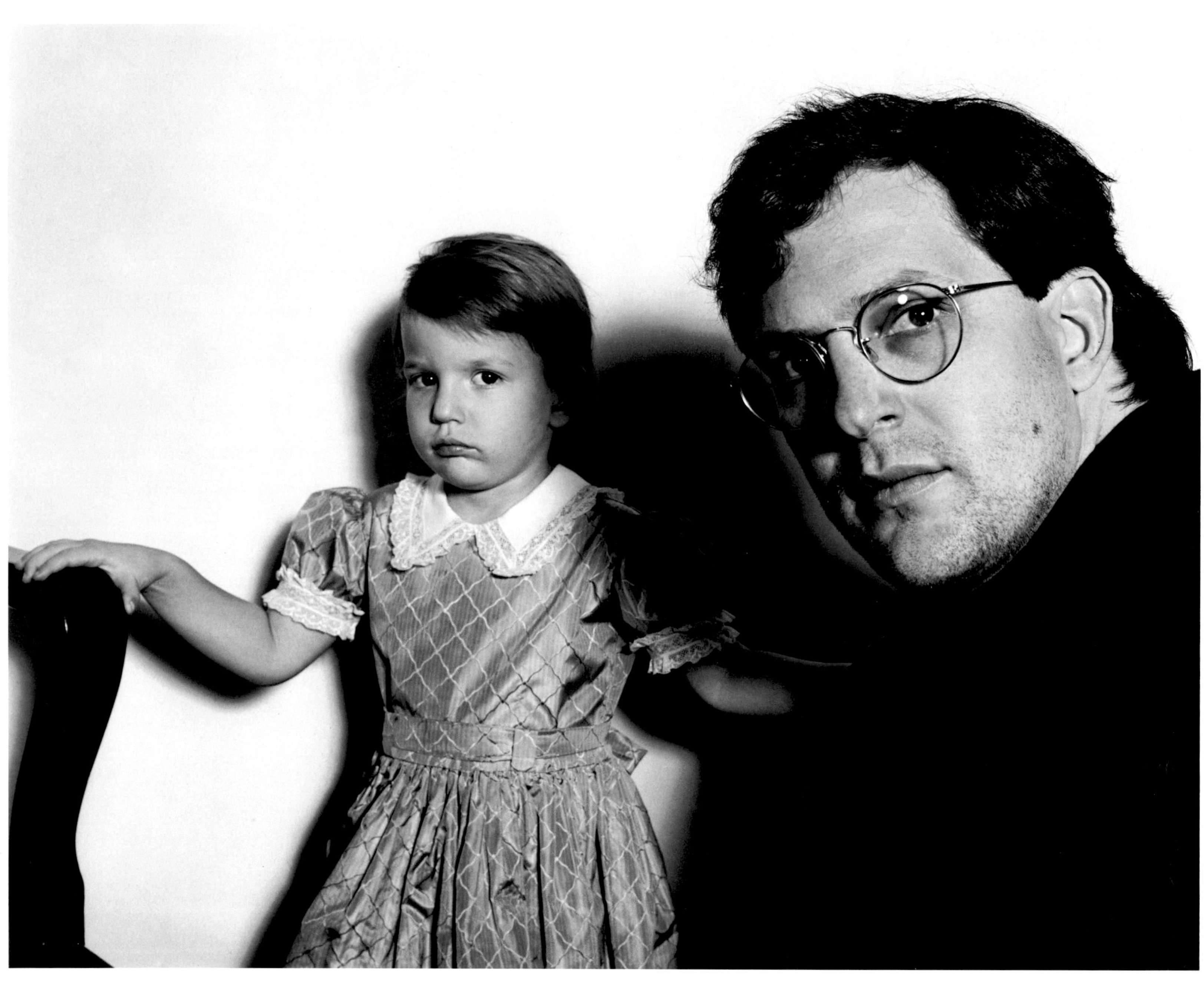

John Coplans · *Frances and Donald* · 1984

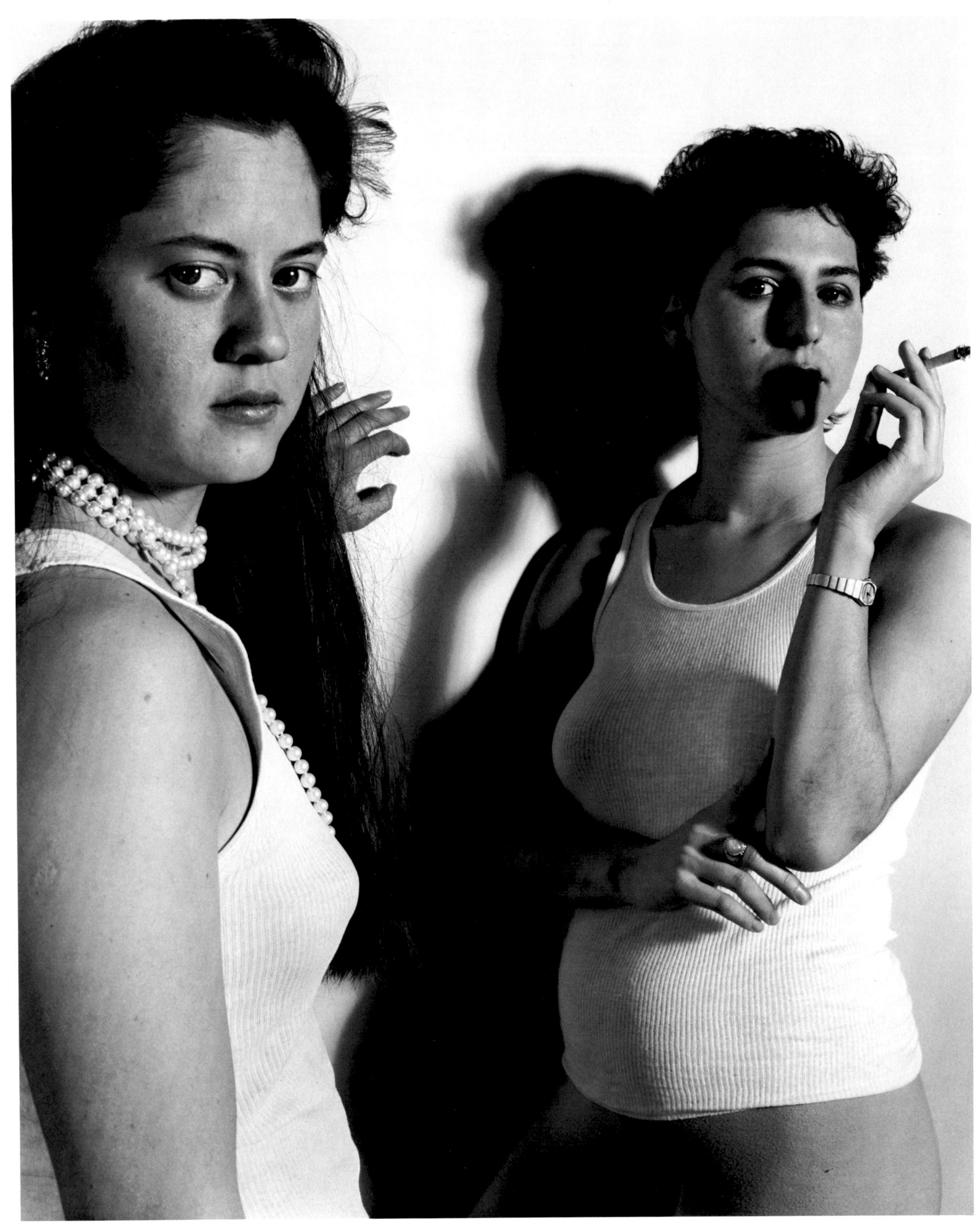

John Coplans · *Sandy and Dana* · 1983

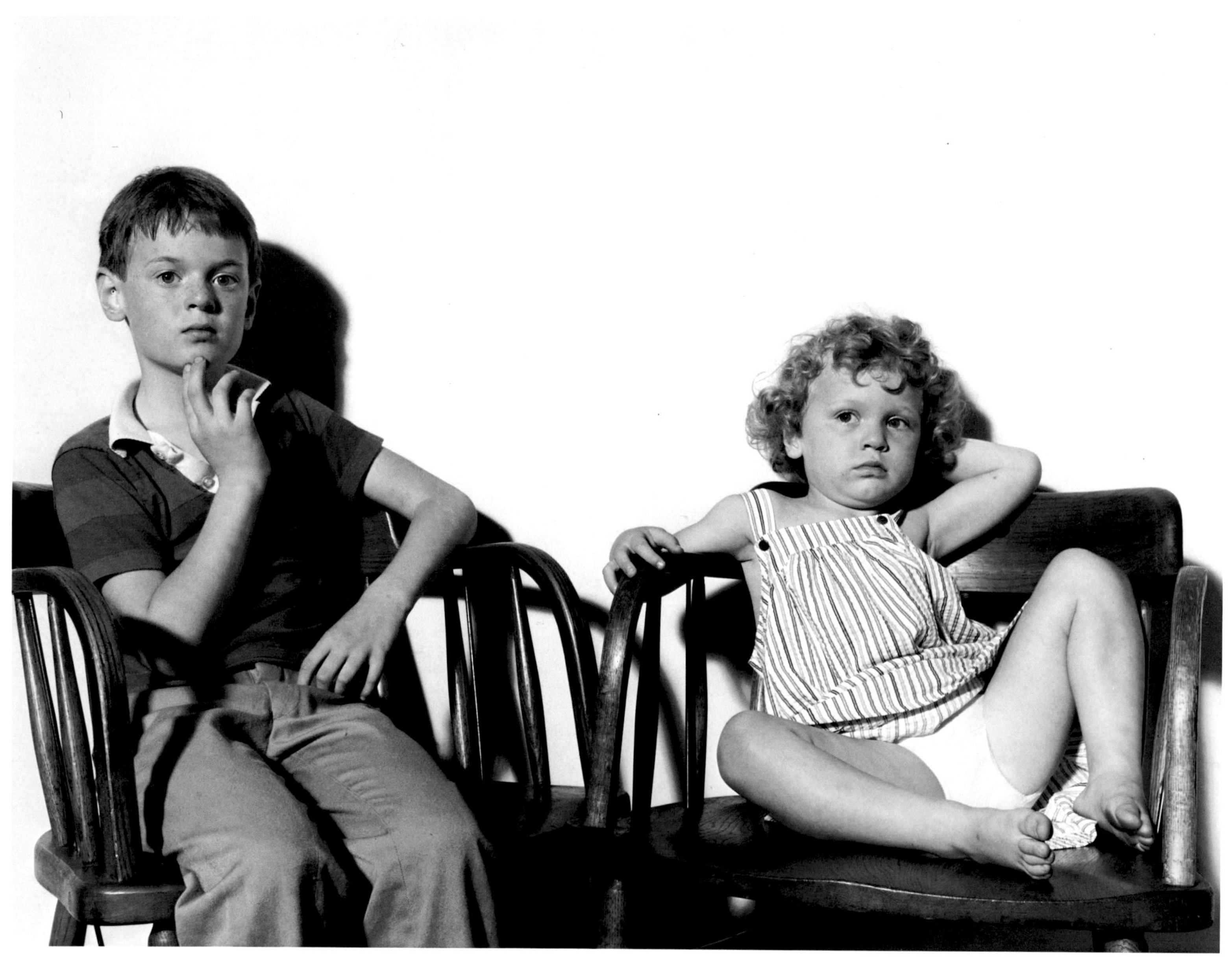

John Coplans · *Edward and Ella* · 1983

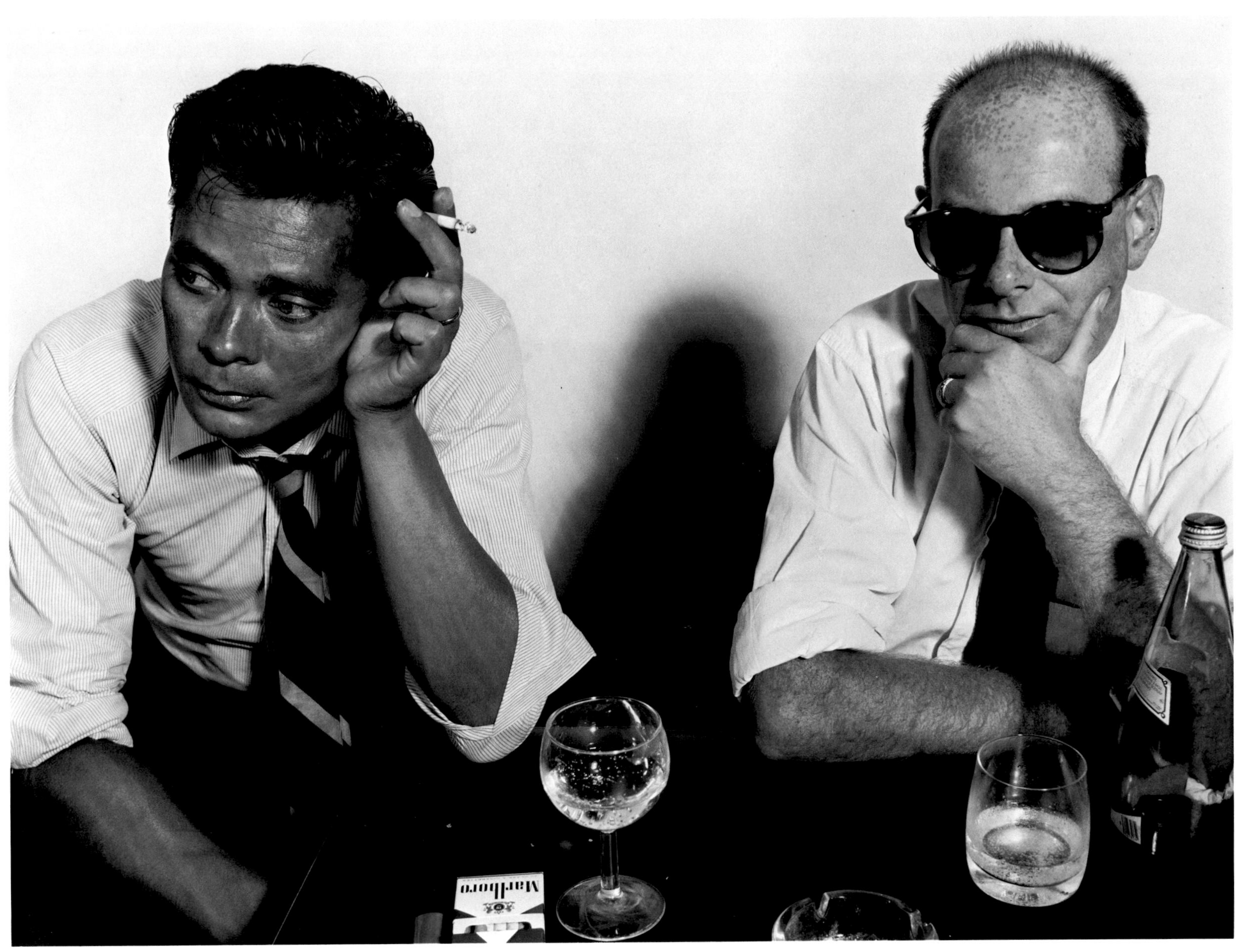

John Coplans · *Rudo and Geoffrey* · 1984

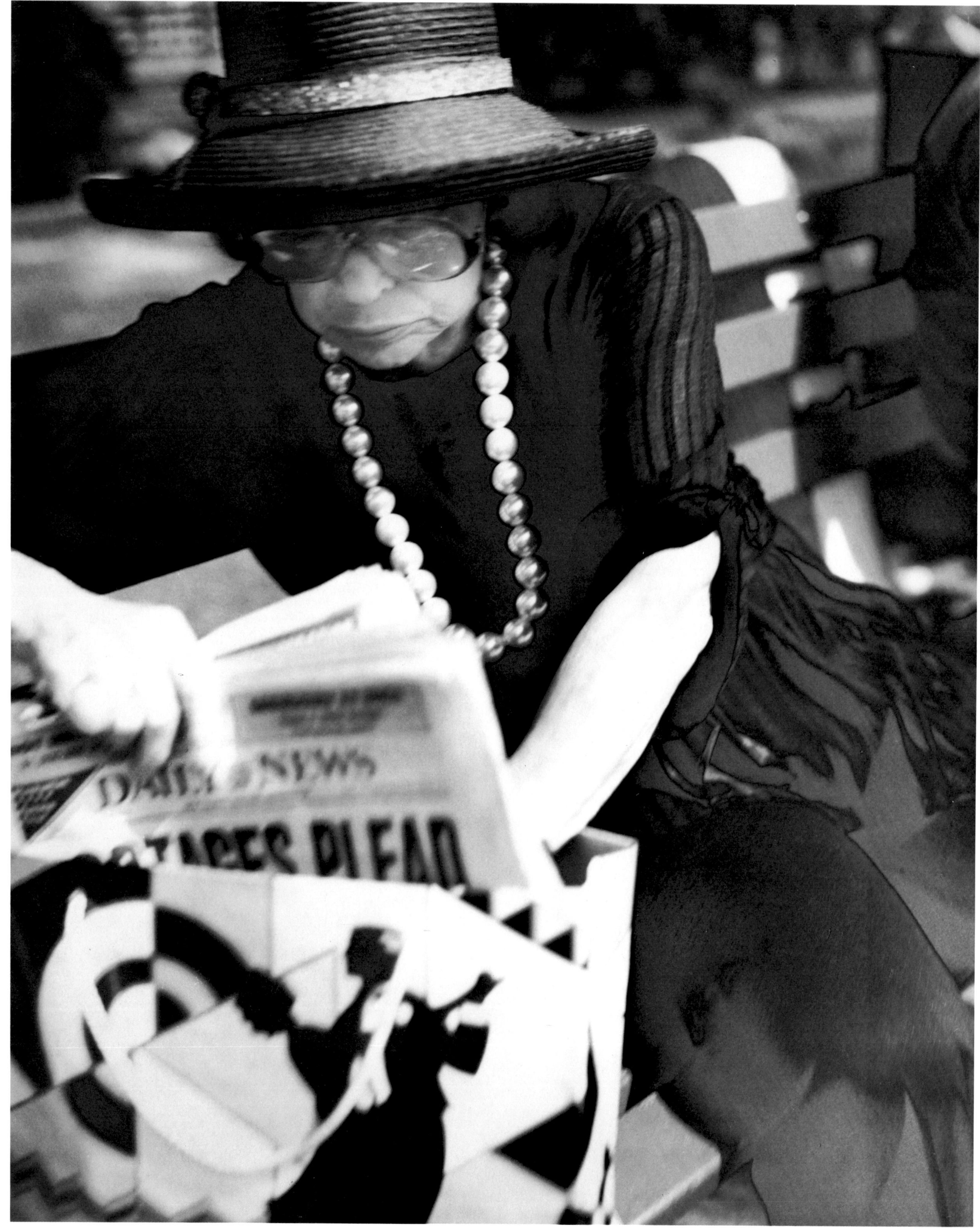

Michael Spano · Untitled · 1985

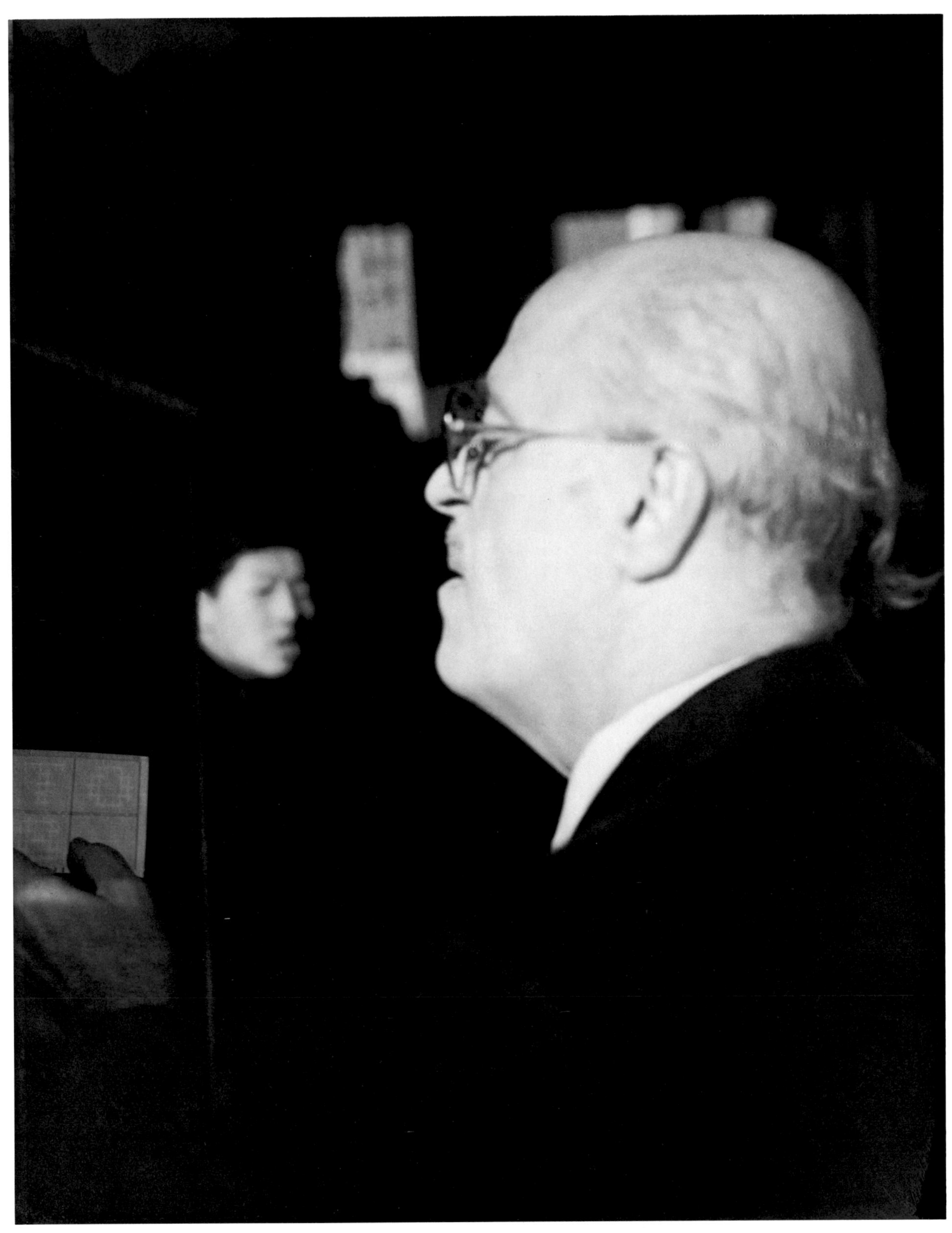

Michael Spano · *Lotto* · 1985

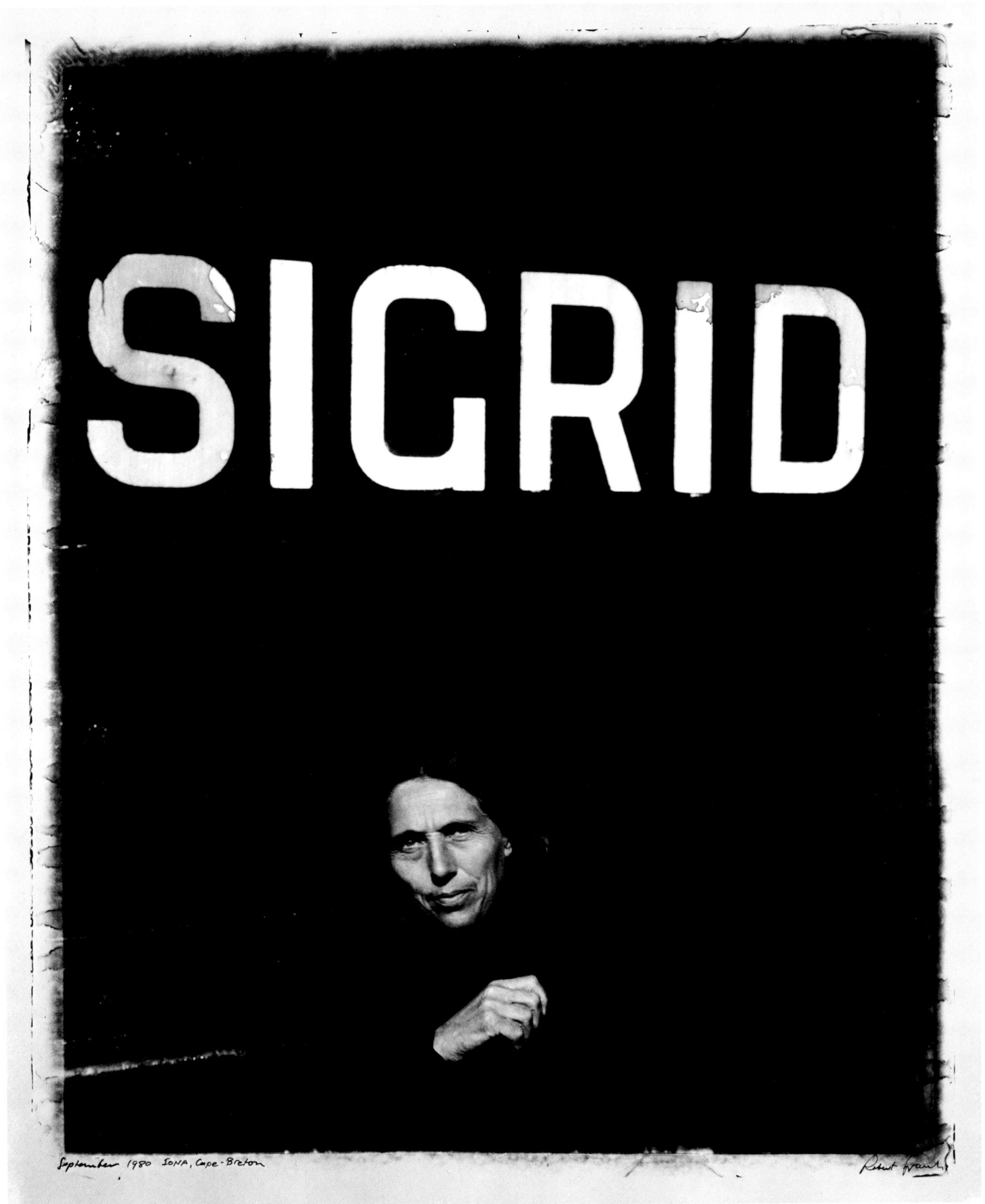

Robert Frank · *September 1980, Iona, Cape Breton*

Following six pages: Robert Frank · *Boston, March 20, 1985*

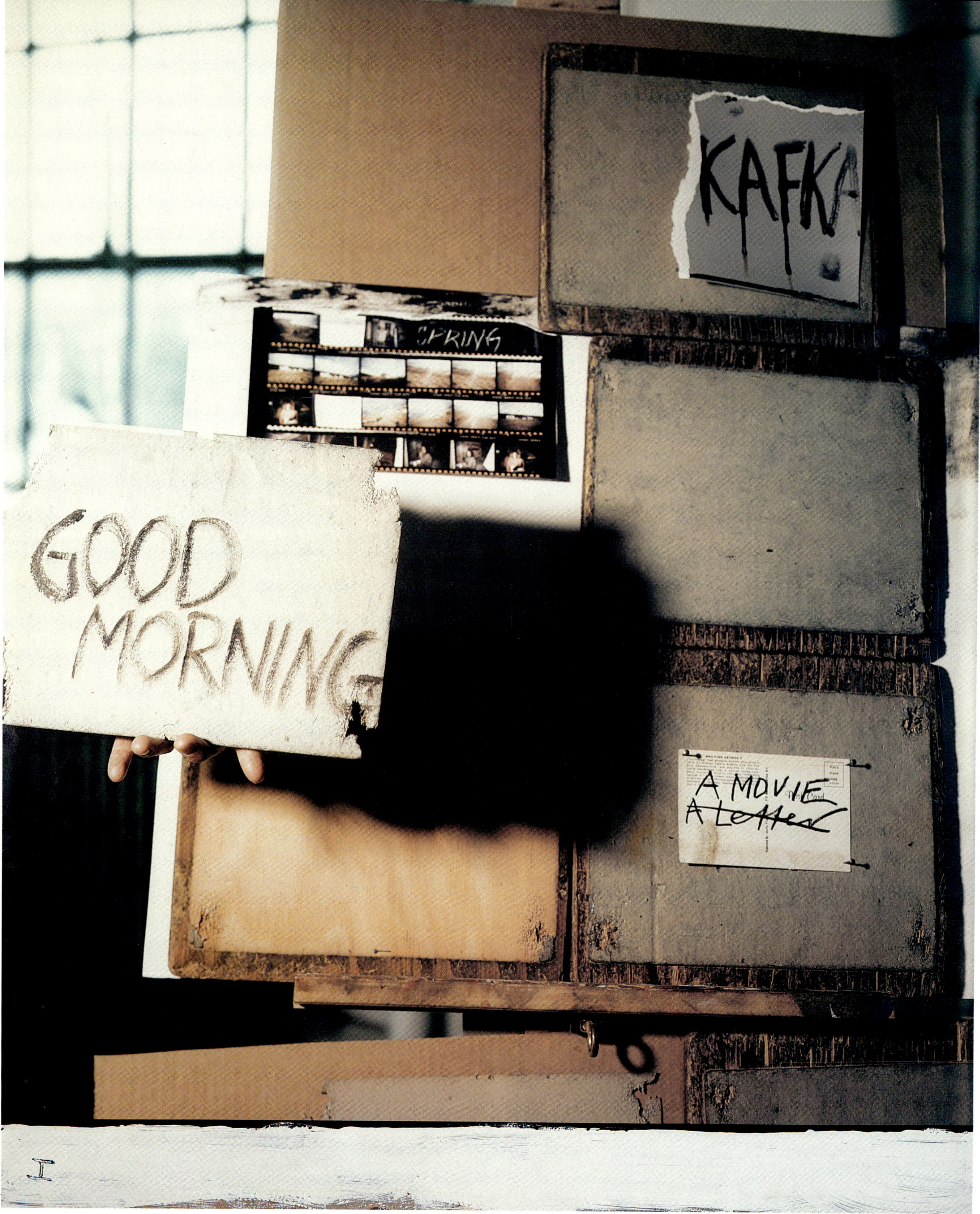
KAFKA
SPRING
GOOD MORNING
A MOVIE
~~A Letter~~

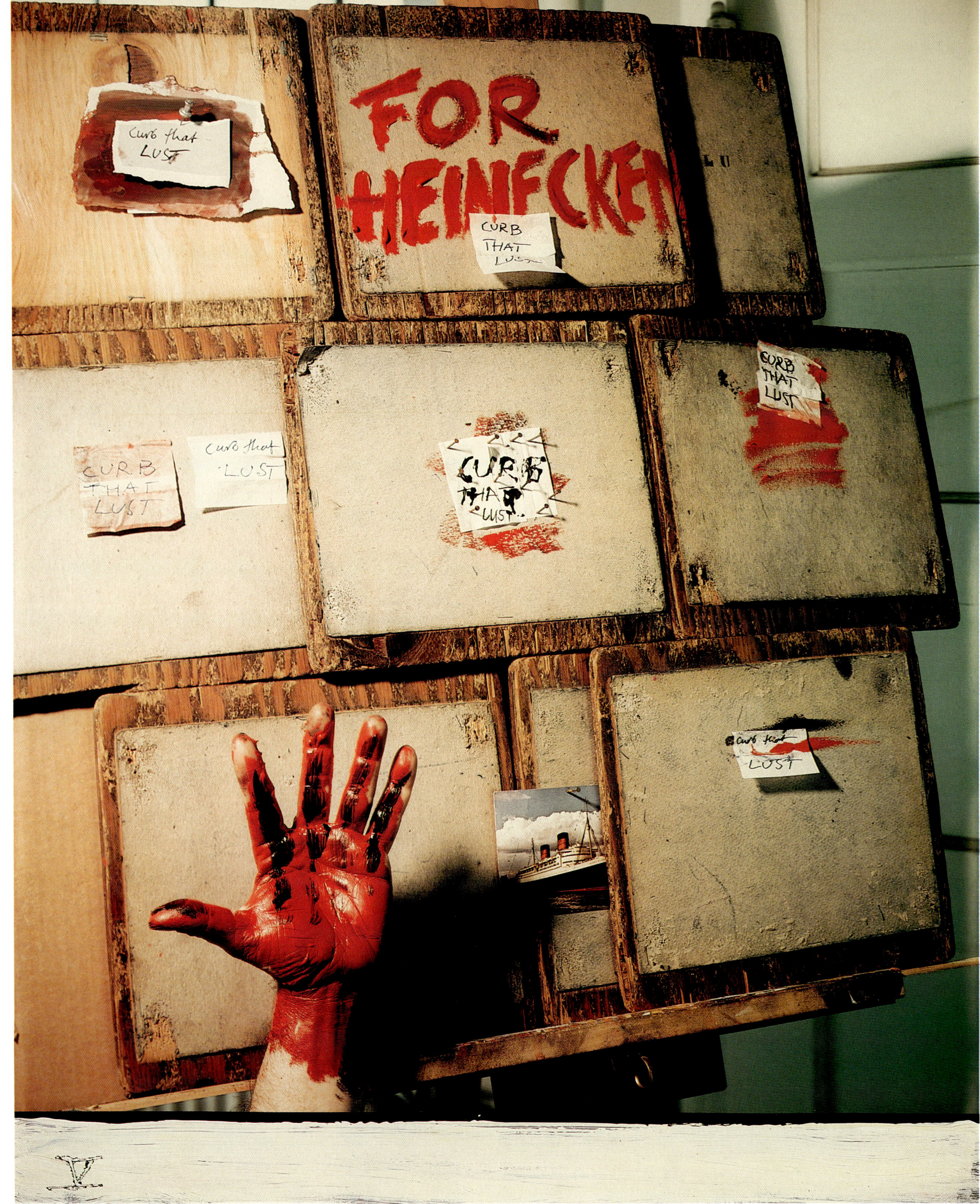

Curb that LUST
FOR HEINECKEN
CURB THAT LUST
CURB THAT LUST
Curb that LUST
CURB THAT LUST
CURB THAT LUST
Curb that LUST

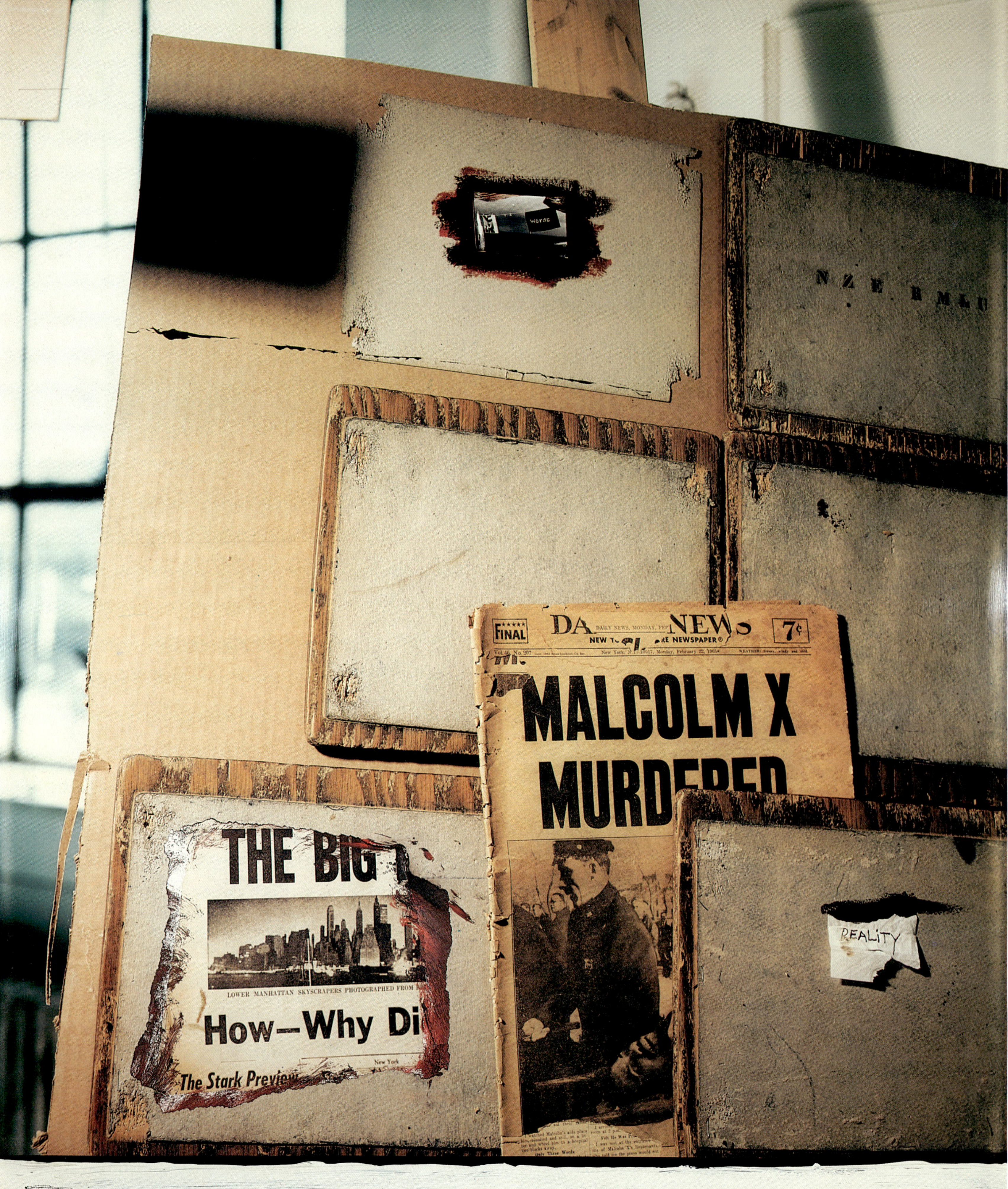

FINAL
7¢
MALCOLM X
THE BIG
LOWER MANHATTAN SKYSCRAPERS PHOTOGRAPHED FROM
How—Why Di
The Stark Preview
REALITY

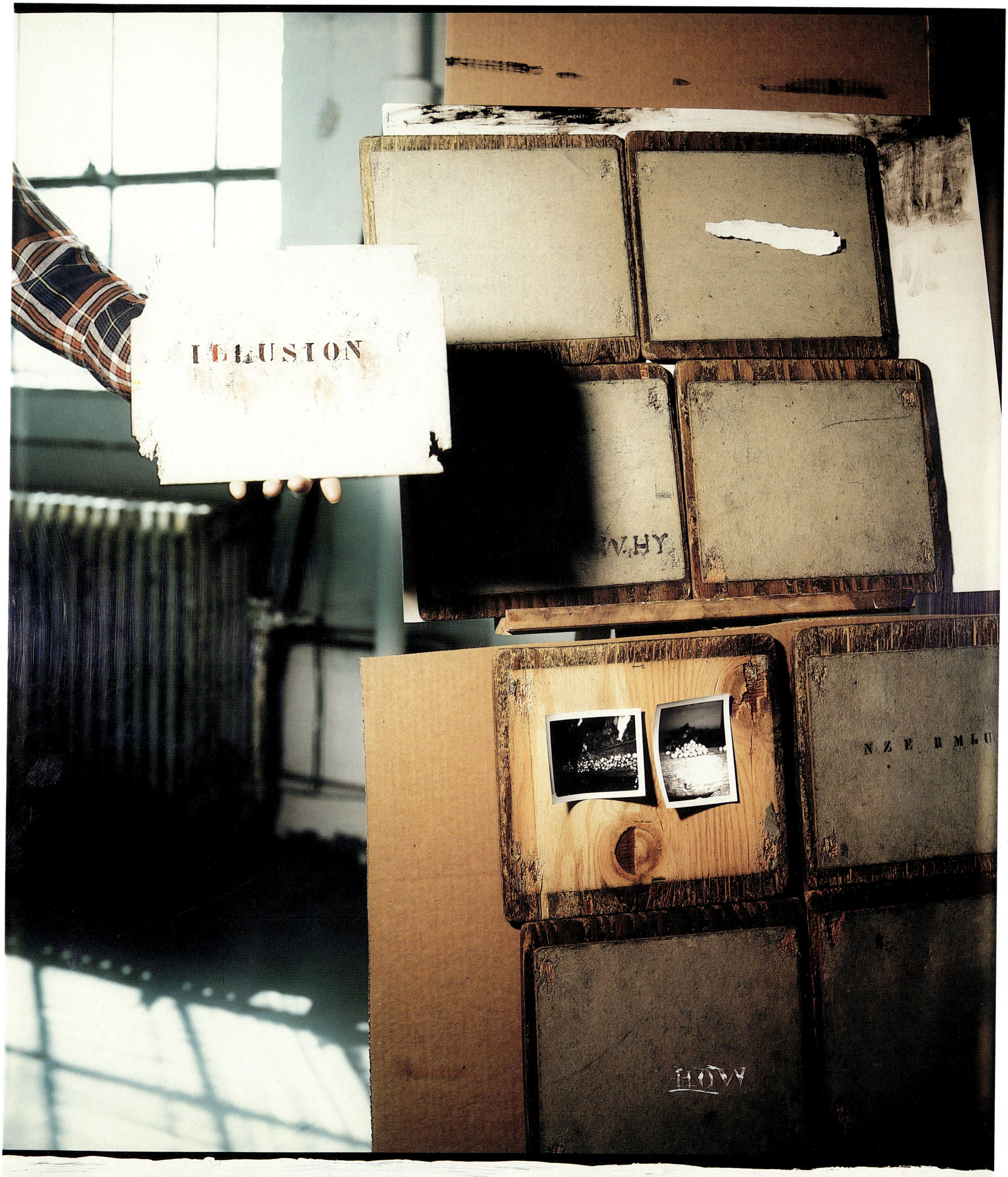

ILLUSION
WHY
NZE RMLU
HOW

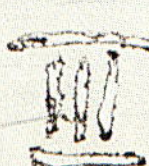

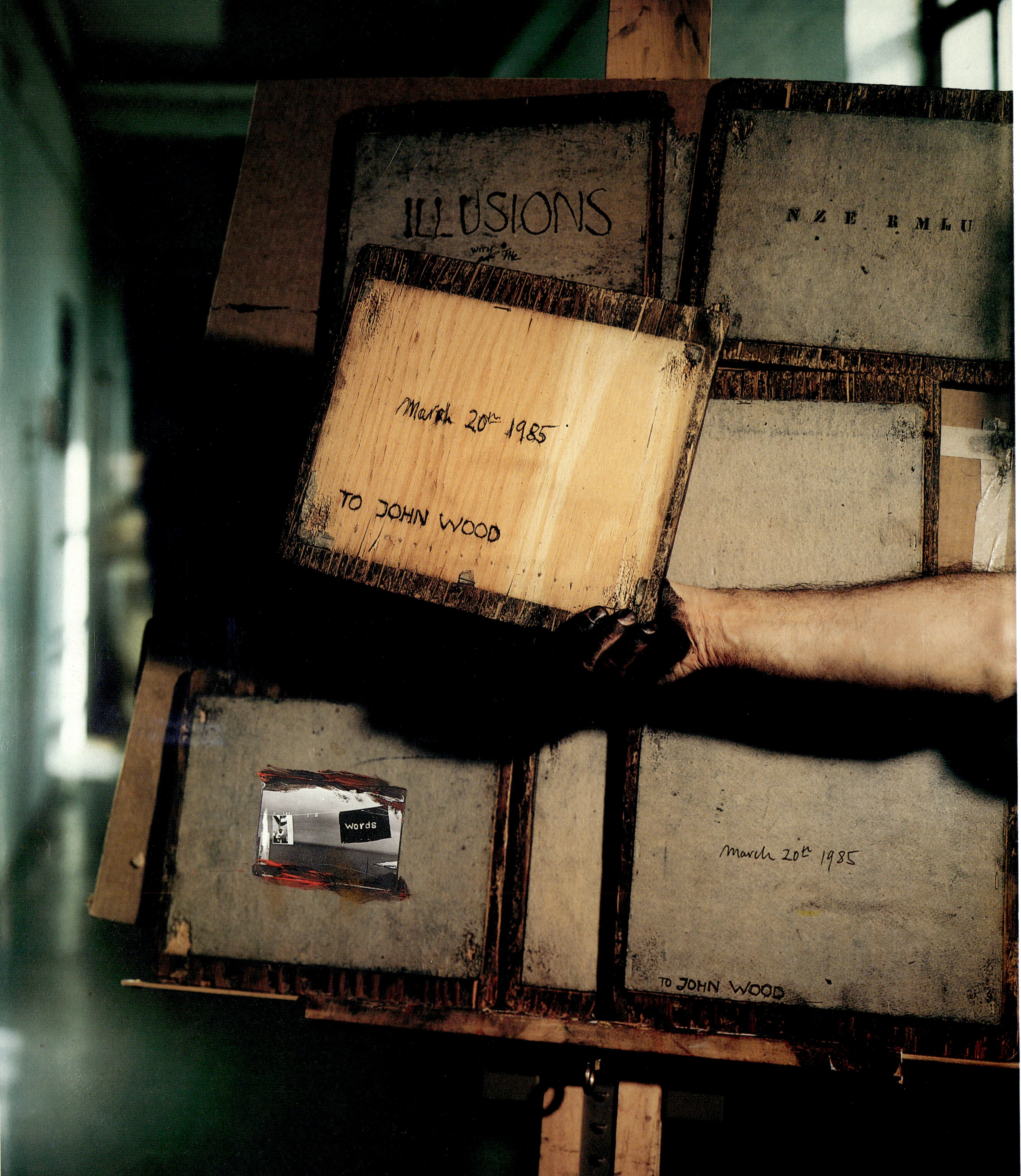
ILLUSIONS
N Z E R M L U
March 20th 1985
TO JOHN WOOD
words
March 20th 1985
TO JOHN WOOD

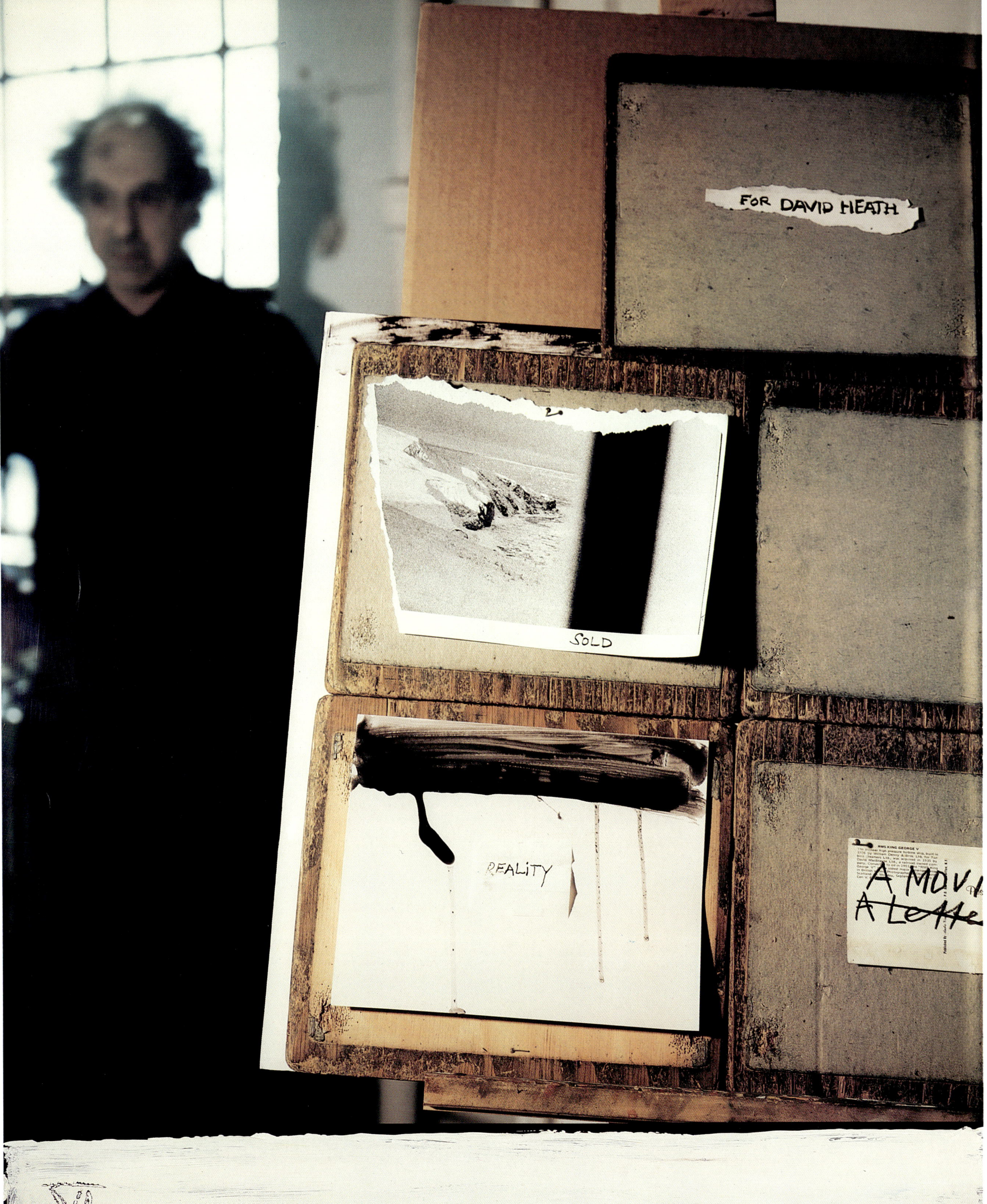
FOR DAVID HEATH
SOLD
REALITY
A MOVI

Robert Frank · *For Sandy and Pablo in Brattleboro, Vermont and the Men and Women—Angels—Horses Everywhere, New York City–Brattleboro* · 1980

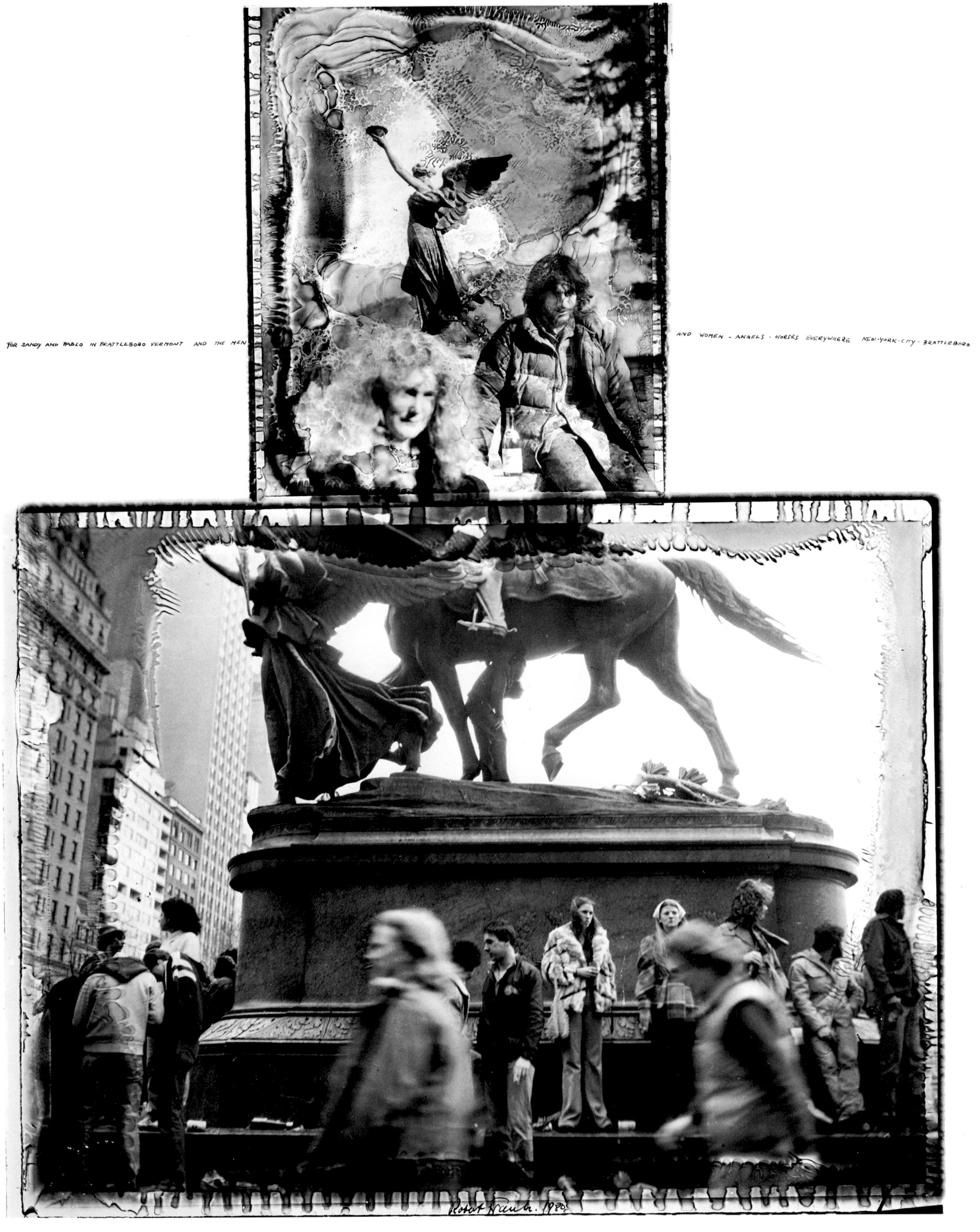

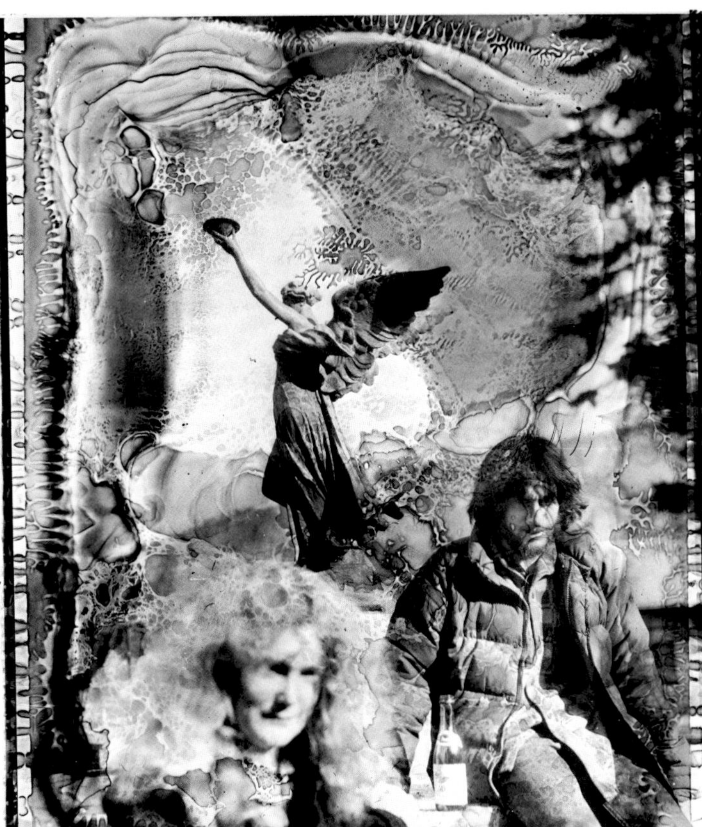

FOR SANDY AND PABLO IN BRATTLEBORO VERMONT AND THE MEN
AND WOMEN - ANGELS - HORSES EVERYWHERE NEW-YORK-CITY-BRATTLEBORO
Robert Frank. 1980

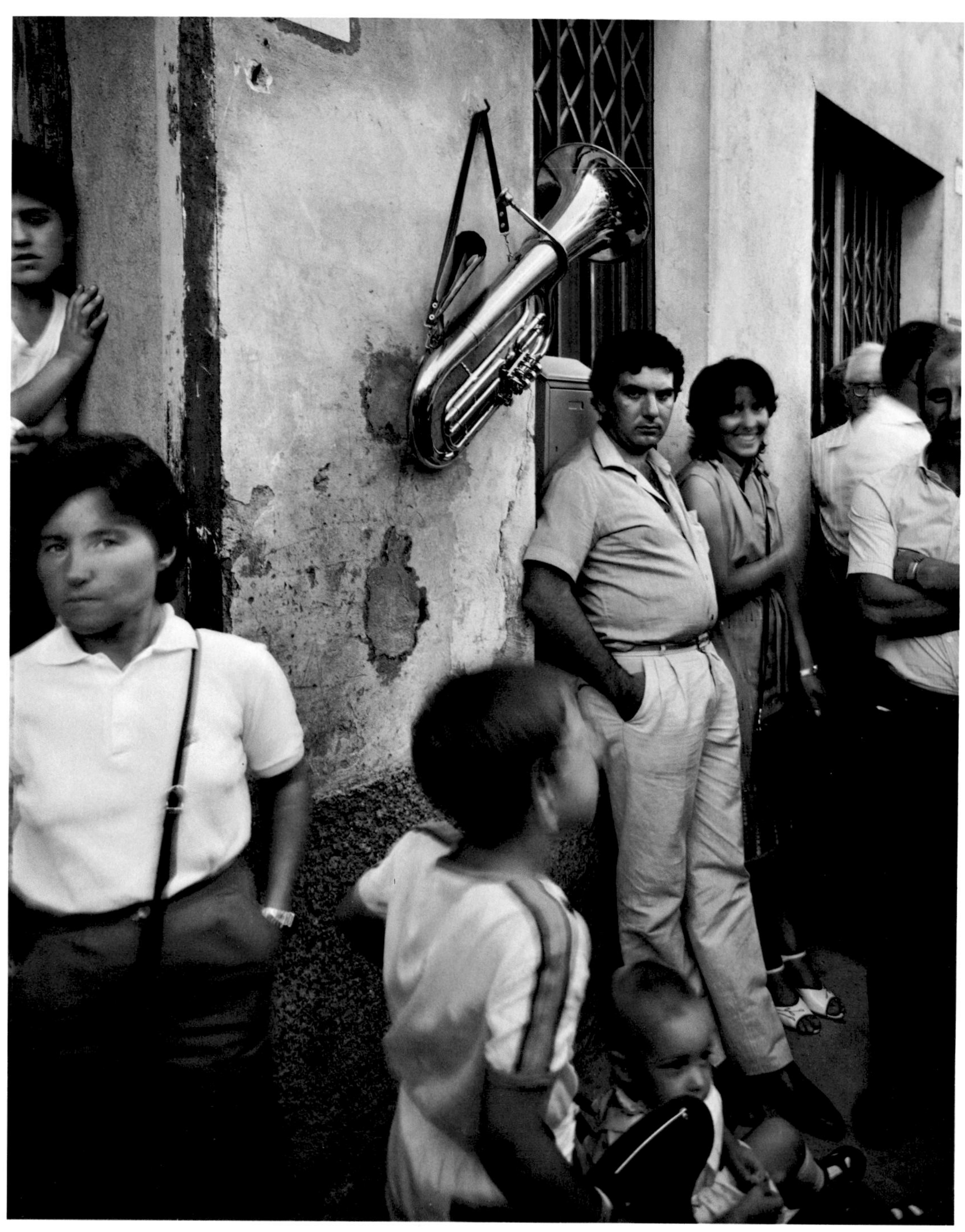

Emmet Gowin · *Pitigliano, Italy* · 1983

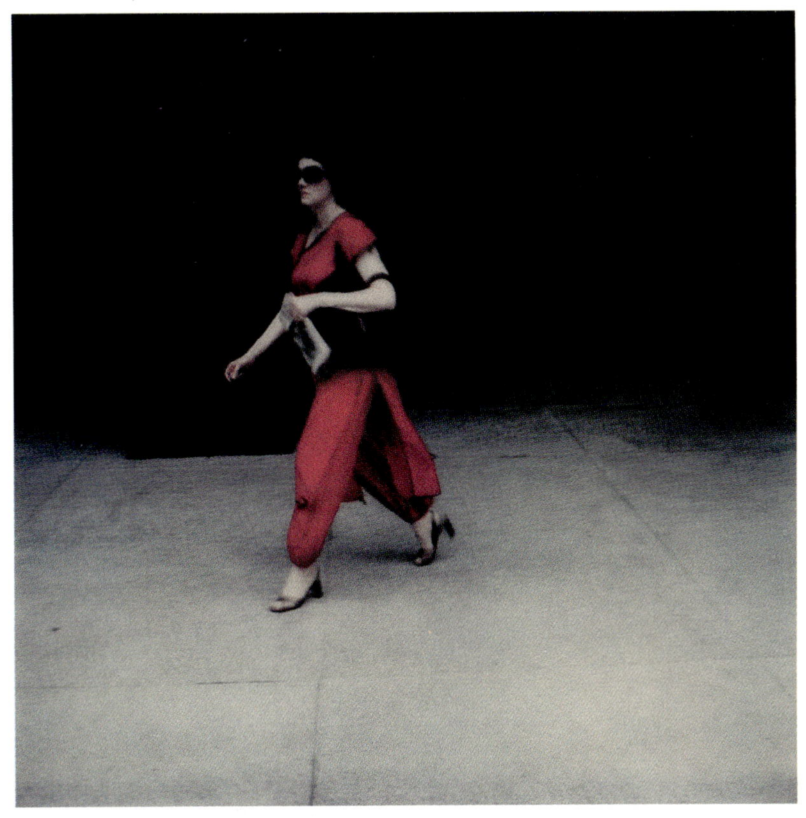

Richard Pare · *Woman in Red Crossing Seagram Plaza* · c. 1975

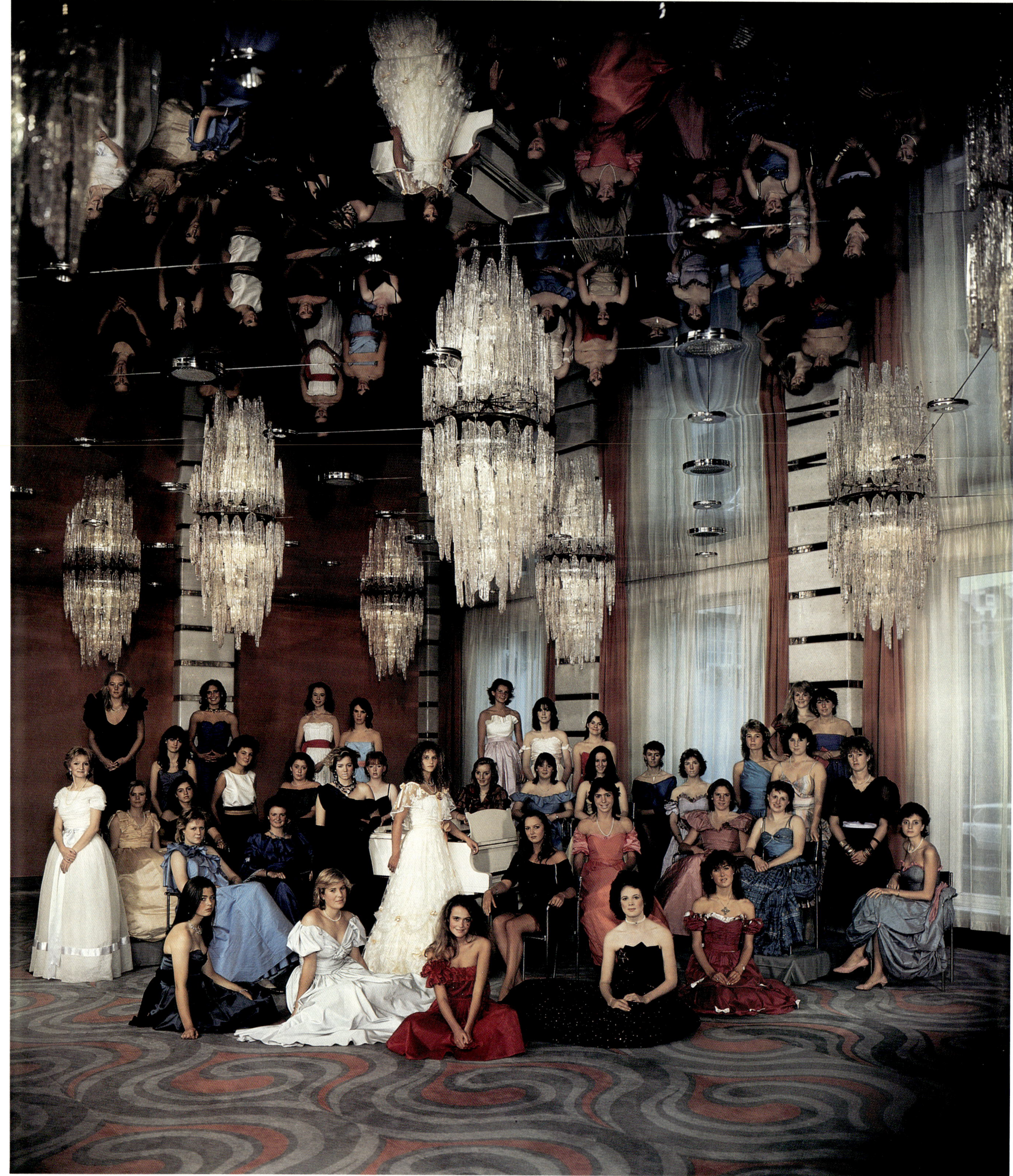

Neal Slavin · *Debutantes of 1983, The Berkeley Hotel, London, 13 September 1983*

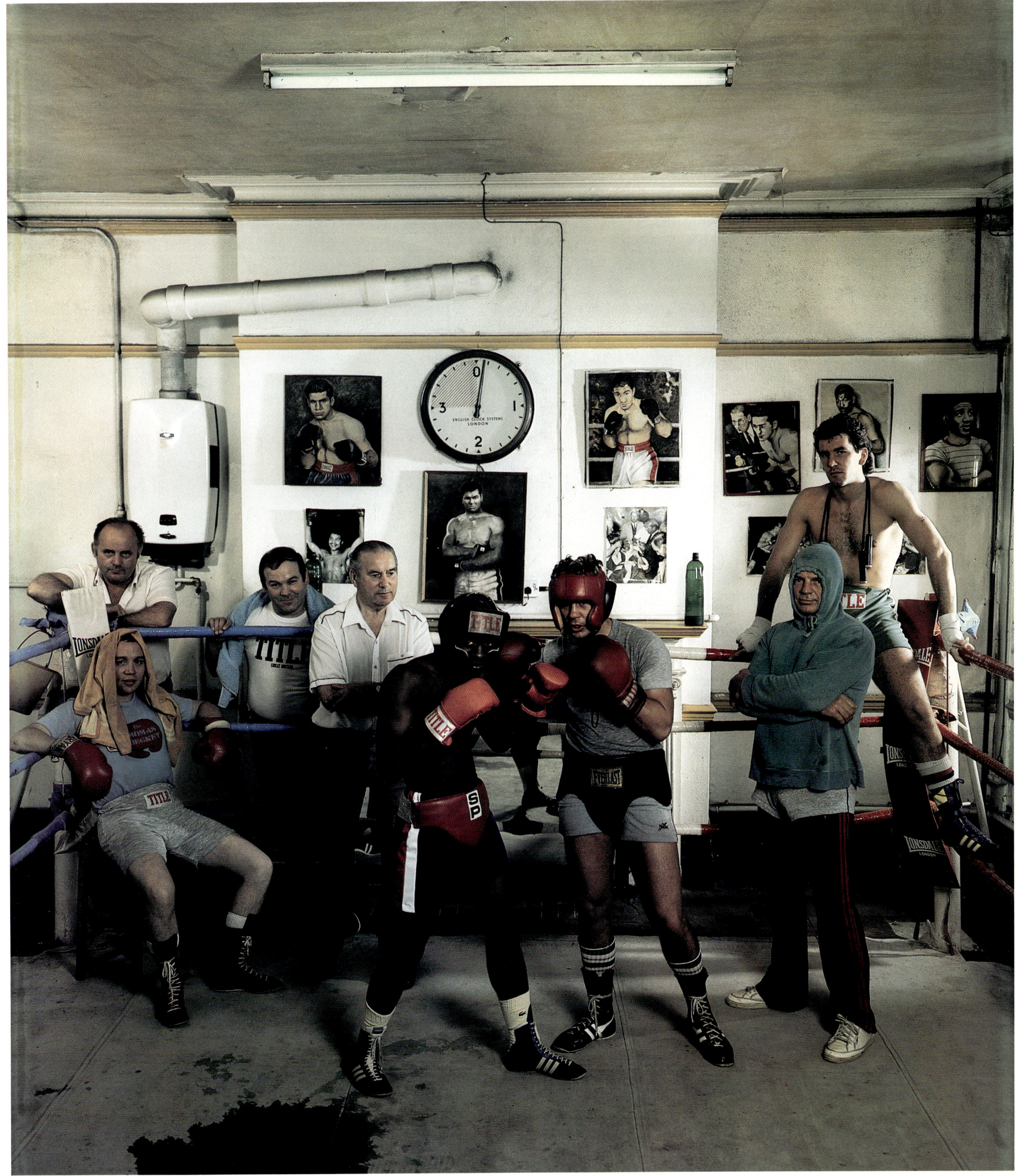

Neal Slavin · *The Thomas A Becket Gymnasium, Old Kent Road, London, 24 July 1984*

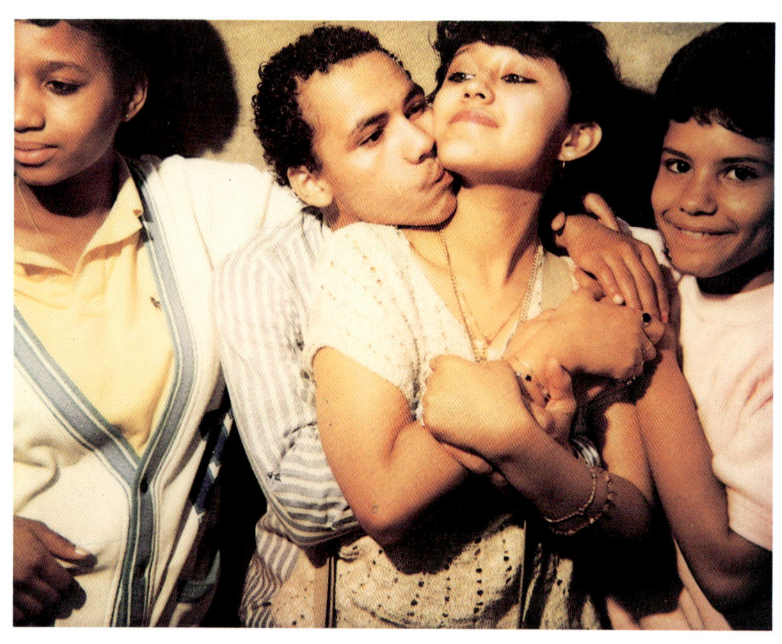

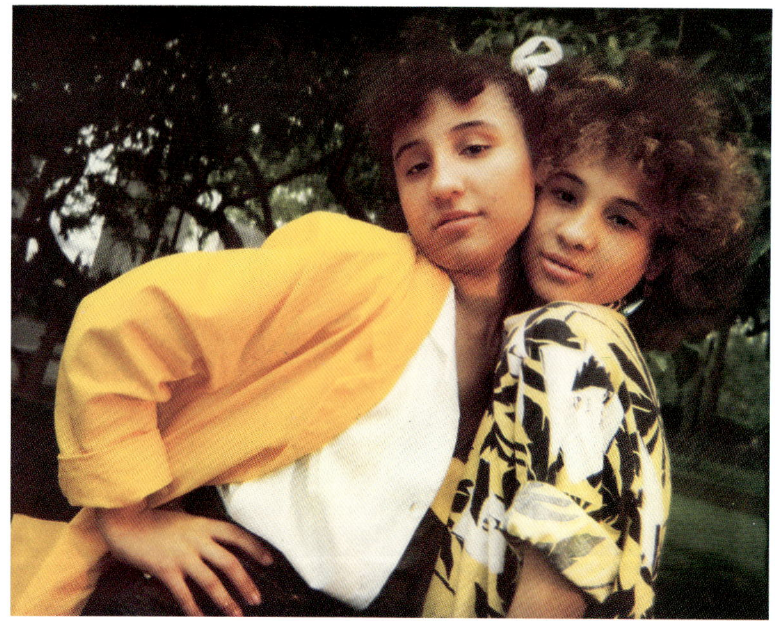

Mary Ellen Mark · *New York City* · 1986

Mary Ellen Mark · *New York City* · 1986

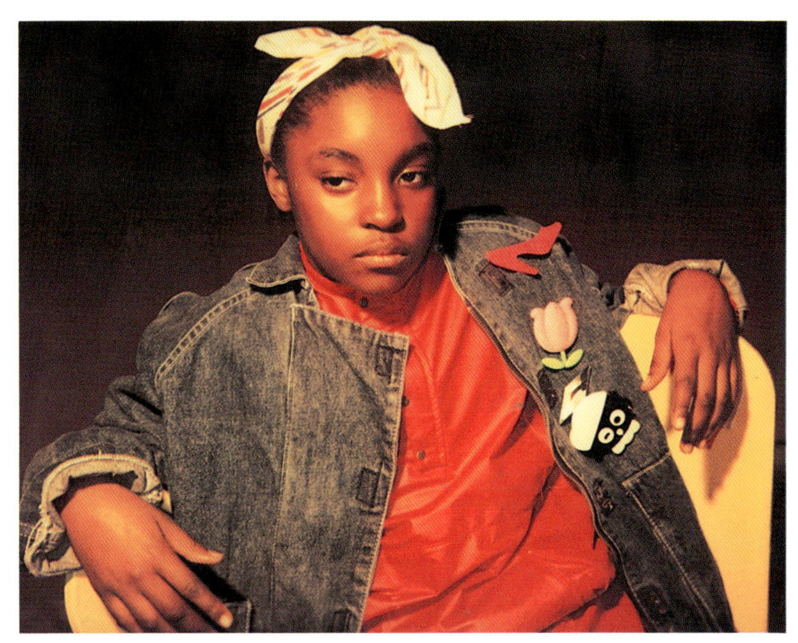

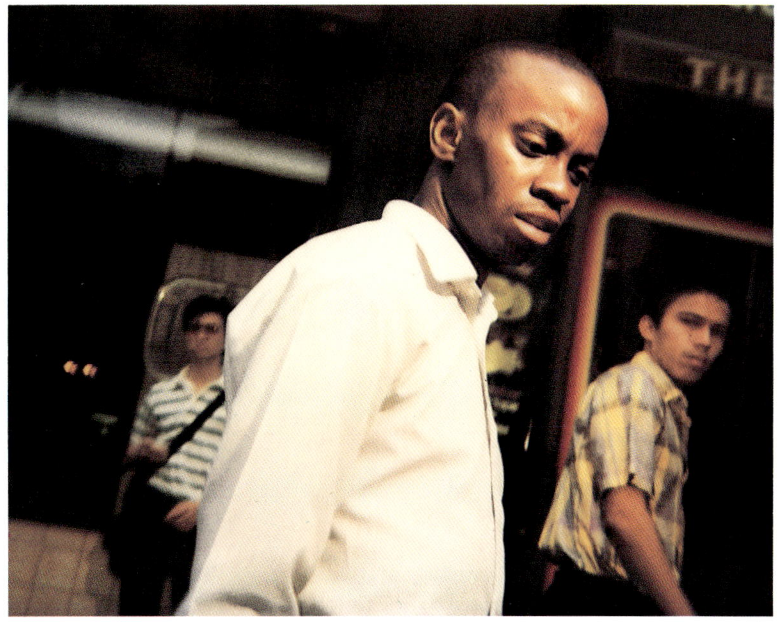

Mary Ellen Mark · *New York City* · 1986

Mary Ellen Mark · *New York City* · 1986

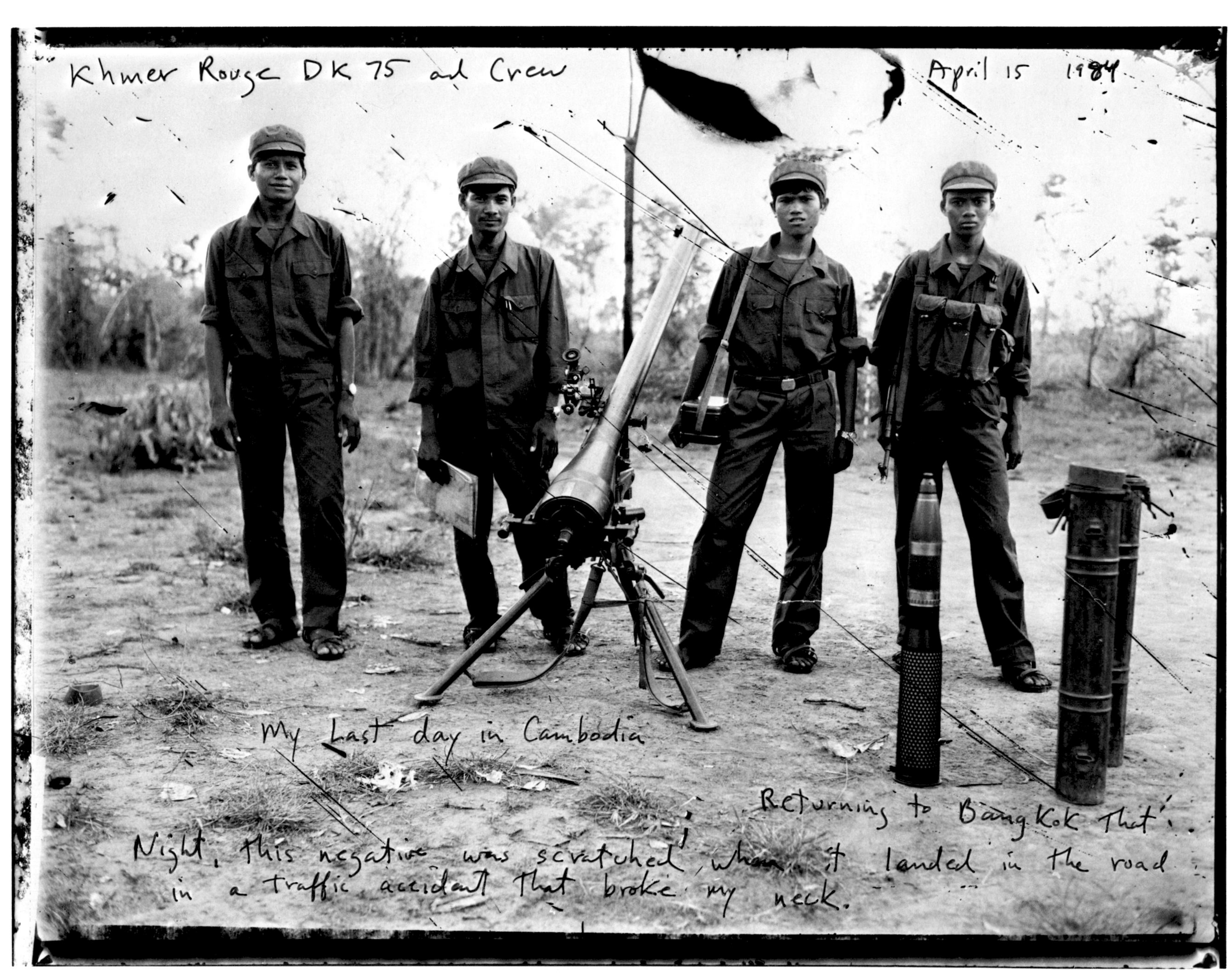

Bill Burke · *Khmer Rouge DK 75 and Crew* · 1984

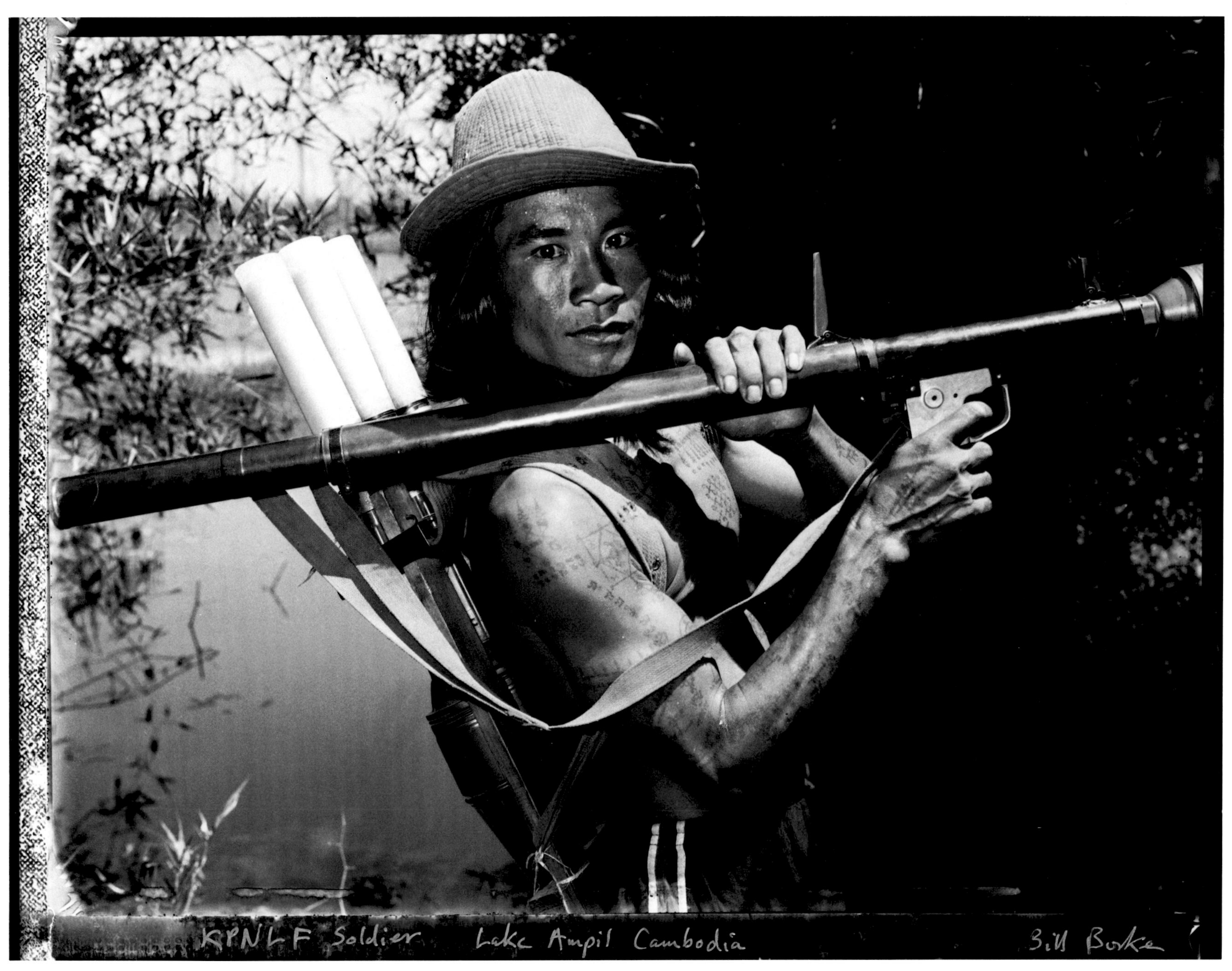

Bill Burke · *KPNLF Soldier, Lake Ampil, Cambodia* · 1984

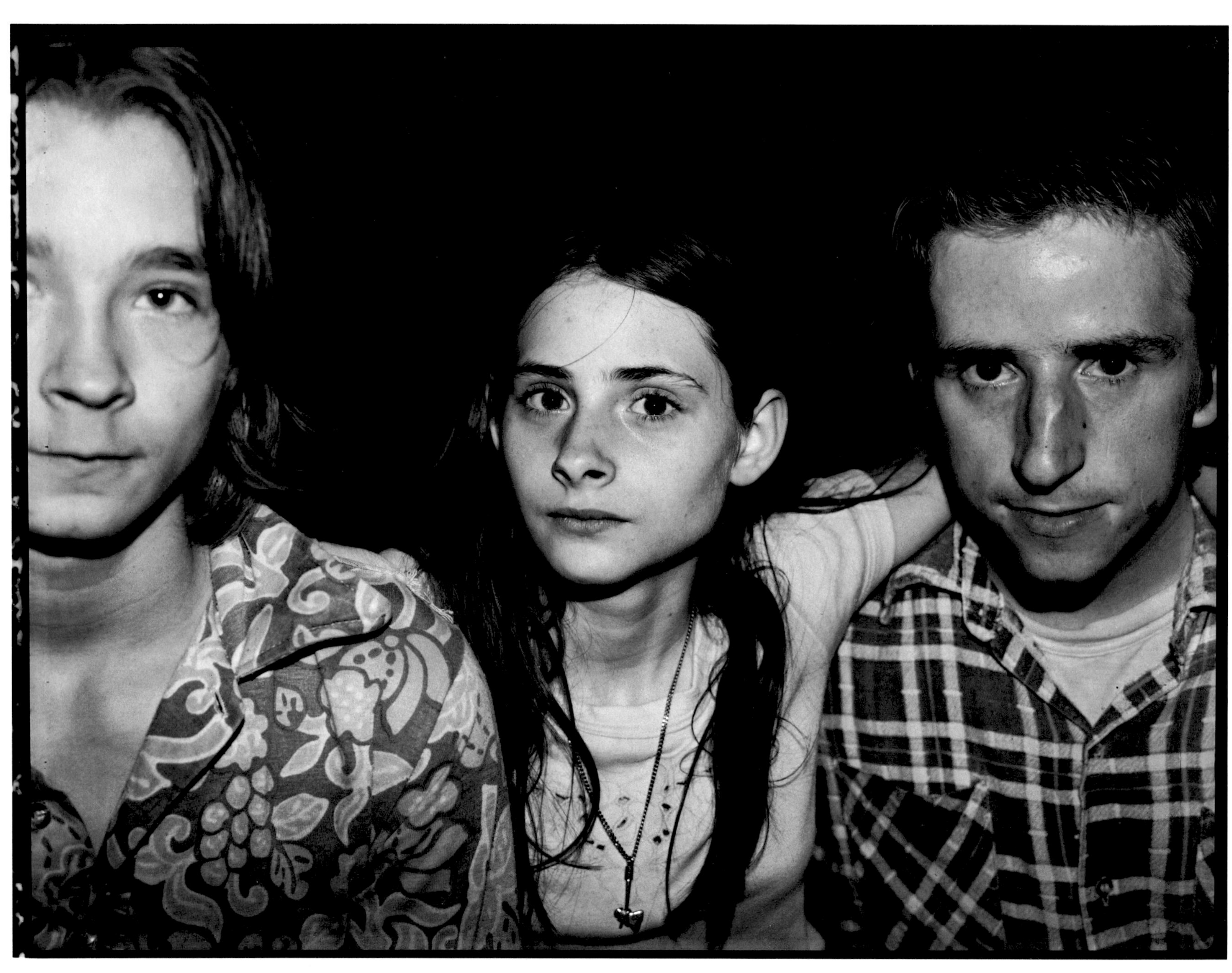

Bill Burke · *Kissing Cousins, Mingo County, West Virginia* · 1979

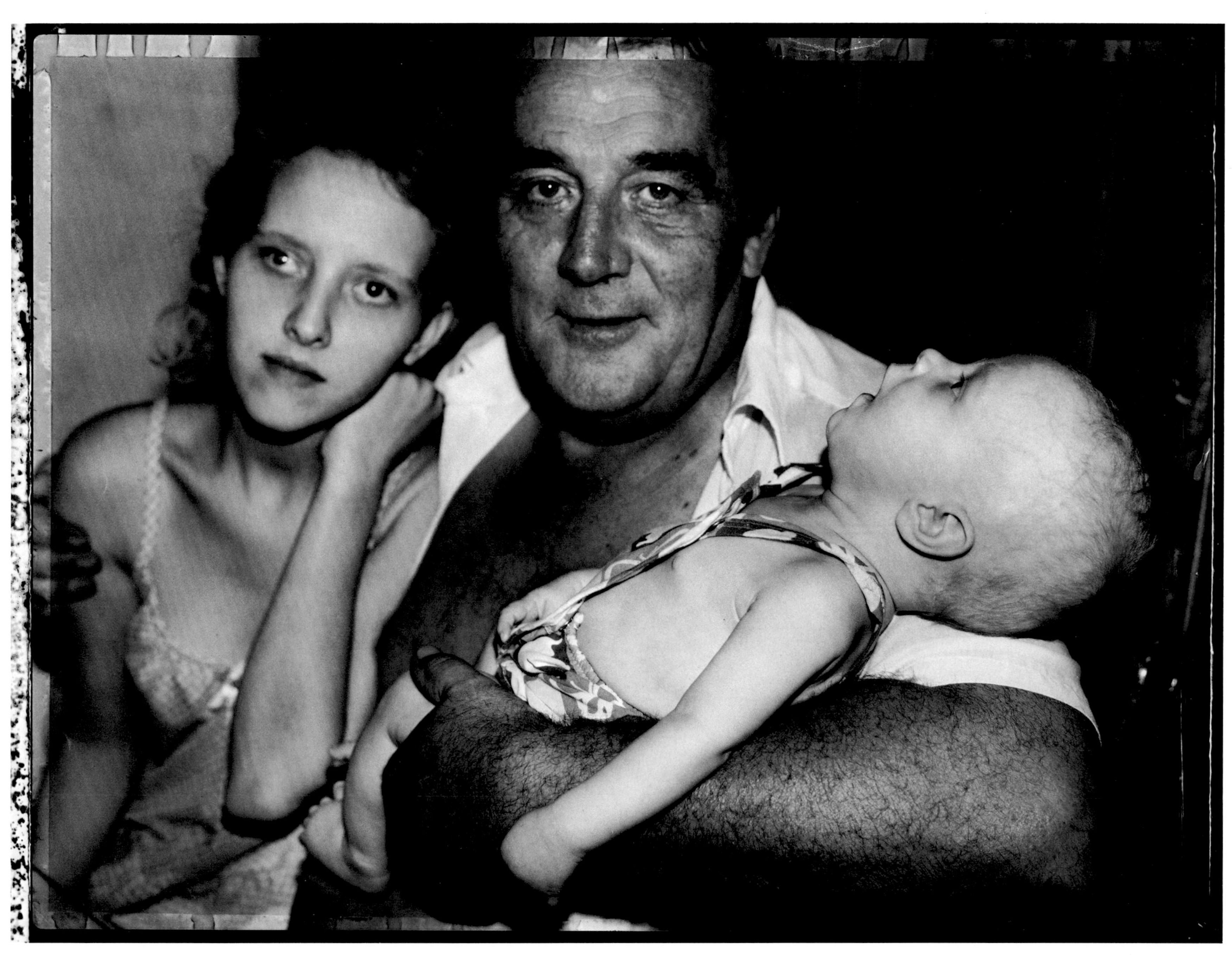

Bill Burke · *Family, Kermit, West Virginia* · 1979

I LOOK AT THIS PICTURE AND I KNOW MY MOTHER KNEW THAT WE WERE THERE AND WE LOVED HER.

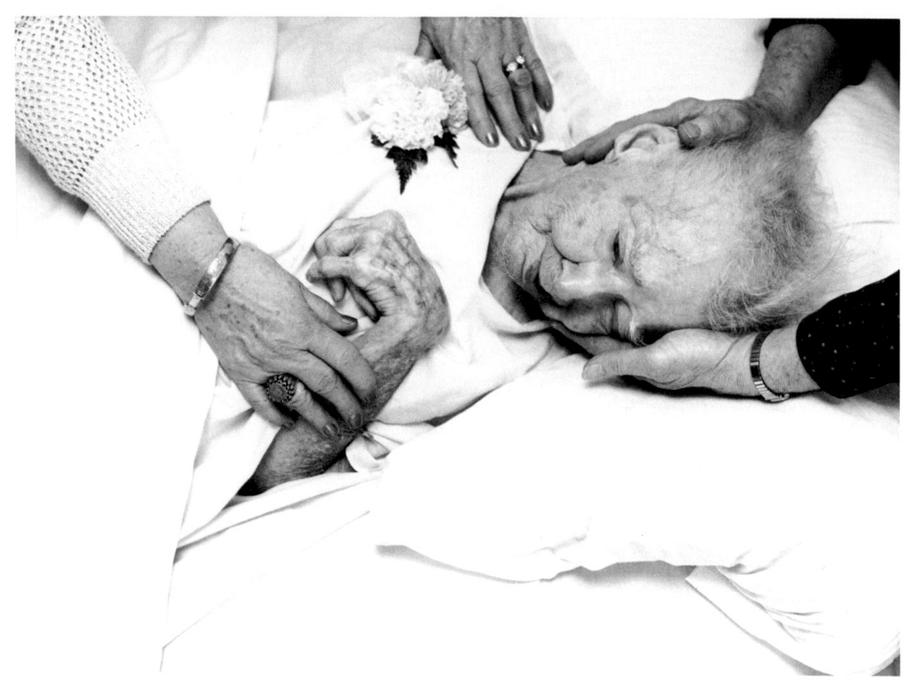

THIS IS MY MOTHER HELPLESS IN HER FINAL DAYS.
SHE WAS WAITING AND TRYING HARD TO DIE
SHE HAD LIVED TOO LONG

THE NURSING HOME GAVE HER THE CARE SHE REQUIRED,
BUT I WISH I COULD HAVE KEPT HER HOME WITH ME—
LIKE A ROSE KENNEDY.

IT IS ALL ECONOMICS AND TIME - IF ONLY I WERE RICH

Edna K. Sheeley
DAUGHTER OF MARY G. SULLIVAN
1885 - 1985
8 CHILDREN
17 GRANDCHILDREN
28 GREAT GRANDCHILDREN

Jim Goldberg · *Nursing Home Series, Cambridge, Massachusetts* · 1985–86

ITS A DAMM GOOD PICTURE

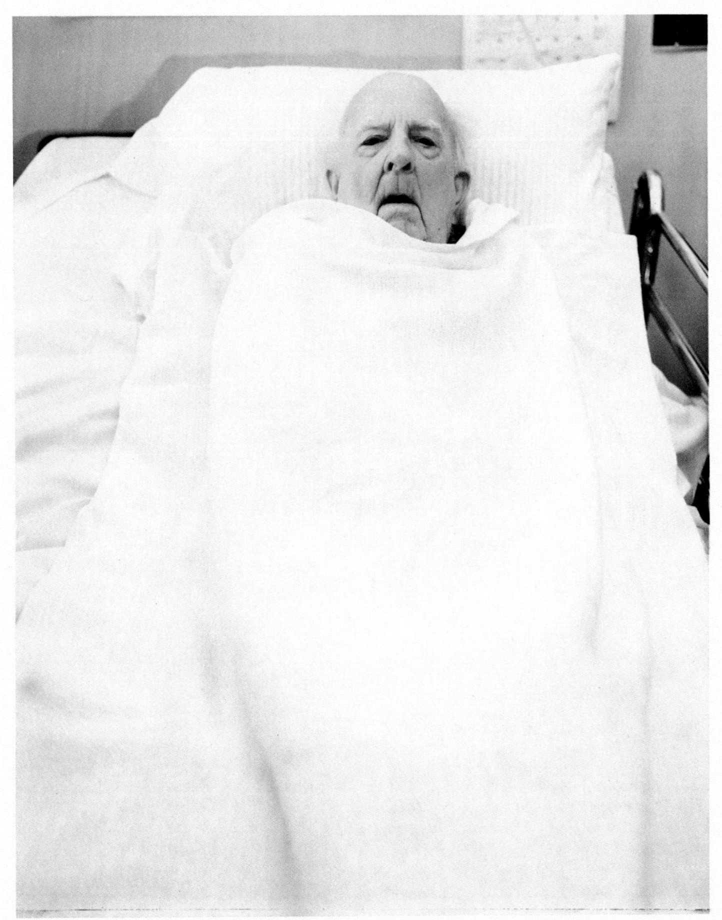

I'VE HAD A ROUGH AND WILD LIFE
I WAS A MERCHANT MARINE
EVERYTHING WAS IN AN UPROAR
WAR - DEPRESSION - WAR
LIFE IS EASIER FOR ME NOW
THEY DO EVERYTHING FOR ME HERE
I LIKE THAT
THIS IS THE GOOD LIFE

H.E. BEAL

I MISS GETTING DRUNK

Jim Goldberg · *Nursing Home Series, Cambridge, Massachusetts* · 1985–86

THE NUDE

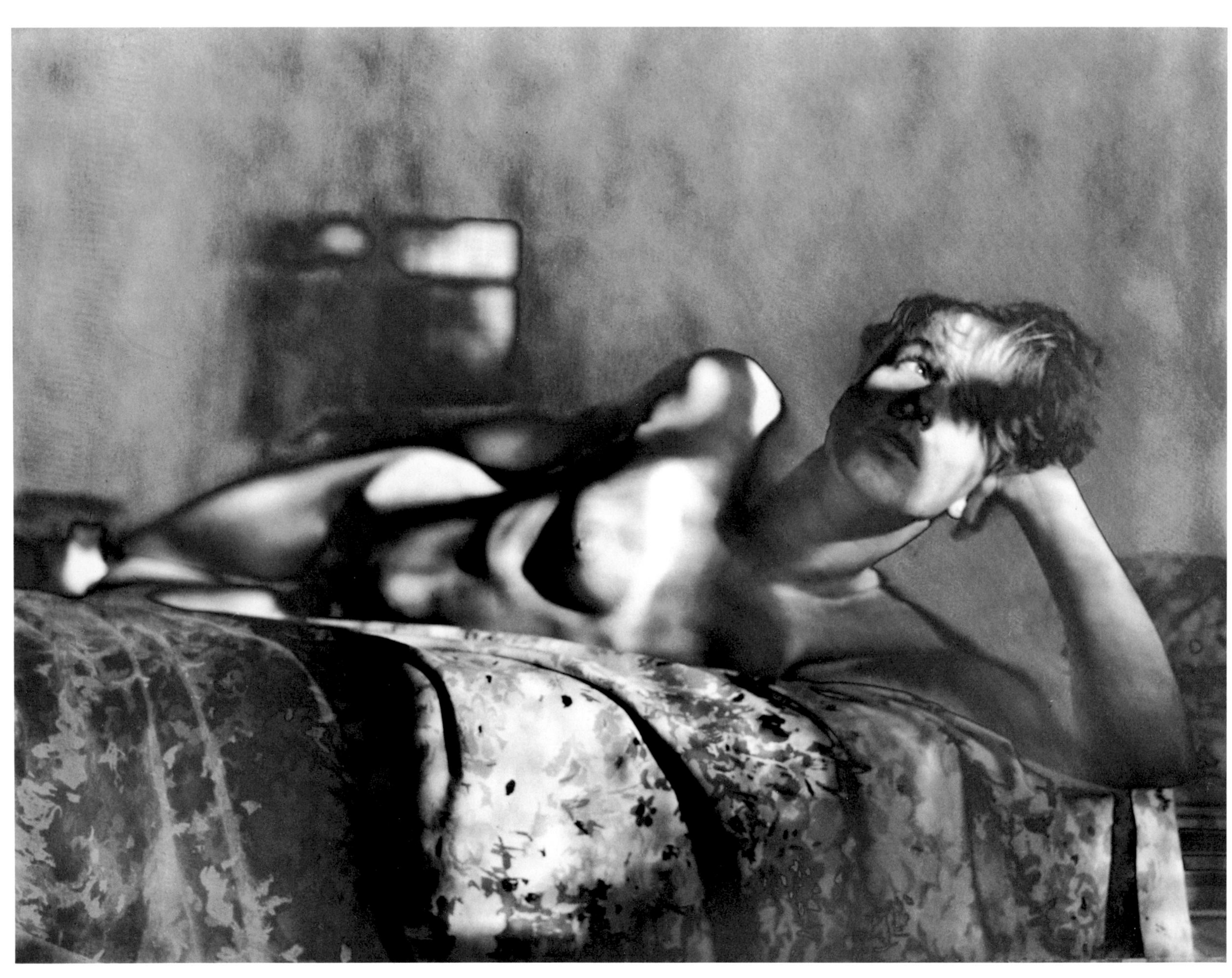

Michael Spano · *Flower Bed* · 1984

In recent decades I have noticed that people attend "legitimate" theaters in order to see other people naked, not in order to see—as formerly in Batista's naughty Havana, 150 miles from home—Sensational Sex Acts. Of course the nakedness of pornography, on stage and page, maintains its old stand; although more accessible than ever, it is scarcely more inviting, scarcely more enviable—only less scarce. But it is not the transactions of an erotic agon that audiences flock to see. Not entirely. Nor is the naked body sought for contemplation as a respectable diversion on the pretext that it offers some sort of rhythmic kinesis or athletic prowess. Not entirely. Nor are the people who pay to see other people naked—or rather, nude—forgetting that they too have bodies much like those they pay to see: it is not a matter of overlooking the universal datum that all of us have a pair of these, or that none of us is born without one of those. Not entirely. There is, I believe, another factor involved in our patronage of these entertainments and of the publications, of every class and circumstance, of photographs of the unclad body. It is not entirely for vicarious sexual gratification that men and women alike seek out the show of nudity today as never before. What we seek is the *form* of the body, not its *accident* in the Thomist sense. I believe that nowadays we pay to see the entire flesh of both sexes disrobed, disclosed, displayed because we no longer possess an imaginative visualization of the human body long vouchsafed us by art. We no longer have a revealed image of the whole person that can sustain and satisfy our yearning for these most elementary notions of order and design within ourselves. Photography may be the only art (and only a pre-modernist aspect of photography at that, an ecstatic, lyric aspect committed to unity of being) that can still resolve our need, can answer our question: what does it mean to be—to look—human?

For five hundred years this need has been fulfilled by representations of the general body in art. As the art critic and psychoanalyst Adrian Stokes has observed in *Reflections on the Nude,* we cannot discover the nude entirely in our own bodies; narcissistic sensitivity obscures contemplation. Rather we must discover such integrity by a massive projection of ourselves, of *an image of ourselves,* onto the external that we then reabsorb. Therefore the conception of the undivided nude that is not ourselves is a singular and significant attainment, probably first achieved by Greek art and the Greek Olympians. For in a sense, without such a notion, such an image, such consciousness, we cannot be at home in a shared adult world. It is, as Stokes concludes, a premise of sanity that we are thus afforded, for this primary, impersonal love of ours for the whole figure is at the root of all human respect. Without what is so resonantly known as the state of nature, no State—or at least no citizens.

Yet despite our perennial cultural needs and political compromises, it is evident that the nude in art has altered its nature and even its aspect, as that art itself has altered. The change is a pervasive one, and it is generally expressed—or specifically identified—by the much-vexed word "modernism." Whatever modernism's manifestations in culture, we may remark this much about it: its modes and mechanisms are those of fragmentation, dissociation, erasure, and opposition. A work of literature, of music, of plastic art or architecture need merely exhibit these divisive, agonistic characteristics and energies with a certain insolence and determination (the names Picasso, Joyce, Pound, Stravinsky, Le Corbusier, Eliot, Webern will serve as a sort of shorthand here), for us to label them, with a certain resignation, a certain setting of the teeth, "modernist." For modernism is habitually the arena of enormous repudiations, erasures, cancellations—in short, of negations. And it is evident that in all the arts, indeed in all the workings of culture, we have shifted from a poetics of *modulation*, whereby continuity is perceived to be the evidence of creative power, to a poetics of *collage*, an abrupt collocation or mosaic of shifting fòci and citations functioning not by transformation but by transgression. I have always been struck by the coincidence of this development, actually of this explosion, with the advent of photography in our societies (photography both as a general practice readily available to any enthusiast, and as a singular art created by trained professionals). And I propose the phrase "the photographic moment" for that period (shall we say 1880? perhaps as early as 1870? the likelihood must in any case occur long before the century's turn) when the great upheavals of modernism took place in our visual culture, irreversible and inseparable from the technology—chiefly the internal-combustion engine and the film-loading camera—that circulated them to the ends of the earth and to the center of our psyches. As a poet I have been immensely taken with the notion that in order to produce most photographic images there must initially be *a negative*. This platitude of photographic technology has become part of the language itself, and most appropriately so.

For modernism is most appropriately taken as an inclusively negative concept, I think, one regarded as a field of conflicting energies, of sudden juxtapositions rather than of continuous modulation. Parody and critique, erasure and collage, are the characteristic dynamics of modernism, and they preside over, if they do not bring about, the disappearance of the old order, the structures and hierarchies of Western culture. Photography has of course been pursued and practiced as an art since its inception, and naturally its history contains instances and achievements that, although occurring within the chronological bounds of modernism, transcend negation. "The photographic moment" knows contradictions; the nudes of Weston and of Stieglitz are glorious examples of a virtually classical apprehension of wholeness, an almost Hellenic attainment of the whole nude. Yet I suggest that photography-as-technology made possible a sweeping, indeed a seismic, alteration in consciousness—or rather, it made possible a seismic alteration in the *manifestation* of consciousness in our societies. The destruction of the nude as a harmonious balance of forces is a representative process of modernism in *all* the showings of our visual culture; and such a carnage was most likely empowered by the (often horrified, certainly alarmed) recognition that for the first time in many centuries the nude body was not inevitably an entity in which to take pride.

The better to comprehend what has happened to ourselves (for there is an interrelation between our conception of the nude and our assessment of ourselves), I suggest that three significant new dimensions have appeared in our recognition of art that have immitigably converted what we understand, specifically, by the nude in art. This assertion concerns *all* the arts, those of time as well as of space, poetry, and music quite as much as those of imagery, plastic representation, and design.

Contemporary with and related to the assimilation of photography as a universal practice, we have assimilated three transmutations in our notion of what art might, indeed must, be. These three new organizations, or dimensions, oppose all that our forefathers held dear by way of critical determinations in high culture. They have implications so extreme they cannot yet be labeled with any neatness of phraseology, for they have not receded into the comfort of historical periods. If obliged to offer an identification, I should suggest "unconscious art." (Is the photograph not the supreme manifestation, as Roland Barthes has suggested in his essay *Camera Lucida*, of an art capable of emblemizing, of *embodying*, the unconscious?) Dissatisfied with labels, let me put it crudely in terms of our representations of the nude: for the first time in historical memory, we acknowledge in self-representation the Art of the Primitive (or the archaic, the tribal, the aboriginal—what cultural chauvinism calls "the savage"); the Art of Unreason (or of irrationality, madness, the absurd); and the Art of the Child (or of the infantile, the untaught, what Sir Herbert Read calls the innocent eye). It is easy to remark, in the very proliferation and slipperiness of this vocabulary, a considerable tendency to overlap. Frequently we are reluctant to distinguish between or among the art of the mad, the art of the tribe, and the art of the child—for are they not all crystallizations or floodings of what the poet Wallace Stevens identified as *a tidal undulation underneath*, an eruption of forces no longer ordered by those amassed and cumulative disciplines that were in place until "the photographic moment"?

Yet the remarkable thing is that we are nowadays quite convinced by our museum curators, our art schools, our aesthetic philosophers that all three dimensions are intrinsic to art. We are prepared to forswear all the salon pieties and to acknowledge that the Sepik mask, the schizophrenic's drawing, and the six-year-old's clay bogeyman (wherein the doll and the idol are indissociable) function as authentic avatars of art, an art that once dared not speak its name but that now fulfills its unspeakable purposes of terror, ecstasy, and apotropaism.

And it is through the lens of this triple transformation that we must perceive the image of the modern nude. First of all, though, we have discovered that the naked body can be parceled out, can be fragmented, the more readily to be fetishized. It is here, I think, that photography assumes its greatest responsibility. I believe Rodin was the first artist to exhibit (not produce) as a complete work a fragment of the body, creating an erotic fixation upon a separate limb. And Rodin (along with Degas) is probably the first sculptor to make use of photography in the creation of his works.

From the fixated, fetishized, fragmented nude it was but a step to that impersonal cutting up of collage, which became the most distinctive invention of modern art. Where once—say from Phidias to Canova—we were obliged to conceive the nude body as a complex of thrusts and tensions whose reconciliation symbolized the principle of all the "figure arts," we now know that the naked body can be a "heap of broken images," of barely salvaged pieces, even a staccato dissolution whereby for the first time perhaps since Rodin's *Adam* (which in Hebrew means "red clay") man is unmade in his own image. If photography has identified itself with the glorious totalizing emblems of the past, it has as often dramatized the possibilities of the fragment and the fetish, thereby constituting much of the evidence of our knowledge.

The great witness to this transformation from the whole to the fragment-as-symbol-of-the-whole is of course the poet Rilke, whose account of the headless torso of an archaic Apollo ("archaic" is another of those ambiguous words we use when we are uncertain about the historical status of the "primitive," the "tribal") is the first great modern nude in poetry (the latest is surely Irving Feldman's ecphrasis of George Segal's white plaster bodies in "All of Us Here"). Without a head, Apollo's body looks at Rilke, and at us, from all its remaining flesh ("his gaze, only turned down, lingers and gleams"). There is no place in this flesh, Rilke says, that does not *see us*. Here the reversal of categories is ocular—the observer is being observed, in turn, by the fragmentary statue that has been transformed into a single though total eye. The reversal is possible precisely because the sculpture is broken, fragmentary. If the nude had actually incorporated Apollo's head, Apollo's eyes, the reversal could not occur. The absent eyes allow for an imaginary vision to come into being, making the eyeless sculpture into an Argus-eye capable of engendering by itself all the dimensions of space. It is absence that creates the space necessary for the reversal; it is fragmentation that finally leads to a totalization it seemed, at first, to make impossible.

The art of the child, the vision of the innocent eye, has had particular consequences for the envisioned nude. Think of the work of Paul Klee, of Joan Miró, of Jean Dubuffet, of Paula Modersohn-Becker, in easel painting alone, and it is apparent that the child's apprehension of function has triumphed over the post-Renaissance artist's comprehension of structure: in the art of the child, as it has been assimilated by the nude in modern art, there is no attempt whatever to separate the person from that person's body: every virtue resides in or is symbolized by the flesh, together with all humiliation, threat, and squalor. This indissociability is what modern nudity has learned from the art of infantilism. Indeed we note that children, perhaps because they are the portion of humanity most unceremoniously habituated to nakedness, do not make a point of representing the human figure as specifically unclothed. Of course there is nakedness in children's art, but there is no nudity, that idealized construct. For the child, nakedness is neither a customary nor an assumed condition; it is a functional dimension, and can quite readily be perceived *through clothes*, which become transparent indicators of status or category, but never hamper the perception of an infantile fantasy that has, so to speak, corporeal intent. But if the nude as an idealized whole is not a distinctive category for the child, the fragmented, partial body is very much one, and as such has entered into the canons of modernism. The "distorted" perspectives of the child create a strange proximity of certain organs, the impinging might of certain members, producing not so much a represented body in the child's artwork but a graphism of forces, a redistribution of powers that surrealist photography, for instance, has been quick to acknowledge. If nakedness exists at all in the child's art, it is as a version of need; and the grotesquerie of human need has assumed a certain grandeur in modern art.

This is one dramatic and vigorous transformation of the nude, and perhaps one of the most evident: what was once conceived of as an enduring figuration, a temple of the integrated adult psyche, is in modernism materialized—and often *broken down*—as a diagram of momentary interferences, sometimes with the character of an oppressive weight or listlessness left by the child's terrors and thefts, as well as by infantile delights and satisfactions. The celebrated commonplace once uttered so dismissively in galleries before a canvas by Jackson Pollock or Cy Twombly: "My five-year-old could do that!" has become a sort of accolade, the recognition of a truth of vision over and above any mere transmutation of matter into ideal form, of which the nude for centuries had remained the most complete example.

In the art that our Western societies have persistently called primitive, barbarian, archaic, there is also no such thing as the nude, nor even—as in children's art—the naked. There is the body, variously decorated and embellished, scarred and marked with ritual significances, but no state of "undress." The costume of the unclothed, when intended to be looked at, is subject to its own standards of what we call fashion, but it does not acknowledge the body in itself as in any way irregular or arresting. To some degree, this sense of the body's propriety—"a woman is always clothed in the dignity of her own nakedness," as our models are sometimes told—has pertained to the nude in

Western art as well, but with an ever-fading sense of the sacramental, or the transgressive, and a constant trivialization of beholding that in modernism has been revitalized, even revolutionized, by a mimicry of tribal practices, as we could observe at the 1984 exhibition "Primitivism in 20th Century Art" at the Museum of Modern Art in New York. Although objects of African and Oceanic provenance, cult, and ceremony had been in some sense "available" in Europe since the 1880s—what I am calling "the photographic moment"—it was only in the first years of the twentieth century that they all at once became a numinous presence for modern artists in their representation of the nude: for Picasso, for Giacometti, for Modigliani, for Man Ray. These artists, and many others around them and following them, retained the notion of the nude, certainly as the consequence of a love of rational proportion. Yet the pattern of perfection that since the Renaissance has gradually become blurred, blunted, and bleached out required this unexpected and often frightening union of sex and geometry that was observably sacred, observably part of a spiritual function not to be evaded by even the handsomest obeisances to studio convention (Matisse) or to the integrity of materials (Brancusi). The idea of offering the naked body for its own sake as a serious object of contemplation nowadays erects a certain barrier of misunderstanding that I believe only our response to the primitive can overcome. It is a sad paradox that even as we have erased the reality of tribal cultures from our world, we have conceded the force, even the necessity, of their human representations among us. Malraux and Robert Goldwater pointed out in the 1930s that there is no modernity without primitivism—art's images of the body must reject the salon or not exist. Much of the work of Lucas Samaras and Robert Mapplethorpe, for example, is evidence of this, although "our" salon has managed to transform its thresholds in order to capitalize on their achievements. As André Breton once proclaimed, "Beauty must be convulsive or not be at all." The insertion of the primitive, the intercession of the tribal in our arts, has been so pervasive and so inveterate that we are in danger of forgetting—as when we look at Man Ray's famous photograph of the-nude-as-minotaur—that there was once a working method among Western arts that "proved" by representations of the human form that the gods were like men and could be praised for their life-giving beauty rather than for their death-dealing powers.

Most recent, I believe, of the three transmutations that have so profoundly altered our vision of the nude is the onset and acknowledgment of the art of the mad. The insistences of Surrealism—that first constituted cultural movement whose artistic expression always included photography as a major resource—celebrate the unconscious as a version of what is commonly called madness, the irrational (popularly, the "wacky"), unreason; not so much the nonhuman as the nonhumanistic in culture. Yet Surrealism and psychoanalysis are but two frequently interwoven currents of a stream that has many other tributaries.

Cruelty, brutality, and affectlessness are perceived to have their part in the story. The great body of works—objects of the most diverse provenance, often made by children and by "savages," of course—that constitute Jean Dubuffet's *Musée de l'Art Brut* (and how are we to translate *brut* save as: unmediated by consciousness and by culture—primitive, infantile, and crazy?) entirely reorganizes our received and traditional notions of what a created work, *a work of art*, might be. And particularly with regard to representations of the human body, the irrational, the unreasonable, even the irresponsible, have their metamorphic contribution to make to our modernity. The celebrated photographs of funhouse-like distortions of the nude by André Kertész remind us, by their seeming reference to absurdity and nonsense, how much we have recuperated since Nietzsche, van Gogh, and Artaud from what was once dismissed as raving chaos. Henceforth, it is impossible for representations of stabilizing myths and beliefs to appear to encompass our actuality adequately. Among those myths and beliefs is the confidence that the displayed naked human body is something in which to take pride as a source of meaning and delight. No longer a reconciliation and a harmony, the nude is often represented in our art as an interrogation of existence, as problematic of pleasure, and as a reliable cancellation of identity: so many corollaries of the art of the mad.

If we are to recover our respect for the general body, which is the seal upon our respect for other human beings as such, we must regain the vision of the nude in art that these momentous transformations of the infantile, the barbaric, and the irrational have so often alienated us from (though it is to be seen, and celebrated, that photography has often been one means of a recuperation of the classic ideals and idealizations, the source of a recovery often despaired of in the other figure arts). I do not mean, of course, that we can squeeze the child, the primitive, and the madman out of our consciousness, as Chekhov said it was our human task to squeeze the slave out of ourselves. We know they are there, are part of being human, and in some sense the nude must henceforth be the container for the sum of their meanings, while it is also from a concatenation of their meanings that the nude, *the form of the body*, is constructed. Our innocence is irrecoverable, and therefore the reappearance of the nude as a whole and harmonious creation—what might be meant by the old phrase *the body politic*—will necessarily be a new invention, a new discovery.

Is it not possible that the audience for photographic versions of the nude are the catechumens of an elementary art, a new culture (of the nude) that might again afford us what we pursue so hungrily, so desperately: the rudiments of a civil art?

RICHARD HOWARD

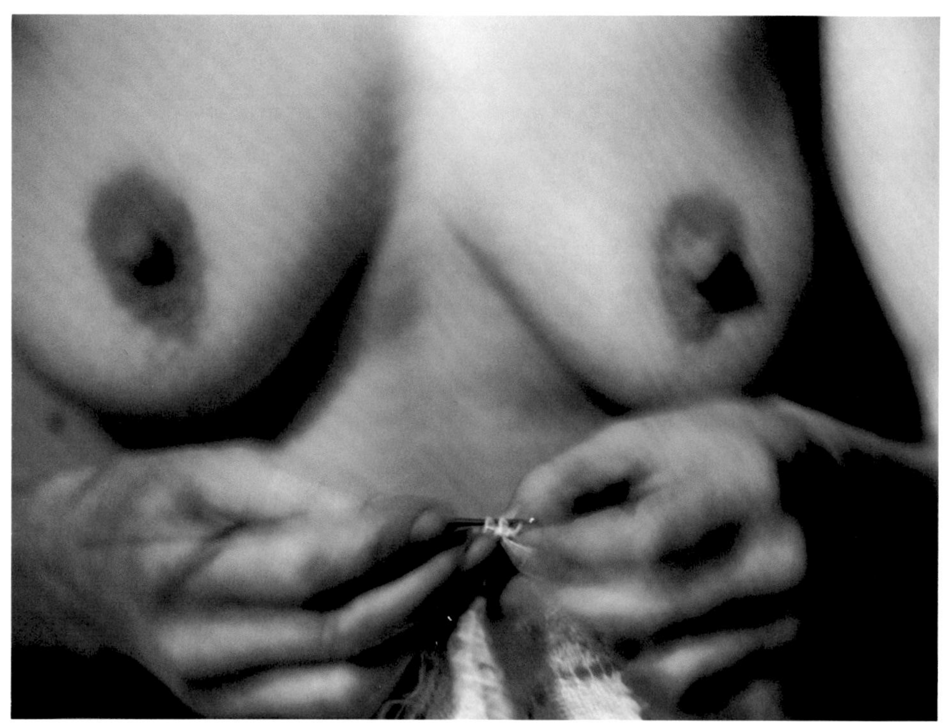

Walter Chappell · *Nancy Crocheting, Wingdale, New York* · 1962

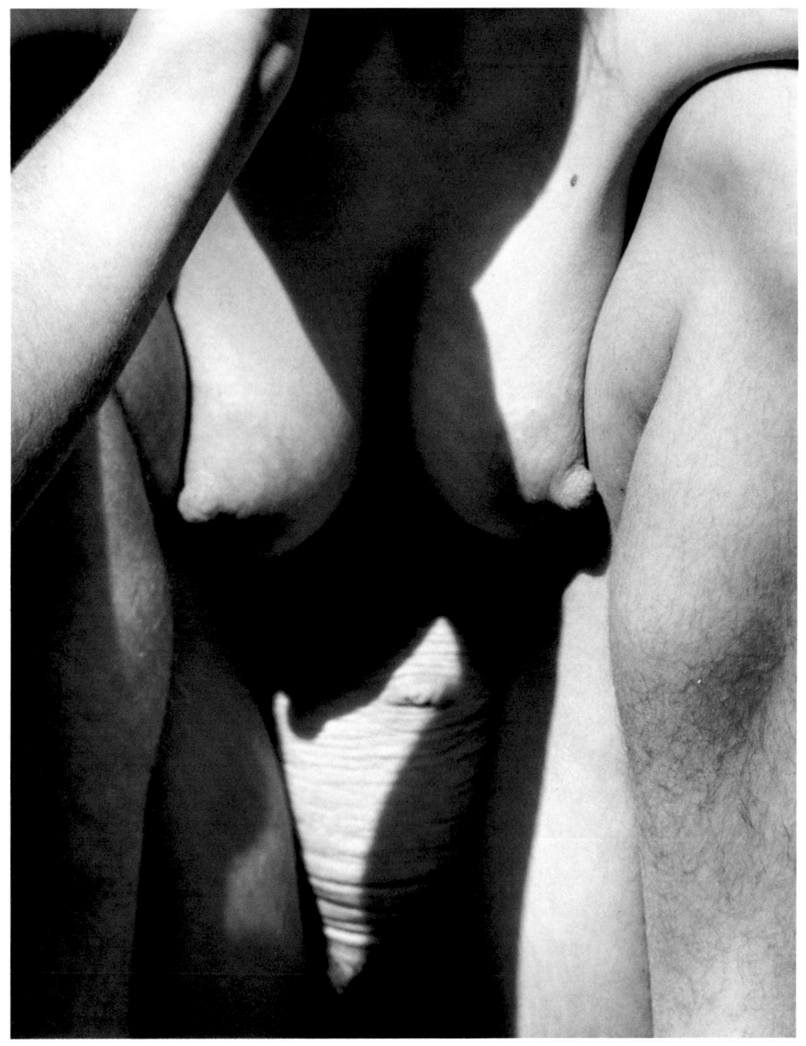

Walter Chappell · *Nude Torso between Legs, Wingdale, New York* · 1962

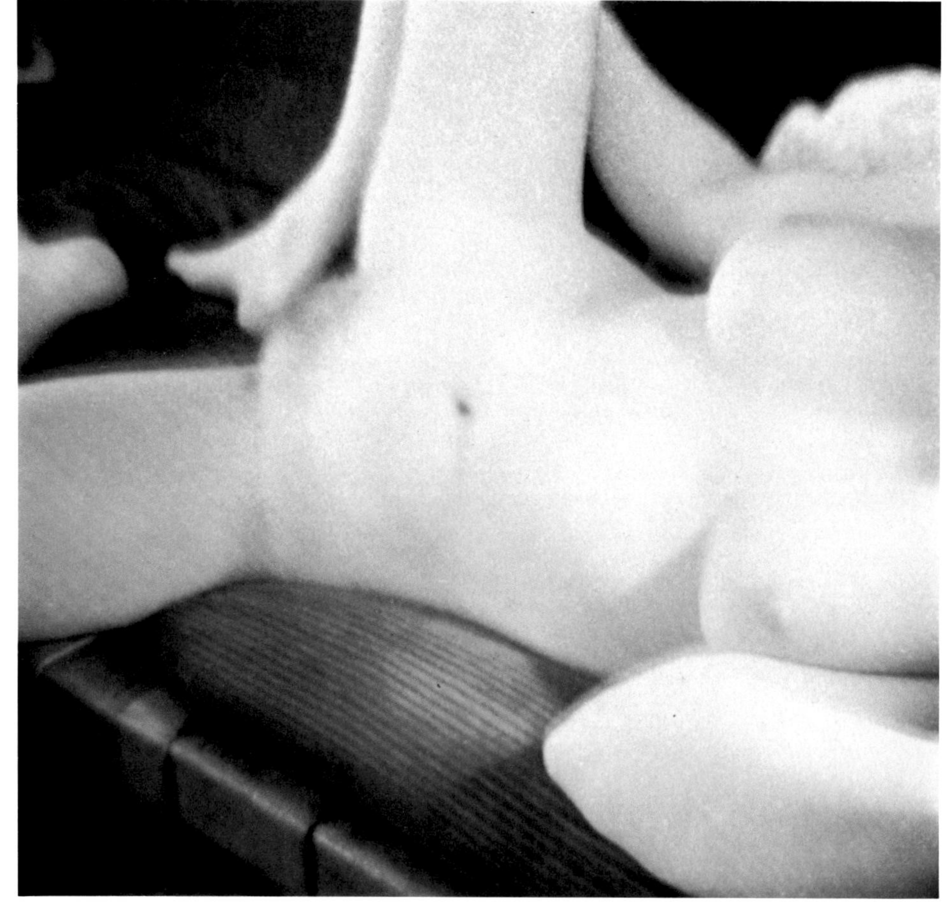

Ann Zelle · Untitled · 1978

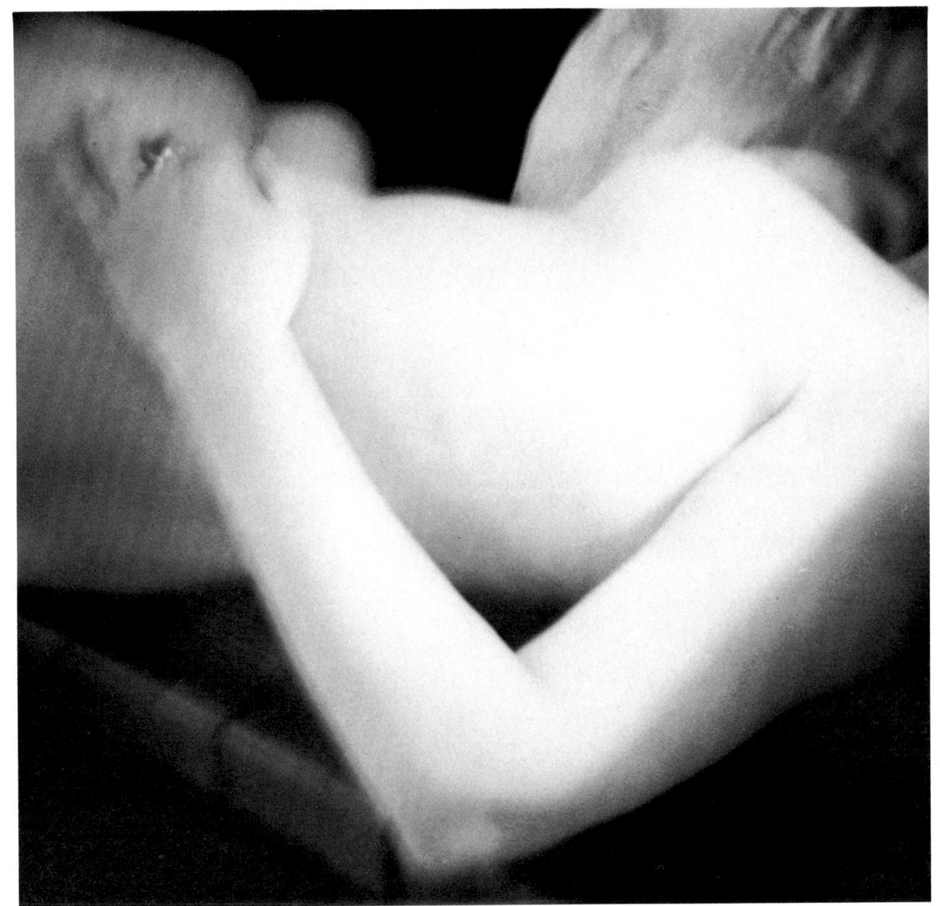

Ann Zelle · Untitled · 1978

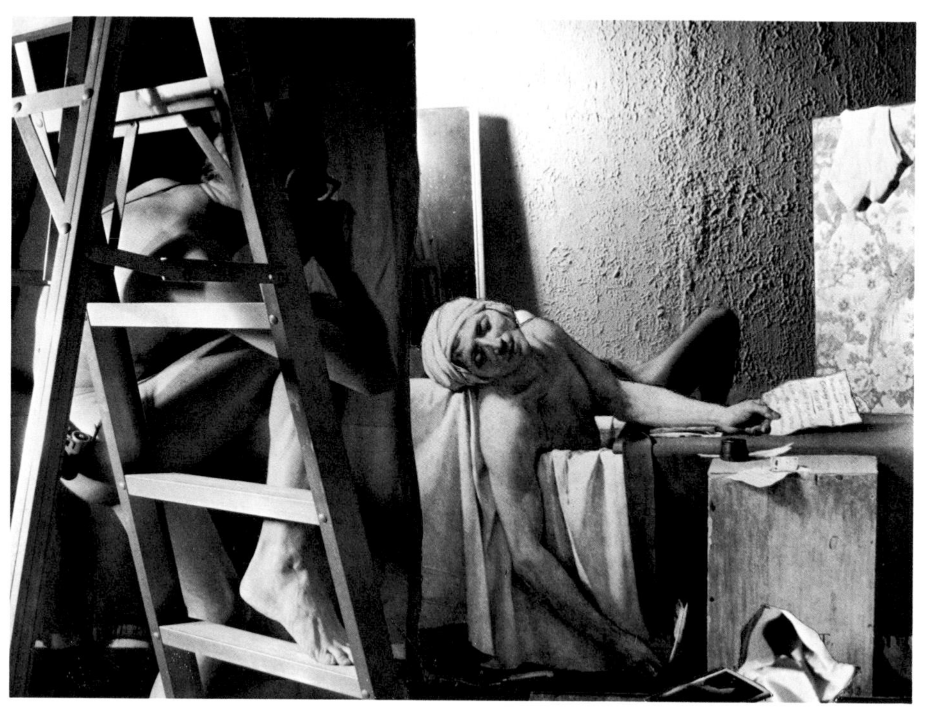

John O'Reilly · *Shooting Marat* · 1985

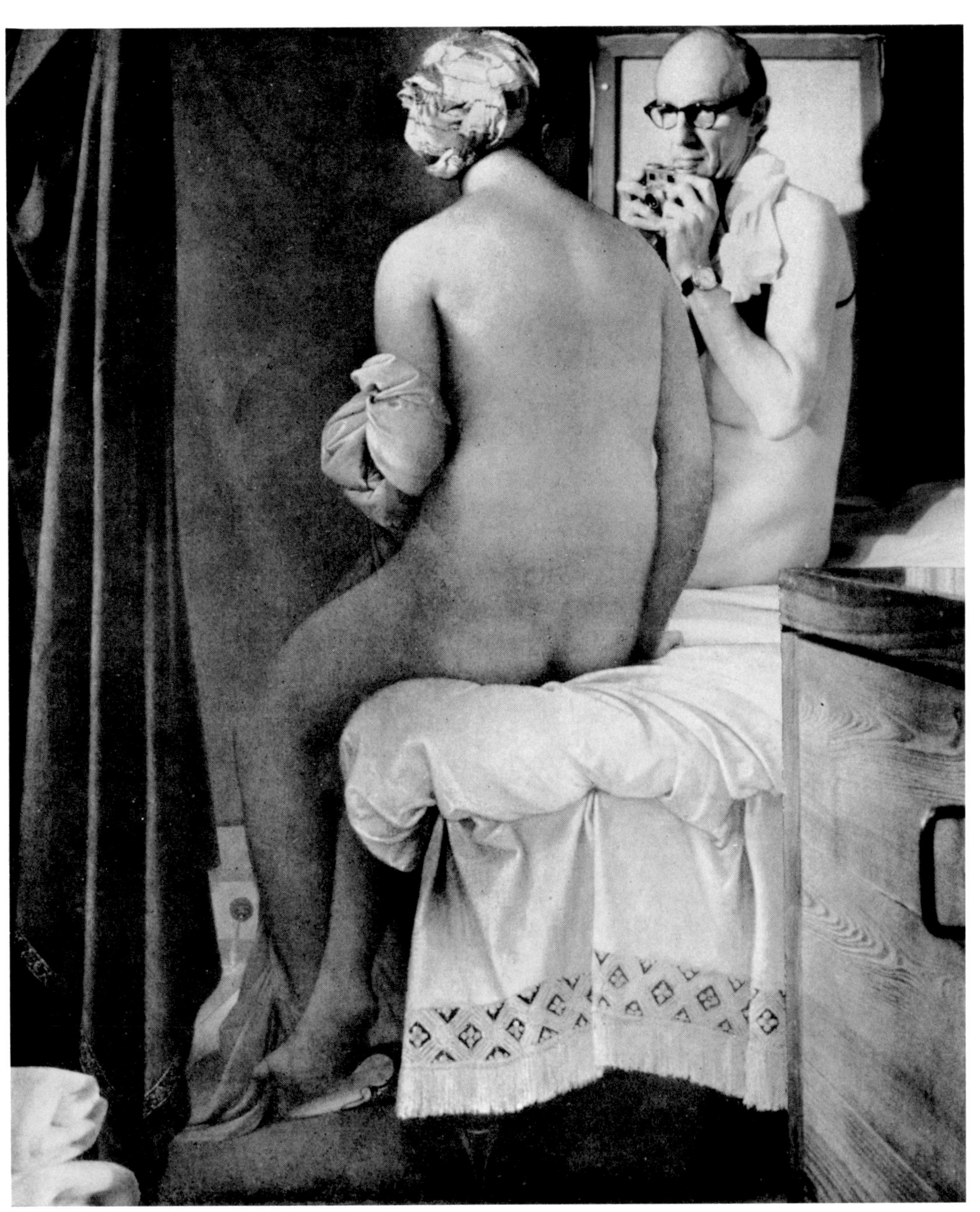

John O'Reilly · *Self-Portrait with Model* · 1984

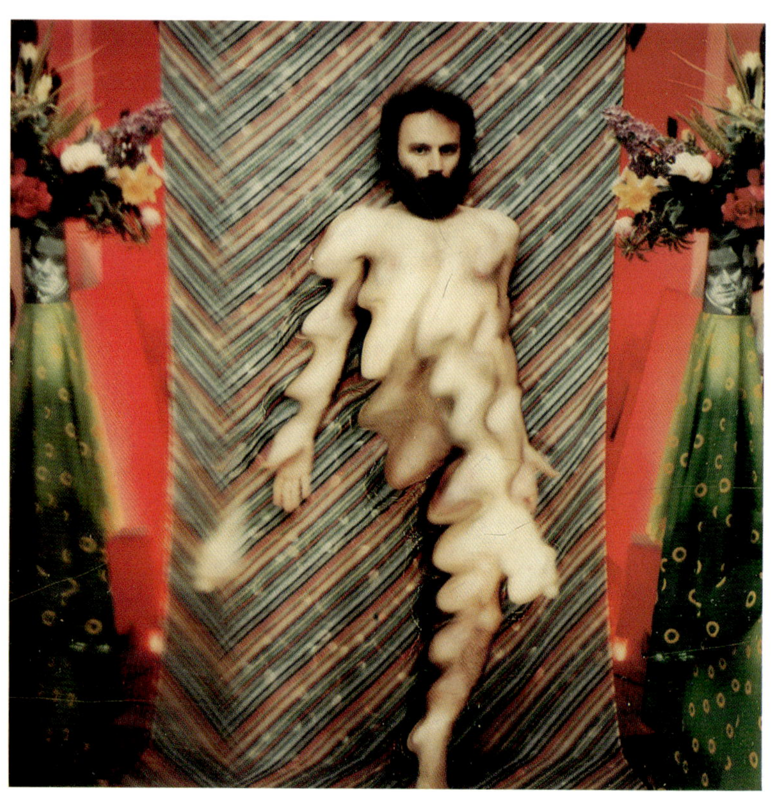

Lucas Samaras · *Photo-transformation, 8/19/76*

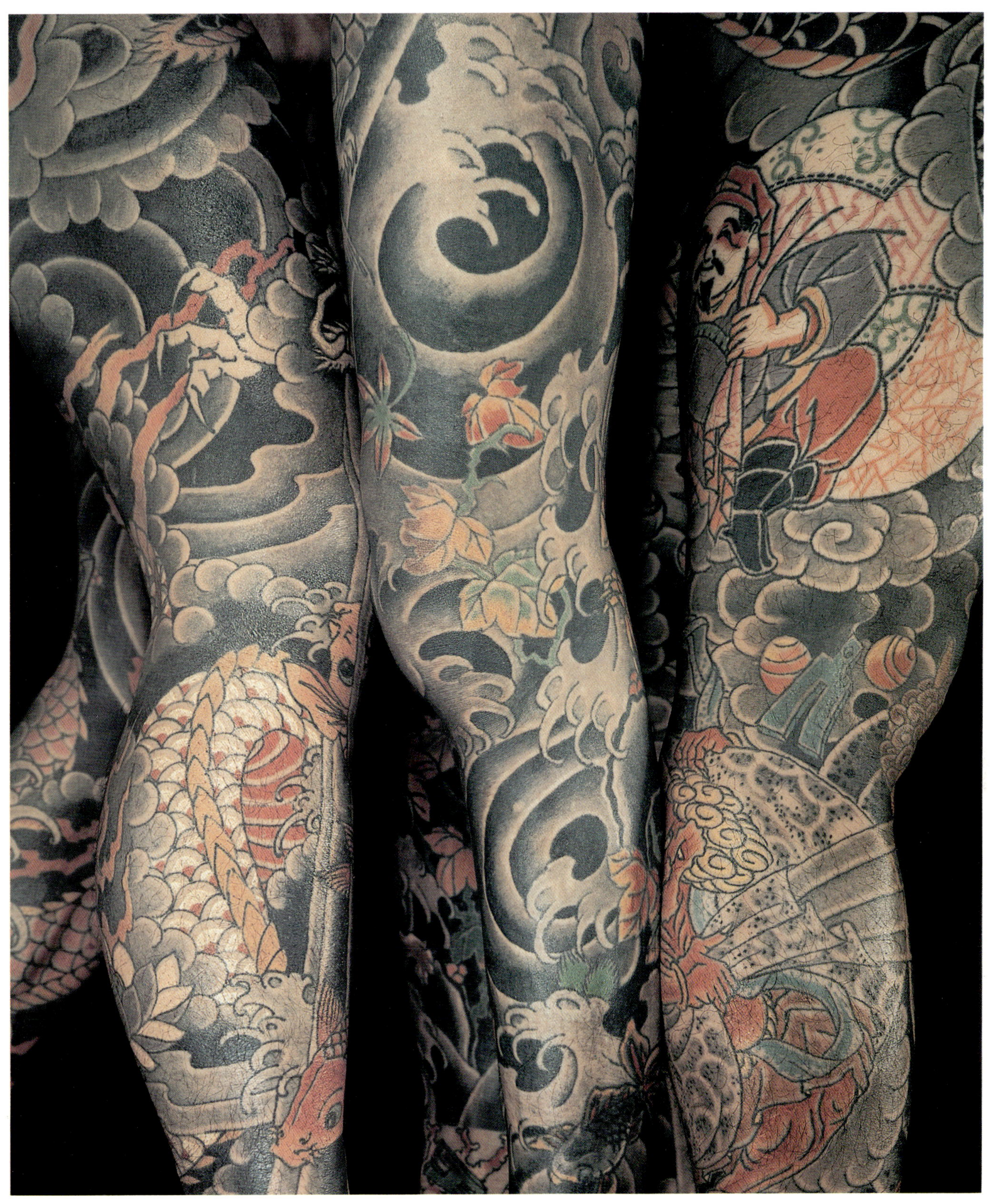

Sandi Fellman · *Fire and Water II* · 1984

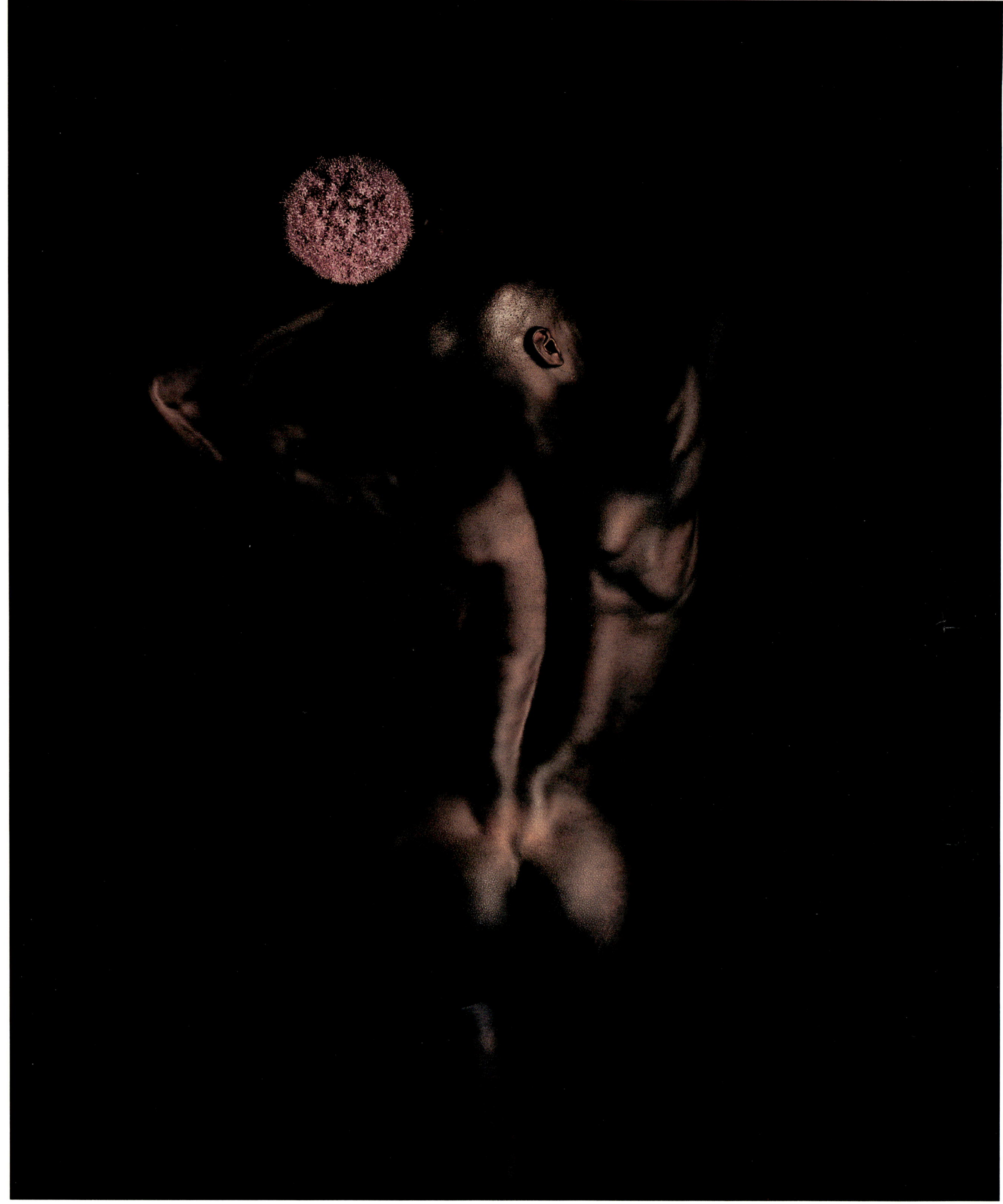

Robert Mapplethorpe · *Ken Moody* · 1984

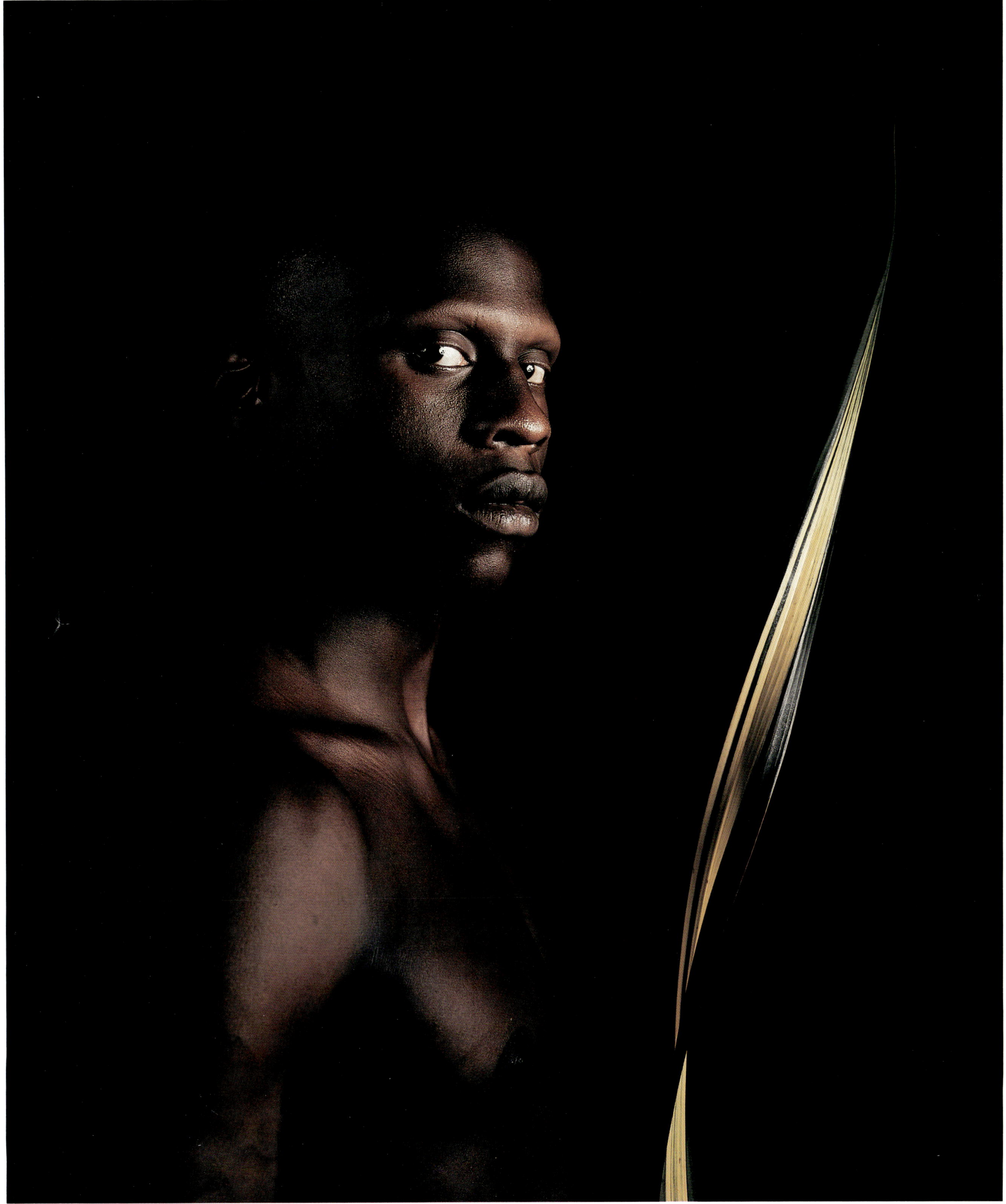

Robert Mapplethorpe · *Ken Moody* · 1984

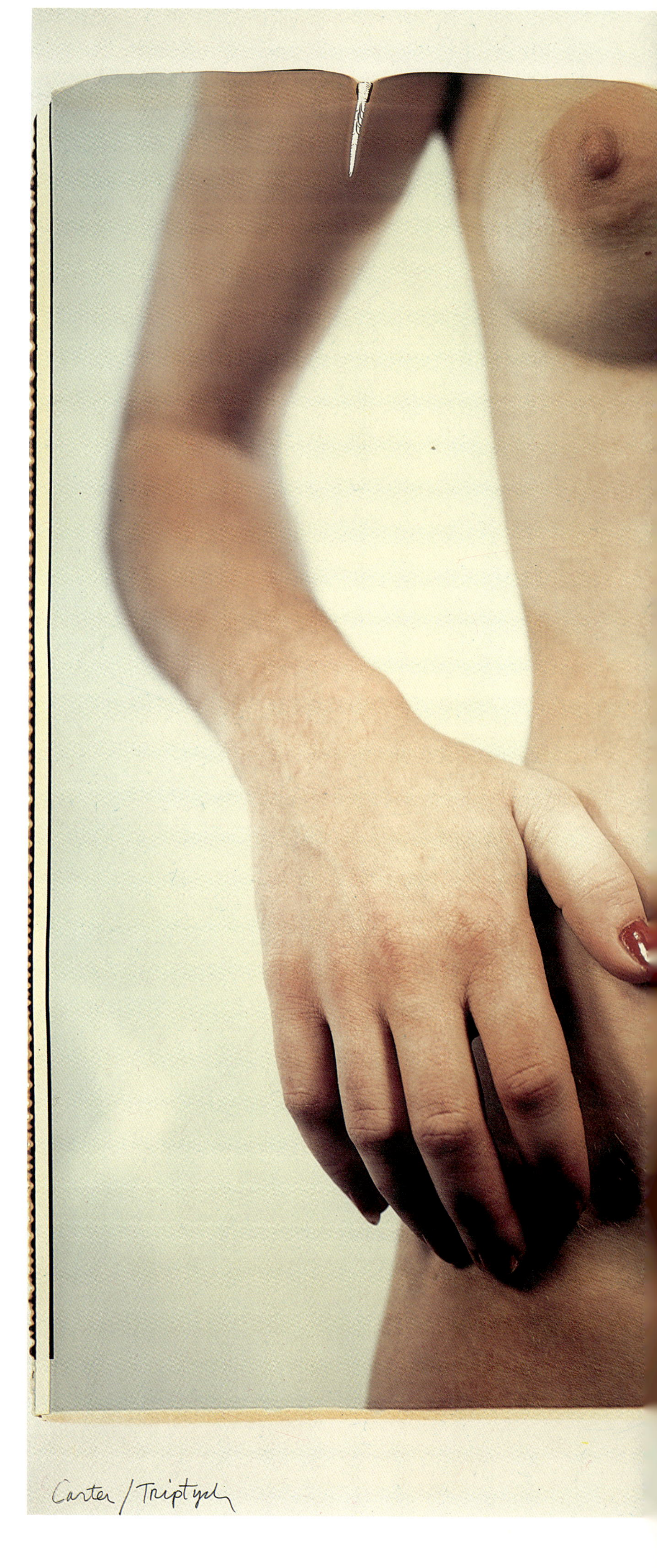

Chuck Close · *Carter* (triptych) · 1984

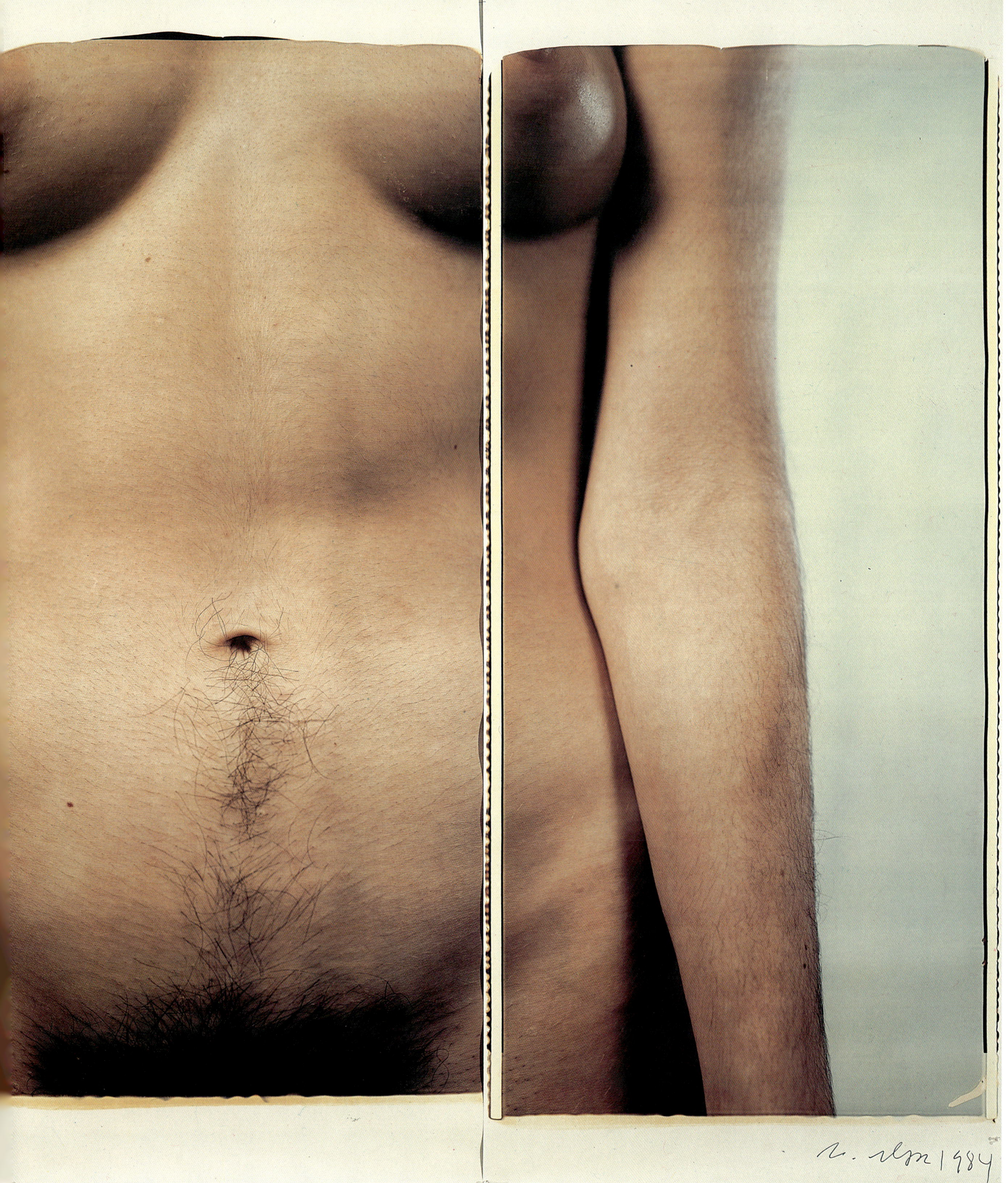

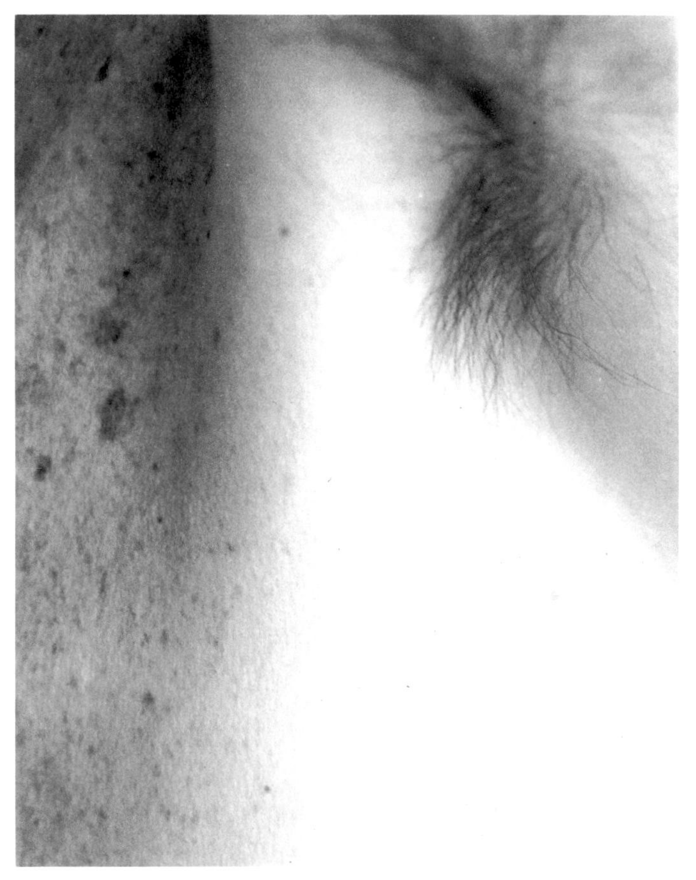

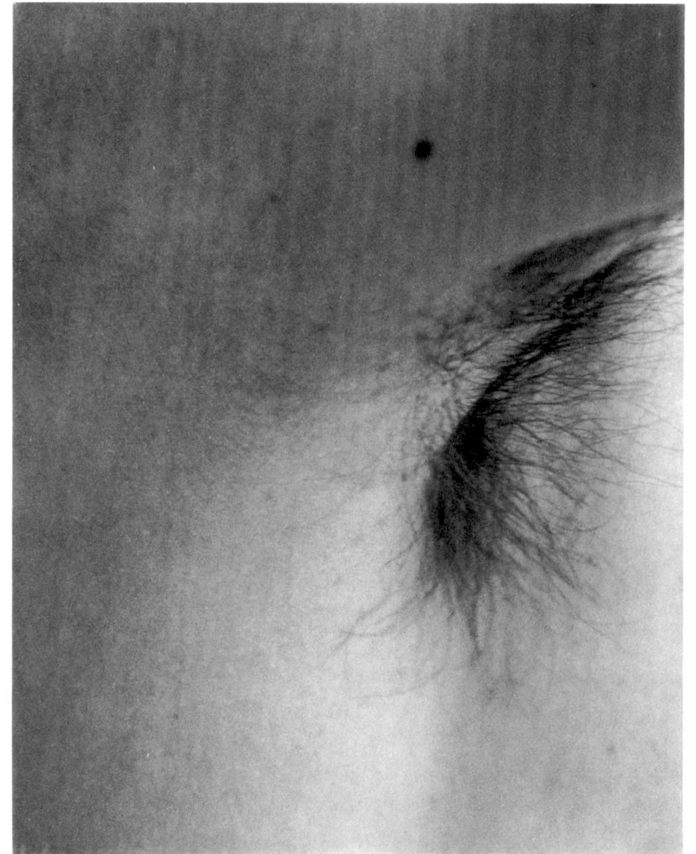

Nancy Hellebrand · Untitled · 1985

Nancy Hellebrand · Untitled · 1985

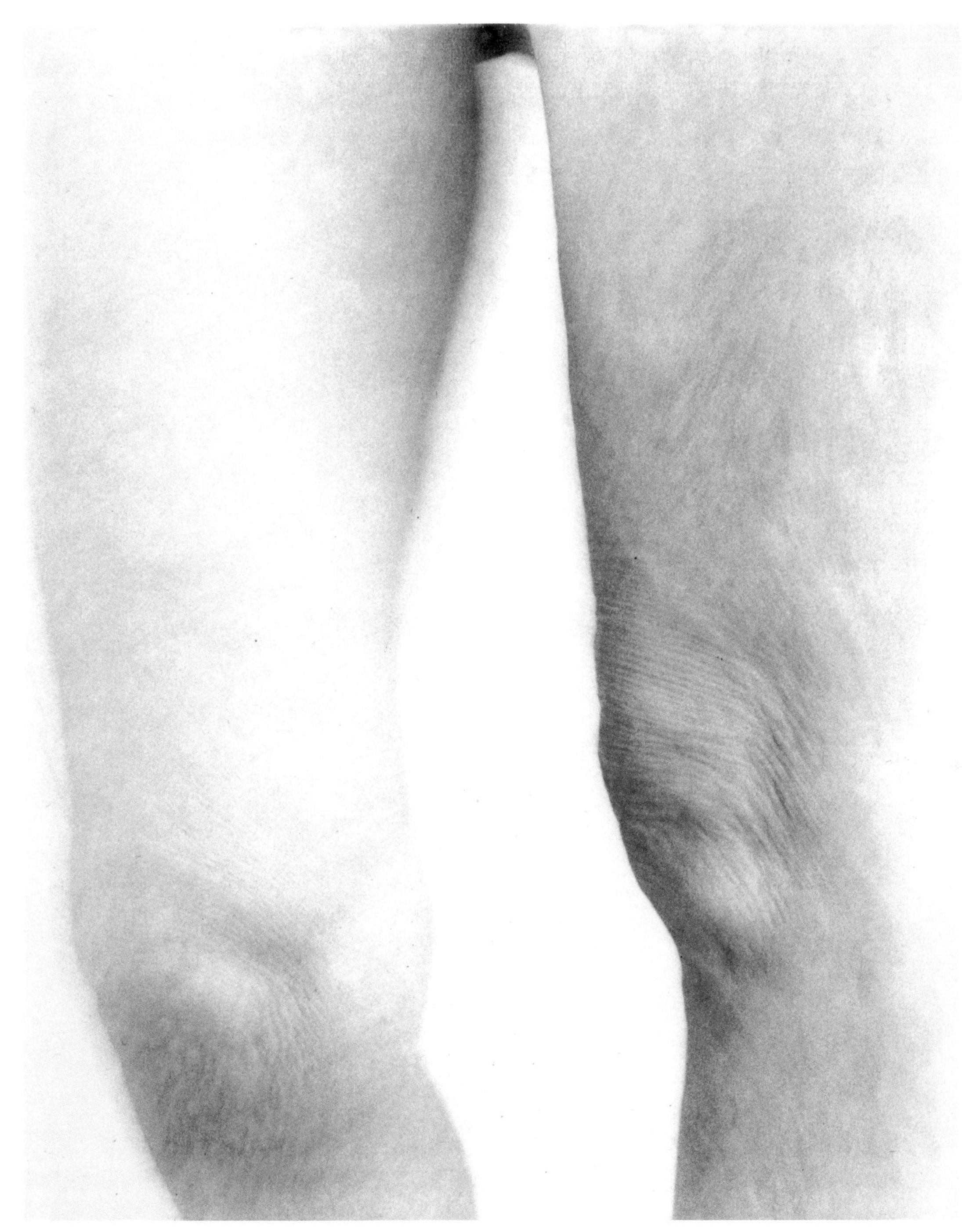

Nancy Hellebrand · Untitled · 1985

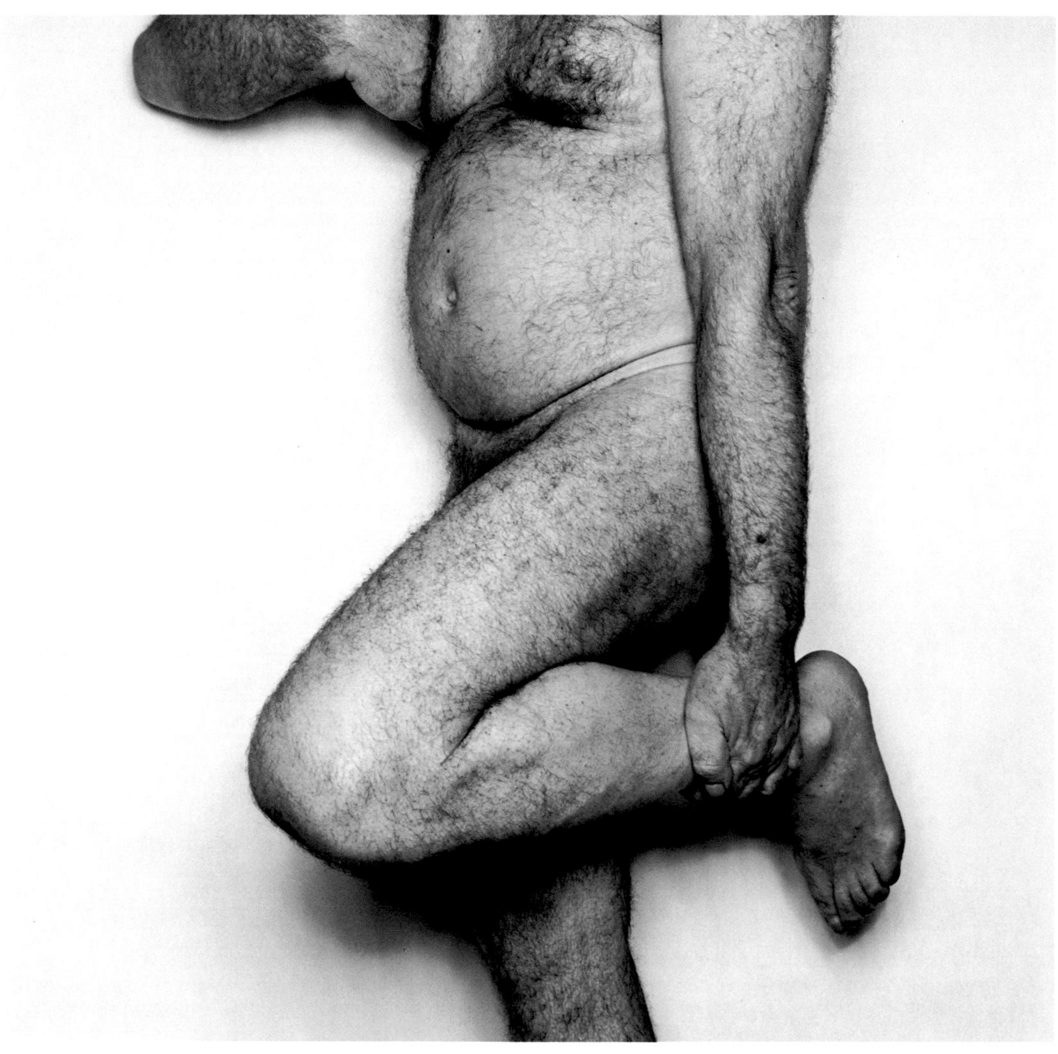

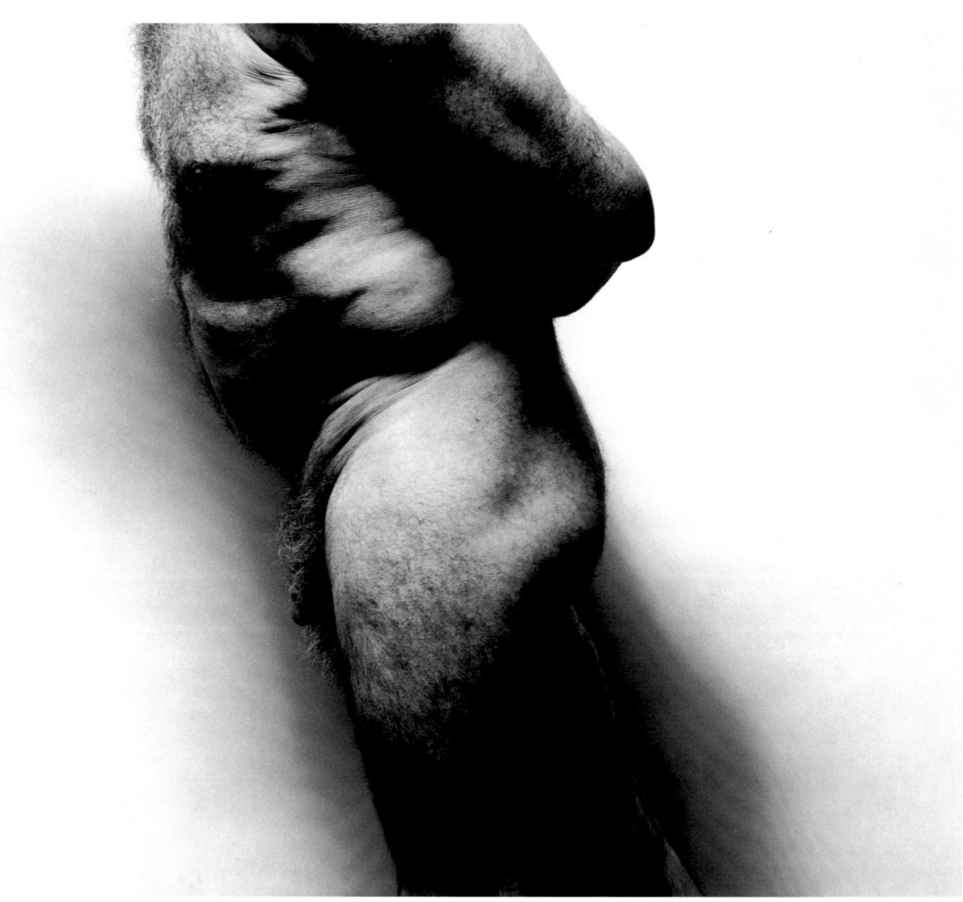

John Coplans · *Self-Portrait: Standing Figure, Hand Holding Leg* · 1986

John Coplans · *Self-Portrait: Side Torso Bent with Large Upper Arm II* · 1985

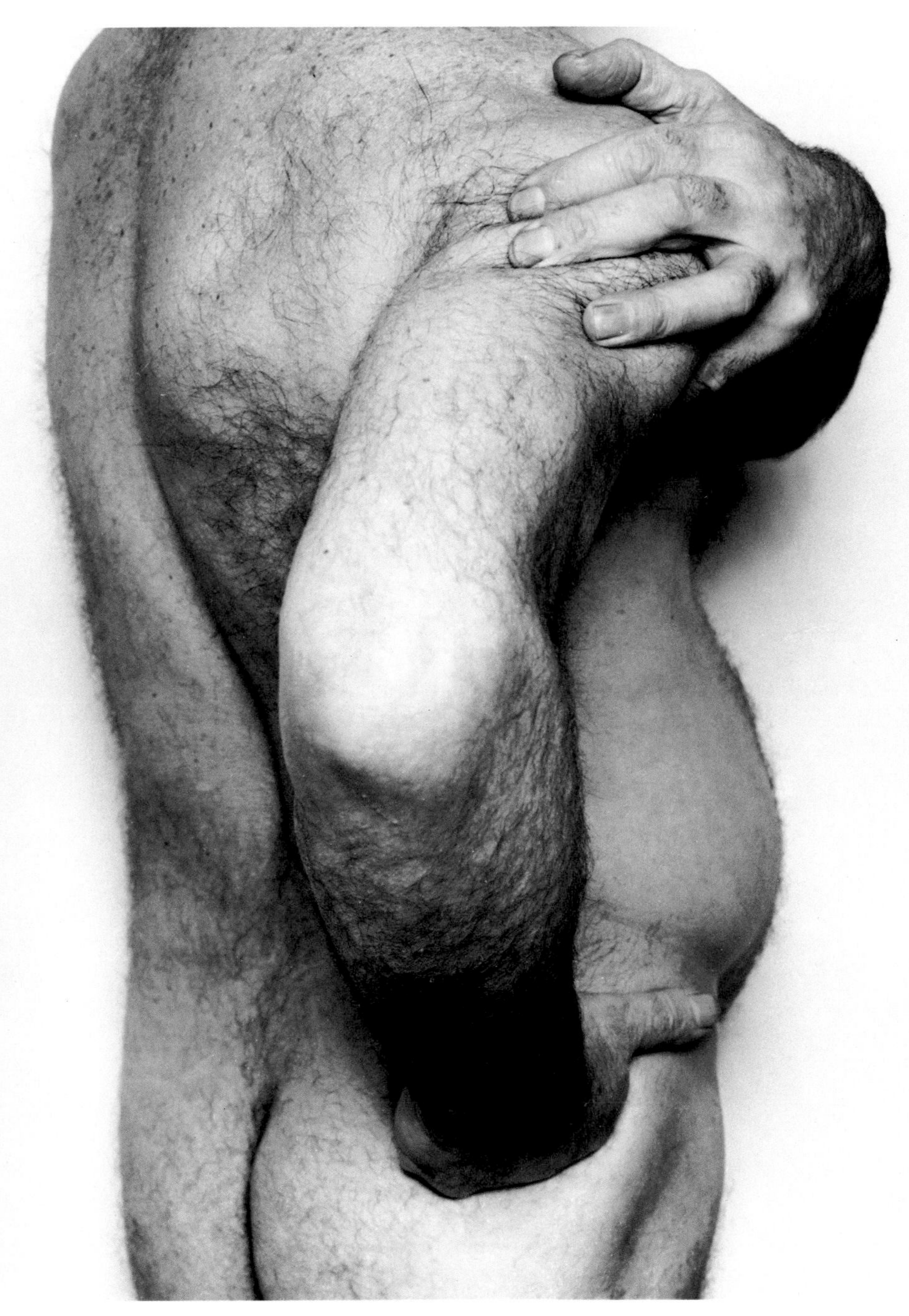

John Coplans · *Self-Portrait: Torso* · 1984

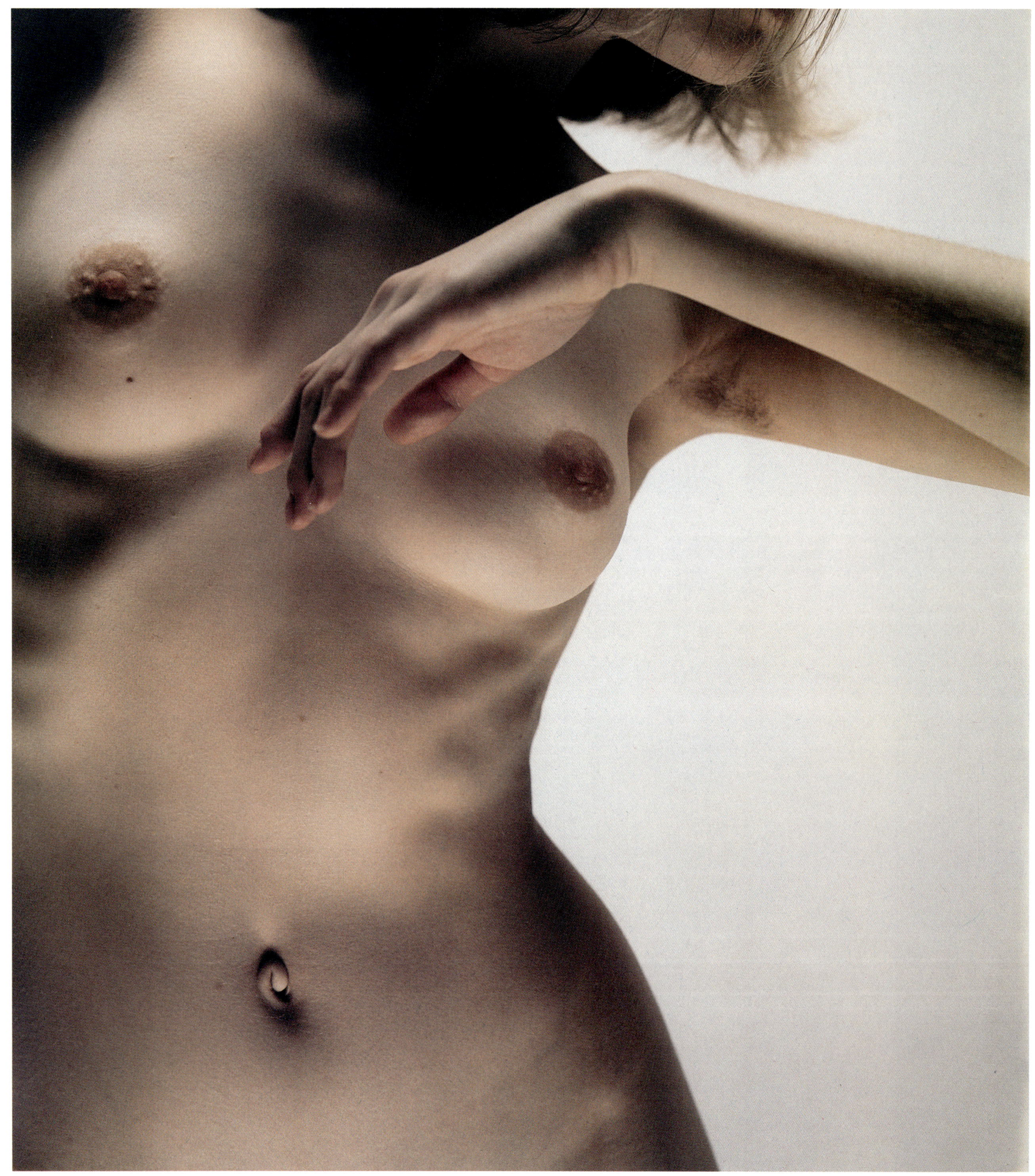

Richard Pare · *Belle Bonarius* (triptych) · 1987

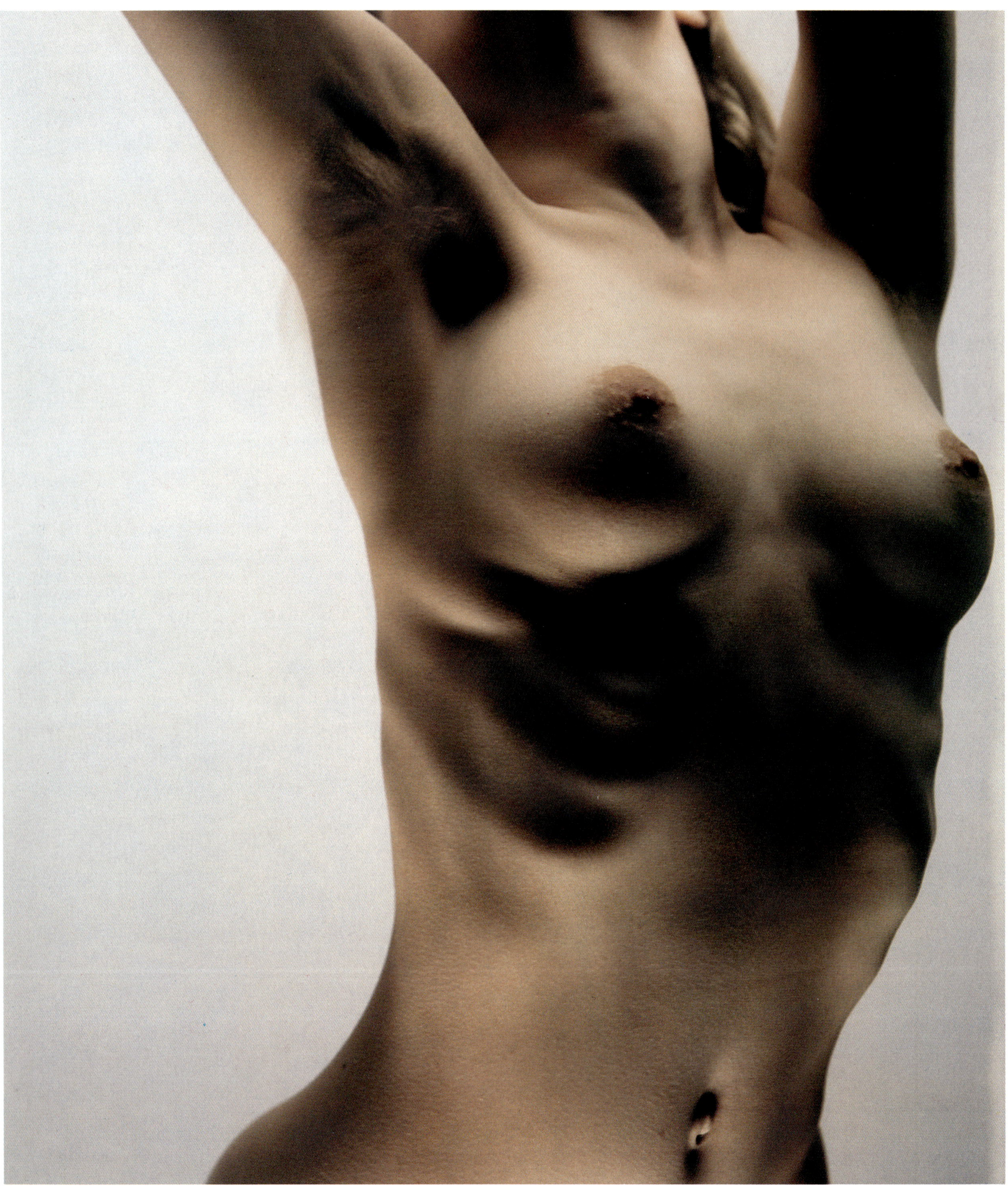

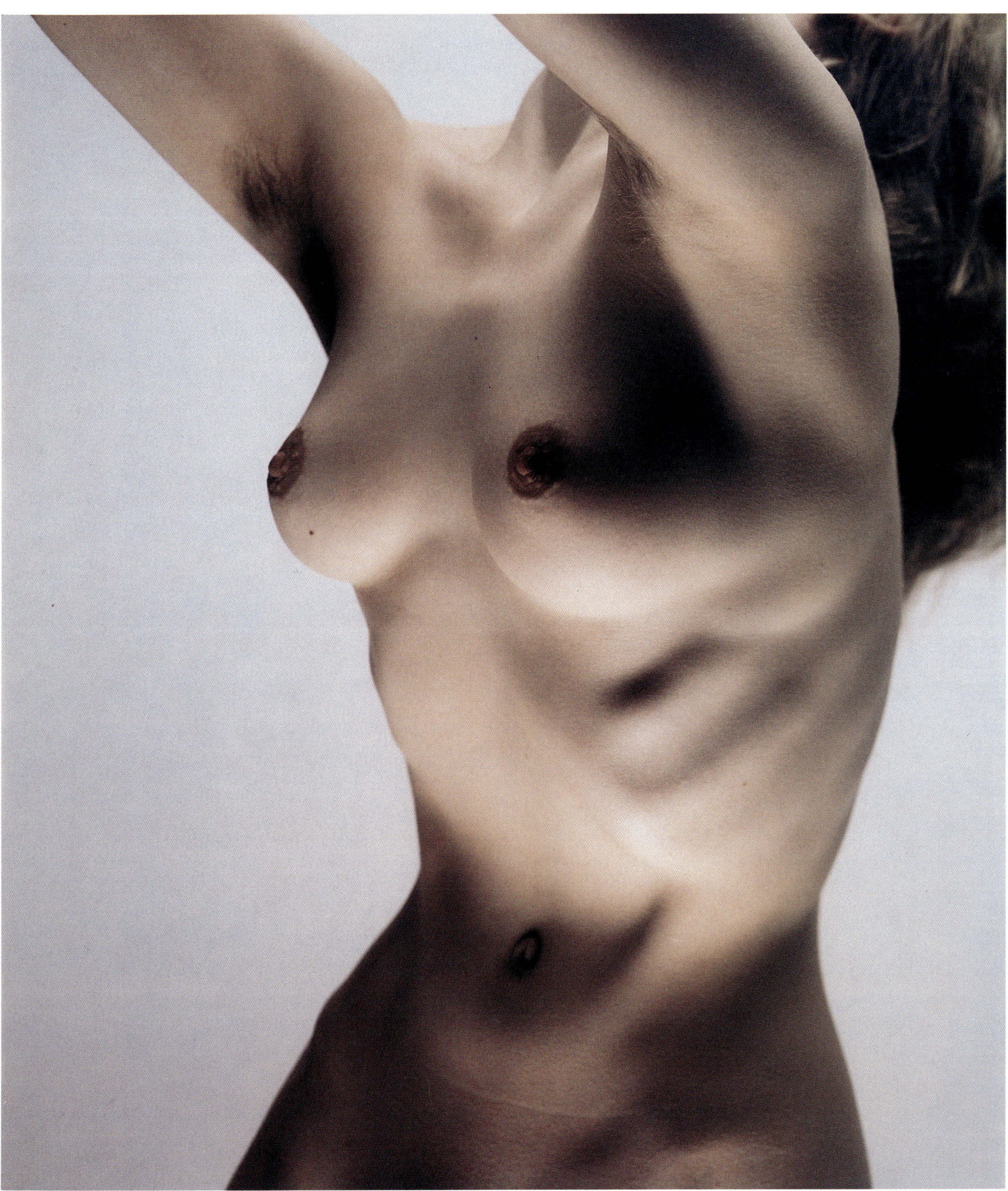

OBJECT AND FORM

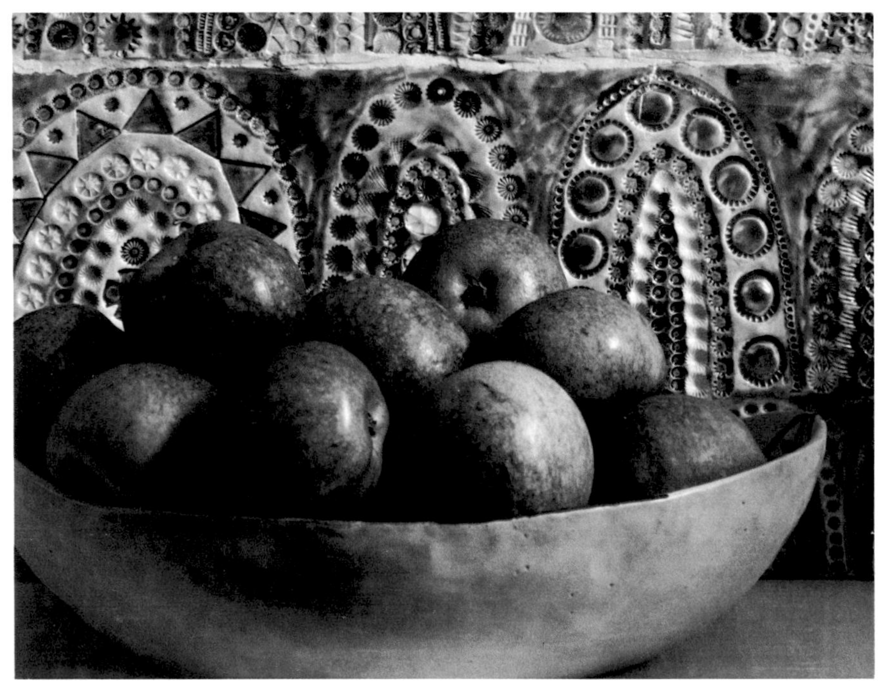

Paul Caponigro · *Fruit Bowl, Stockbridge, Massachusetts* · c. 1967

"In my grandmother's dining room there was a glass-fronted cabinet and in the cabinet a piece of skin. It was a small piece only, but thick and leathery, with strands of coarse, reddish hair. It was stuck to a card with a rusty pin. On the card was some writing in faded black ink, but I was too young then to read. . . . Never in my life have I wanted anything as I wanted that piece of skin."

Bruce Chatwin's description from *In Patagonia* captures, for most of us, our first experience of desire. The child views with wild desire some object, usually something out of reach, behind glass, in a vitrine or museum or shop, unattainable. The wish is to touch and to own this untouchable object.

What object is it? Some memento of the family's history, or of the past of the world (Bruce Chatwin's grandmother's shred of skin, she said, was from a brontosaurus). It may be a treasure, a display of wealth, or merely something beautiful, delightful to the eye; or something useful, sometimes an instrument of power—the child may desire a red pencil or silver skates—adornment, or some badge of another station or class, or culture; or some piece of one's own culture or history. Above all, objects are magic, totemic, protective.

Often an object connects us to a vanished past—to our grandmother, or to our own vanished, smaller self. If we cannot possess the object, we would rather have a picture of it than not. Before pictures people had "memories," which they spoke of in a way that sounds today as if memory was a kind of spacious depository, like an album, where inner pictures were kept framed and stored, available to be summoned up before the inner eye in a way our modern eyes, trained in the fitful flicker of the television, cannot do.

In the beginning treasured objects were pieces of the natural world: protective, beautiful stones or shells. No doubt the first kings' ransoms consisted of precious souvenirs from nature. Travelers brought back wonderful tusks and skins. With the dinosaur's skin would come a dream of the prehistoric world, and the idea that you were there or that it was here, a world continuous and strange. I heard a group of famous women poets on a stage answer the question, not about their rhyme or meter but, "What are your amulets?" And each had an amulet of some kind of natural substance—turquoise or lapis. Mine is a round stone from China that hangs on a necklace of braided silk; and I have another, a pre-Columbian stone of the same size and dark-green color with a face carved in, perhaps by a poet, to guard her spirit. The painter Paul Klee wrote that "the object expands beyond the bounds of its appearance by our knowledge that the thing is more than its exterior presents to our eyes," and, of course, it stirs our desire because it is more powerful than we are. One thinks of the early crowns of Carolingian kings, where the jewels are set in just the form in which they must have been found: round, lumpish, fondled into shapes if shaped at all. And I have a Persian jewel that must have been carried by a simple fighter or a peasant woman: a piece of crystal backed by a piece of tinfoil to make it glisten. A good object, it seems, should be made by hand, and will contain the soul of its maker. After the Industrial Revolution, the factory-made object became a symbol of man's degradation, at least in the Ruskinian view.

Words cannot preserve or present a cherished object or scene. Apart from Maupassant's comb and watch chain, one can think of very few objects in books. Sometimes they are avoided, like the mysterious object manufactured by the Newsome family in Henry James's *The Ambassadors*, although James was one of the few, until the French new novelists, who tried at other times to render vases, flowers, necklaces. Yet his Golden Bowl seems to lack the magical beauty of a real bowl, and for some reason we would not want a photograph of it, for the same reason that we do not like to see in books photographs of actresses playing our favorite characters, blighting with their actuality the lovely friend who has taken form in the eye of the mind.

When I was a child I had a little cabinet, and in it tiny objects: chairs and a table, vases and cooking pots, and a tiny pistol that would really shoot, they told me, had I had the minute bullets it took, and real gunpowder to fire it. In the vase I put the smallest of flowers—coral bells and spring beauties—and there were plaster carrots to cook in the pots. I loved this cabinet and its tiny objects, of course, but what I also noticed was that the adults loved it more. It was they, when they brought me something for my cabinet, who would rearrange the chairs and set the table with the cutlery the size of pins. Aunts and even uncles brought little rugs and miniature pictures in gilt frames. And I recall that the cabinet was called a shadow box, preserving the idea that in it you could assemble the tiny necessaries of a shadow world. The box itself created a frame around the world, as if it were a picture.

At that time many children were taken to see a wonderful dollhouse that had belonged to an actress, Colleen Moore. Perhaps she was one of those who had not succeeded in the talking films; at any rate she had devoted herself to a dollhouse of fanciful beauty—designed for the fairy queen Titania, I think—and it was filled with artifacts from other fairy tales: a cushion embroidered in seed pearls upon which the prince had returned Cinderella's slipper, tiny renditions of Gainsborough's *Blue Boy*, or perhaps wonderfully small Rembrandts, on canvases of one inch square.

In England children view a dollhouse that belonged to the young Victoria, in which as a child she could rearrange the tiny, homely objects of an imaginary and perhaps longed-for bourgeois life. Gaston Bachelard has written that "miniature is an exercise that has metaphysical freshness; it allows us to be world conscious at slight risk. And how restful this exercise on a dominated world can be! For miniature rests us without ever putting us to sleep. Here the imagination is both vigilant and content." In the dollhouse life can be arranged and controlled; we can move its objects around with ease. In China they have always had those little houses and barnyards made of clay to take to the grave, with the chickens and horses the soul will need in the next world; and nowadays there are paper bluejeans to send along.

In the world he dominates, the painter or photographer arranging his tablescapes of flowers and apples, a vase and a knife, will miniaturize it, taking pleasure in the way it is under his control. He can make the light strike the side of the porcelain vase in just such a manner, can straighten up the drooping stalks and put in pleasing order the scattered fruit. The term "still life," or as the French would have it, *nature morte*, is not really paradoxical but expressive of the charm of this subject, where nature cannot go on to wither and brown and droop and die, but remains forever fresh. "Happy, happy boughs that cannot shed your leaves," as Keats put it. The photographer, the painter produce miniature copies of the perfectly ordered world they have composed, metaphors for immortality.

Both painters and photographers have long felt a mystical association with objects. Photographers, especially, respond to the inner light, the reflection, the physical properties of emanation. They want to catch these and transmit them to the print. A photograph of a significant or beautiful object is like the object behind glass, or it is the object enhanced, itself an object beautiful and desired, and unlike the painting, attainable. Susan Sontag says that photographs as objects are themselves "the most mysterious of all the objects that make up and thicken the environment we recognize as modern. Photographs really are experience captured, and the camera is the ideal arm of consciousness in its acquisitive mode." The distance between us and the beautiful object in the photograph is also the distance of our memory of childhood desire.

One feels the same desire to possess the photograph or painting of a still life. Miniature, brightened, perfect, it will fit into our lives in a way that some vast, troubled Tintoretto would not. Portrait photographs are drenched in the sadness we feel if their subjects are dead, but sadness is never present in the eternally living flowers and fruit here.

Even, curiously, the still life that contains dead animals is not sad. Kandinsky wrote: "everything that is dead quivers . . . even a white trouser button glittering out of a puddle in the street . . . everything has a secret soul, which is silent more often than it speaks." Even the images of death—skulls, bones, stuffed trophy heads, bare branches of trees—are in a way images of endurance and a celebration of the inner structure, the creation of living things. Beyond this, though, is another affirmative thing. In *Camera Lucida* Roland Barthes refers to the odd, perverse confusion between the two concepts of the Real and the Live in photographs: "by attesting that the object has been real, the photograph surreptitiously induces belief that it is alive, because of that delusion which makes us attribute to Reality an absolutely superior, somehow eternal value; . . . Hence it would be better to say that Photography's inimitable feature . . . is that someone has seen the referent (even if it is a matter of objects) in flesh and blood . . . in person." The photograph is different from painting, for although the painter has also seen the object, he is changing it into something else, not testifying to its actuality. The photographer wins the argument with death.

It is interesting that one of the earliest photographs (made by Niépce around 1827) was a still life. But painters used to believe, and perhaps still do (perhaps photographers believe it too), that other subjects are nobler than the still life: historical subjects, portraits, landscapes, even buildings or animals somehow outranked, in the traditional view of it, the simple bowl of fruit or vase of flowers. The photograph has taken the place of testimony, in the sense Barthes uses. History is recorded now altogether by photography, which for this use is so far superior to painting. It can bring back the dead in that although the pictured bodies or victims are dead, the photograph is alive as photograph, and the photographer as witness.

The nature that opens before the naked eye, or before the painterly eye, is different from the nature that reveals itself to the camera—if only because of the difference between the innocent, inadvertent glance and the intentional, shaping gaze of the photographer. The camera intervenes with its lowerings and liftings, its interruptions and framing, its wide angle or its stop action, its enlargements and miniaturization. "The camera introduces us to unconscious optics as does psychoanalysis to unconscious impulses," says Barthes.

The old still-life painters also believed that some miniature tablescape worlds were more worth copying than others—those with a moral clearly to be perceived were favored: those displaying allegories of *vanitas*, or those with hunting trophies such as dead rabbits. Is that a statement about man's control over his world? They also preferred the still lifes that have musical instruments and manuscripts and spectacles, for these also glorify human accomplishment. But it is really the vase of flowers that one desires, or rather the image of the vase of flowers, or of fruit stilled and forever perfect, for these possess what Schopenhauer called "tranquillity of soul."

All great simple images reveal the psyche. The primitively satisfying—because flat—world of the tabletop is above all graced with vases, and most of these have flowers in them; you imagine they are there because you have to put the flowers in something. Some still lifes have just the vase—enduring female symbol—arranged with other objects for the sake of their pleasing forms, and for their symbolic contribution to the idea of life. The vase full of flowers is a particularly life-giving image, a dream of giving birth to flowers. A vase of flowers is, above all, affirmative. And flowers are themselves like tiny worlds, or tiny women with petaled skirts, and with the anatomical resemblance that has never gone unremarked.

Beauty, that intangible array of choices, guides the arrangement of these flowers and of these rich, bellied, voluptuous pears. Of course the photographers here are at their most painterly, and the spontaneity prized in photographs is necessarily absent. Some people have said that in order to be "good," a photograph must be the most itself, the most not-a-painting. But even the formally composed subject is animated by the photographer's conflicting desires to express—to "externalize the inner images," as historian Siegfried Kracauer would have it—and to render the objective form. And thus, in the occasional coincidence between the two, and because of the penetrating powers of camera and film, the photographer (the viewer too, of course) can discover things in the photograph he did not exactly put there: accidents of light, brilliance of color, detail suddenly significant. We find photographs beautiful in part because of this connection with exploration and surprise.

And yet, for rather puritanical reasons, arrangements of objects, whether seen or pictured, but above all pictured, have not always been admired. They have been thought incapable of offering moral instruction—they do not teach us anything—and of course they are not "real." But we might remember the story of Zeuxis, who competed in a painting contest with Parrhasius. Zeuxis painted grapes that were so lifelike that birds flew down and tried to peck them. Nobody could paint more realistically than that! Then when in triumph Zeuxis went to remove the cloth covering Parrhasius's effort, it was discovered that the cloth was the painting! Parrhasius was considered the victor because his drapery was even more "real" that Zeuxis's grapes. It is harder to fool men than birds, the judges said. (This may or may not be true.) But what is clear from this ancient tale, if we did not already know, is our endless fascination with the image as life improved upon, testified to, preserved, and portable, as delightful deception. And there is a moral, if we like: life can indeed be improved upon by photography.

DIANE JOHNSON

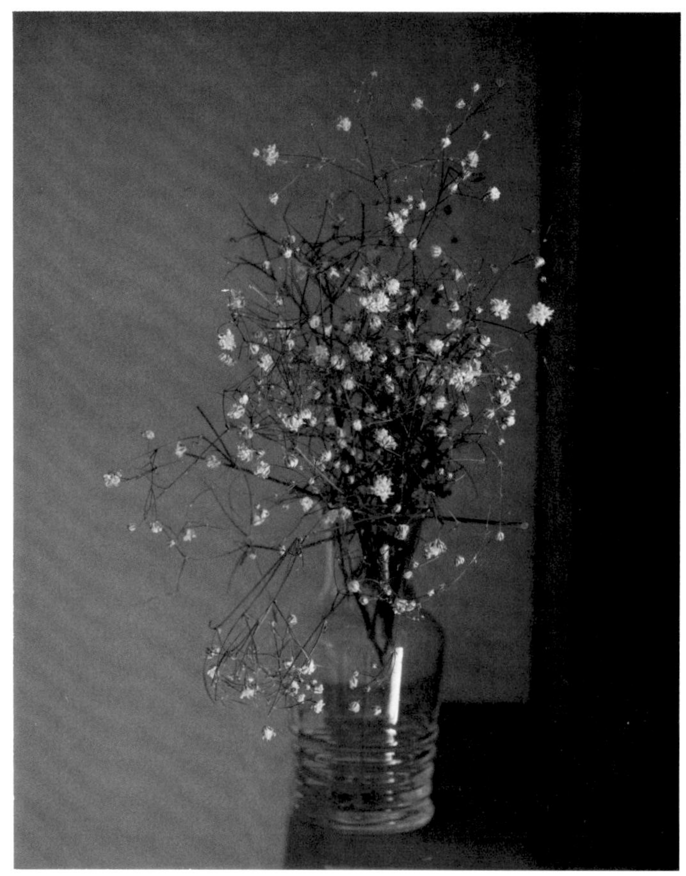

William Clift · *Baby's Breath, Cambridge, Massachusetts* · 1971

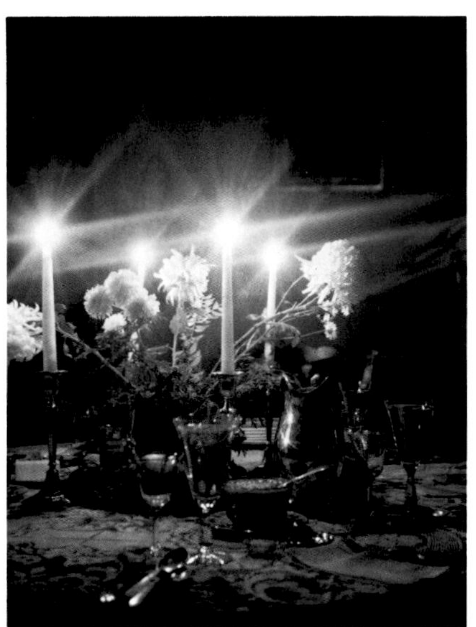

William Clift · *Barbara's Table, Beacon Hill, Boston, Massachusetts* · 1956

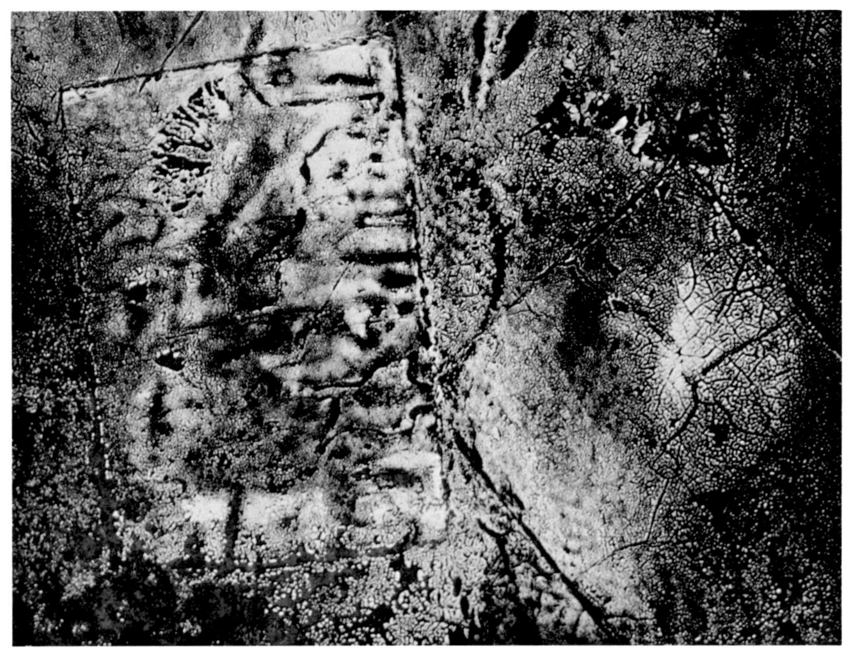

Ansel Adams · *Weathered Oil Drum, Yosemite Valley, California* · c. 1976

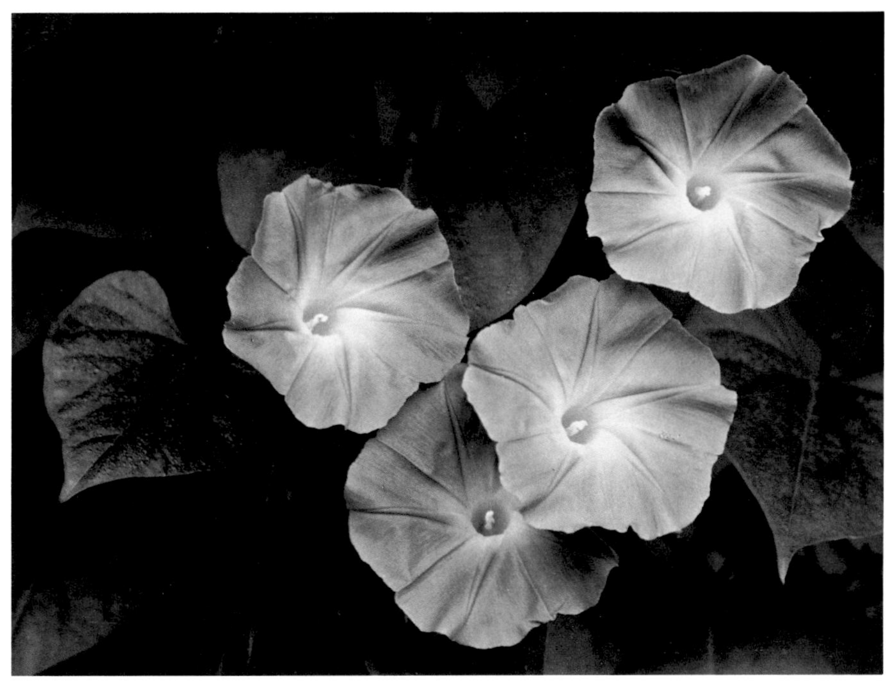

Ansel Adams · *Morning Glories, Massachusetts* · 1958

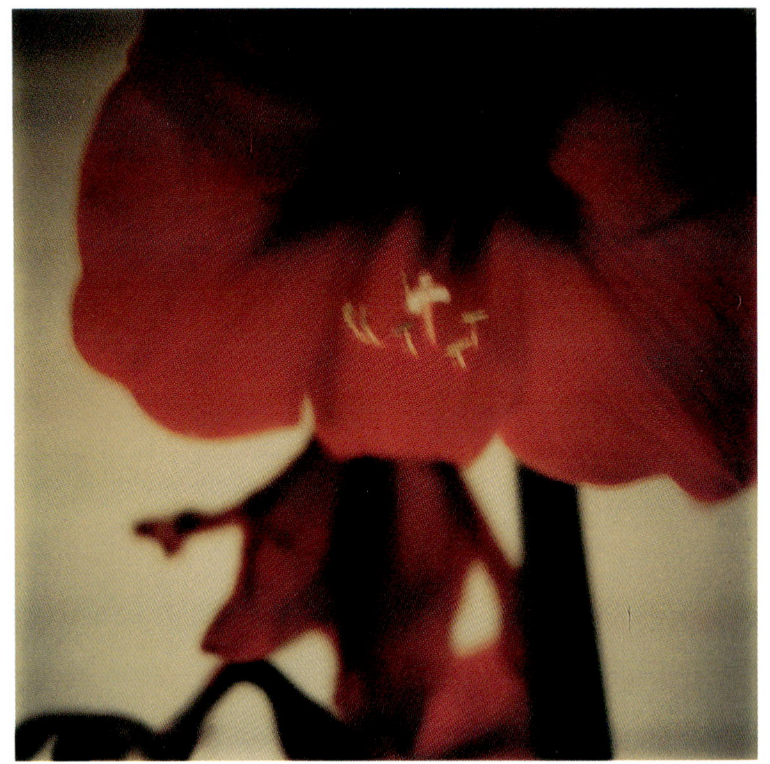

Minor White · Untitled · 1976

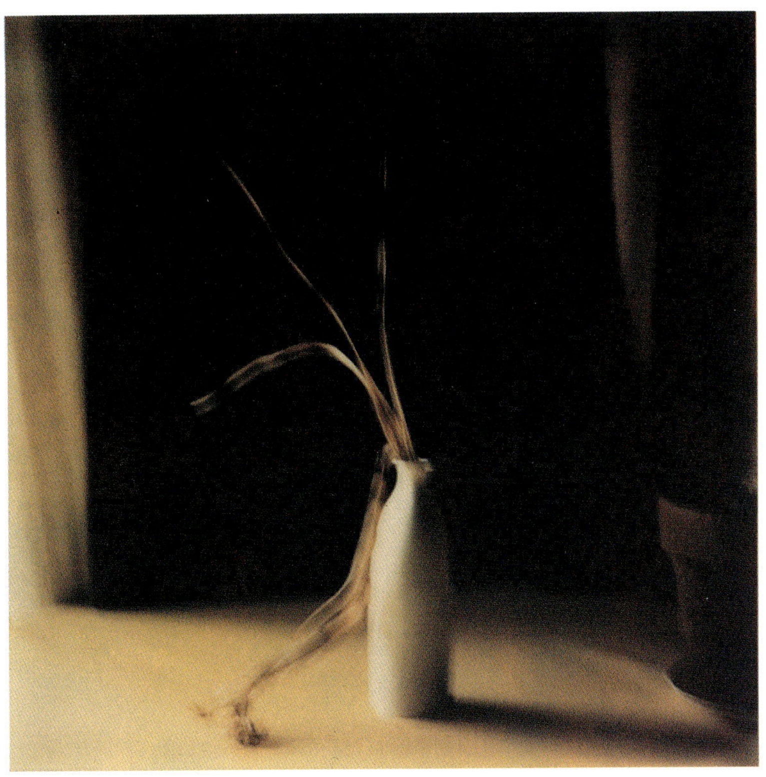

Minor White · Untitled · 1976

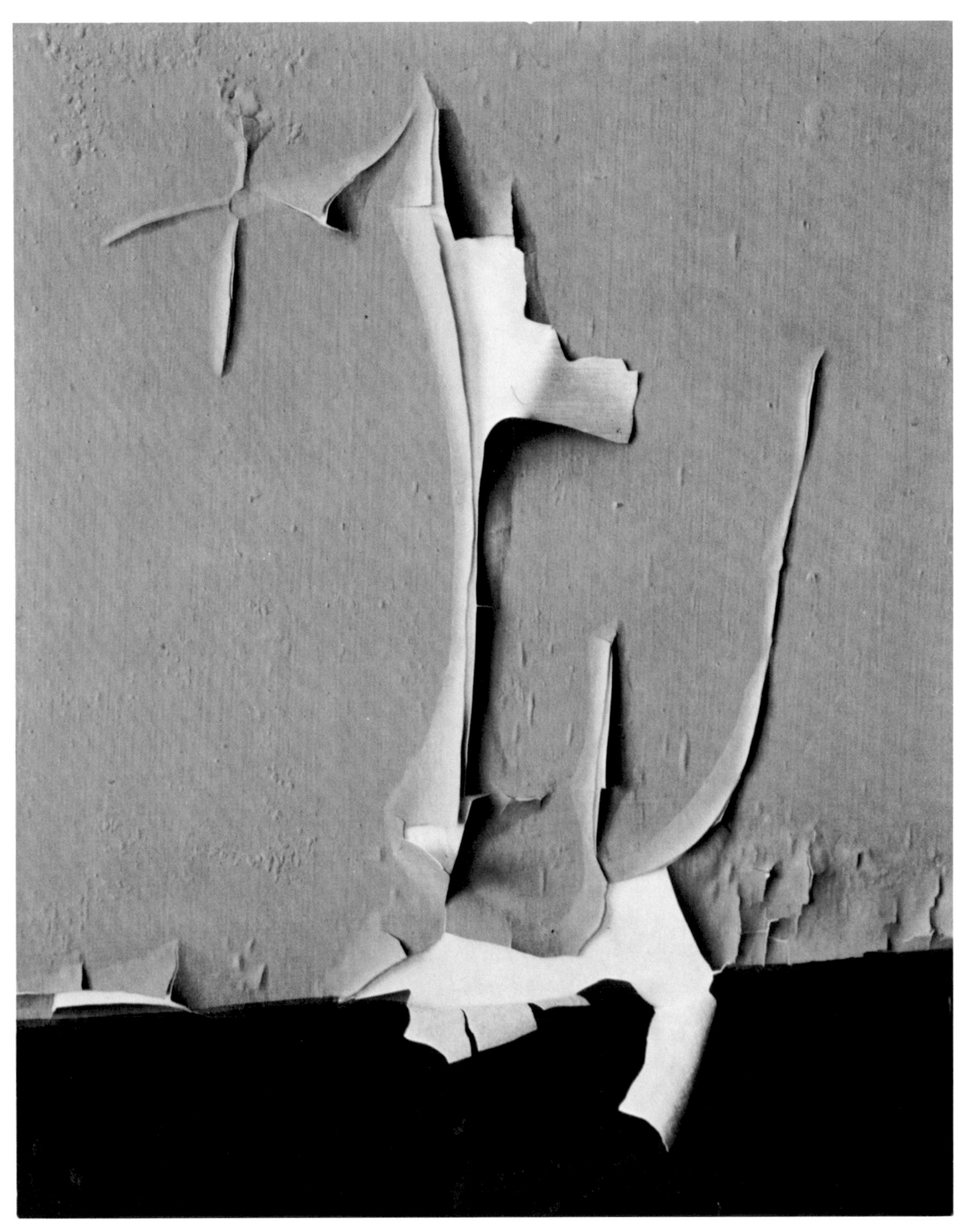

Minor White · *Peeled Paint, Rochester, New York* · 1959

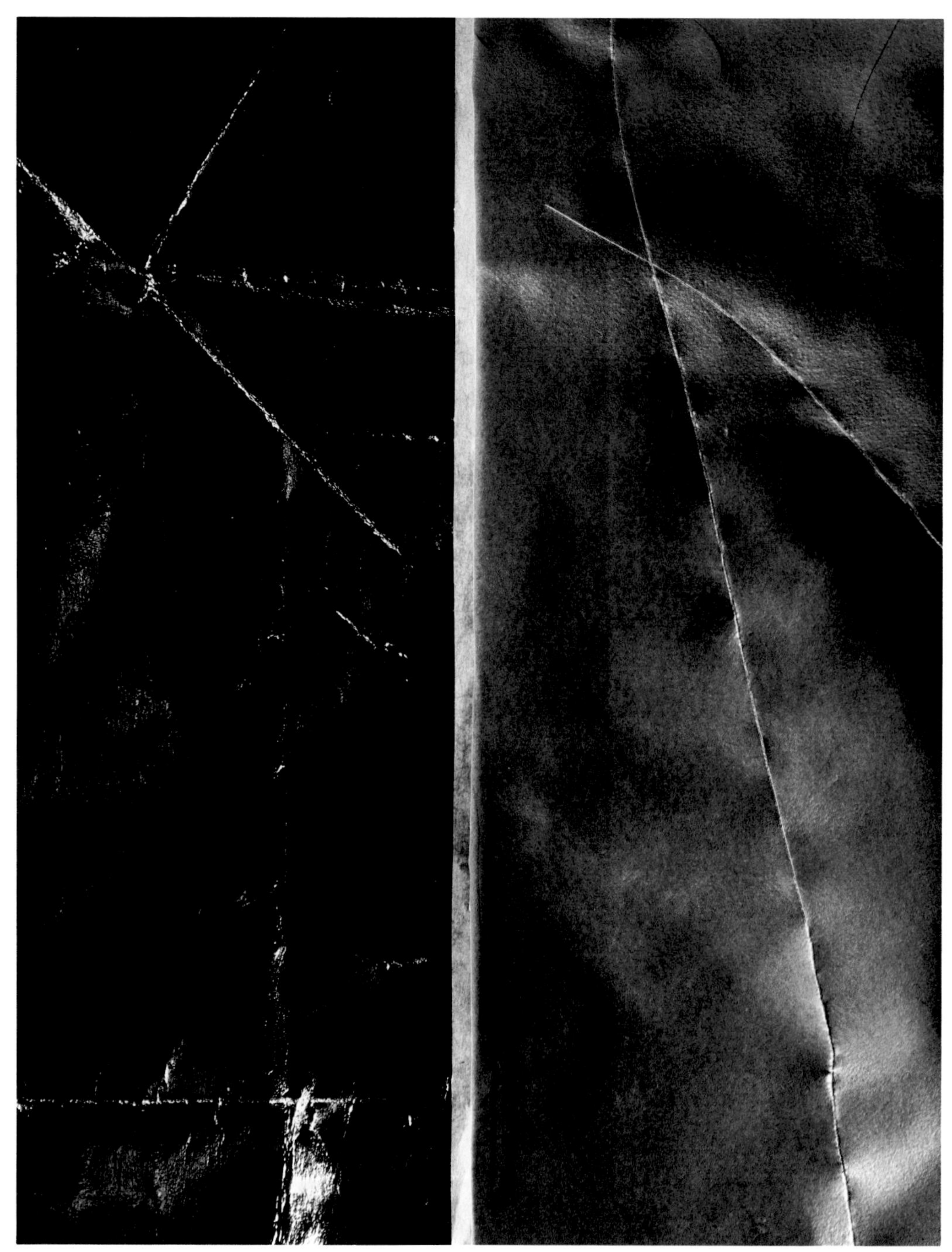

Carl Chiarenza · *Menotomy 268* (from diptych) · 1982

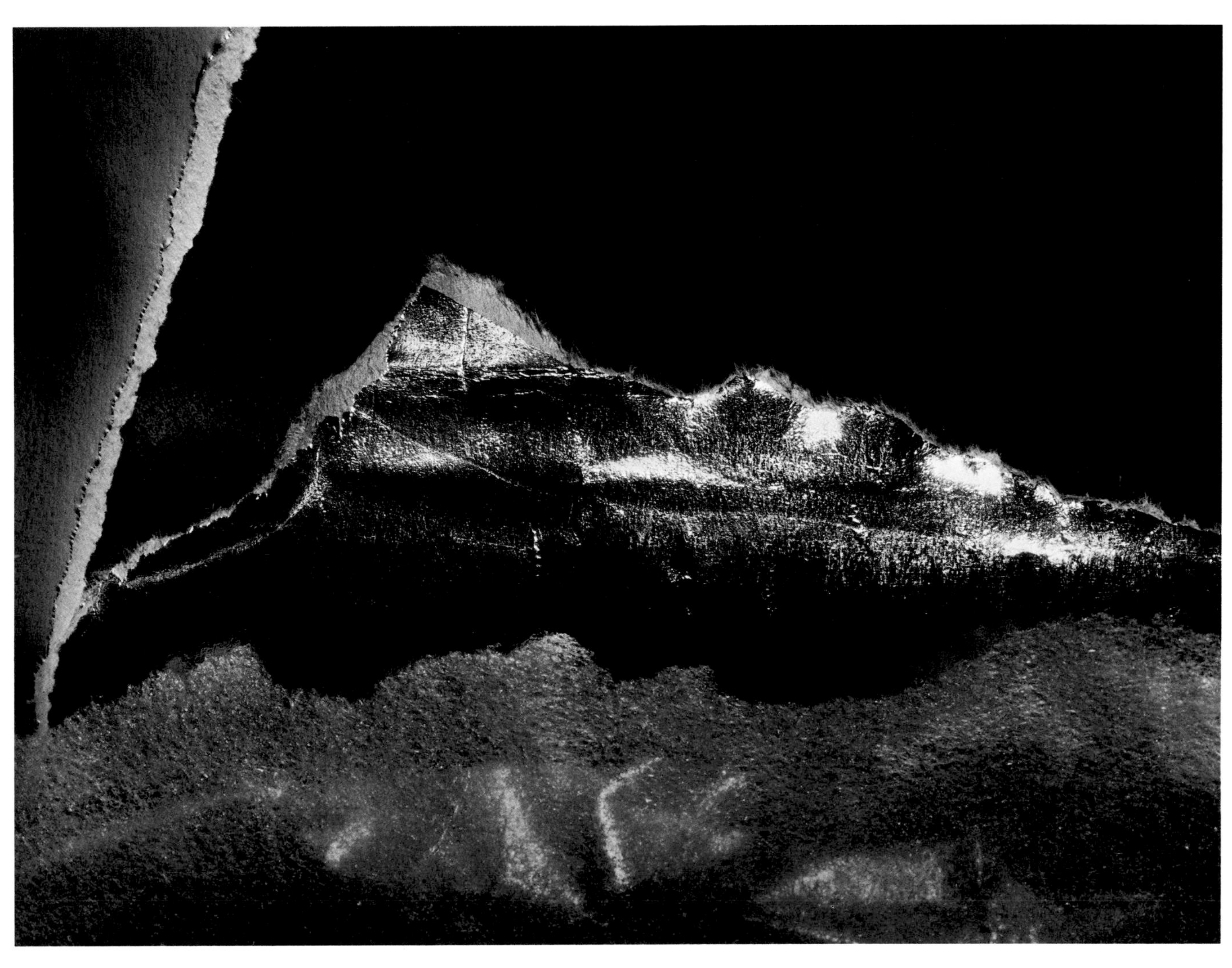

Carl Chiarenza · *Menotomy 293* (from triptych) · 1982

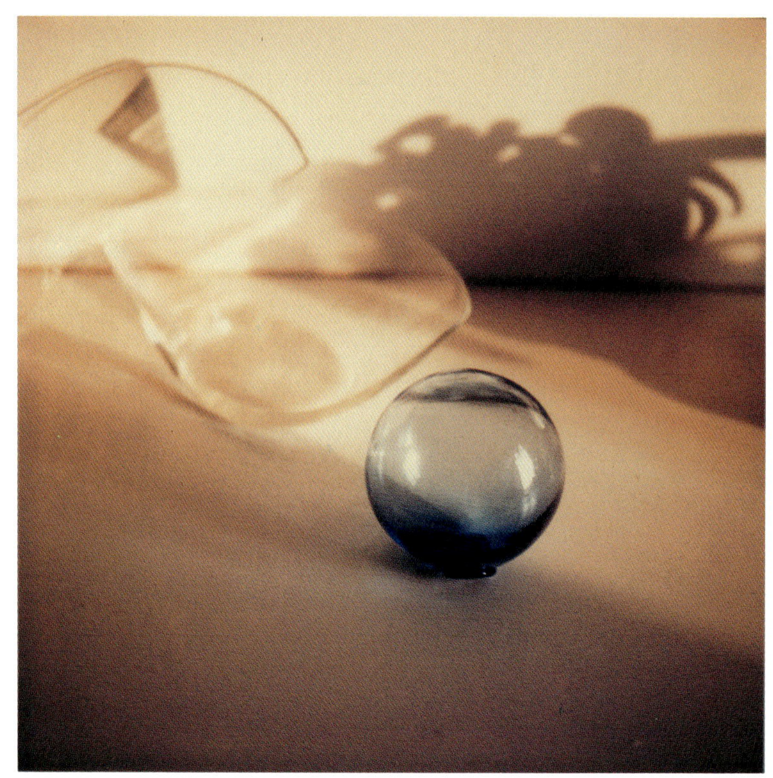

André Kertész · Untitled · 1982

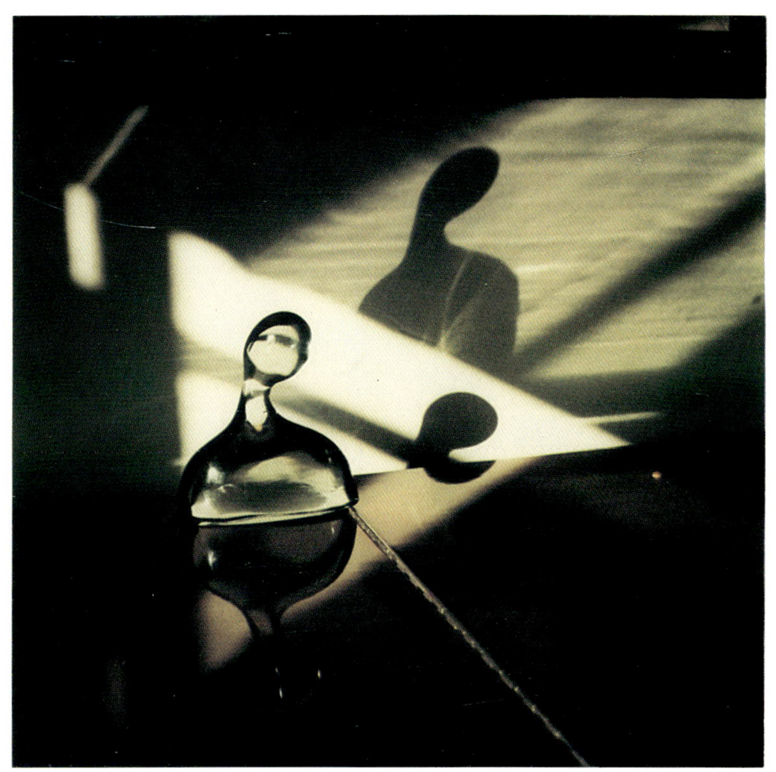

André Kertész · Untitled · 1979

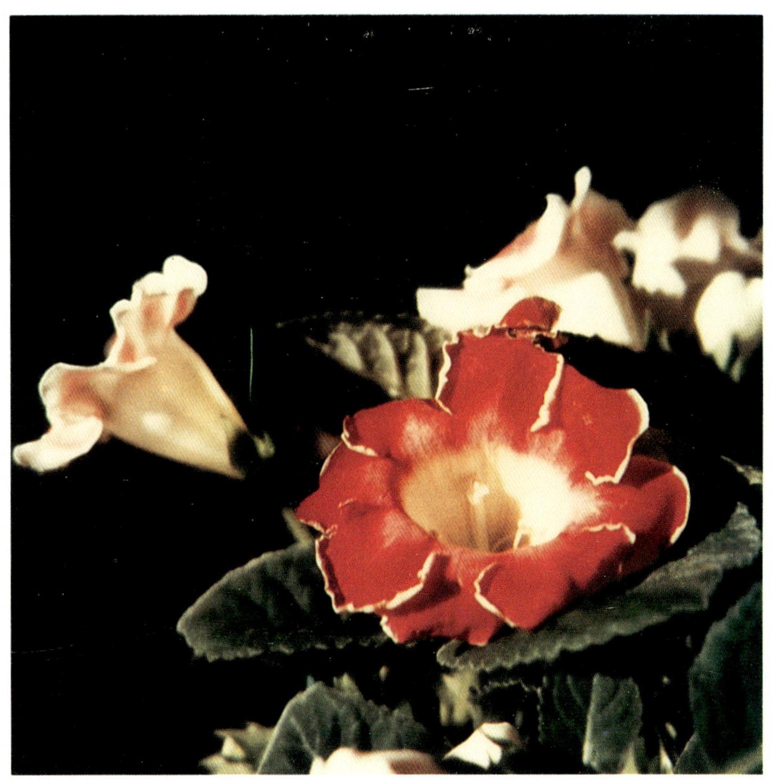

André Kertész · Untitled · 1980

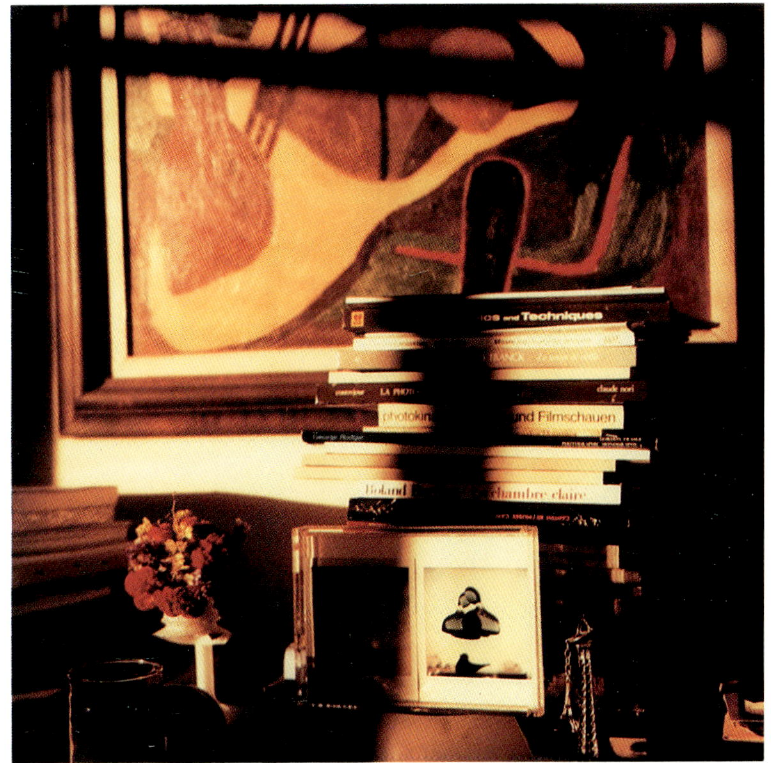

André Kertész · Untitled · 1982

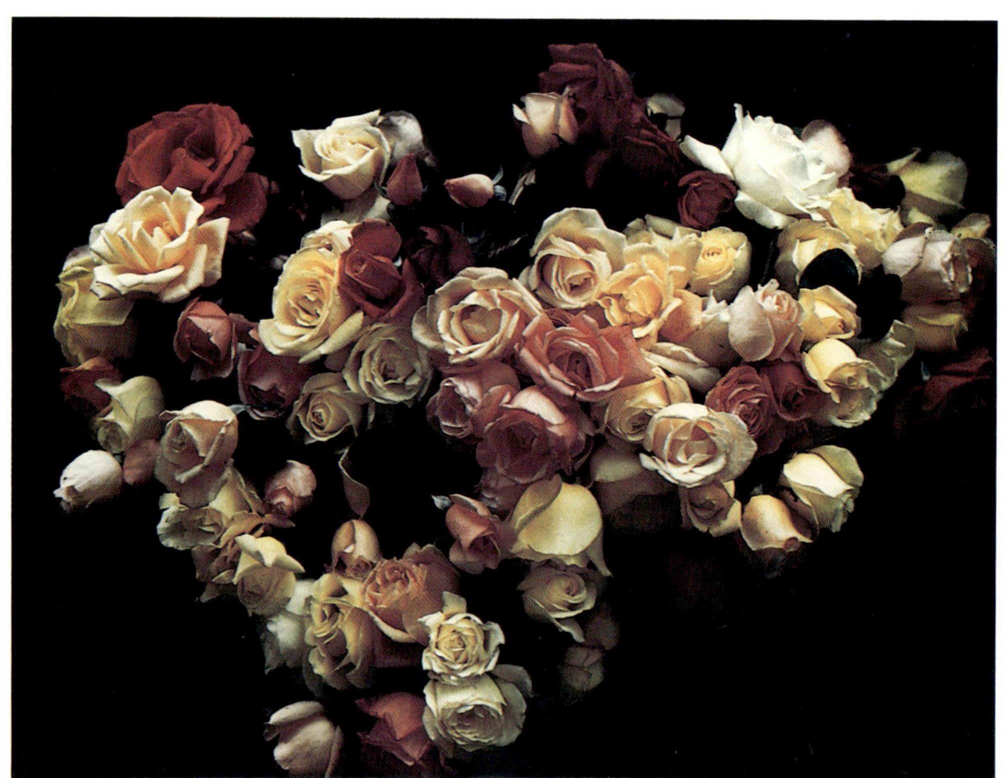

Marie Cosindas · *Roses, Mexico* · 1966

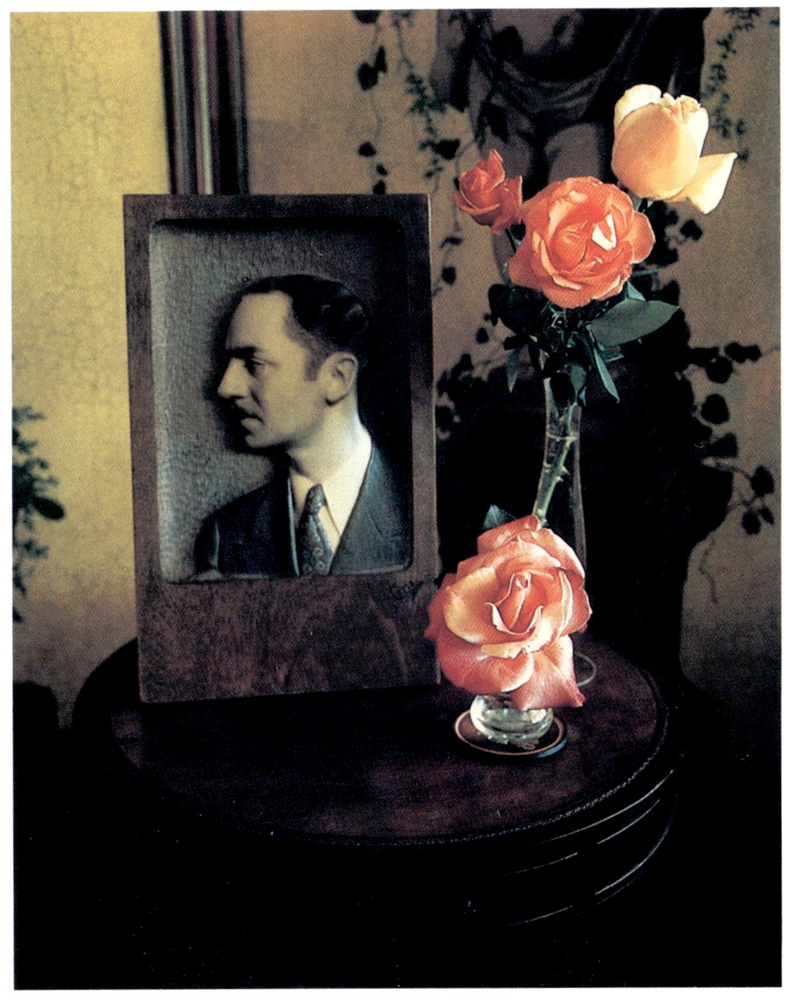

Marie Cosindas · *William Powell Still Life* · 1985

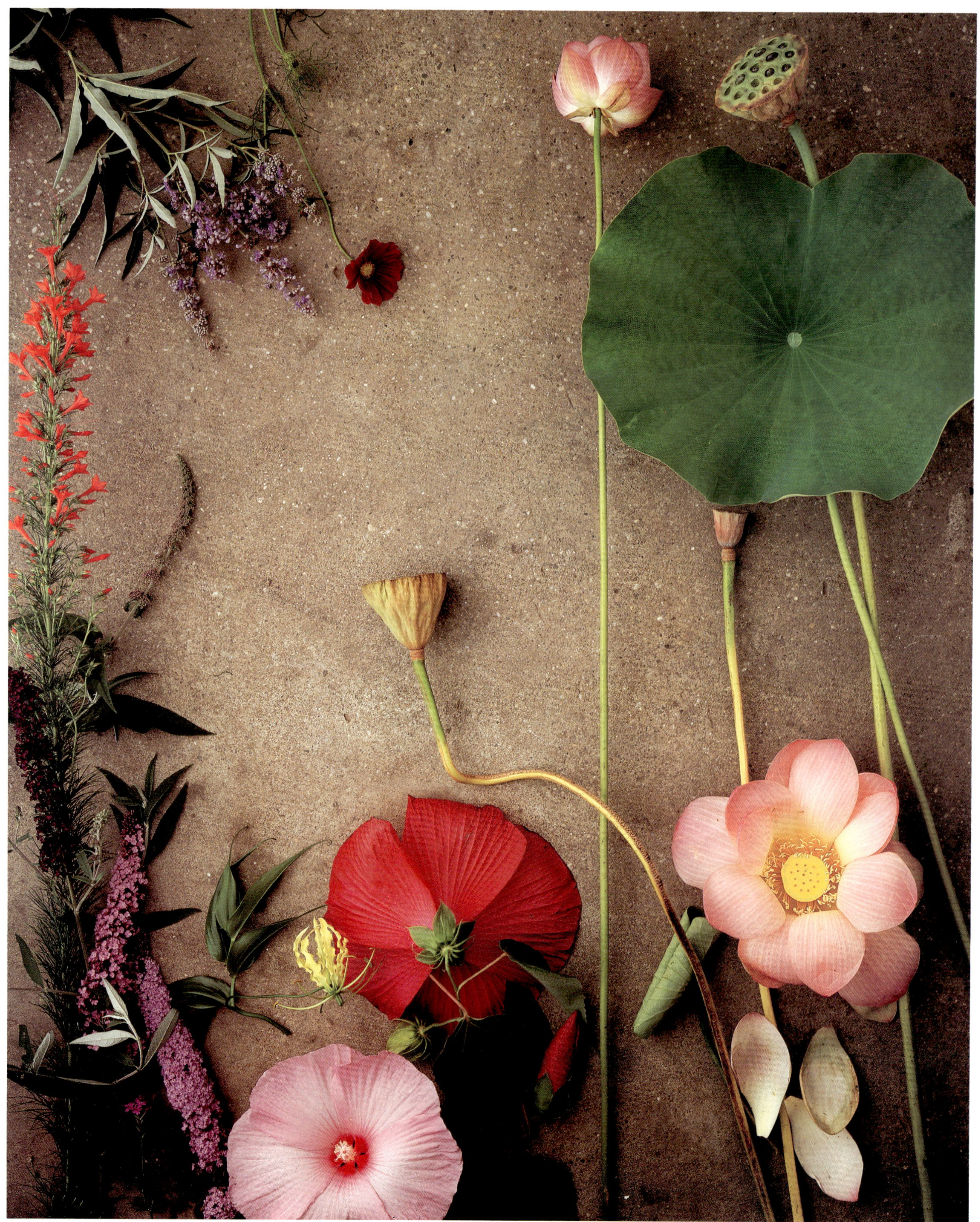

Michael Geiger · *Summer Lotus* · 1982

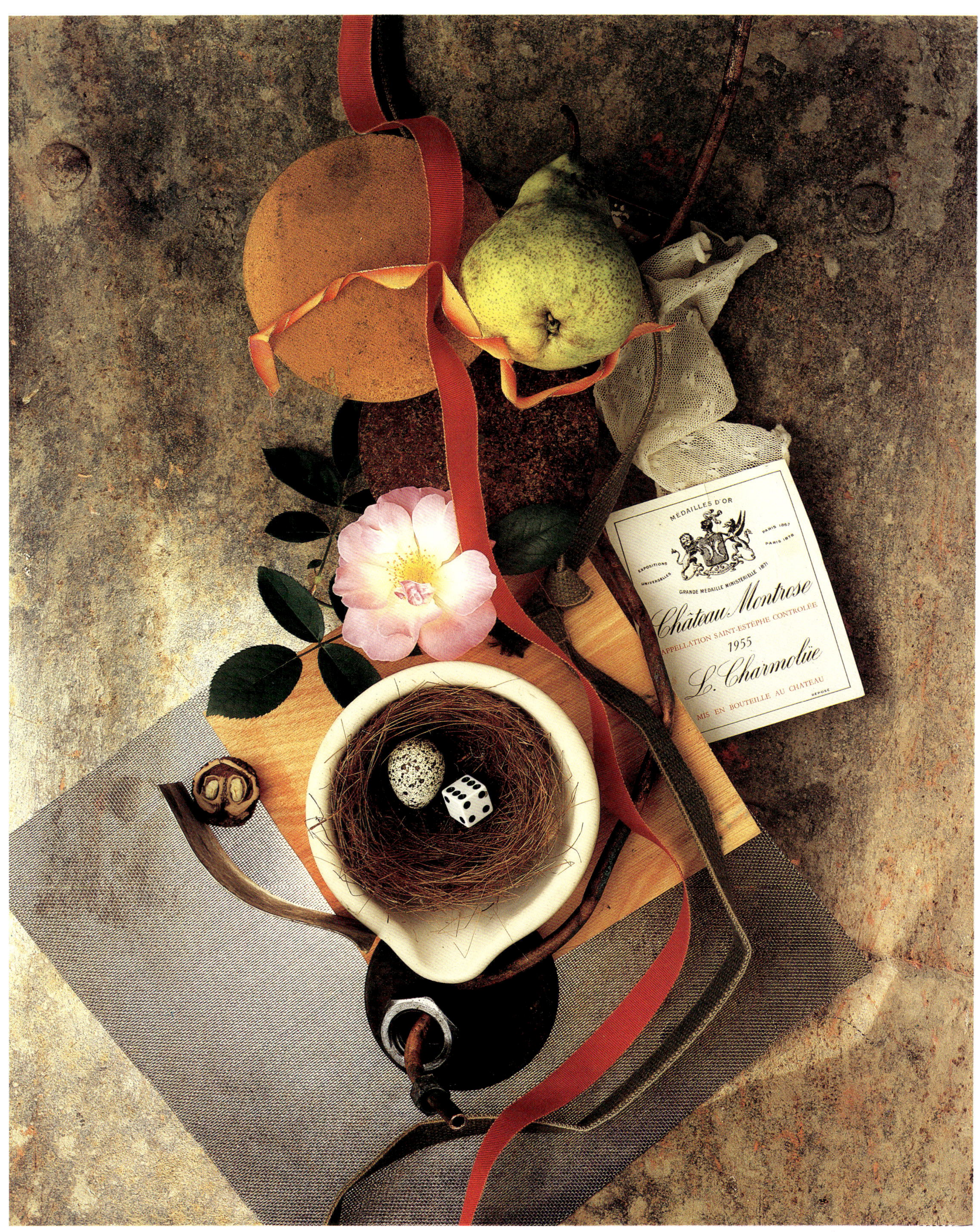

Michael Geiger · *Konstructions (Chateau Montrose)* · 1984

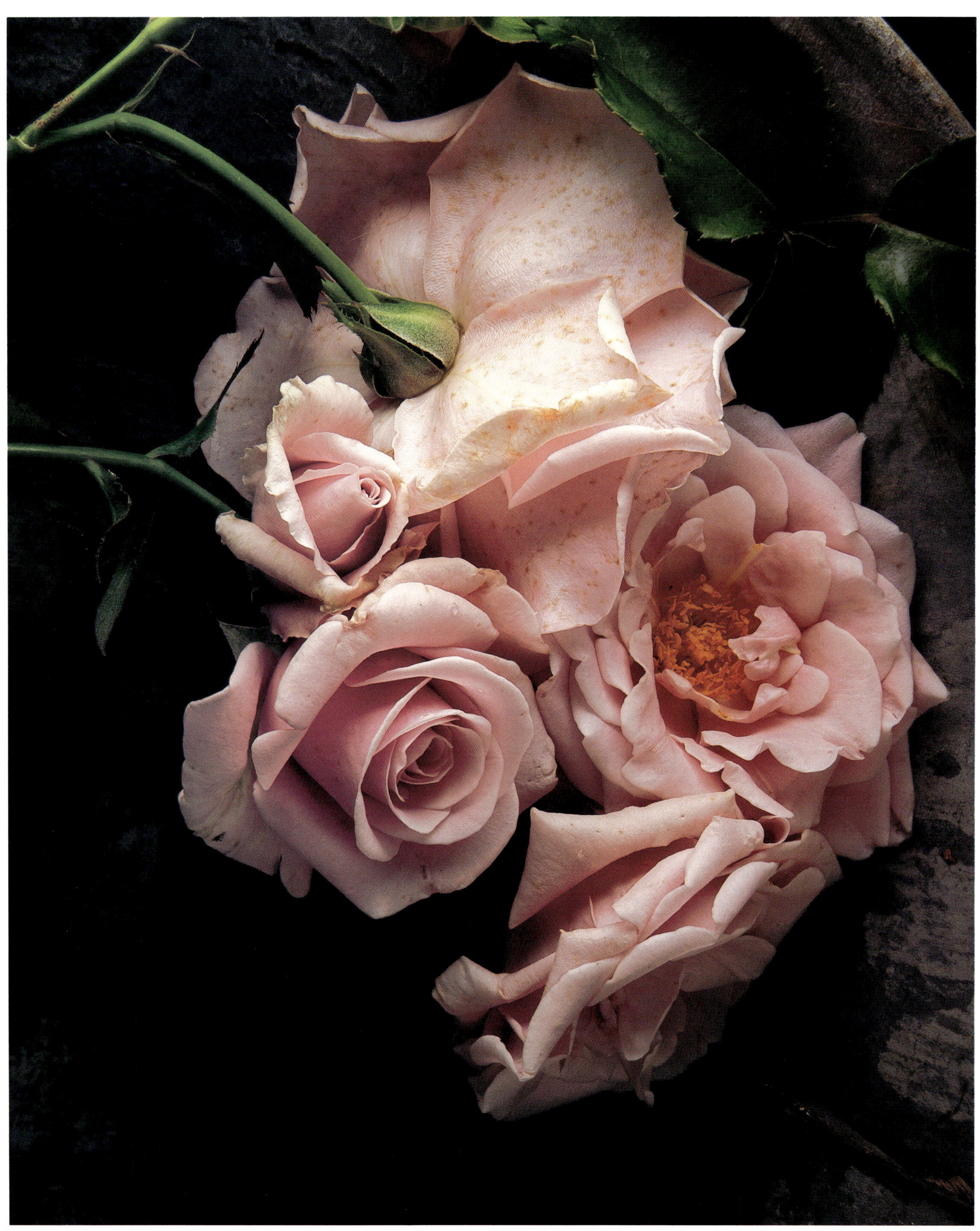

Michael Geiger · *Garden Roses (Sterling Silver)* · 1986

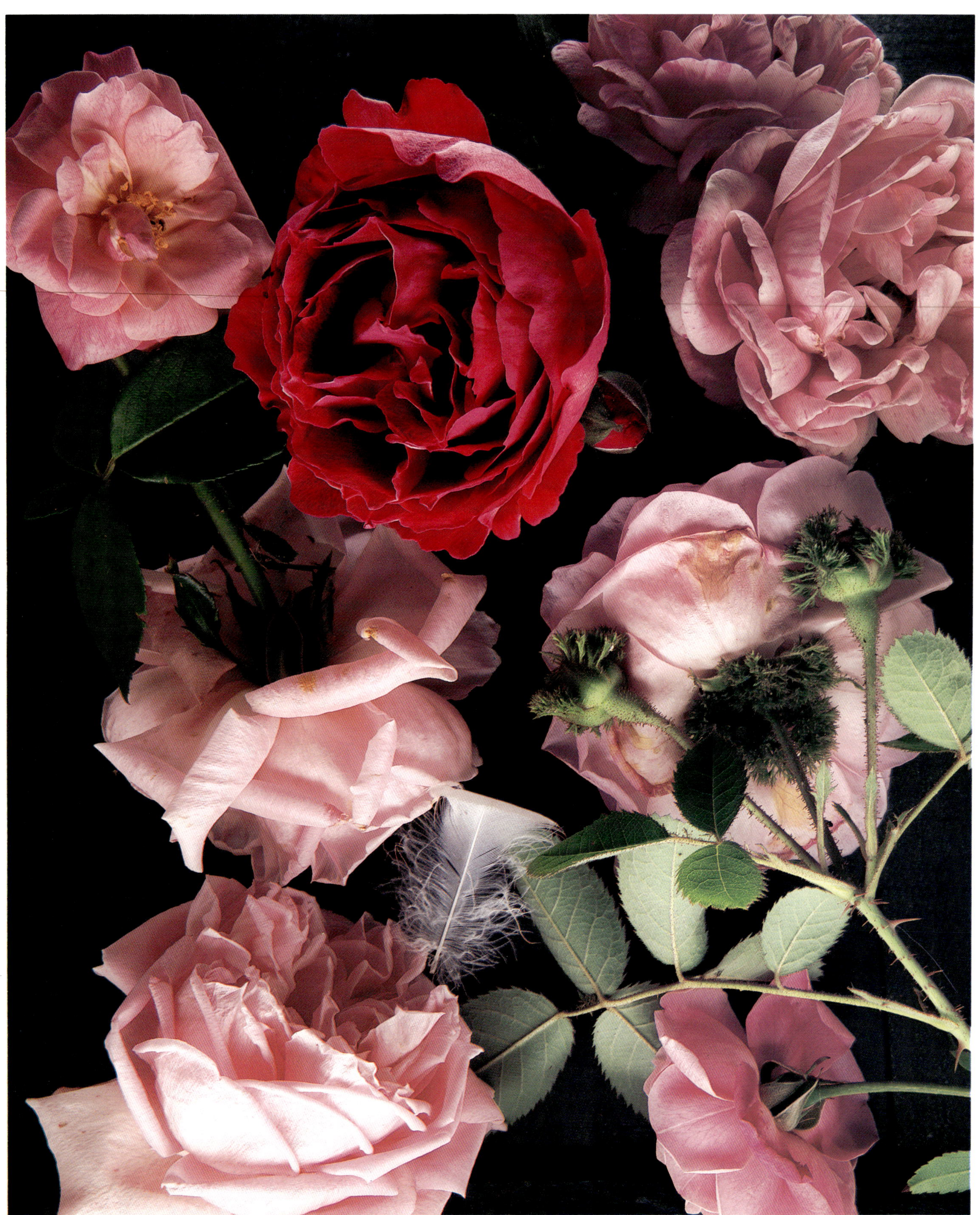

Michael Geiger · *Garden Roses with Feather, No. 26* · 1986

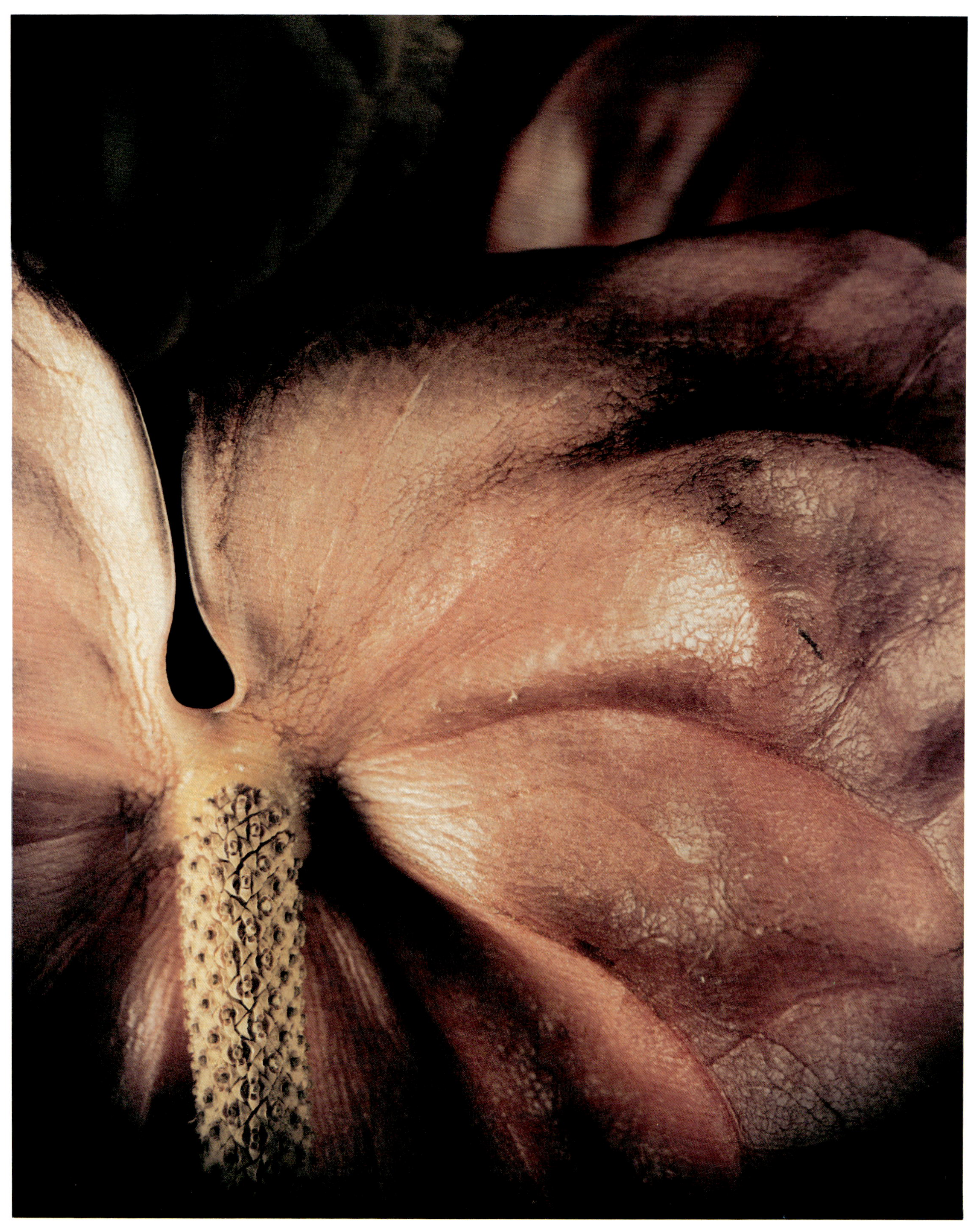

Chris Enos · Untitled, Flower Series · 1980

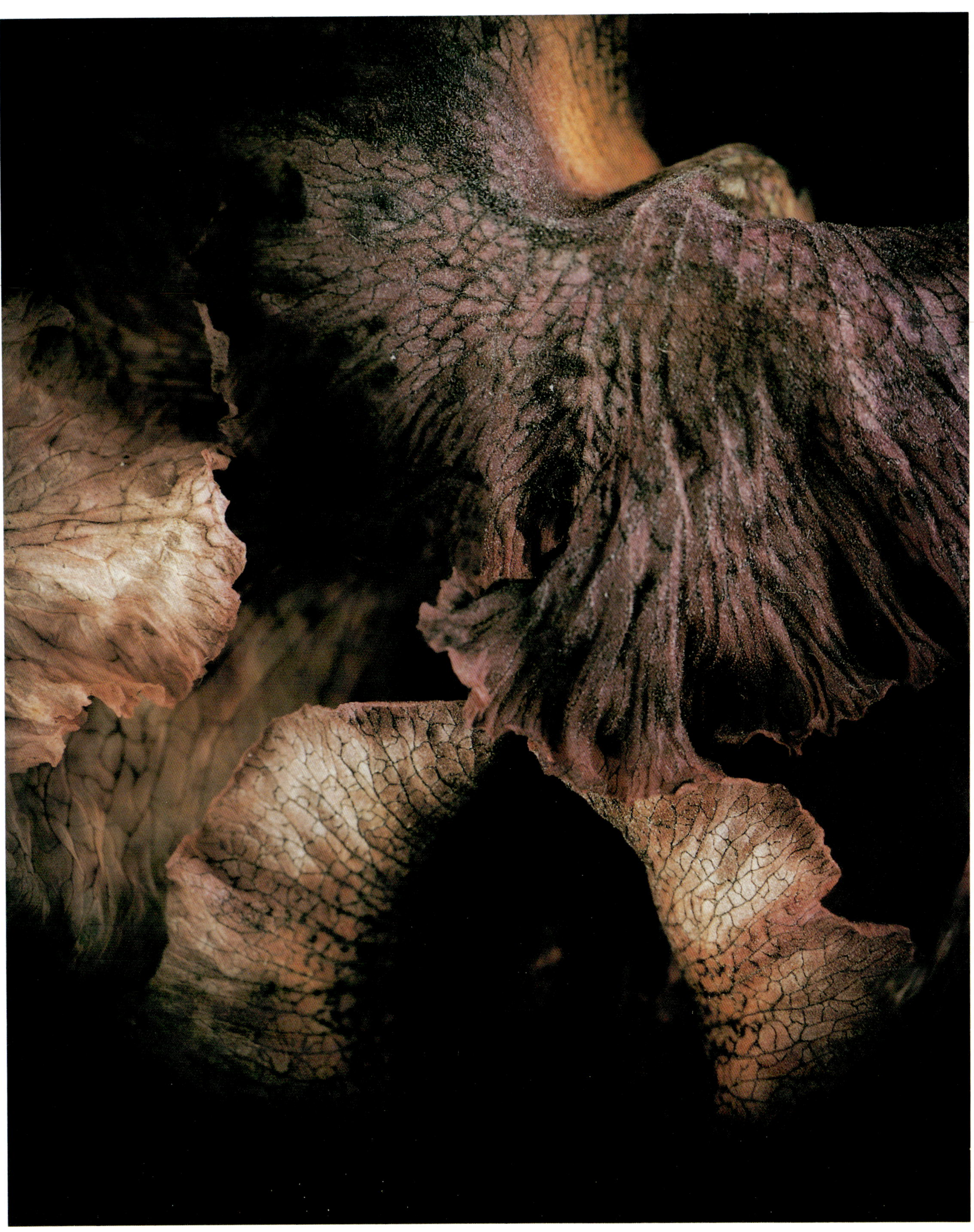

Chris Enos · Untitled, Flower Series · 1980

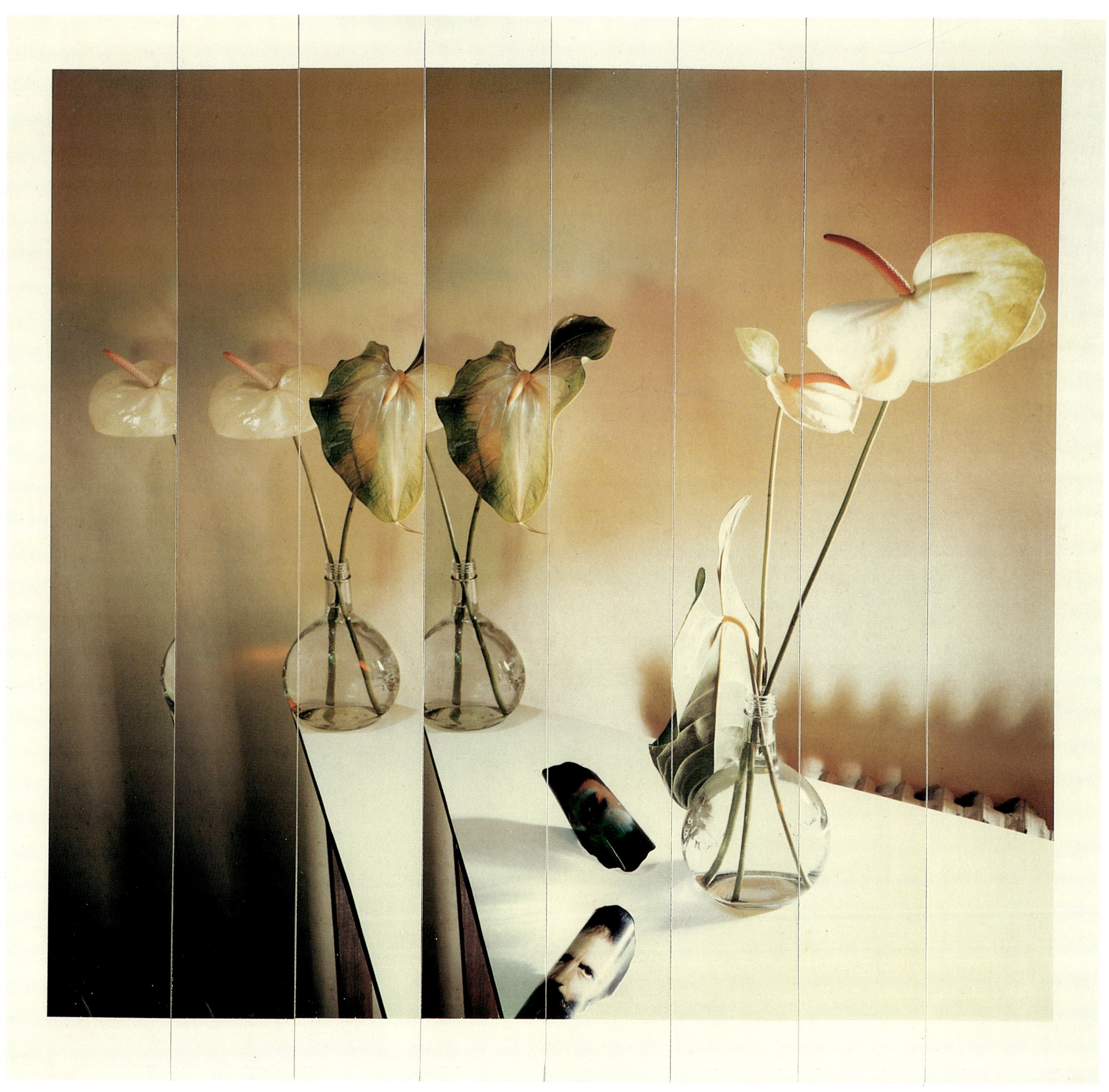

Lucas Samaras · *Panorama, 11/5/84*

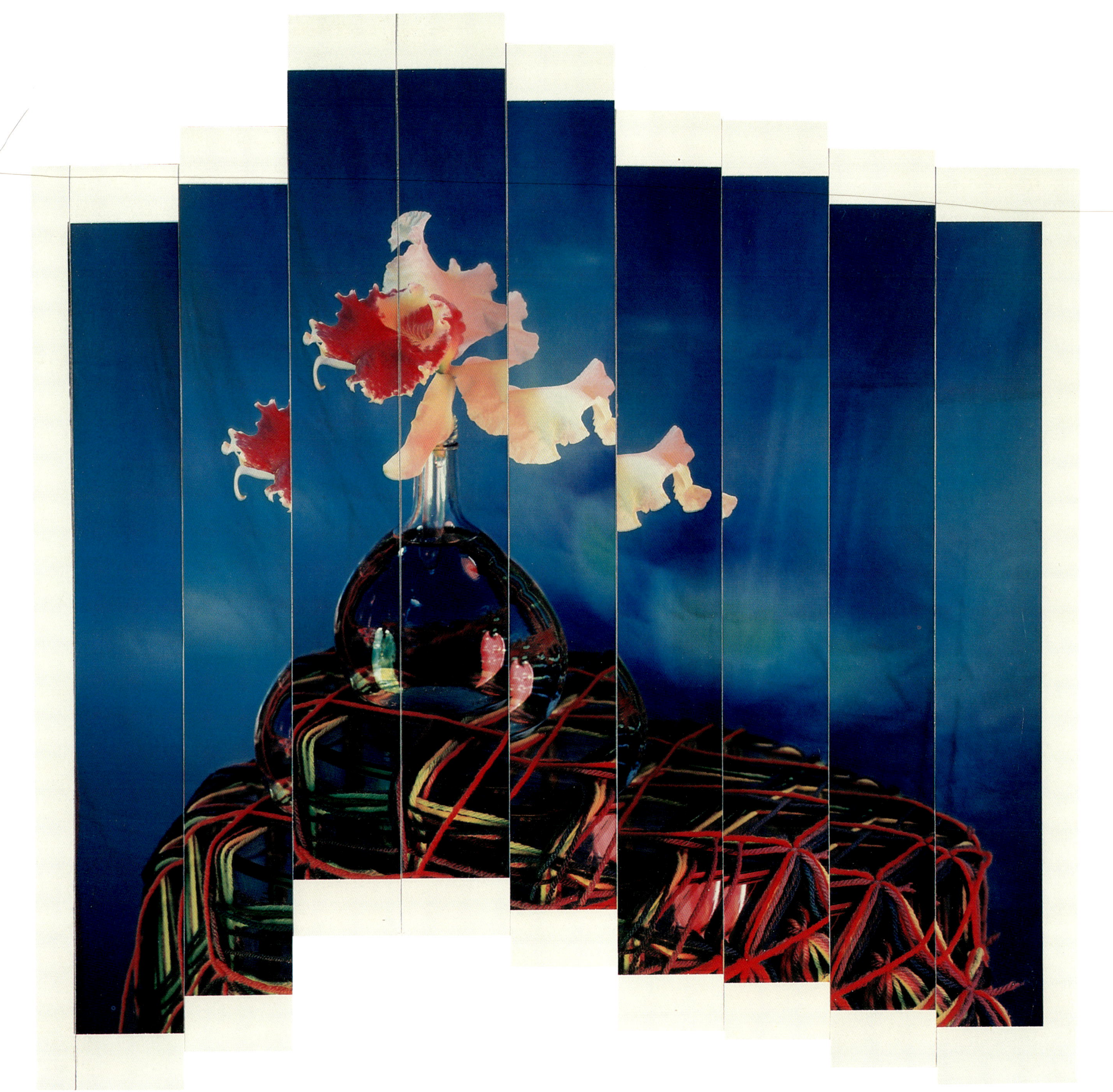

Lucas Samaras · *Panorama, 11/19/84*

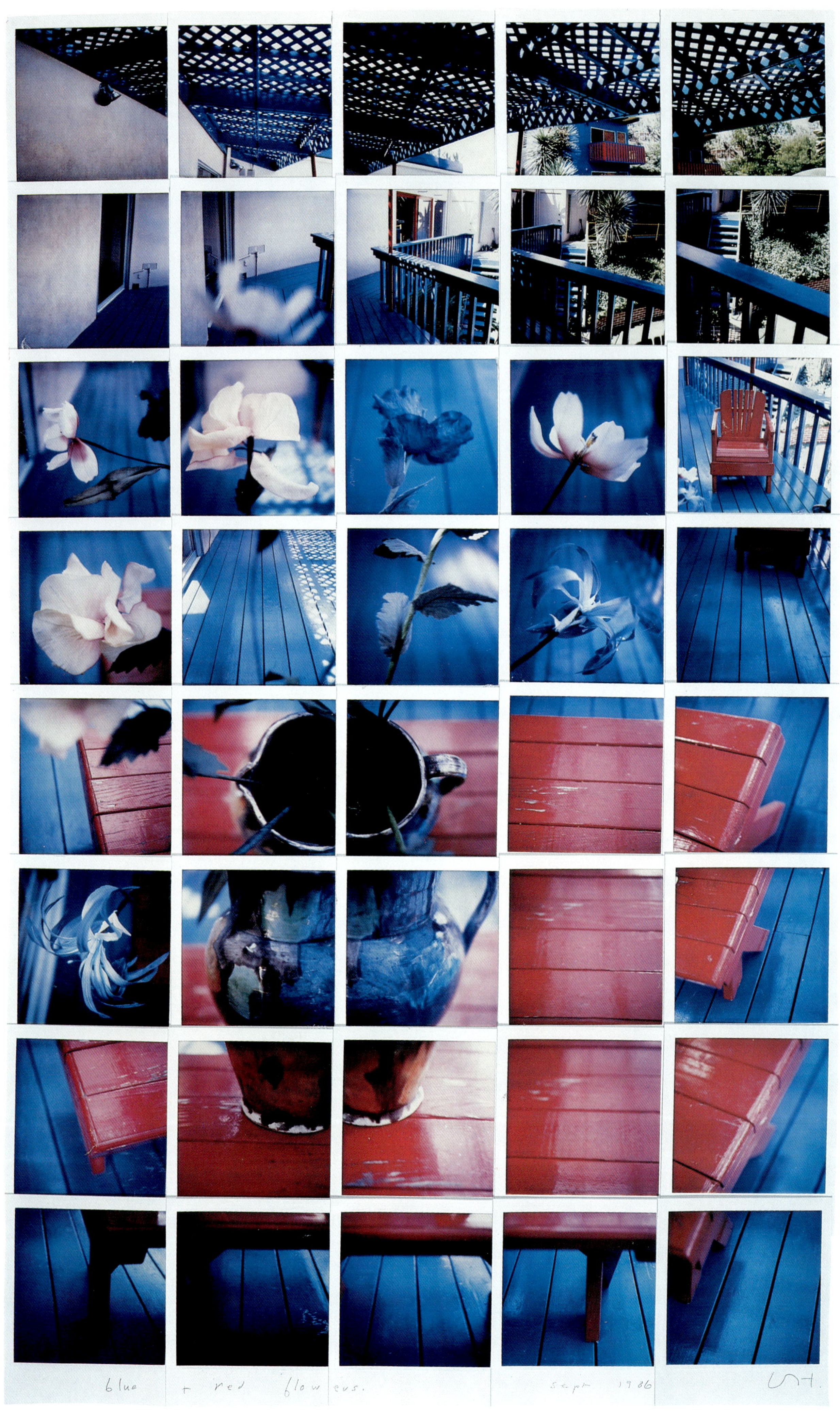

David Hockney · *Blue & Red Flowers, September 1986*

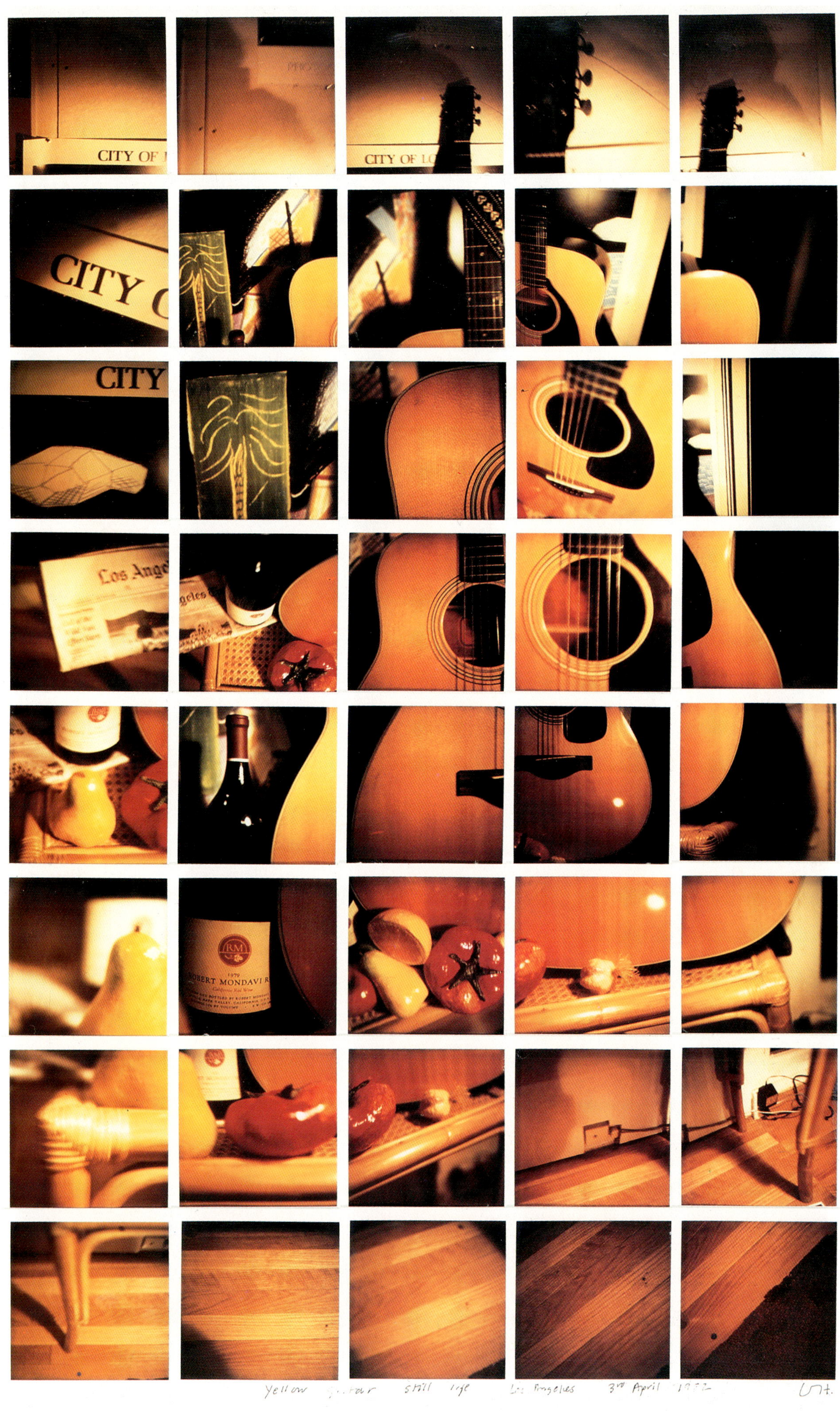

David Hockney · *Yellow Guitar, Still Life, L.A., 3rd April 1982*

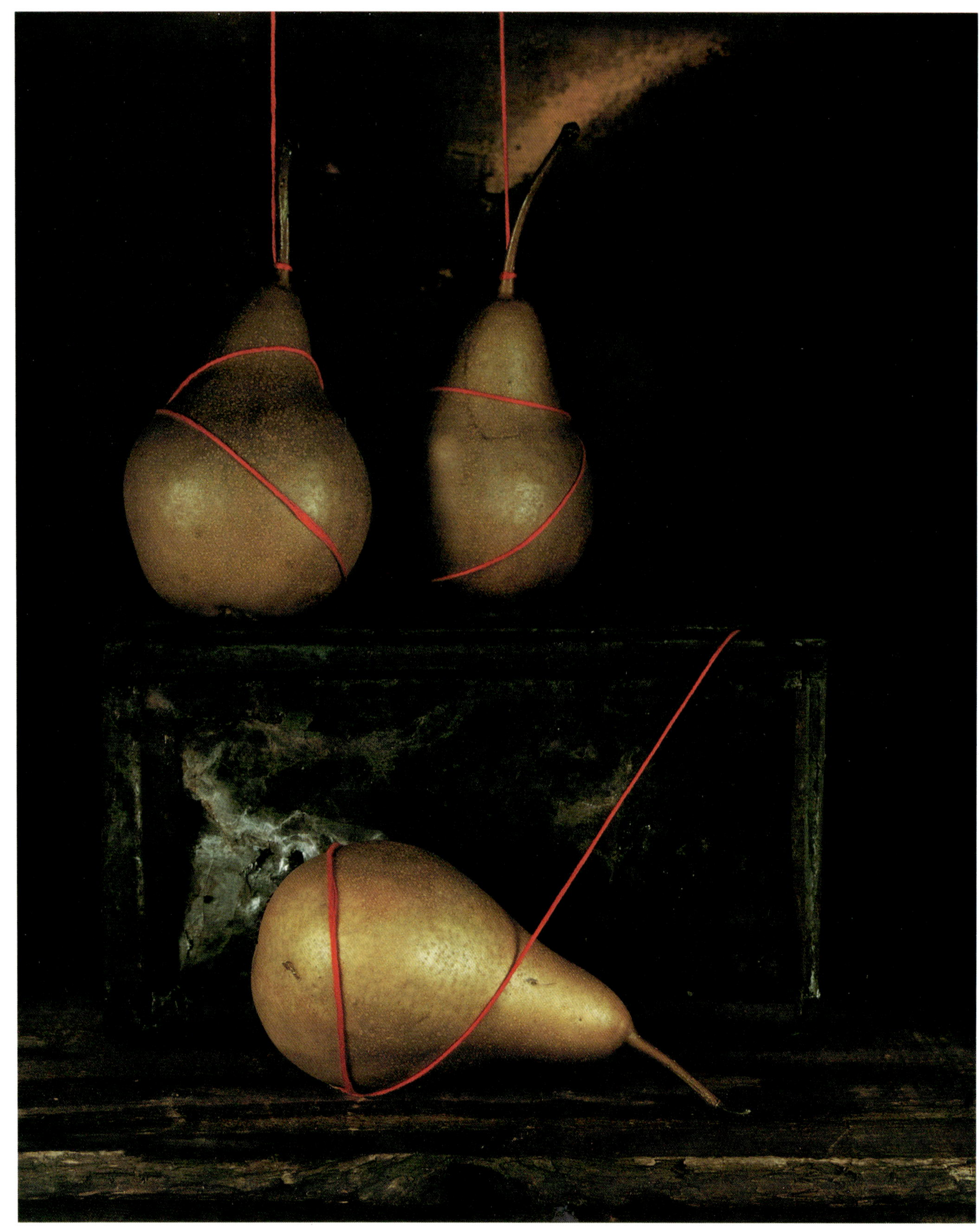

Olivia Parker · *Golden Pears* · 1979

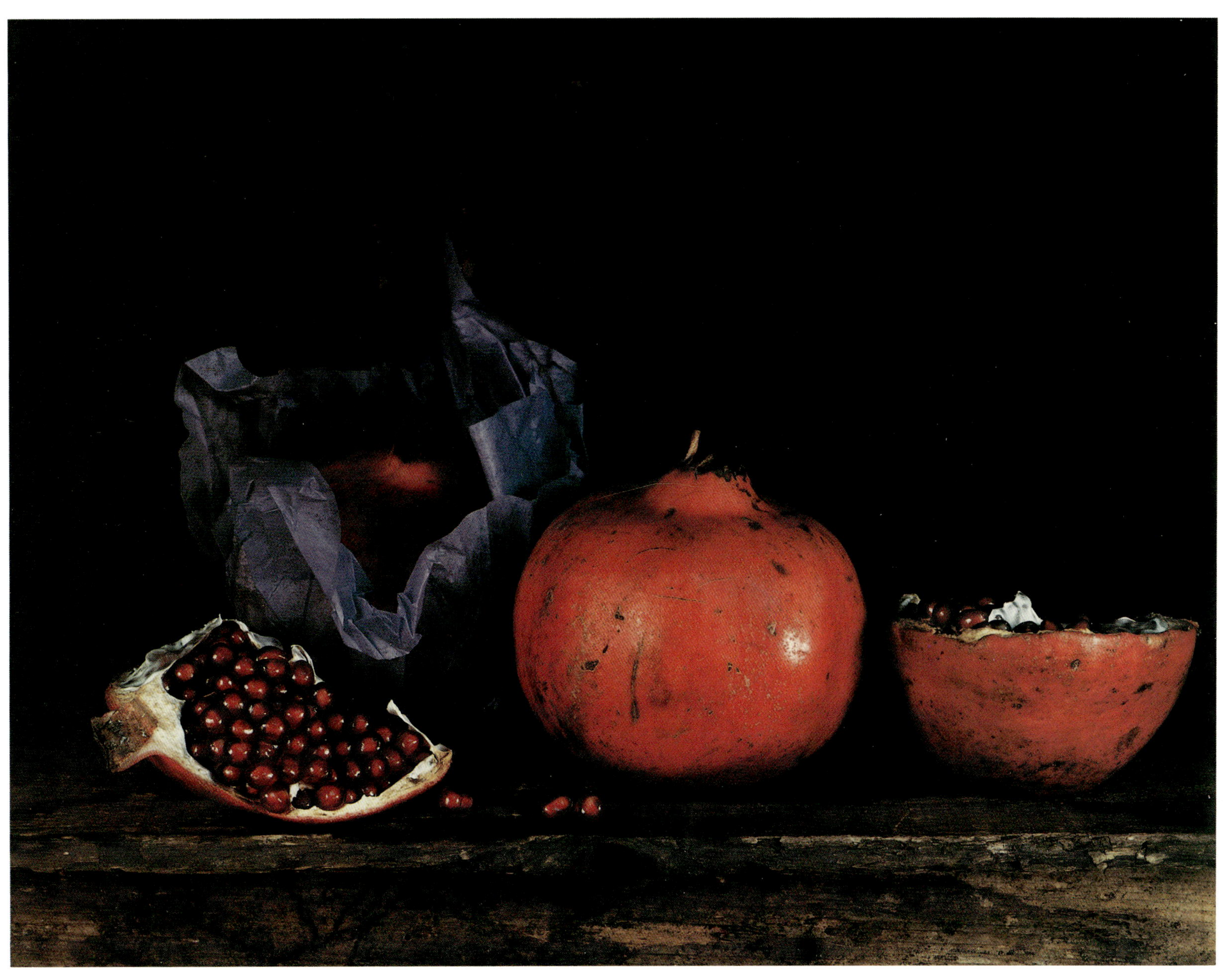

Olivia Parker · *Pomegranates* · 1979

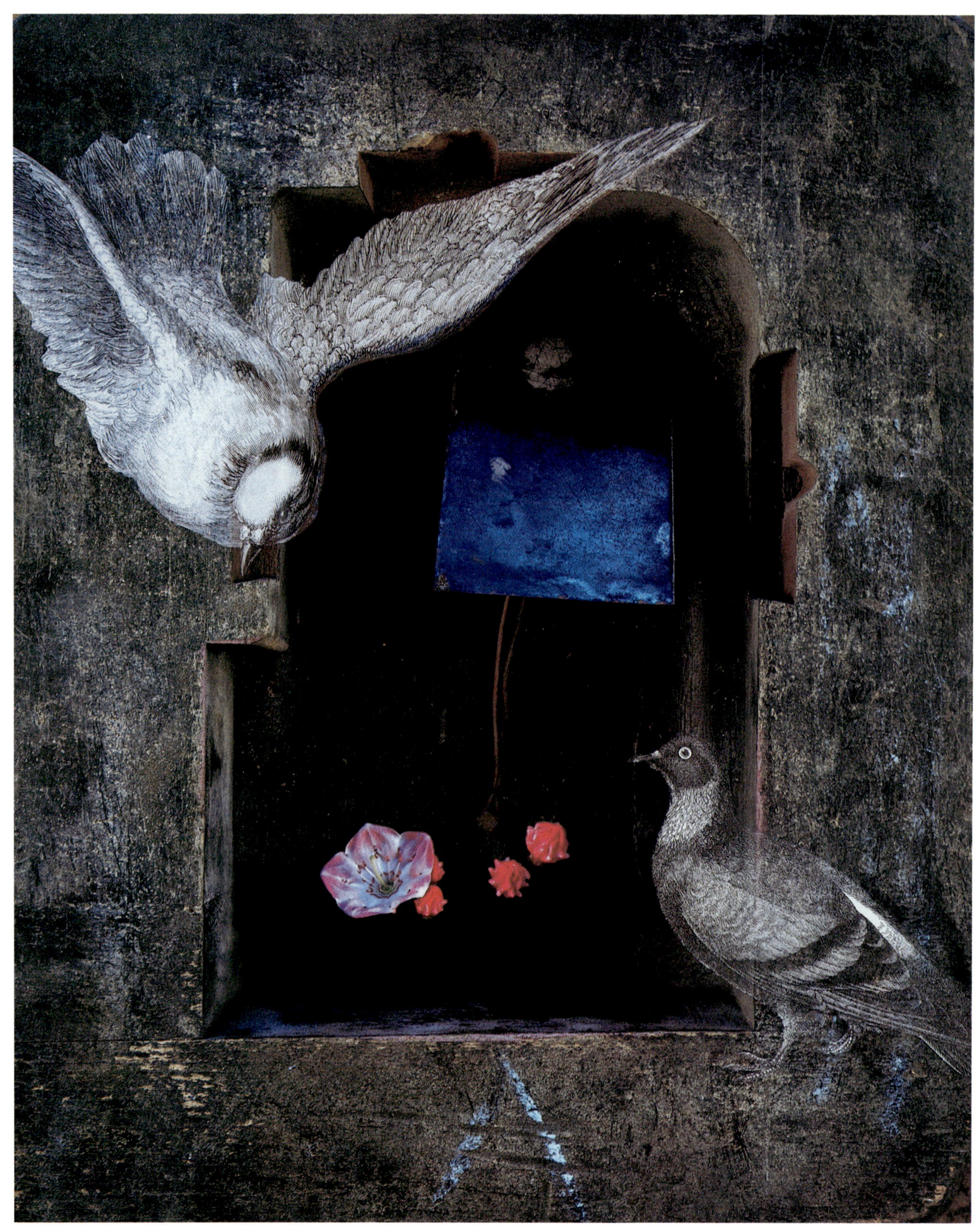

Olivia Parker · *Lares* · 1984

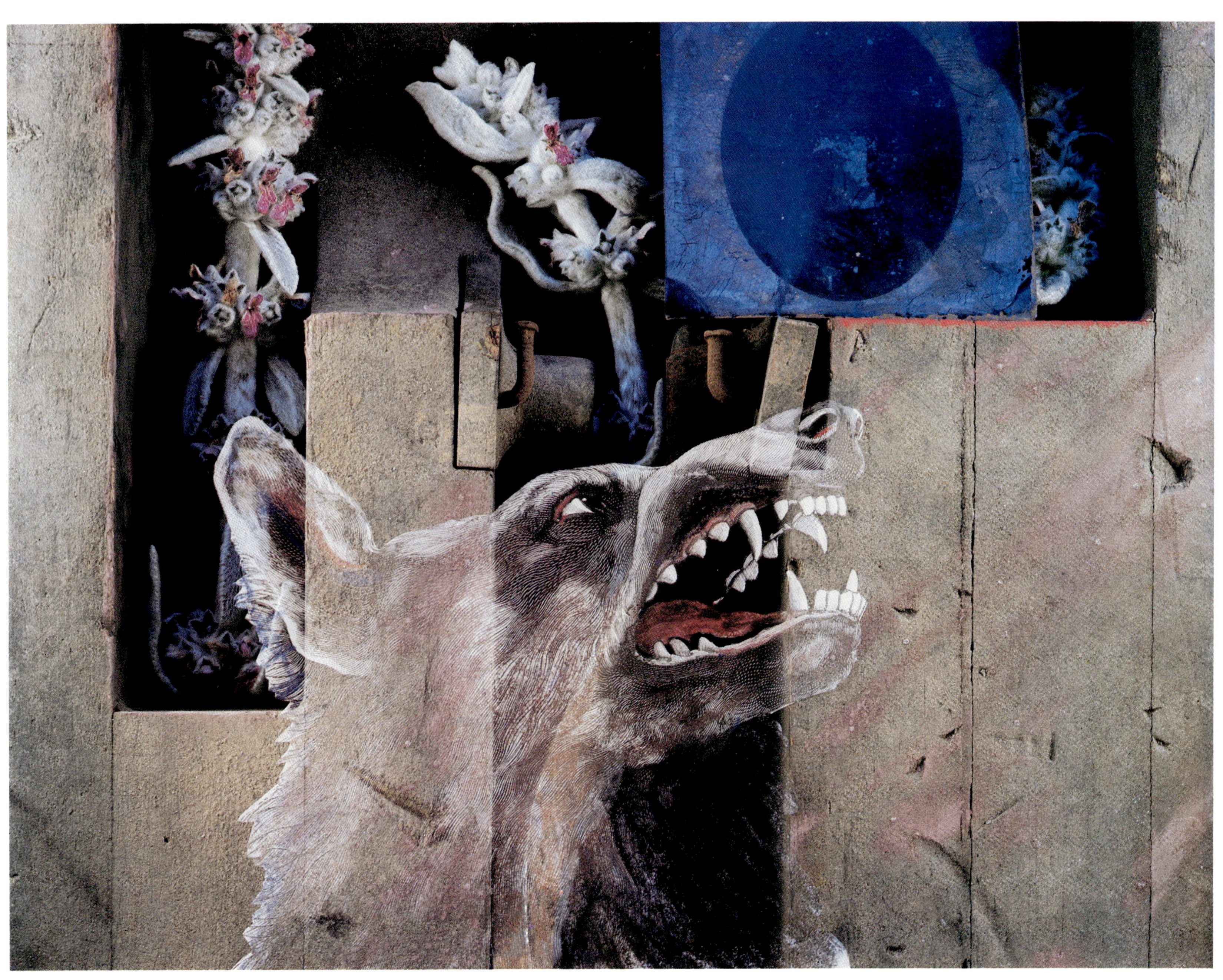

Olivia Parker · *The Wolf in the Door* · 1984

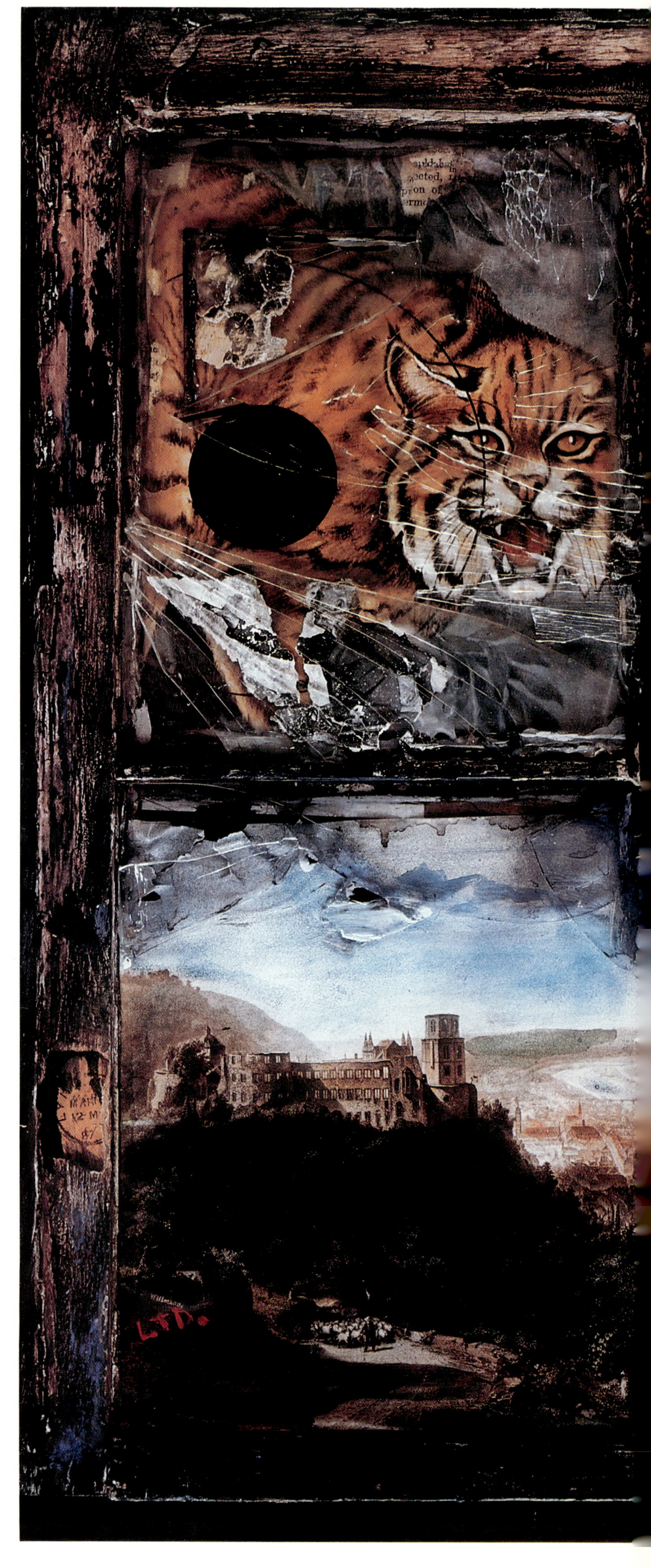

Rosamond Purcell · *Landscape Ltd.* · 1984

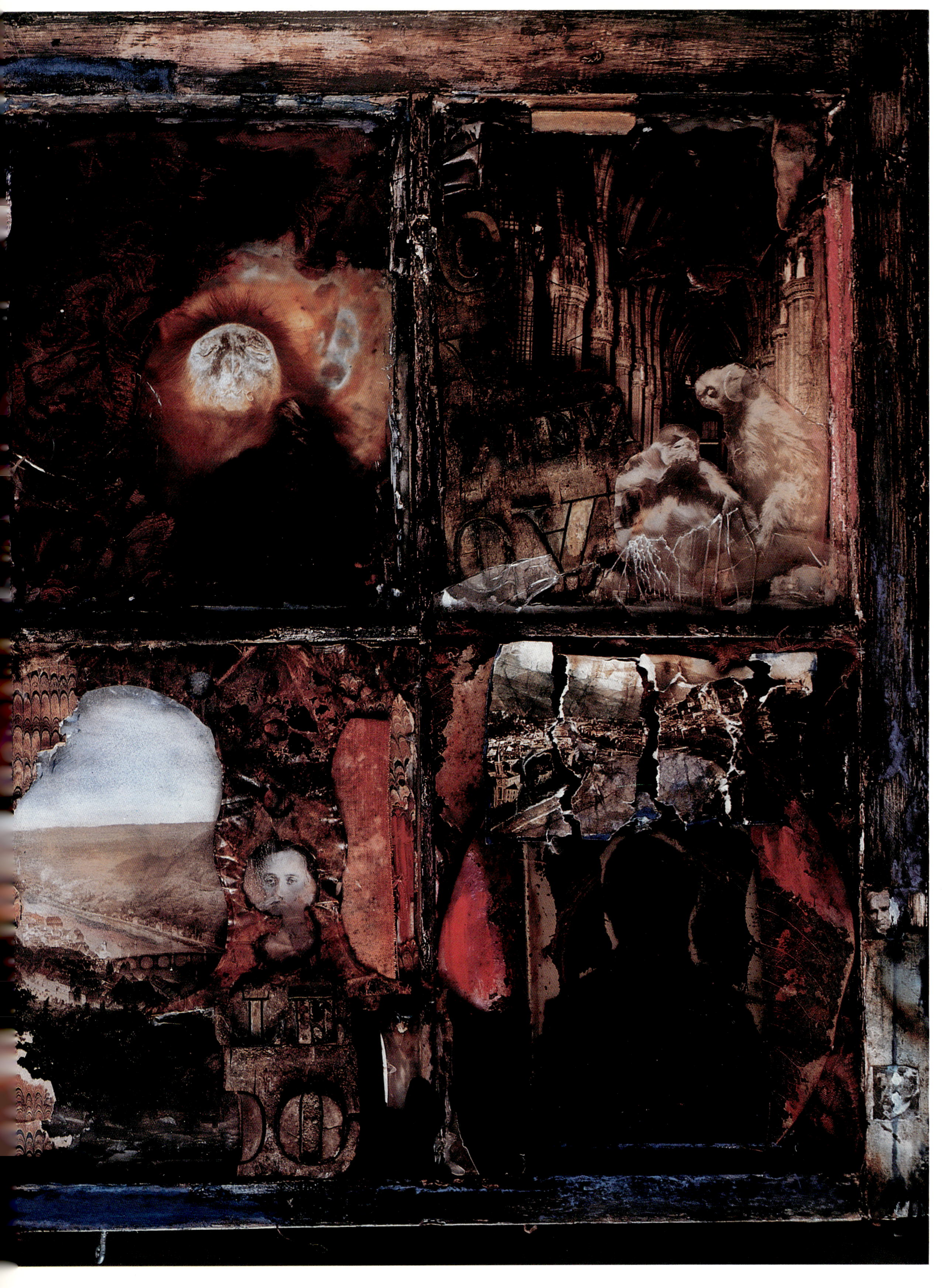

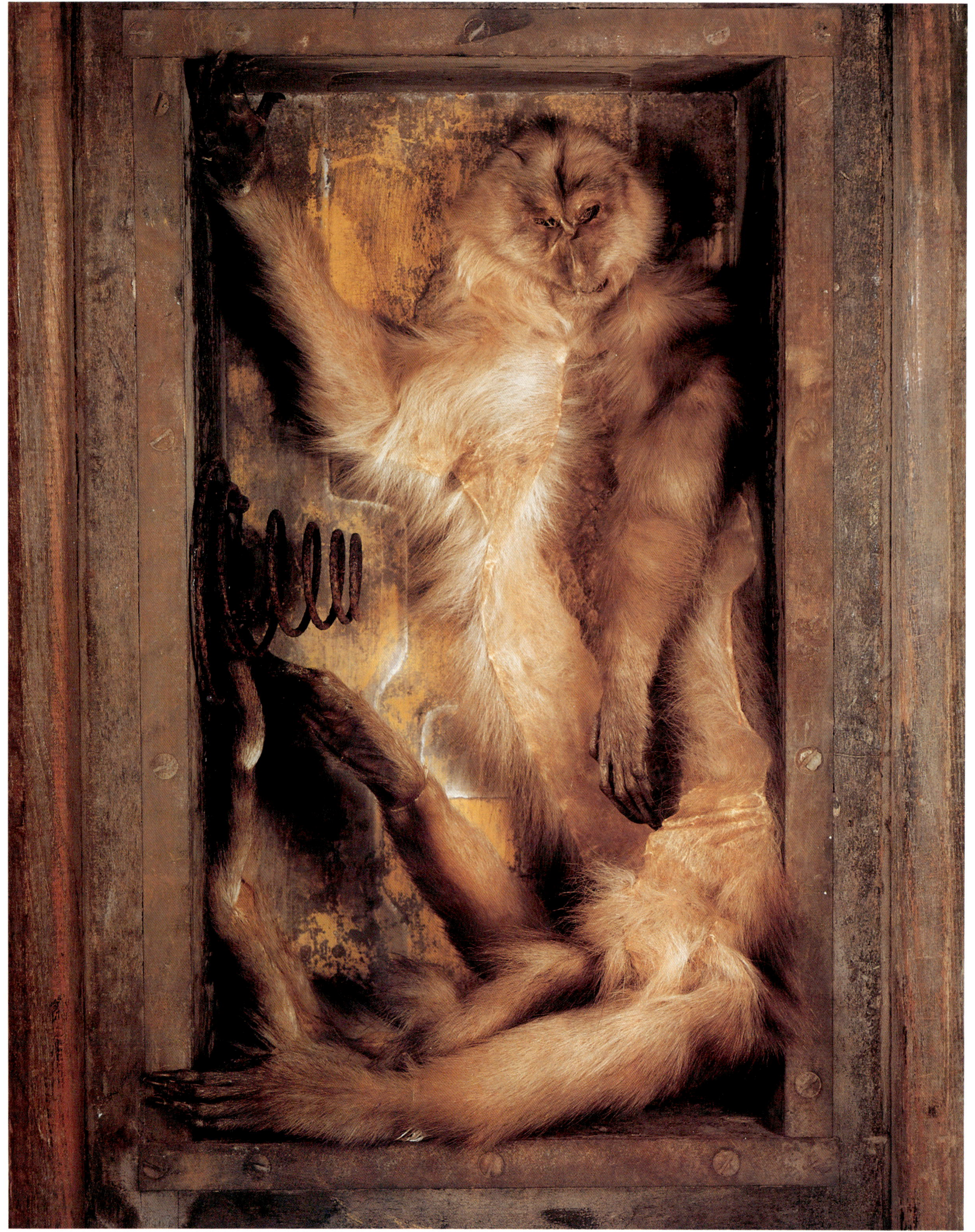

Rosamond Purcell · *Cebus albifrons* · 1984

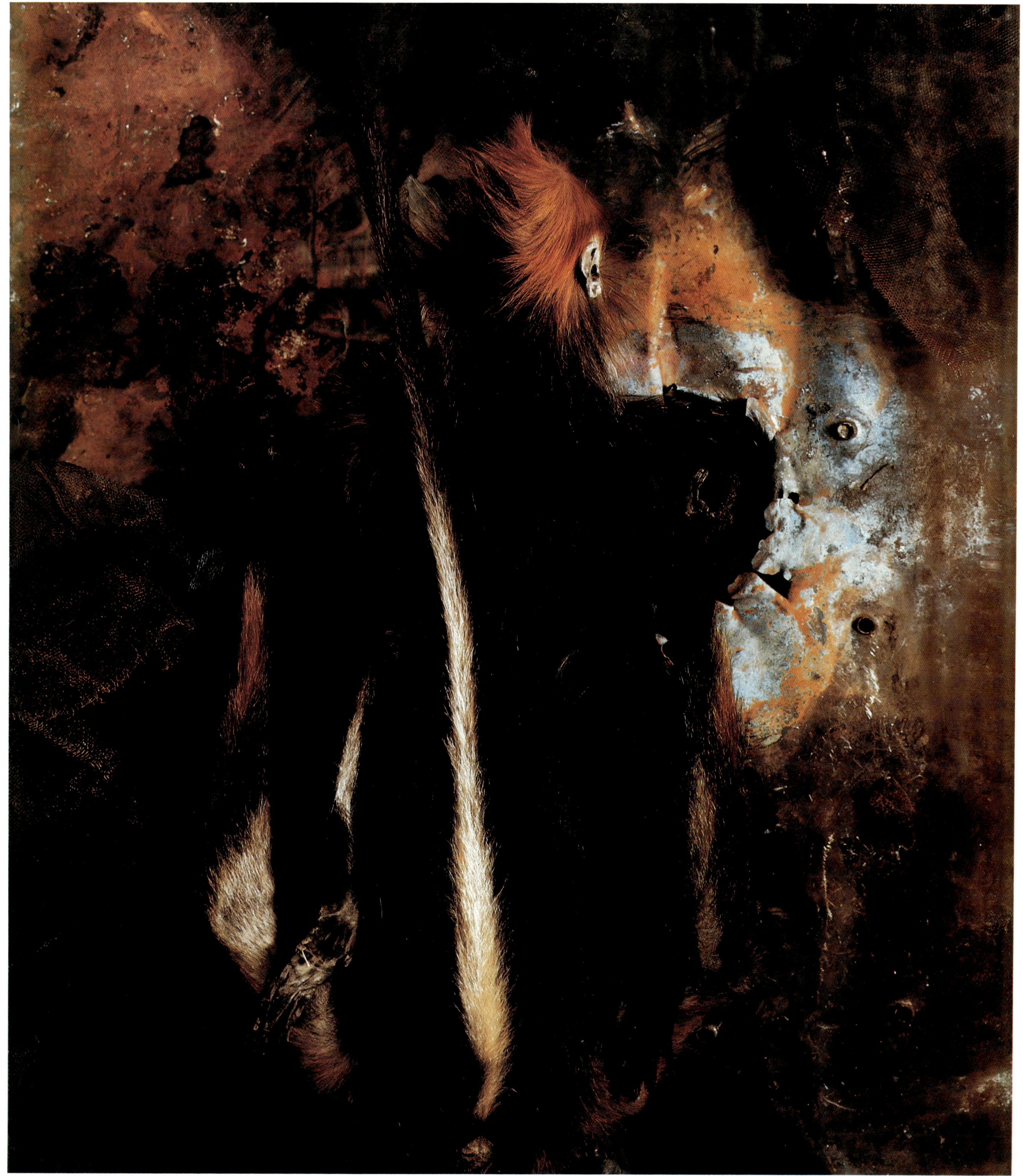

Rosamond Purcell · *Monkey/Ear* · 1983

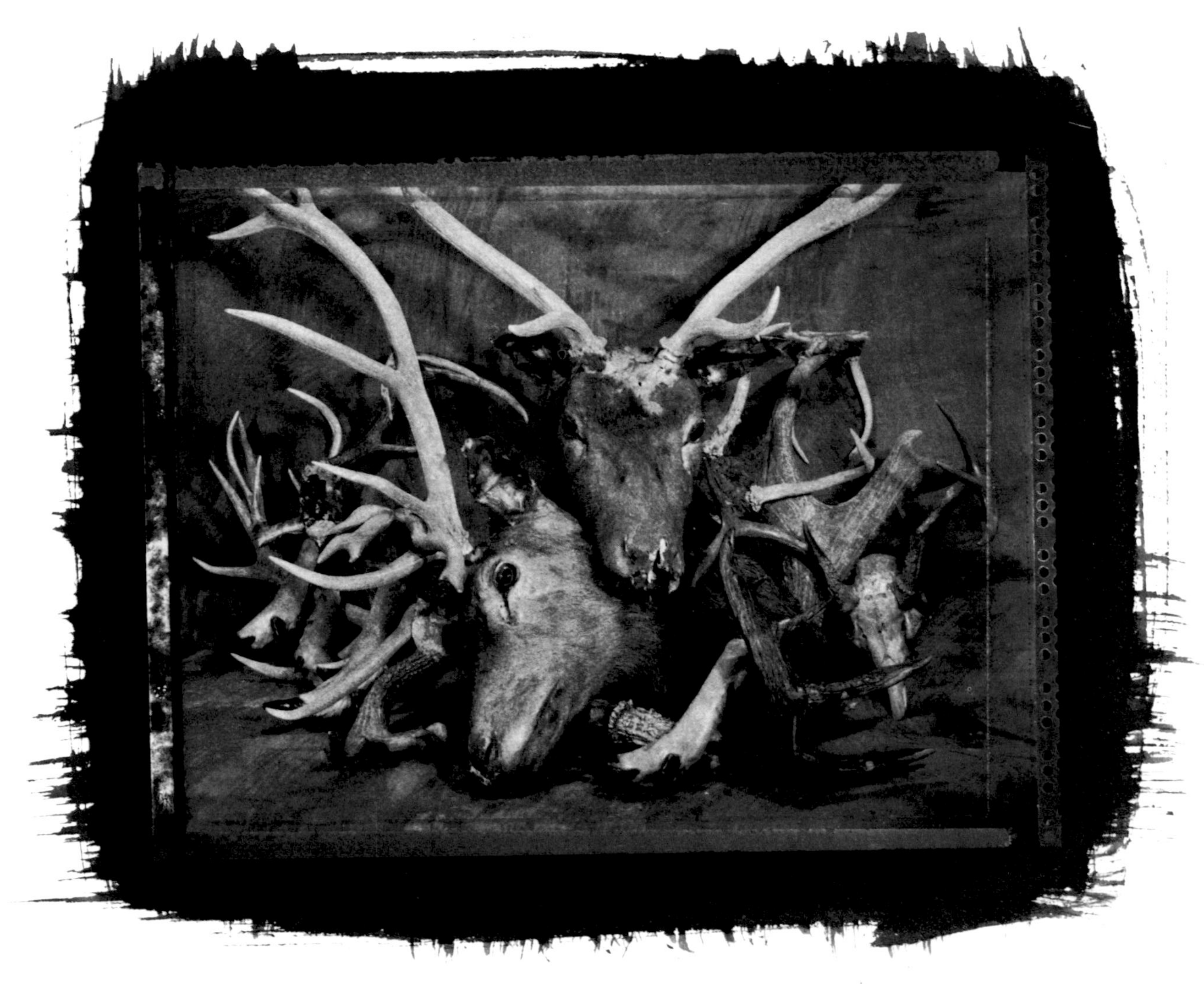

Gwen Akin and Allan Ludwig · *Elk Head Series, #24* · 1987

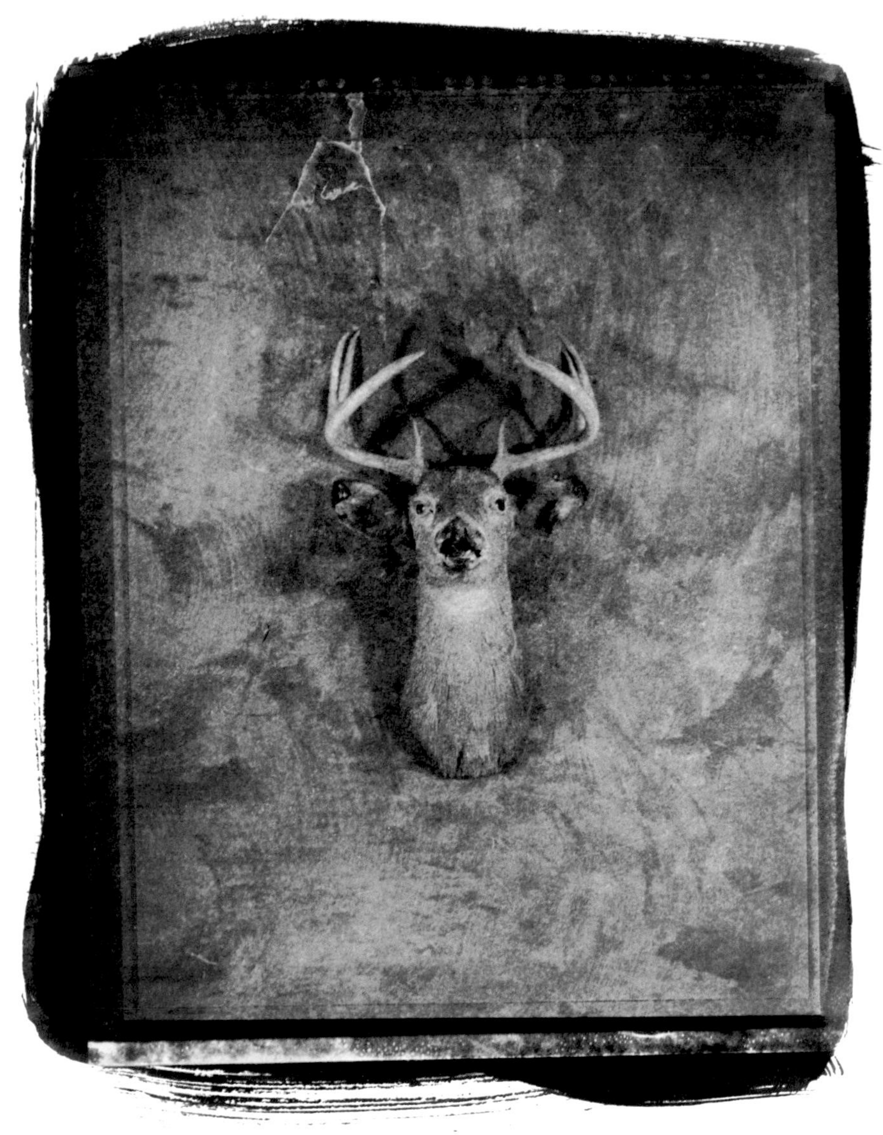

Gwen Akin and Allan Ludwig · *Elk Head Series, #18* · 1987

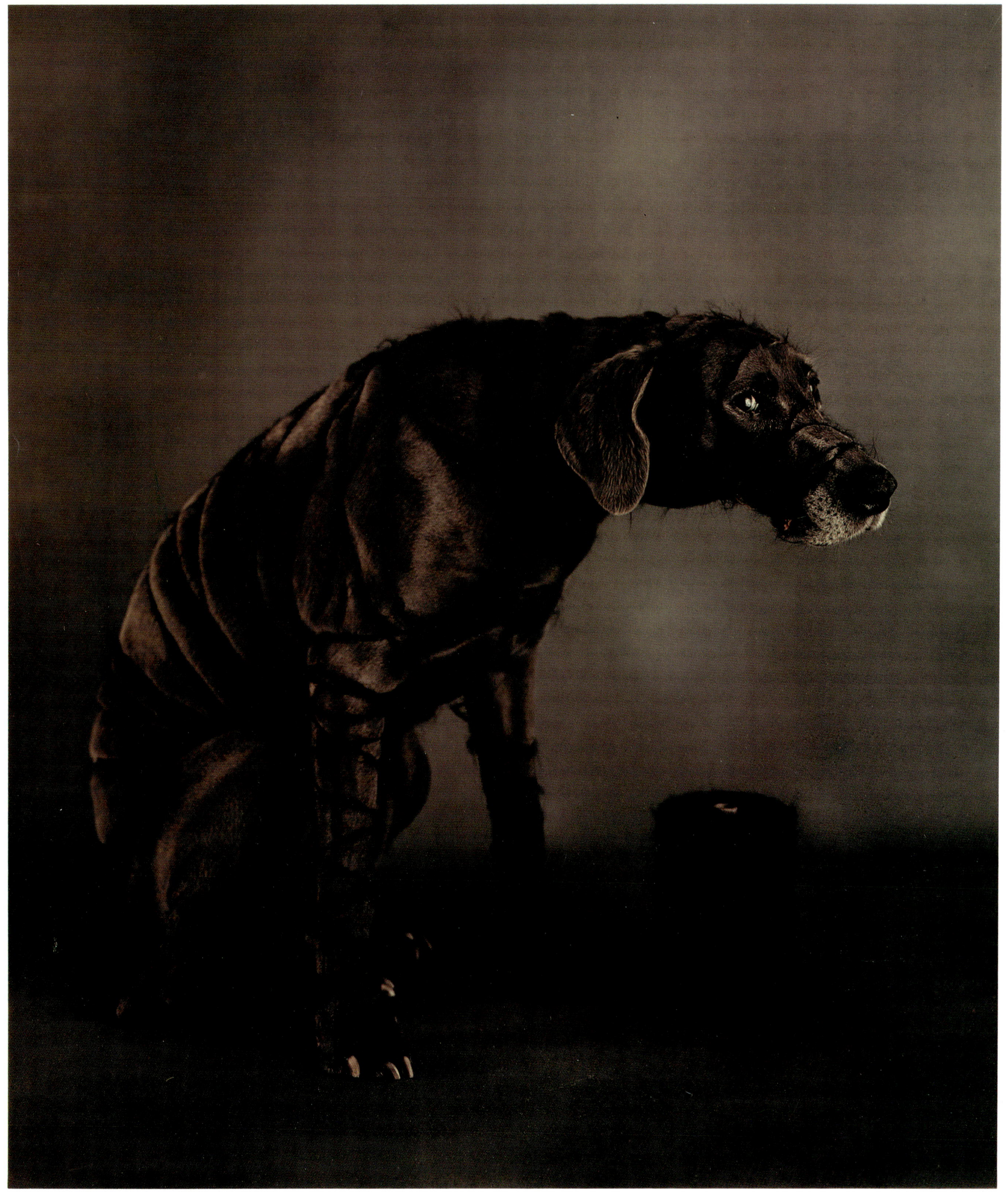

William Wegman · *Yarn (Chardin)* · 1982

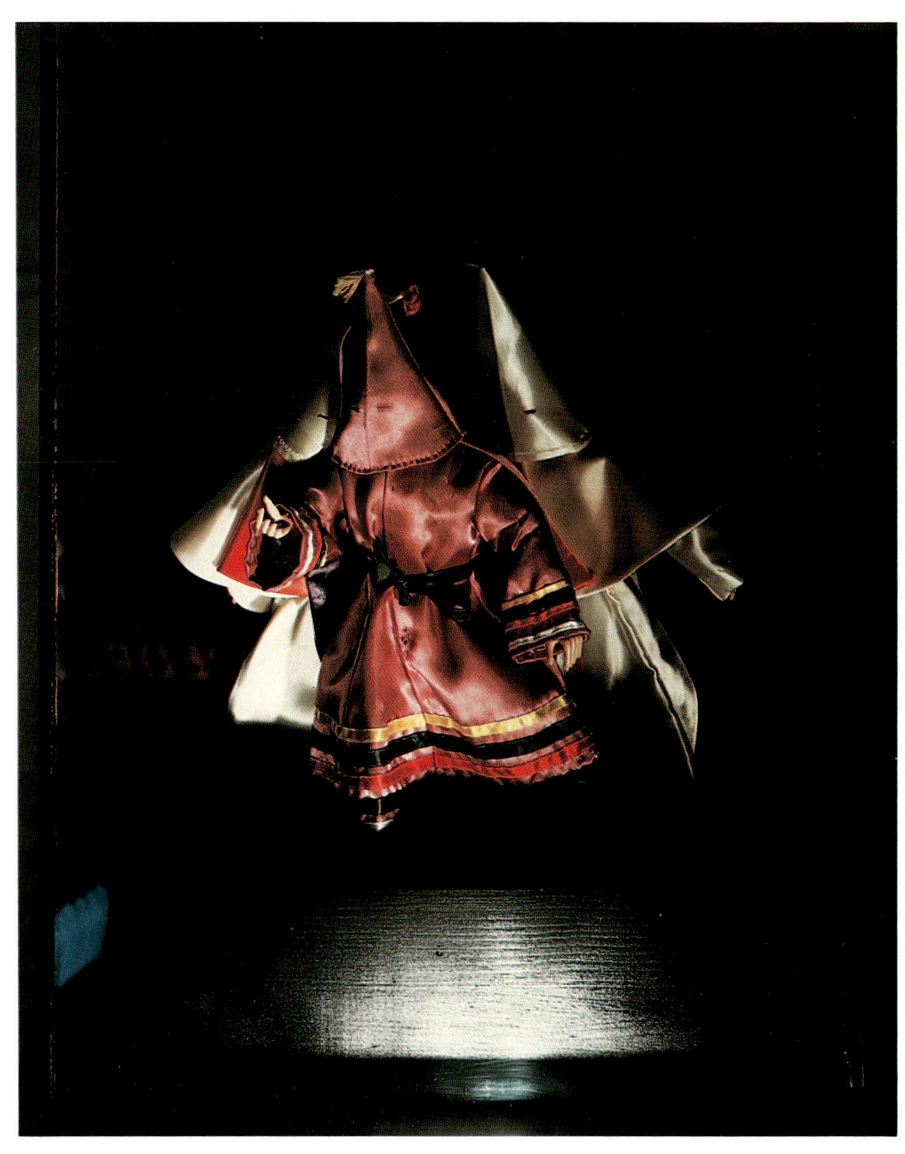

William Christenberry · *From the Klan Room* · 1978

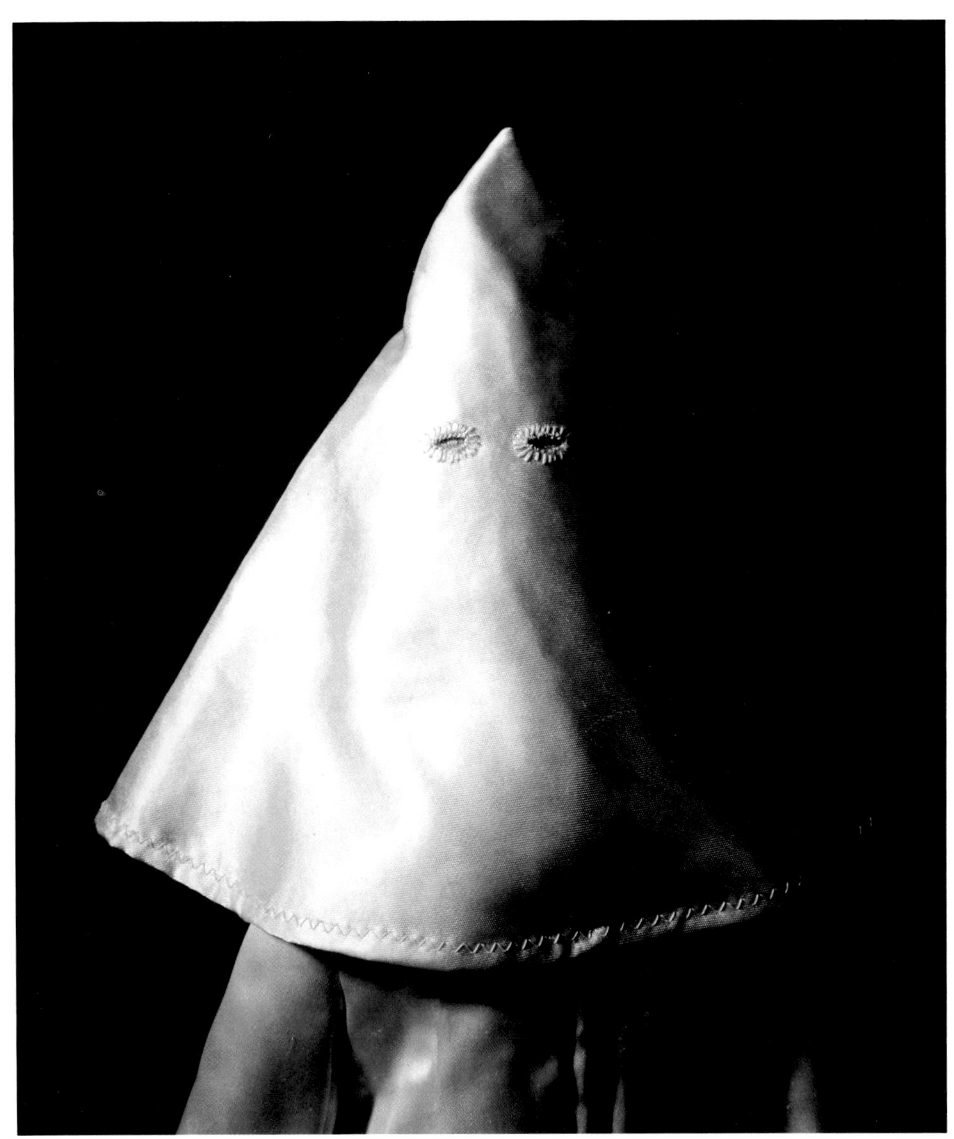

William Christenberry · *From the Klan Room* · 1984

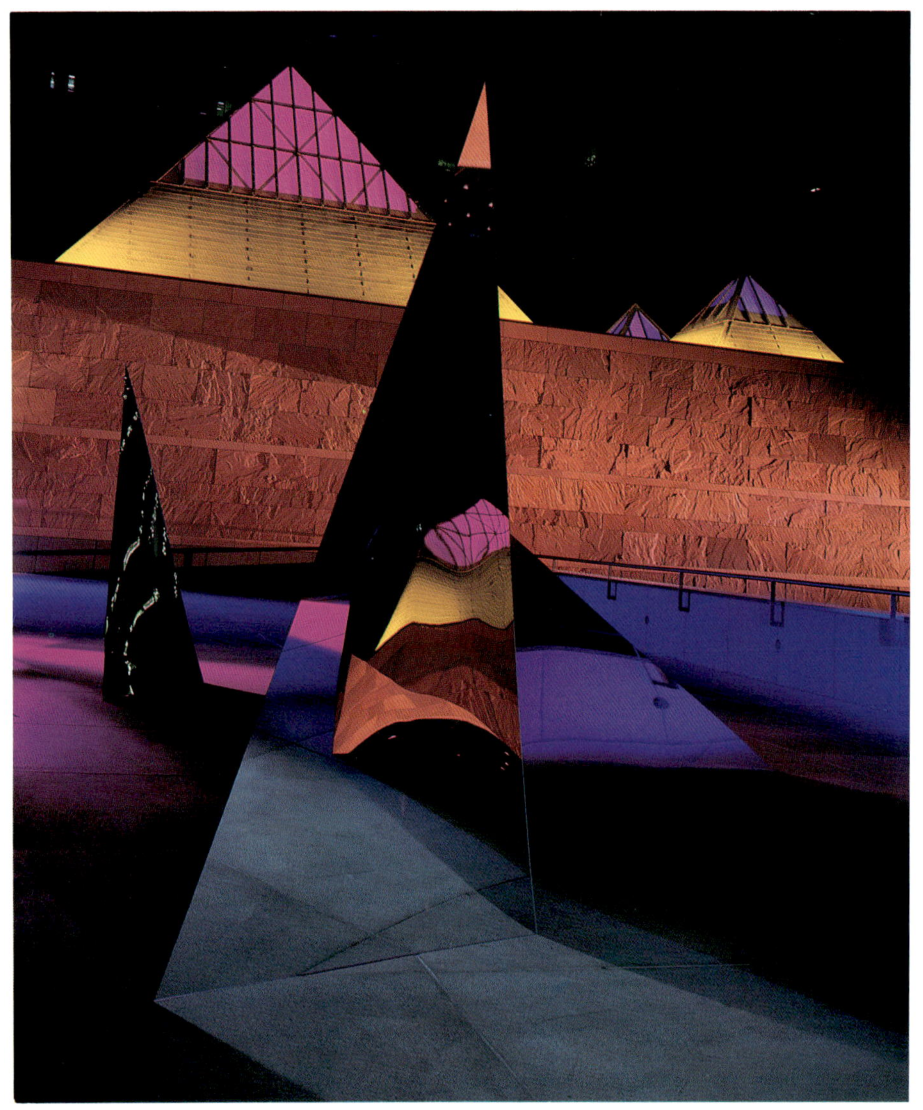

Barbara Kasten · *Architectural Site 10* · 1986

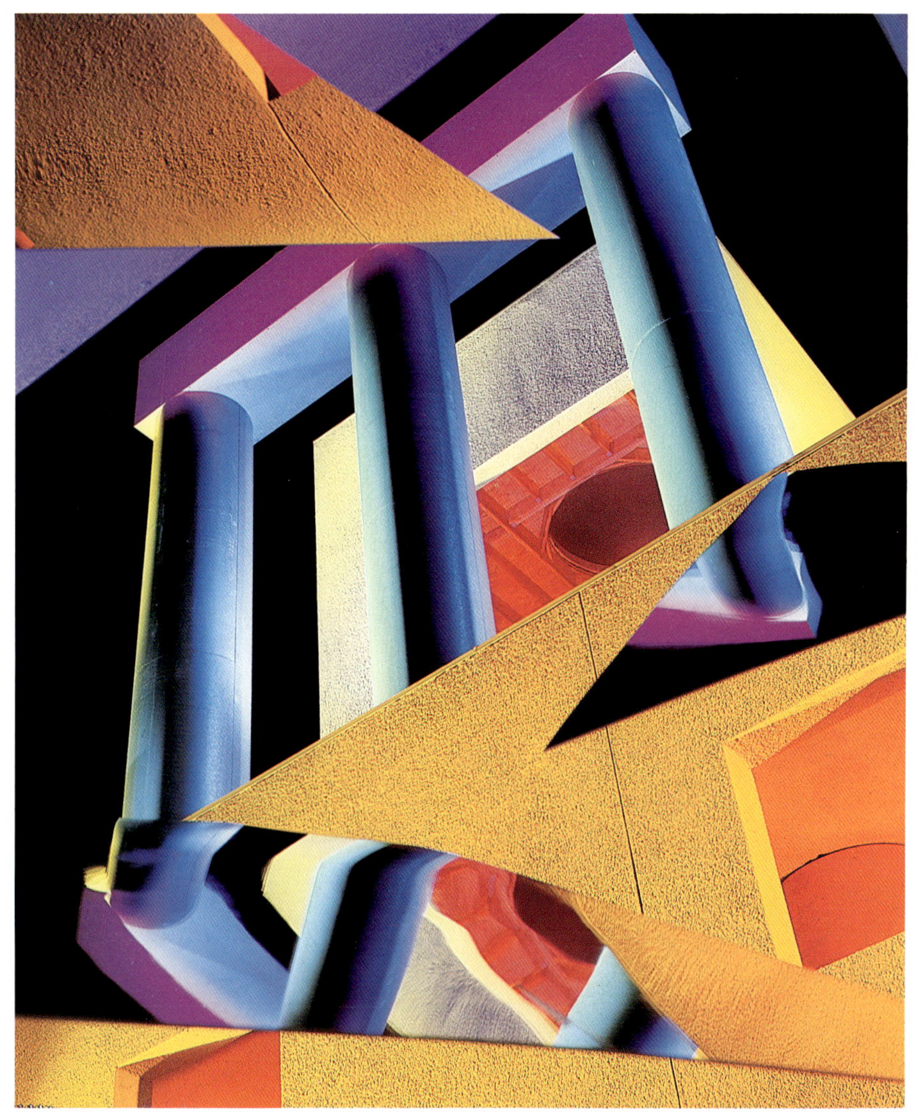

Barbara Kasten · *Architectural Site 8* · 1986

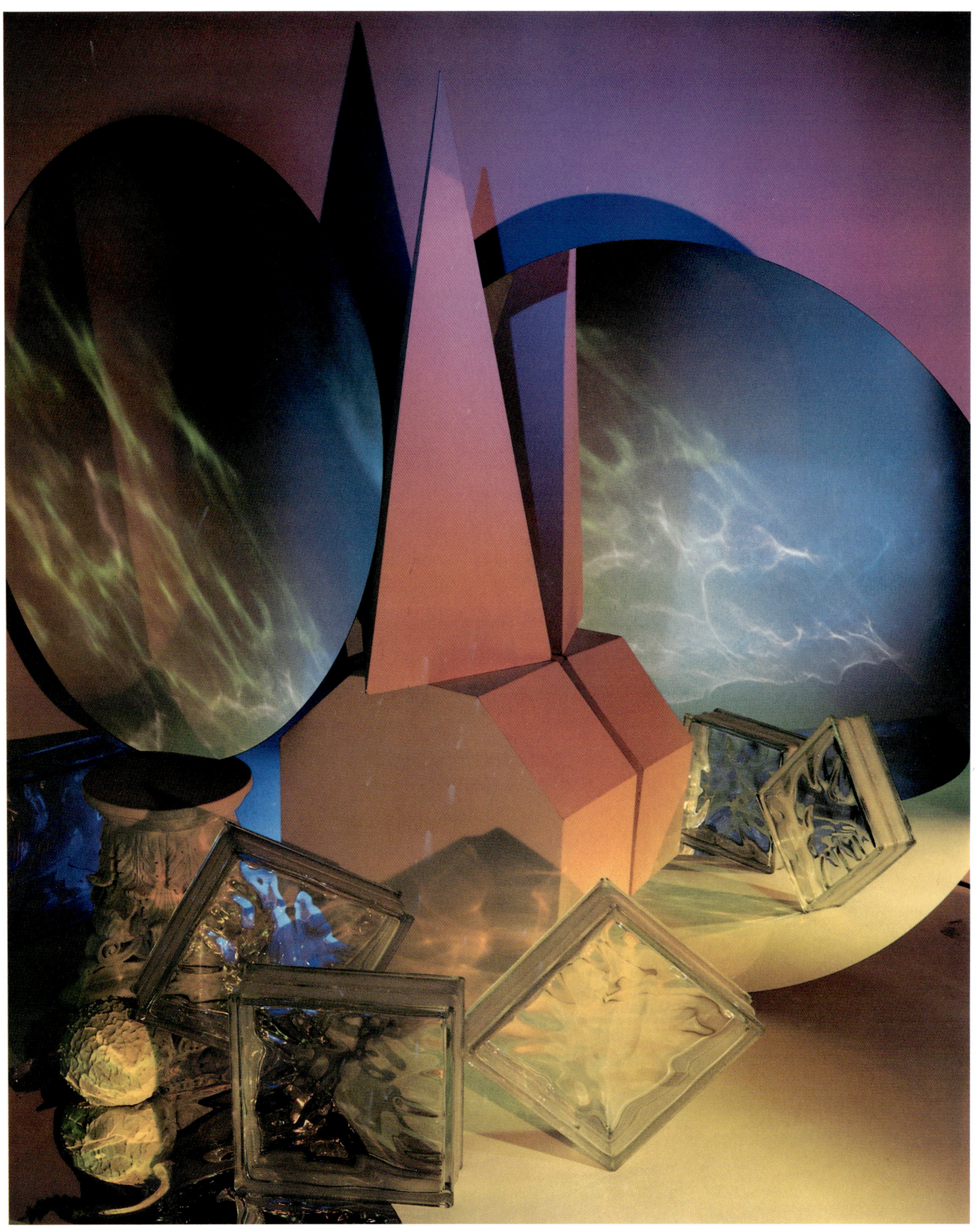

Barbara Kasten · *AP Metaphase 8* (diptych) · 1986

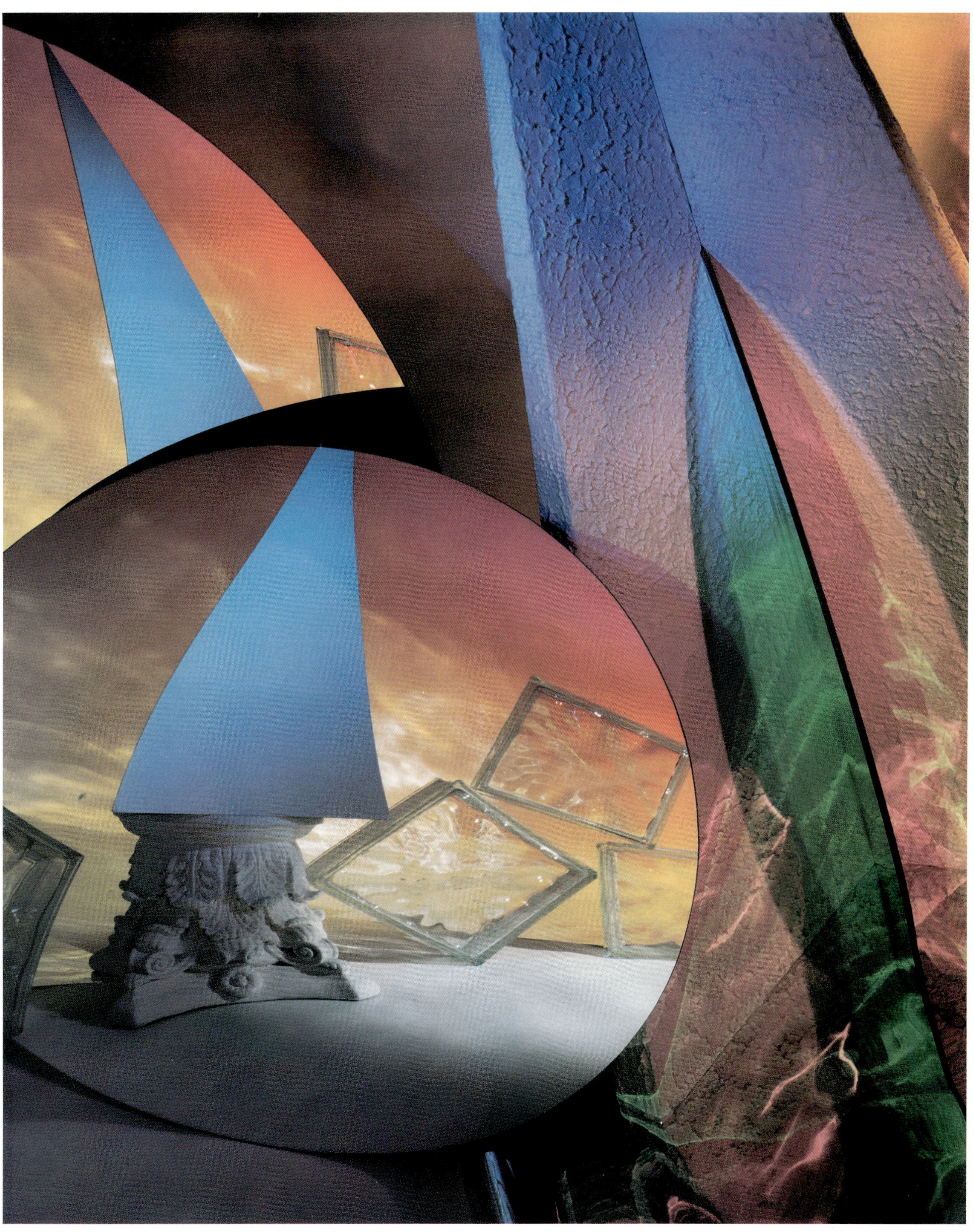

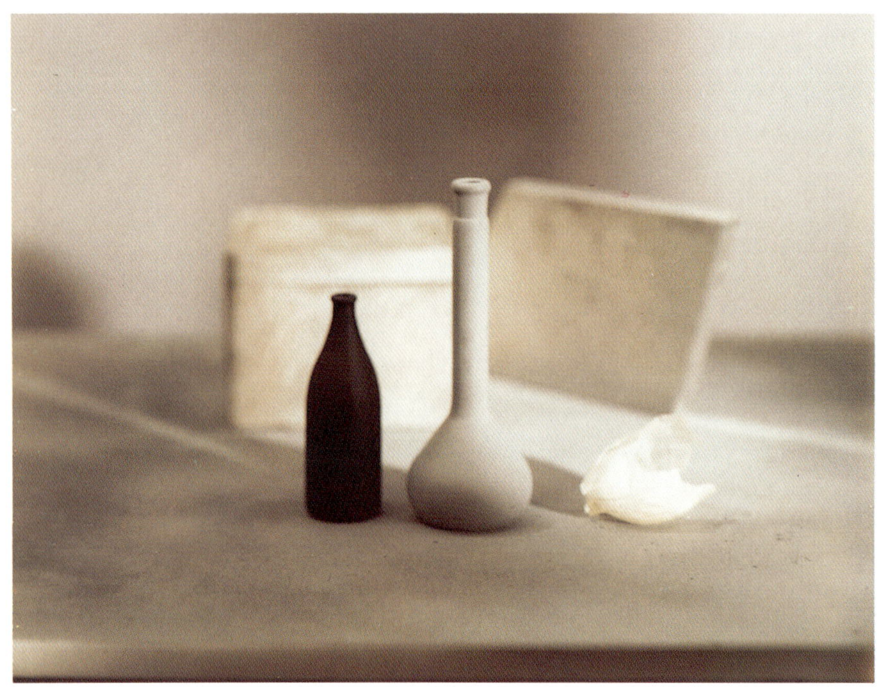

Jan Groover · Untitled · 1986

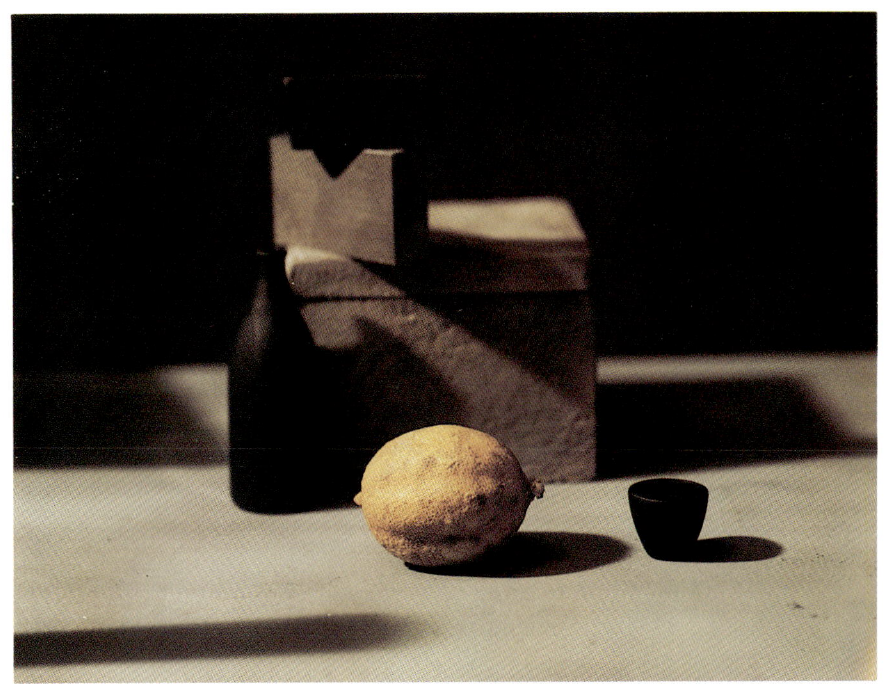

Jan Groover · Untitled · 1986

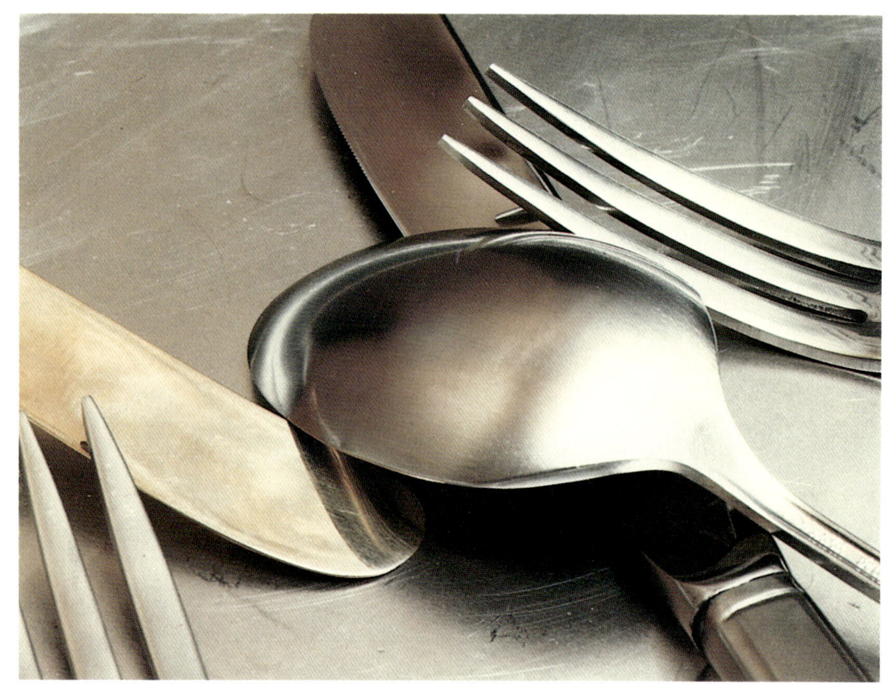

Jan Groover · Untitled · 1979

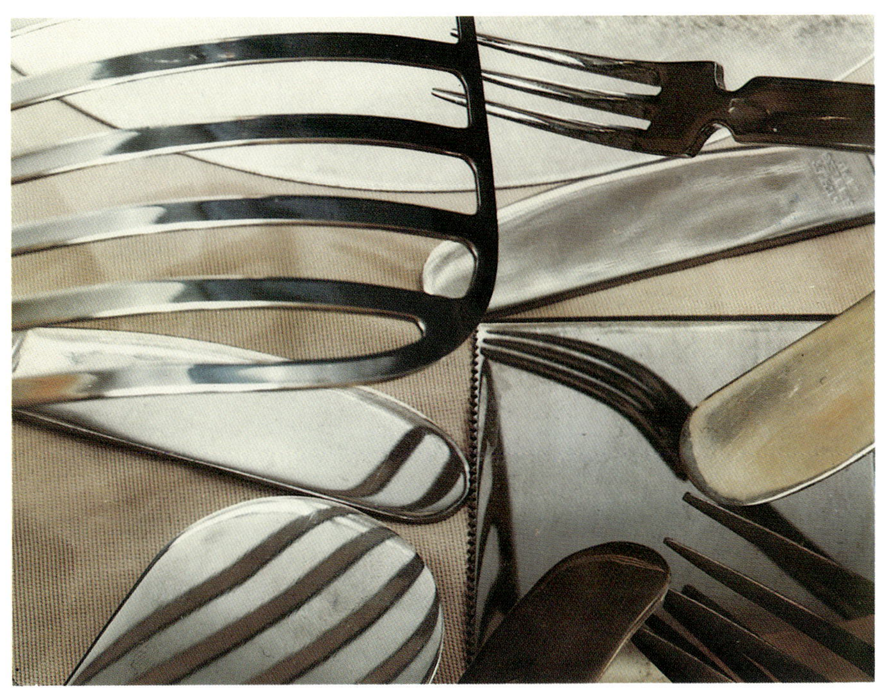

Jan Groover · Untitled · 1979

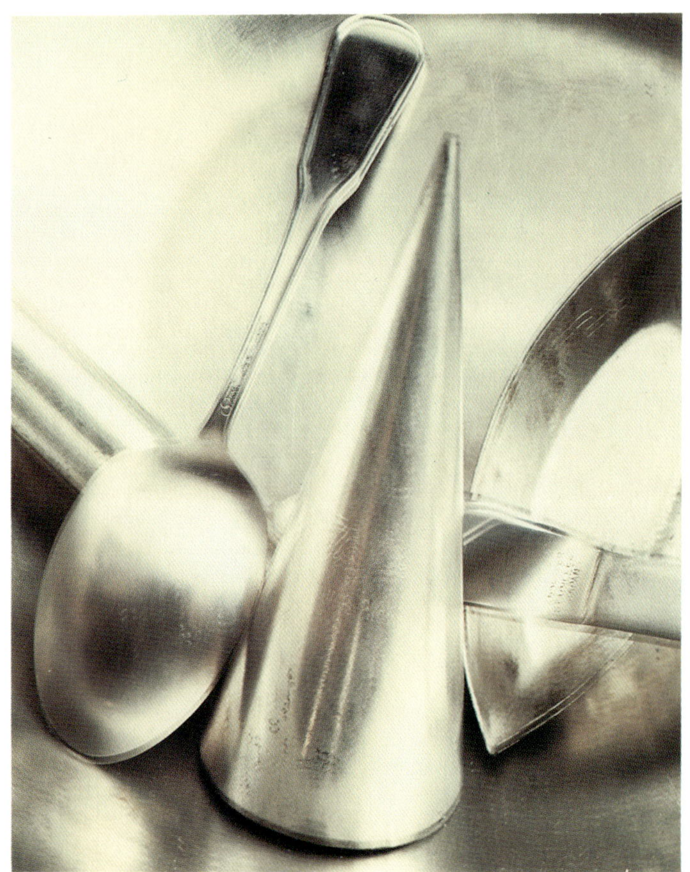

Jan Groover · Untitled · 1980

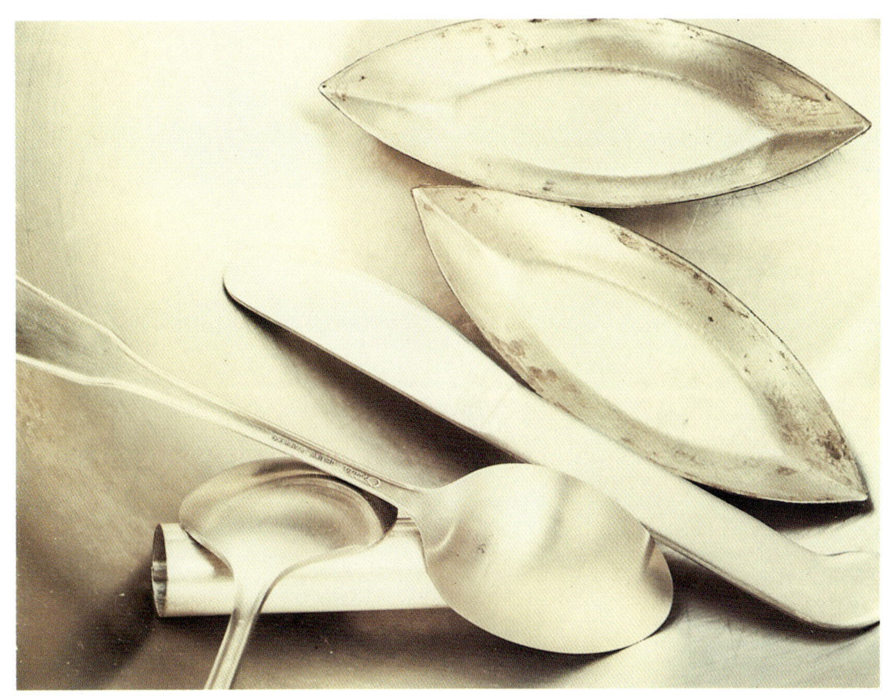

Jan Groover · Untitled · 1980

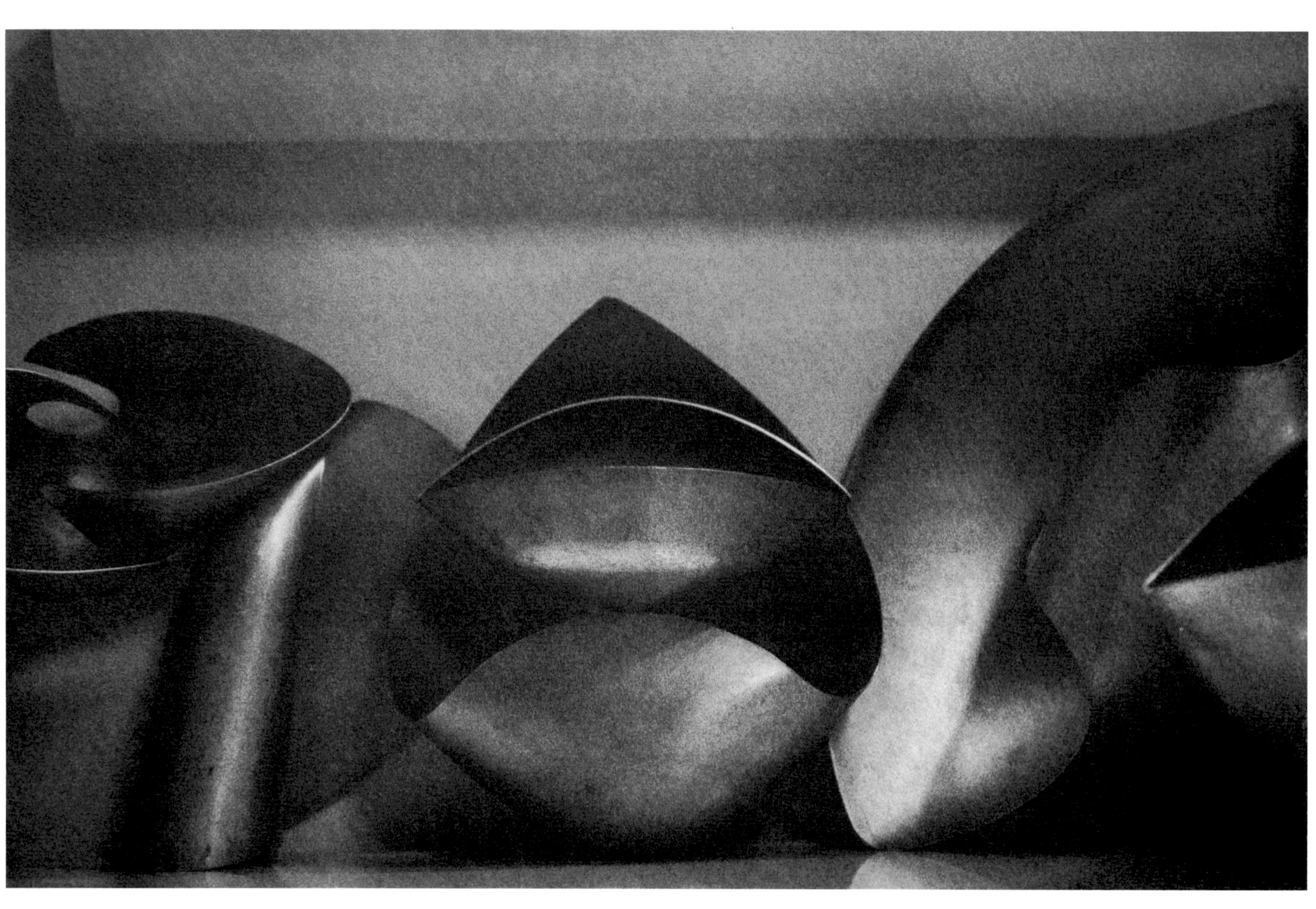

Sheila Metzner · *Mouillé Shapes* · 1986

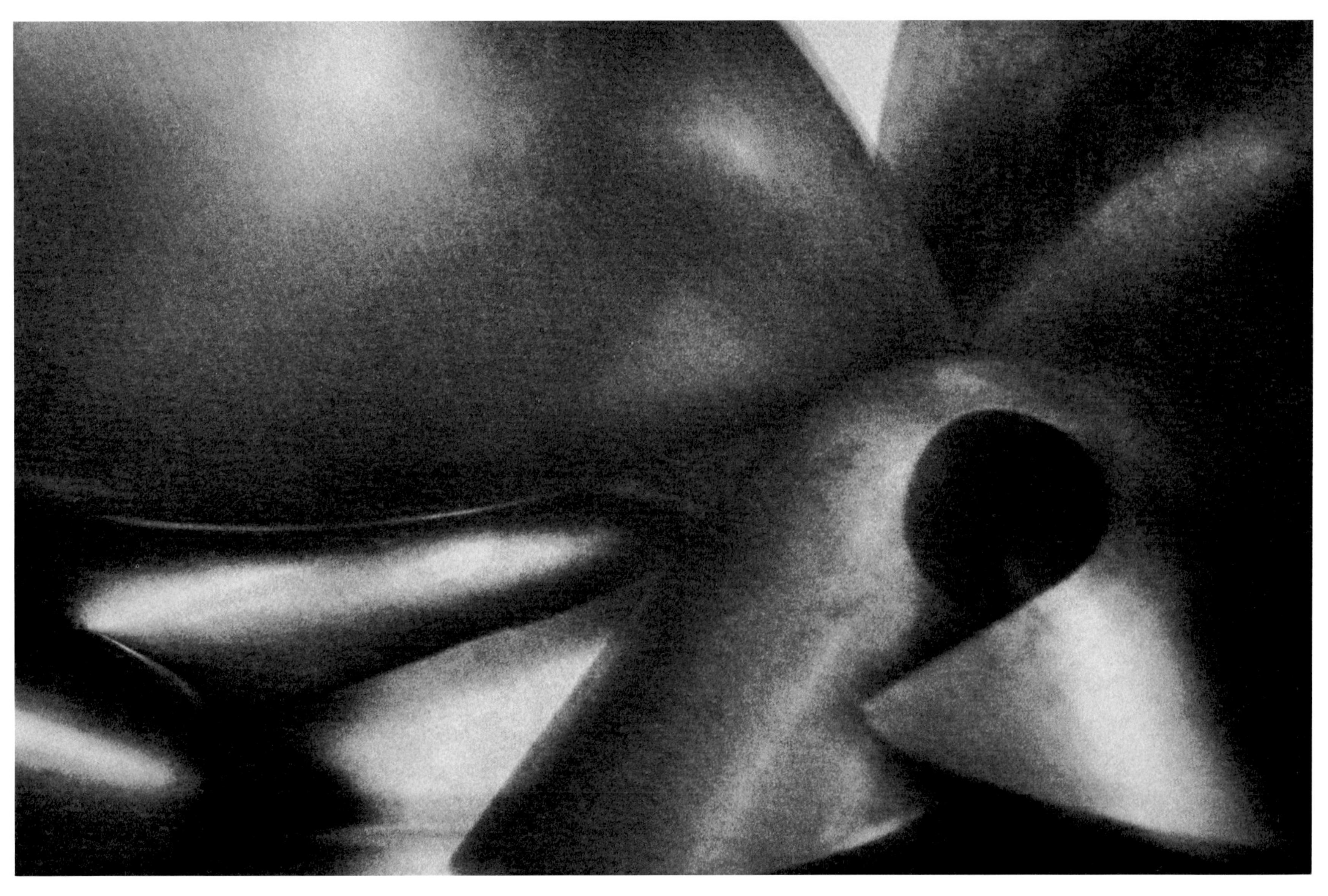

Sheila Metzner · *Mouillé Shapes* · 1986

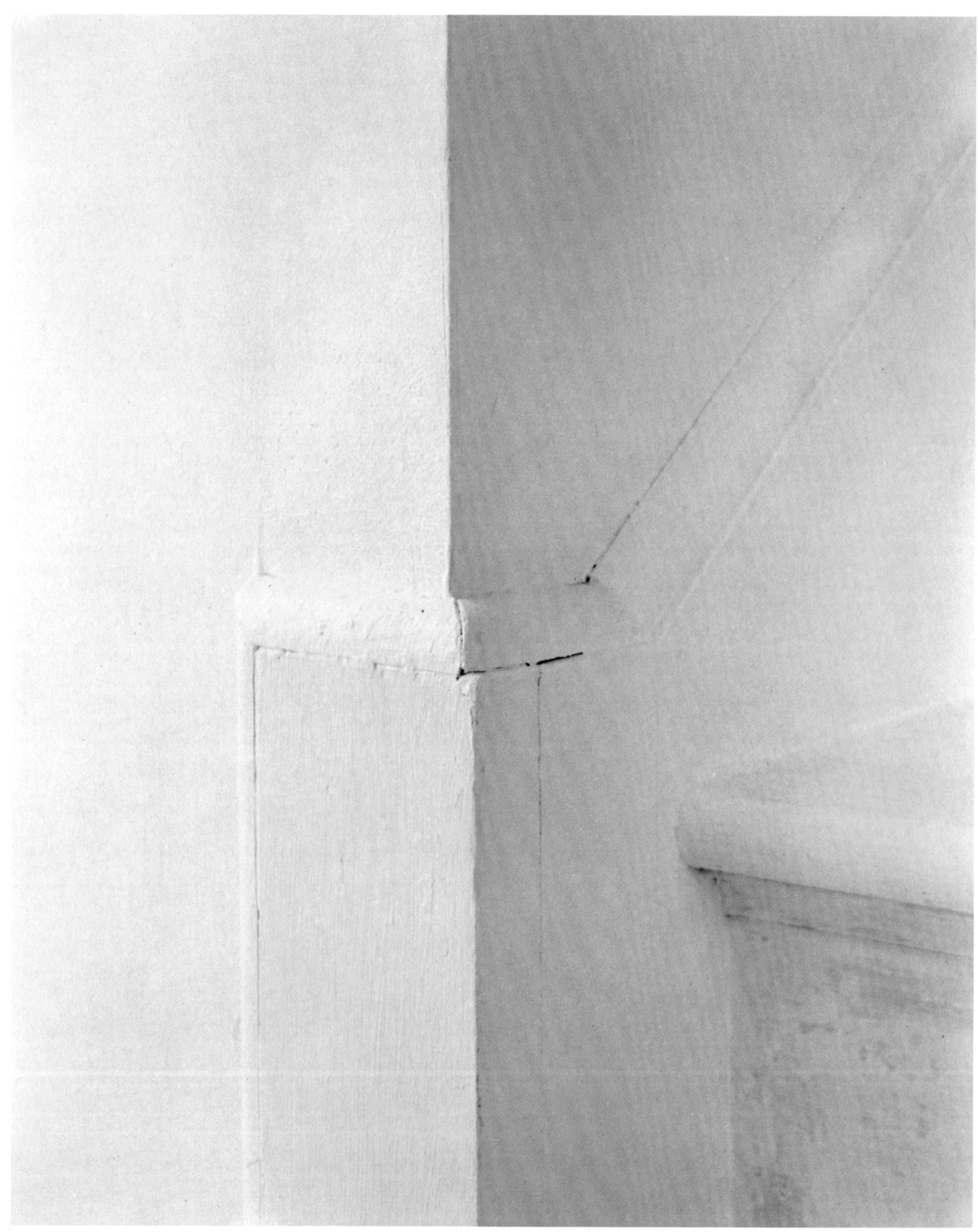

Grace Knowlton · *Stair Turning* · 1984

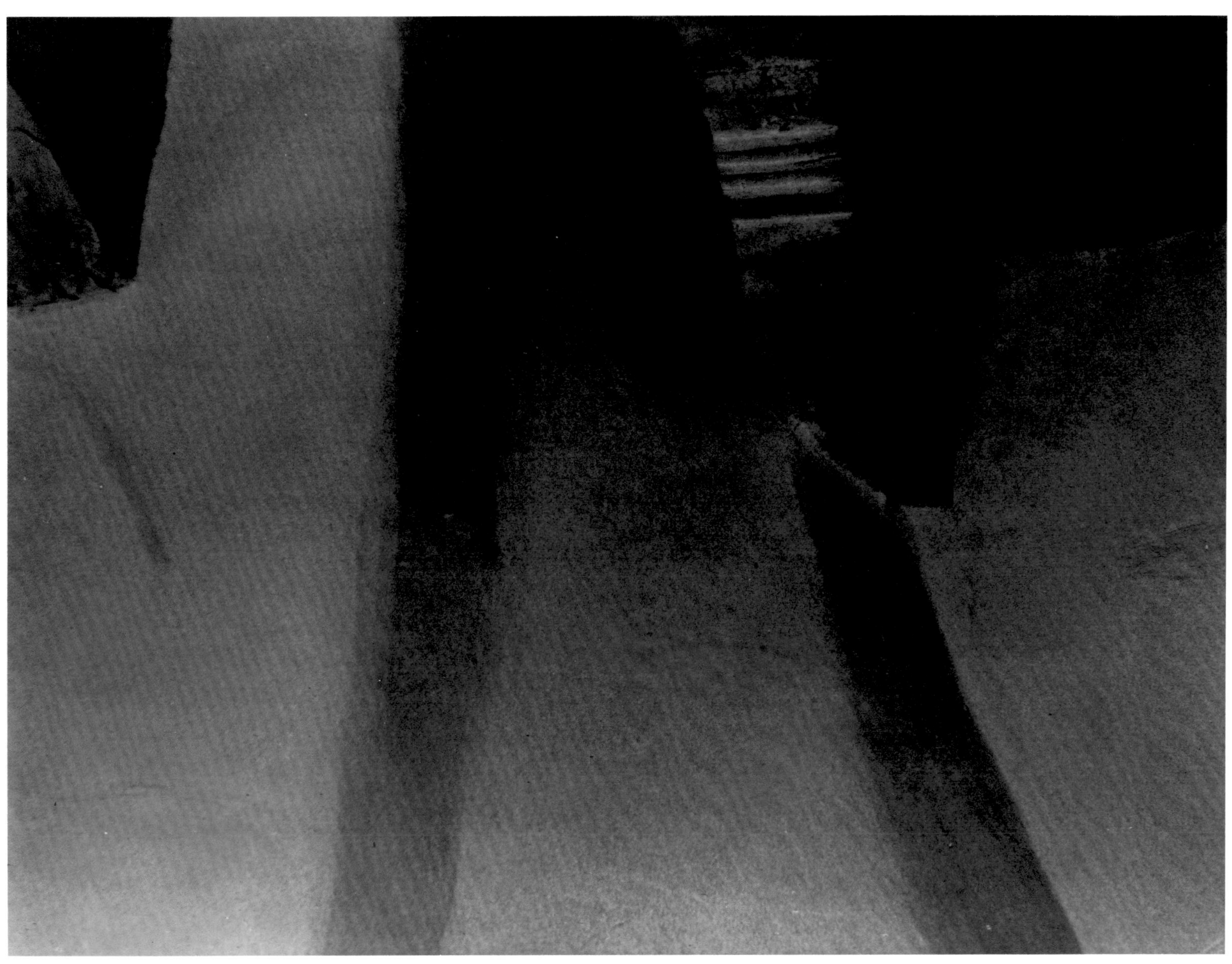

Grace Knowlton · *Adobe Chimney, Cerro Gordo* · 1985

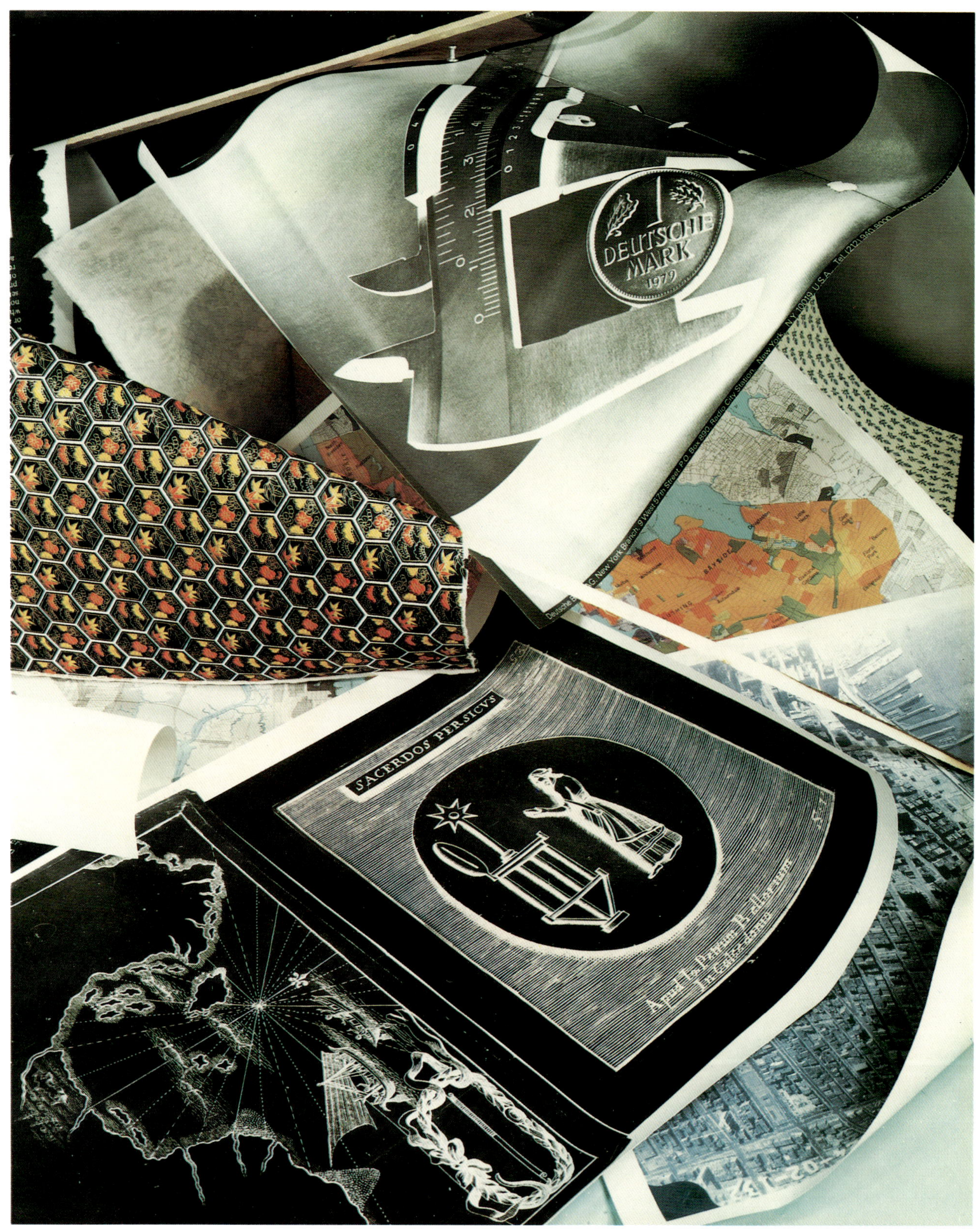

Victor Schrager · Untitled (Deutsche mark) · 1979

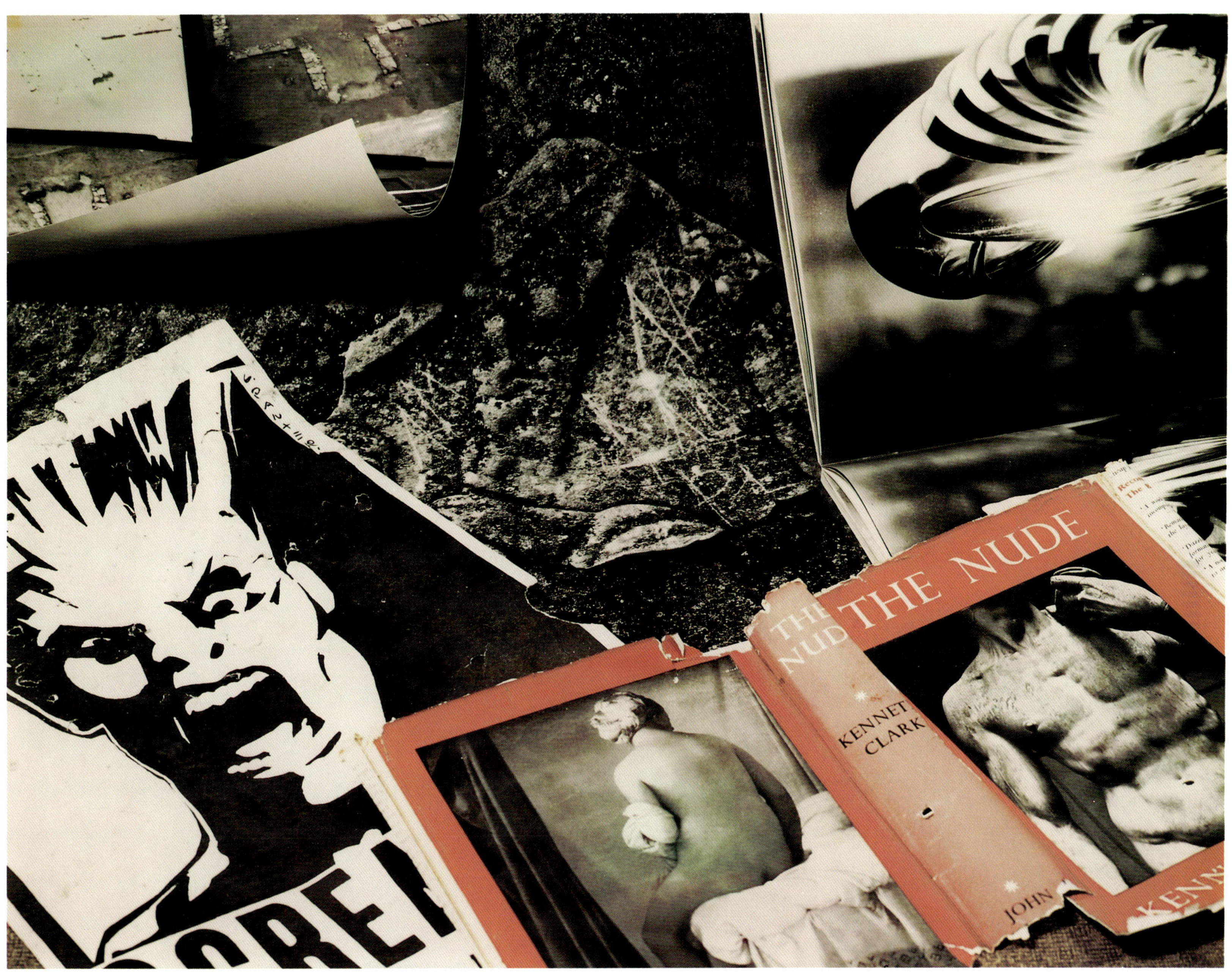

Victor Schrager · Untitled *(The Nude)* · 1978

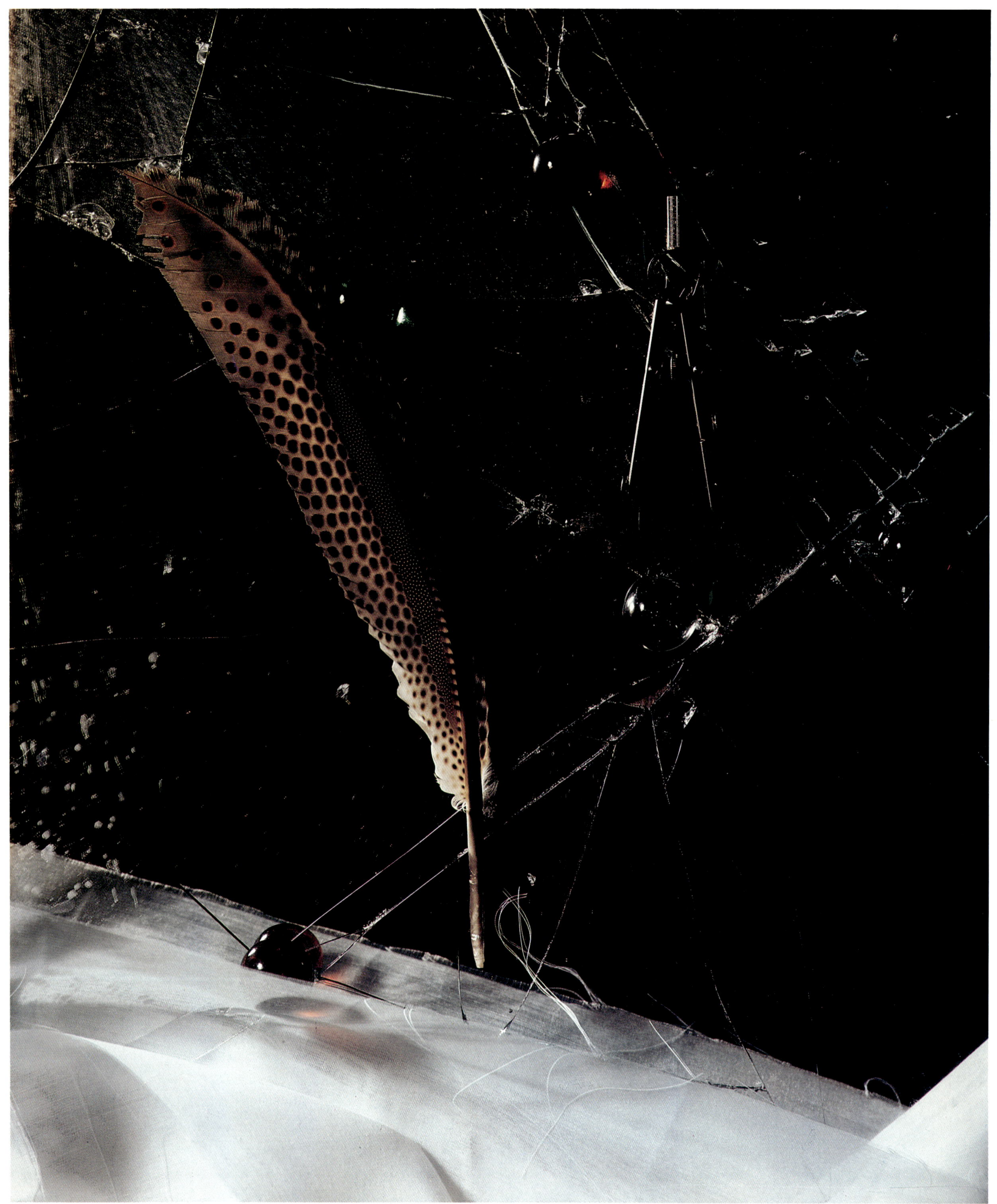

Gyorgy Kepes · Untitled · 1987

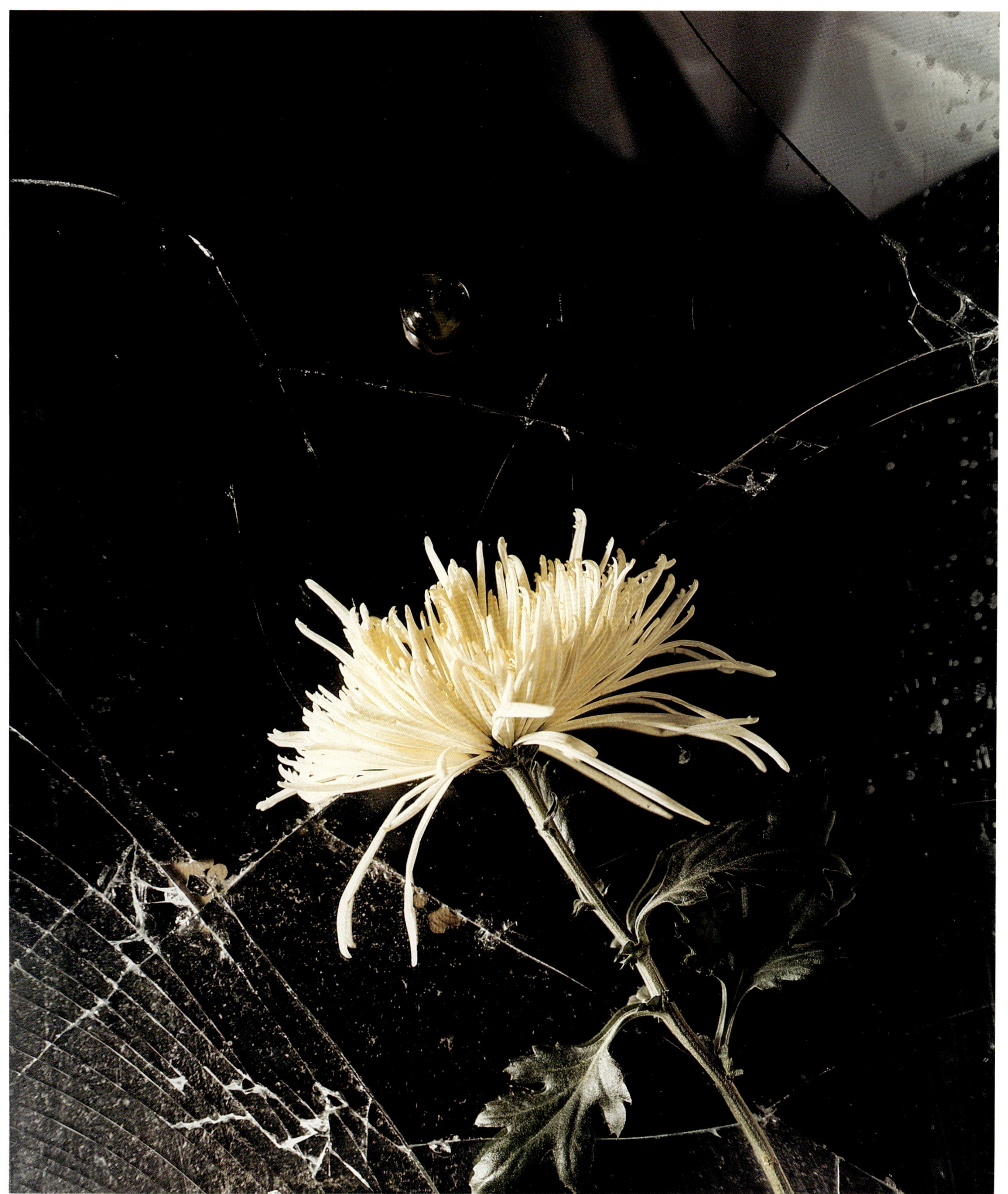

Gyorgy Kepes · Untitled · 1987

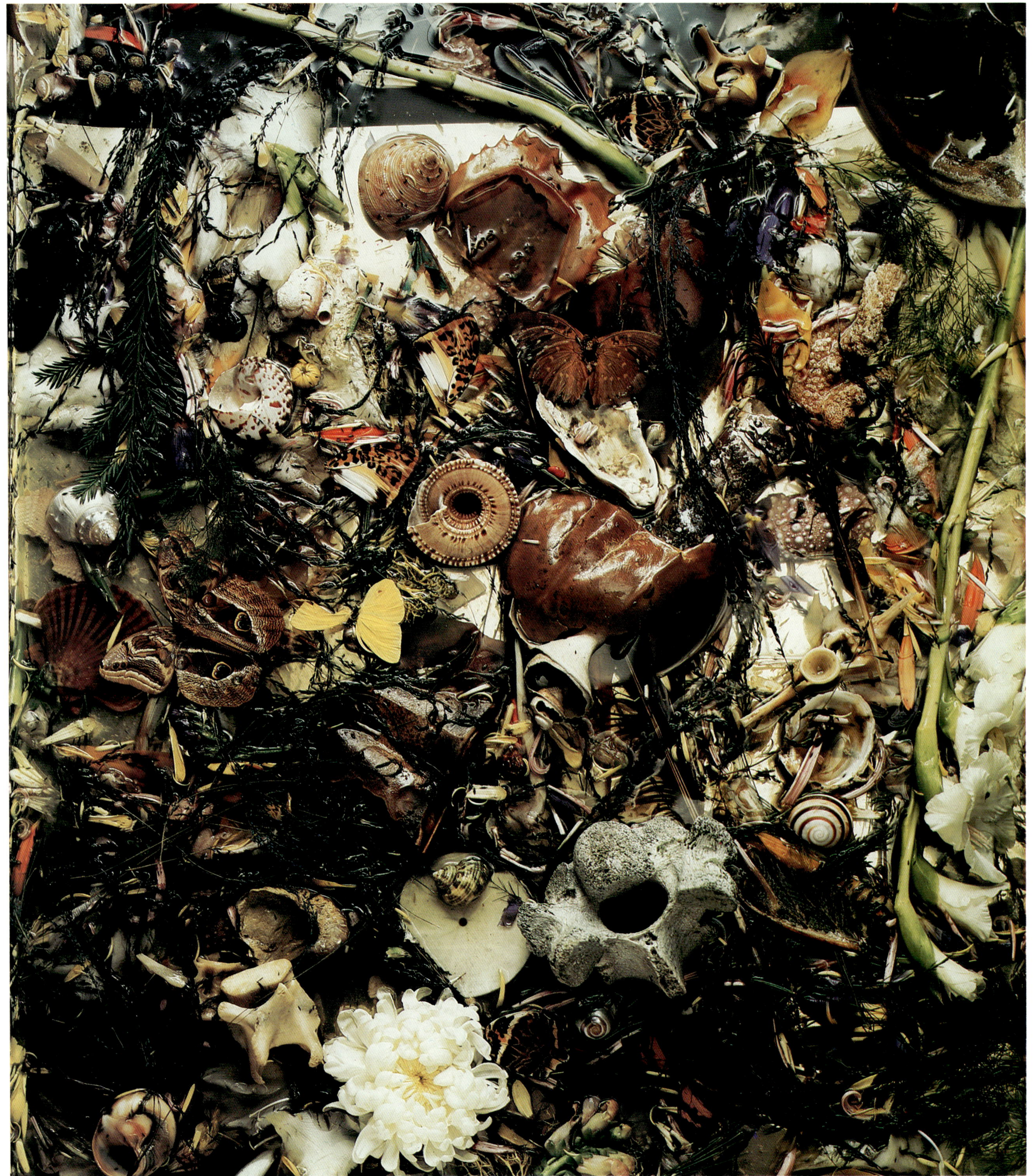

Frank Gillette · Untitled · 1981

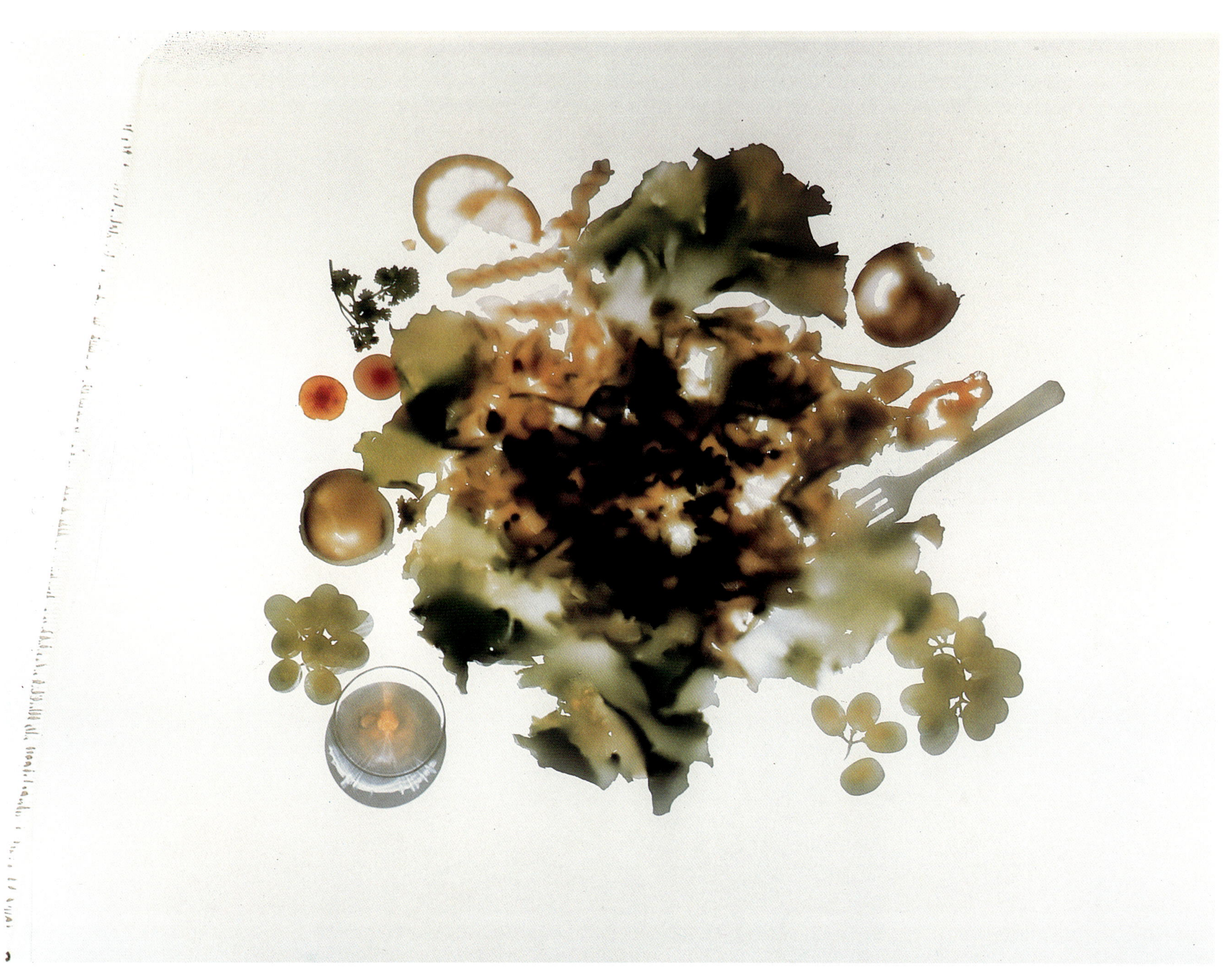

Robert Heinecken · *Pasta Salad (Chopped Olives, Red Pepper, Lettuce, Parsley, Lemon Slices, Grapes, Cherry Tomatoes, Red Wine)* · 1983

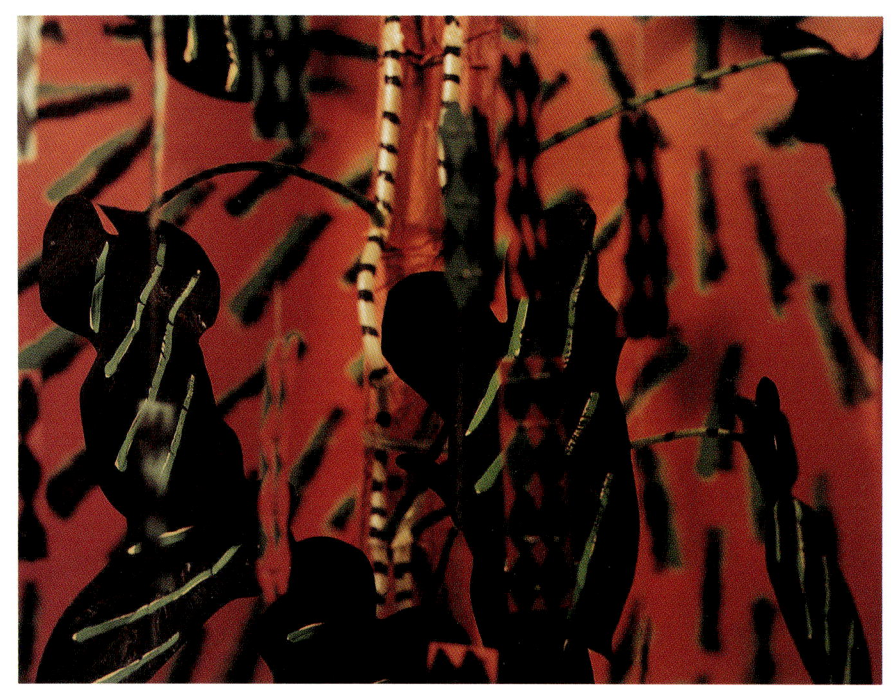

Lawrie Brown · *Black Philodendron* · 1984

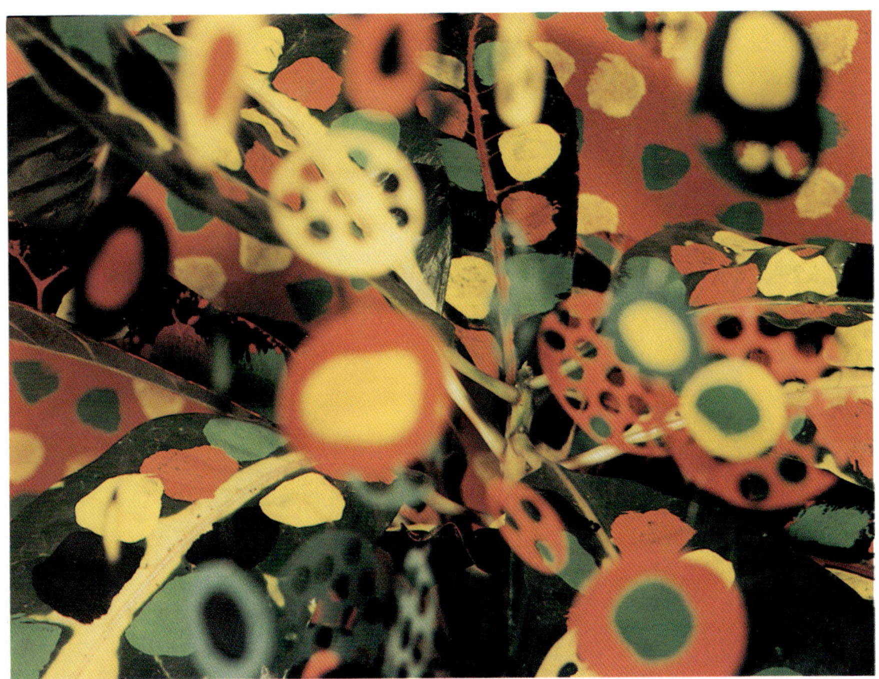

Lawrie Brown · *Spotted Croton Plant* · 1985

ACKNOWLEDGMENTS

The preparation and production of this book involved many people who gave generously of their time and expertise. We wish to thank, first and foremost, the artists who allowed us to include their photographs.

We are grateful to the following executors of estates, museum curators, and gallery administrators who made material available for consideration and reproduction, or offered advice, ideas, and criticism. Mary Alinder, Ansel Adams Trust, Carmel, California; Rondal Partridge, The Imogen Cunningham Trust, Berkeley, California; John Hill, The Estate of Walker Evans, Bethany, Connecticut; Jose Fernandez and Alexander Hollander, Estate of André Kertész, New York; Peter Bunnell, Minor White Archive, Princeton University; James L. Enyeart, Director, Terence Pitts, Curator, and Larry Fong, Registrar, Center for Creative Photography, University of Arizona, Tucson; Jane Livingston, Associate Director, and Frances Fralin, Assistant Curator, Corcoran Gallery of Art, Washington, DC; James Alinder, Friends of Photography, Carmel, California; Weston J. Naef, Curator of Photography, J. Paul Getty Museum, Malibu, California; Anne Hoy, Curator, and Willis Hartshorn, Director of Exhibitions, The International Center of Photography, New York; Kathleen Gauss, Curator of Photography, Los Angeles County Museum of Art; Maria Morris Hambourg, Curator, Department of Prints and Photographs, The Metropolitan Museum of Art, New York; Carroll T. Hartwell, Curator of Photography, Minneapolis Institute of Arts; Clifford Ackley, Curator of Photography, Museum of Fine Arts, Boston; Anne Tucker, Curator of Photography, Museum of Fine Arts, Houston; John Szarkowski, Director, and Susan Kismaric, Associate Curator, Department of Photography, The Museum of Modern Art, New York; William Stapp, Curator of Photographs, The National Portrait Gallery, Washington, DC; Therese Heyman, Curator of Prints and Photography, The Oakland Museum; Van Deren Coke, Curator of Photography, San Francisco Museum of Modern Art; Jeffrey Fraenkel, Fraenkel Gallery, San Francisco; Susan Harder, New York; G. Ray Hawkins, G. Ray Hawkins Gallery, Los Angeles; Peter MacGill, Director, and Amy Brady Legg, Pace/MacGill Gallery, New York; Howard Read, Robert Miller Gallery, New York; Marcuse Pfeifer, Marcuse Pfeifer Gallery, New York; Eun-Mo Griebsch, Sander Gallery, New York; Teresa Schmittroth, Registrar, Holly Solomon Gallery, New York; Brent Sikkema, Vision Gallery, Boston; Joyce Nereaux, John Weber Gallery, New York; and Kathy Ishizuka, Witkin Gallery, New York. Leland Rice, Marvin Heifferman, and Floyd Yearout also offered suggestions about photographers and significant work. Robert Hennessey advised us about duotone negatives with exceptional skill. Original prints were photographed for reproduction by Scott Hyde, Allen Hess, and Jan van Steenwijk.

The book could not have been realized without the contributions of certain people at Polaroid Corporation: Sam Yanes's interest and enthusiasm made this project possible; Eelco Wolf and Barbara Hitchcock supported the book and graciously provided material from the International Polaroid Collection; Linda Benedict-Jones and Nasrin Rohani loaned work from the Polaroid Collection and Polaroid Corporate Archives and furnished technical information.

Essential to the book were Katy Homans's fine design sensibility and her, and Jody Hanson's, tireless attention to detail. Susan Weiley's intelligent, sensitive reading and editing of the text was deeply valued. Lastly, of great benefit were Vicky Wilson's understanding and appreciation; her ideas and suggestions were always helpful.

LIST OF PLATES

Plates are listed according to page numbers. Unless otherwise indicated, photographs were obtained from individual photographers.

16. Ansel Adams, *Poplars, Cemetery near Mount Diablo, California*, 1960. The Metropolitan Museum of Art, gift of Virginia Best Adams and Polaroid Corporation. Courtesy of the Trustees of the Ansel Adams Publishing Rights Trust. All rights reserved. Polaroid PolaPan 4 × 5 Land Film Type 52.

22. Ansel Adams, *The Tetons, Meadow and Fog*, c. 1965. Polaroid Corporate Archives. Courtesy of the Trustees of the Ansel Adams Publishing Rights Trust. All rights reserved. Polaroid PolaPan 4 × 5 Land Film Type 52.

23. Ansel Adams, *Merced River, Winter, Yosemite National Park*, c. 1959. Polaroid Corporate Archives. Courtesy of the Trustees of the Ansel Adams Publishing Rights Trust. All rights reserved. Polaroid PolaPan 4 × 5 Land Film Type 52.

24. Ansel Adams, *Bridal Veil Fall and Cathedral Peaks, Yosemite National Park*, 1968. Polaroid Corporate Archives. Courtesy of the Trustees of the Ansel Adams Publishing Rights Trust. All rights reserved. Polaroid Positive/Negative 4 × 5 Land Film Type 55.

25. Ansel Adams, *El Capitan and Valley View to Half Dome, Yosemite National Park*, 1968. Polaroid Corporate Archives. Courtesy of the Trustees of the Ansel Adams Publishing Rights Trust. All rights reserved. Polaroid Positive/Negative 4 × 5 Land Film Type 55.

26. Ansel Adams, *Arches, Mission San Xavier del Bac, Tucson, Arizona*, 1968. Polaroid Corporate Archives. Courtesy of the Trustees of the Ansel Adams Publishing Rights Trust. All rights reserved. Polaroid PolaPan 4 × 5 Land Film Type 52.

27. Ansel Adams, *New England Barn, Peterborough, New Hampshire*, c. 1960. Polaroid Corporate Archives. Courtesy of the Trustees of the Ansel Adams Publishing Rights Trust. All rights reserved. Polaroid PolaPan 4 × 5 Land Film Type 52.

28. Paul Caponigro, *Detail of Ruined Church, Glendalough, County Wicklow, Ireland*, 1966. Polaroid Positive/Negative 4 × 5 Land Film Type 55.

29. Paul Caponigro, *Monastic Site, Glendalough, County Wicklow, Ireland*, 1966. Polaroid Collection. Polaroid Positive/Negative 4 × 5 Land Film Type 55.

31. Paul Caponigro, *Yosemite Valley, Yosemite National Park*, 1974. Polaroid PolaPan 4 × 5 Land Film Type 52.

32. Paul Caponigro, *Frozen Pond, Coventry, Connecticut*, c. 1962. Polaroid Collection. Polaroid PolaPan 4 × 5 Land Film Type 52.

33. Paul Caponigro, *Tide Pool, Nahant, Massachusetts*, c. 1965. Polaroid Collection. Polaroid PolaPan 4 × 5 Land Film Type 52.

34. Mark Klett, *Longest Day: Last Light of the Solstice, Carefree, Arizona, 6/21/84*. Courtesy of Pace/MacGill Gallery, New York. Silver print from Polaroid Positive/Negative 4 × 5 Land Film Type 55.

35. Mark Klett, *Sandy Fishing the Colorado at High Water, Lee's Ferry, 9/16/83*. Courtesy of Pace/MacGill Gallery, New York. Silver print from Polaroid Positive/Negative 4 × 5 Land Film Type 55.

36. Mark Klett, *Campsite Reached by Boat through Watery Canyons, Lake Powell, 8/20/83*. Courtesy of Pace/MacGill Gallery, New York. Silver print from Polaroid Positive/Negative 4 × 5 Land Film Type 55.

37. Mark Klett, *Linda Photographing the Petrified Forest, Arizona, 6/10/83*. Courtesy of Pace/MacGill Gallery, New York. Silver print from Polaroid Positive/Negative 4 × 5 Land Film Type 55.

38. Emmet Gowin, *Matera, Italy*, 1983. Polaroid Collection. Toned gelatin silver print from Polaroid Positive/Negative 4 × 5 Land Film Type 55.

39. Emmet Gowin, *Matera, Italy*, 1983. Courtesy of Pace/MacGill Gallery, New York. Toned gelatin silver print from Polaroid Positive/Negative 4 × 5 Land Film Type 55.

40. Emmet Gowin, *Pitigliano, Italy*, 1983. Courtesy of Pace/MacGill Gallery, New York. Toned gelatin silver print from Polaroid Positive/Negative 4 × 5 Land Film Type 55.

41. Emmet Gowin, *Matera, Italy*, 1983. Courtesy of Pace/MacGill Gallery, New York. Toned gelatin silver print from Polaroid Positive/Negative 4 × 5 Land Film Type 55.

42. Philip Trager, *Villa Godi*, 1984. Silver print from Polaroid Positive/Negative 4 × 5 Land Film Type 55.

43. Philip Trager, *Villa Godi*, 1984. Silver print from Polaroid Positive/Negative 4 × 5 Land Film Type 55.

44. Philip Trager, *Villa Pojana*, 1984. Silver print from Polaroid Positive/Negative 4 × 5 Land Film Type 55.

45. Philip Trager, *Villa Pojana*, 1984. Silver print from Polaroid Positive/Negative 4 × 5 Land Film Type 55.

46. Walker Evans, Untitled, c. 1973. Courtesy of the Estate of Walker Evans. Polaroid SX-70 Time-Zero Supercolor Film.

46. Walker Evans, Untitled (Connecticut), c. 1973. Courtesy of the Estate of Walker Evans. Polaroid SX-70 Time-Zero Supercolor Film.

47. Walker Evans, Untitled, c. 1973. Courtesy of the Estate of Walker Evans. Polaroid SX-70 Time-Zero Supercolor Film.

47. Walker Evans, *Strand Theater, Old Saybrook, Connecticut*, c. 1973. Courtesy of the Estate of Walker Evans. Polaroid SX-70 Time-Zero Supercolor Film.

48. Jim Dow, *Cervantes Theatre, from the Stage, Buenos Aires*, 1986. Polaroid Polacolor ER 8 × 10 Land Film Type 809.

49. Jim Dow, *The Grand Splendid Theatre, Buenos Aires*, 1986. Polaroid Polacolor ER 8 × 10 Land Film Type 809.

50–51. Danny Lyon, *IGA, Clintondale*, 1986. Collage made from Polaroid High-speed Land Film Type 107 prints.

52–53. Danny Lyon, *Newburg City Library*, 1986. Collage made from Polaroid High-speed Land Film Type 107 prints.

54. Robert Frank, *Mabou Storm, New Year's Day*, 1981. Courtesy of Pace/MacGill Gallery, New York. Silver print from Polaroid Positive/Negative 4 × 5 Land Film Type 55.

55. Robert Frank, *Pour la Fille*, 1980. Courtesy of Pace/MacGill Gallery, New York. Silver print from Polaroid Positive/Negative 4 × 5 Land Film Type 55.

58. Ansel Adams, *Gerry Sharpe, San Francisco, California*, 1960. The Metropolitan Museum of Art, gift of Virginia Best Adams and Polaroid Corporation. Courtesy of the Trustees of the Ansel Adams Publishing Rights Trust. All rights reserved. Polaroid PolaPan 4 × 5 Land Film Type 52.

64. Philippe Halsman, *Edith Sitwell*, 1958. © 1958 Philippe Halsman. Courtesy of the Center for Creative Photography, University of Arizona. The John Wolbarst Collection. Polaroid Coaterless 4 × 5 Instant Sheet Film Type 53.

65. Philippe Halsman, *Randall Jarrell*, 1958. © 1958 Philippe Halsman. Courtesy of the Center for Creative Photography, University of Arizona. The John Wolbarst Collection. Polaroid Coaterless 4 × 5 Instant Sheet Film Type 53.

66. Imogen Cunningham, *Portrait of a Woman*, n.d. Copyright © 1978 The Imogen Cunningham Trust. Polaroid Positive/Negative 4 × 5 Land Film Type 55.

67. Imogen Cunningham, *Portrait of a Woman 2*, n.d. Copyright © 1978 The Imogen Cunningham Trust. Polaroid High-speed 4 × 5 Land Film Type 57.

68. Imogen Cunningham, *Under my Fig Tree*, n.d. Copyright © 1978 The Imogen Cunningham Trust. Polaroid PolaPan 4 × 5 Land Film Type 52.

69. Minor White, [Bill] *LaRue and Tree Root, Cape Meares, Oregon*, 1961. The Art Museum, Princeton University, The Minor White Archive. © 1987 Trustees of Princeton University. Polaroid PolaPan 4 × 5 Land Film Type 52.

70. Paul Caponigro, *Don Harrison, Brewster, New York*, c. 1963. Polaroid Collection. Silver print from Polaroid Positive/Negative 4 × 5 Land Film Type 55.

71. Paul Caponigro, *Italian Boy, North End, Boston, Massachusetts*, c. 1961. Polaroid PolaPan 4 × 5 Land Film Type 52.

72. William Clift, *Wendy, Boston, Massachusetts*, 1956. Polaroid PolaPan Land Film Type 32.

73. William Clift, *Barbara Pearmain, Cape Cod, Massachusetts*, 1967. Polaroid PolaPan 4 × 5 Land Film Type 52.

74. William Clift, *Sandy and Jody, Boston, Massachusetts*, 1962. Polaroid PolaPan 4 × 5 Land Film Type 52.

75. William Clift, *Carola, Santa Fe, New Mexico*, 1987. Polaroid Spectra System Film.

76. Sheila Metzner, *Stella, Mouillé Shapes*, 1986. Fresson print from Polaroid PolaPan CT 35mm Film.

77. Sheila Metzner, *Louie, Mouillé Shapes*, 1986. Fresson print from Polaroid PolaPan CT 35mm Film.

78. Sally Mann, *Virginia in Bed*, 1987. Courtesy of Marcuse Pfeifer Gallery, New York. Polaroid Polacolor ER 8 × 10 Land Film Type 809.

79. Sally Mann, *Jessie's Hands*, 1987. Courtesy of Marcuse Pfeifer Gallery, New York. Polaroid Polacolor ER 8 × 10 Land Film Type 809.

80. Danny Lyon, *Wright's Farm, Ireland Corners*, 1986. Collage made from Polaroid High-speed Land Film Type 107 prints.

81. Danny Lyon, *Gabe*, 1984. Collage made from Polaroid High-speed Land Film Type 107 prints.

82–83. Danny Lyon, *At Addie's Beach*, 1986. Collage made from Polaroid High-speed Land Film Type 107 prints.

84. Jim Bengston, Untitled, Slow Motion Series, 1978. Silver print from Polaroid Positive/Negative Land Film Type 105.

84. Jim Bengston, Untitled, Slow Motion Series, 1977. Silver print from Polaroid Positive/Negative Land Film Type 105.

85. Jim Bengston, Untitled, Slow Motion Series, 1977. Silver print from Polaroid Positive/Negative Land Film Type 105.

85. Jim Bengston, Untitled, Slow Motion Series, 1979. Silver print from Polaroid Positive/Negative Land Film Type 105.

86. Jim Bengston, Untitled, Slow Motion Series, 1977. Silver print from Polaroid Positive/Negative Land Film Type 105.

87. Jim Bengston, Untitled, Slow Motion Series, 1979. Silver print from Polaroid Positive/Negative Land Film Type 105.

88. Judith Black, *Self with Children*, 1984. Silver print from Polaroid Positive/Negative 4 × 5 Land Film Type 55.

89. Judith Black, *Laura and Dylan*, 1984. Silver print from Polaroid Positive/Negative 4 × 5 Land Film Type 55.

90. Michael Spano, *With Lily*, 1986. Silver print from Polaroid Positive/Negative Land Film Type 665.

91. Michael Spano, *Portrait*, 1984. Silver print from Polaroid Positive/Negative Land Film Type 665.

92. Ann Zelle, *Father and Daughter*, 1983. Toned silver print from Polaroid Positive/Negative 4 × 5 Land Film Type 55.

93. Ann Zelle, *Writer*, 1982. Toned silver print from Polaroid Positive/Negative 4 × 5 Land Film Type 55.

94. Joel Meyerowitz, *Dean Rolston*, 1983. Polaroid Polacolor ER 8 × 10 Land Film Type 809.

95. Joel Meyerowitz, *Victoria Brown*, 1983. Polaroid Polacolor ER 8 × 10 Land Film Type 809.

97. Yousuf Karsh, *I.M. Pei*, 1979. © 1979 Karsh, Ottawa. Polaroid Polacolor ER 4 × 5 Land Film Type 59.

98. Arnold Newman, *Joan Miró, Palma, Mallorca*, 1979. © Arnold Newman. Polaroid Polacolor ER 8 × 10 Land Film Type 809.

99. Arnold Newman, *Eugene Richards, New York*, 1977. © Arnold Newman. Polaroid Polacolor ER 8 × 10 Land Film Type 809.

100. Marie Cosindas, *Sailors, Key West*, 1966. Polaroid Polacolor ER 4 × 5 Land Film Type 58.

101. Marie Cosindas, *Boston Ladies*, 1982. Polaroid Polacolor ER 8 × 10 Land Film Type 809.

102. David Hockney, *Double Portrait, One Minute*, 1986. © 1986 David Hockney. Polaroid Polacolor ER 40 × 80 Land Film.

103. David Hockney, *Double Portrait, 125th of a Second*, 1986. © 1986 David Hockney. Polaroid Polacolor ER 40 × 80 Land Film.

104. David Hockney, *Gary and Doug, L.A., March 6, 1982*. © 1982 David Hockney. Collage made from Polaroid SX-70 Time-Zero Supercolor Film.

105. David Hockney, *Stephen Spender, L.A., 9th April 1982*. © 1982 David Hockney. Collage made from Polaroid SX-70 Time-Zero Supercolor Film.

106. Joyce Neimanas, *Untitled #3*, 1980. © 1981 Joyce Neimanas. Courtesy of the Center for Creative Photography, University of Arizona. Collage made from Polaroid SX-70 Time-Zero Supercolor Film.

107. Robert Heinecken, *The Excess-70, Sex-Est, Color/Value Test*, 1978. Polaroid Collection. Collage made from Polaroid SX-70 Time-Zero Supercolor Film.

108. Chuck Close, *Richard A.*, 1975. Courtesy of Pace/MacGill Gallery, New York. Polaroid PolaPan 4 × 5 Land Film Type 52.

109. Chuck Close, *Mark*, 1975. Courtesy of Pace/MacGill Gallery, New York. Polaroid PolaPan 4 × 5 Land Film Type 52.

110. Nancy Hellebrand, Untitled, 1985. Courtesy of Pace/MacGill Gallery, New York. Polaroid PolaPan 4 × 5 Land Film Type 52.

111. Nancy Hellebrand, Untitled, 1985. Courtesy of Pace/MacGill Gallery, New York. Polaroid PolaPan 4 × 5 Land Film Type 52.

112–113. William Wegman, *Foamy, Aftershave* (diptych), 1983. Courtesy of Holly Solomon Gallery, New York. Polaroid Polacolor ER 20 × 24 Land Film.

114. Andy Warhol, *Self-Portrait*, 1979. Polaroid Collection. Courtesy of the Estate of Andy Warhol. Polaroid Polacolor 2 20 × 24 Land Film.

115. Andy Warhol, *Self-Portrait*, 1979. Polaroid Collection. Courtesy of the Estate of Andy Warhol. Polaroid Polacolor 2 20 × 24 Land Film.

116. Lucas Samaras, *Panorama, 11/30/84*. Courtesy of Pace/MacGill Gallery, New York. Collage made from Polaroid Polacolor ER 8 × 10 Land Film Type 809.

117. Lucas Samaras, *Adjustment, 1/13/86*. Courtesy of Pace/MacGill Gallery, New York. Collage made from Polaroid Polacolor ER 8 × 10 Land Film Type 809.

118. Ralph Gibson, Untitled (Piazza Navonna, Rome), 1978. Silver print from Polaroid Positive/Negative Land Film Type 665.

119. Ralph Gibson, Untitled (Piazza Navonna, Rome), 1978. Silver print from Polaroid Positive/Negative Land Film Type 665.

120. John Coplans, *Frances and Donald*, 1984. Silver print from Polaroid Positive/Negative 4 × 5 Land Film Type 55.

121. John Coplans, *Sandy and Dana*, 1983. Silver print from Polaroid Positive/Negative 4 × 5 Land Film Type 55.

122. John Coplans, *Edward and Ella*, 1983. Silver print from Polaroid Positive/Negative 4 × 5 Land Film Type 55.

123. John Coplans, *Rudo and Geoffrey*, 1984. Silver print from Polaroid Positive/Negative 4 × 5 Land Film Type 55.

124. Michael Spano, Untitled, 1985. Silver print from Polaroid Positive/Negative Land Film Type 665.

125. Michael Spano, *Lotto*, 1985. Silver print from Polaroid Positive/Negative Land Film Type 665.

127. Robert Frank, *September 1980, Iona, Cape Breton*. Courtesy of Susan MacGill, New York. Silver print from Polaroid Positive/Negative Land Film Type 665.

128–133. Robert Frank, *Boston, March 20, 1985*. Collection, The Museum of Modern Art, New York. Purchased as the gift of Polaroid Corporation. Polaroid Polacolor ER 20 × 24 Land Film.

135. Robert Frank, *For Sandy and Pablo in Brattleboro, Vermont and the Men and Women—Angels—Horses Everywhere, New York City—Brattleboro*, 1980. Polaroid Collection. Silver print from Polaroid Positive/Negative 4 × 5 Land Film Type 55.

136. Emmet Gowin, *Pitigliano, Italy,* 1983. Courtesy of Pace/MacGill Gallery, New York. Silver print from Polaroid Positive/Negative 4 × 5 Land Film Type 55.

137. Richard Pare, *Woman in Red Crossing Seagram Plaza,* c. 1975. Polaroid SX-70 Time-Zero Supercolor Film.

138. Neal Slavin, *Debutantes of 1983, The Berkeley Hotel, London, 13 September 1983*. Polaroid Polacolor ER 20 × 24 Land Film.

139. Neal Slavin, *The Thomas A Becket Gymnasium, Old Kent Road, London, 24 July 1984*. Polaroid Polacolor ER 20 × 24 Land Film.

140. Mary Ellen Mark, *New York City,* 1986. International Polaroid Collection. Polaroid Spectra System Film.

140. Mary Ellen Mark, *New York City,* 1986. International Polaroid Collection. Polaroid Spectra System Film.

141. Mary Ellen Mark, *New York City,* 1986. International Polaroid Collection. Polaroid Spectra System Film.

141. Mary Ellen Mark, *New York City,* 1986. International Polaroid Collection. Polaroid Spectra System Film.

142. Bill Burke, *Khmer Rouge DK 75 and Crew,* 1984. Silver print from Polaroid Positive/Negative 4 × 5 Land Film Type 55.

143. Bill Burke, *KPNLF Soldier, Lake Ampil, Cambodia,* 1984. Silver print from Polaroid Positive/Negative 4 × 5 Land Film Type 55.

144. Bill Burke, *Kissing Cousins, Mingo County, West Virginia,* 1979. International Polaroid Collection. Silver print from Polaroid Positive/Negative 4 × 5 Land Film Type 55.

145. Bill Burke, *Family, Kermit, West Virginia,* 1979. International Polaroid Collection. Silver print from Polaroid Positive/Negative 4 × 5 Land Film Type 55.

146. Jim Goldberg, *Nursing Home Series, Cambridge, Massachusetts,* 1985–86. Silver print with handwriting from Polaroid Positive/Negative Land Film Type 665.

147. Jim Goldberg, *Nursing Home Series, Cambridge, Massachusetts,* 1985–86. Silver print with handwriting from Polaroid Positive/Negative Land Film Type 665.

150. Michael Spano, *Flower Bed,* 1984. Silver print from Polaroid Positive/Negative Land Film Type 665.

158. Walter Chappell, *Nancy Crocheting, Wingdale, New York,* 1962. Silver print from Polaroid Positive/Negative 4 × 5 Land Film Type 55.

159. Walter Chappell, *Nude Torso between Legs, Wingdale, New York,* 1962. Silver print from Polaroid Positive/Negative 4 × 5 Land Film Type 55.

160. Ann Zelle, Untitled, 1978. Palladium print.

161. Ann Zelle, Untitled, 1978. Palladium print.

162. John O'Reilly, *Shooting Marat,* 1985. Courtesy of Allan Stone Gallery, New York. Collage made from Polaroid High-speed Coaterless Land Film Type 667.

163. John O'Reilly, *Self-Portrait with Model,* 1984. Courtesy of Allan Stone Gallery, New York. Collage made from Polaroid High-speed Coaterless Land Film Type 667 and halftone reproductions.

164. Lucas Samaras, *Photo-transformation, 8/19/76*. Courtesy of Pace/MacGill Gallery, New York. Polaroid SX-70 Time-Zero Supercolor Film.

165. Lucas Samaras, *Photo-transformation, 6/8/76*. Courtesy of Pace/MacGill Gallery, New York. Polaroid SX-70 Time-Zero Supercolor Film.

166. Sandi Fellman, *Endurance,* 1983. Courtesy of Witkin Gallery, New York. Polaroid Polacolor ER 20 × 24 Land Film.

167. Sandi Fellman, *Fire and Water II,* 1984. Courtesy of Witkin Gallery, New York. Polaroid Polacolor ER 20 × 24 Land Film.

168. Robert Mapplethorpe, *Ken Moody,* 1984. International Polaroid Collection. Polaroid Polacolor ER 20 × 24 Land Film.

169. Robert Mapplethorpe, *Ken Moody,* 1984. International Polaroid Collection. Polaroid Polacolor ER 20 × 24 Land Film.

170–171. Chuck Close, *Carter* (triptych), 1984. Courtesy of Pace/MacGill Gallery, New York. Polaroid Polacolor ER 40 × 80 Land Film.

172. Nancy Hellebrand, Untitled, 1985. Courtesy of Pace/MacGill Gallery, New York. Polaroid PolaPan 4 × 5 Land Film Type 52.

172. Nancy Hellebrand, Untitled, 1985. Courtesy of Pace/MacGill Gallery, New York. Polaroid PolaPan 4 × 5 Land Film Type 52.

173. Nancy Hellebrand, Untitled, 1985. Courtesy of Pace/MacGill Gallery, New York. Polaroid PolaPan 4 × 5 Land Film Type 52.

174. John Coplans, *Self-Portrait: Standing Figure, Hand Holding Leg,* 1986. Silver print from Polaroid Positive/Negative 4 × 5 Land Film Type 55.

174. John Coplans, *Self-Portrait: Side Torso Bent with Large Upper Arm II,* 1985. Silver print from Polaroid Positive/Negative 4 × 5 Land Film Type 55.

175. John Coplans, *Self-Portrait: Torso,* 1984. Silver print from Polaroid Positive/Negative 4 × 5 Land Film Type 55.

176–178. Richard Pare, *Belle Bonarius* (triptych), 1987. Belle Bonarius dances with the National Ballet of Holland in Amsterdam. Polaroid Polacolor ER 20 × 24 Land Film.

182. Paul Caponigro, *Fruit Bowl, Stockbridge, Massachusetts,* c. 1967. Polaroid Collection. Polaroid High-speed 4 × 5 Land Film Type 57.

188. William Clift, *Baby's Breath, Cambridge, Massachusetts,* 1971. Polaroid PolaPan 4 × 5 Land Film Type 52.

189. William Clift, *Barbara's Table, Beacon Hill, Boston, Massachusetts,* 1956. Polaroid PolaPan Land Film Type 32.

190. Ansel Adams, *Weathered Oil Drum, Yosemite Valley, California,* c. 1976. Twelfth print in *Portfolio VII*. The Museum of Modern Art, New York, gift of the photographer in honor of David H. McAlpin. Courtesy of the Trustees of the Ansel Adams Publishing Rights Trust. All rights reserved. Polaroid High-speed 4 × 5 Land Film Type 57.

191. Ansel Adams, *Morning Glories, Massachusetts,* 1958. The Metropolitan Museum of Art, gift of Virginia Best Adams and Polaroid Corporation. Courtesy of the Trustees of the Ansel Adams Publishing Rights Trust. All rights reserved. Polaroid PolaPan 4 × 5 Land Film Type 52.

192. Minor White, Untitled, 1976. The Art Museum, Princeton University, The Minor White Archive. © 1987 Trustees of Princeton University. Polaroid SX-70 Time-Zero Supercolor Film.

193. Minor White, Untitled, 1976. The Art Museum, Princeton University, The Minor White Archive. © 1987 Trustees of Princeton University. Polaroid SX-70 Time-Zero Supercolor Film.

195. Minor White, *Peeled Paint, Rochester, New York,* 1959. The Art Museum, Princeton University, The Minor White Archive. © 1987 Trustees of Princeton University. Polaroid PolaPan 4 × 5 Land Film Type 52.

196. Carl Chiarenza, *Menotomy 268* (from diptych), 1982. Silver print from Polaroid Positive/Negative 4 × 5 Land Film Type 55.

197. Carl Chiarenza, *Menotomy 293* (from triptych), 1982. Silver print from Polaroid Positive/Negative 4 × 5 Land Film Type 55.

198. André Kertész, Untitled, 1982. © Estate of André Kertész. Courtesy of the Estate of André Kertész. Polaroid SX-70 Time-Zero Supercolor Film.

199. André Kertész, Untitled, 1979. © Estate of André Kertész. Courtesy of the Estate of André Kertész. Polaroid SX-70 Time-Zero Supercolor Film.

200. André Kertész, Untitled, 1980. © Estate of André Kertész. Courtesy of the Estate of André Kertész. Polaroid SX-70 Time-Zero Supercolor Film.

201. André Kertész, Untitled, 1982. © Estate of André Kertész. Courtesy of the Estate of André Kertész. Polaroid SX-70 Time-Zero Supercolor Film.

202. Marie Cosindas, *Roses, Mexico,* 1966. Polaroid Polacolor ER 4 × 5 Land Film Type 59.

203. Marie Cosindas, *William Powell Still Life,* 1985. Polaroid Polacolor ER 4 × 5 Land Film Type 59.

204. Michael Geiger, *Summer Lotus,* 1982. Polaroid Polacolor ER 8 × 10 Land Film Type 809.

205. Michael Geiger, *Konstructions (Chateau Montrose),* 1984. Polaroid Polacolor ER 8 × 10 Land Film Type 809.

206. Michael Geiger, *Garden Roses (Sterling Silver),* 1986. Polaroid Polacolor ER 8 × 10 Land Film Type 809.

207. Michael Geiger, *Garden Roses with Feather, No. 26*, 1986. Polaroid Polacolor ER 8 × 10 Land Film Type 809.

208. Chris Enos, Untitled, Flower Series, 1980. Polaroid Polacolor ER 8 × 10 Land Film Type 809.

209. Chris Enos, Untitled, Flower Series, 1980. Polaroid Polacolor ER 8 × 10 Land Film Type 809.

210. Lucas Samaras, *Panorama, 11/5/84*. Courtesy of Prudential Insurance Company of America. Collage made from Polaroid Polacolor ER 8 × 10 Land Film Type 809.

211. Lucas Samaras, *Panorama, 11/19/84*. Courtesy of Goldman, Sachs & Co. Collage made from Polaroid Polacolor ER 8 × 10 Land Film Type 809.

212. David Hockney, *Blue & Red Flowers, September 1986*. © 1986 David Hockney. Collage made from Polaroid SX-70 Time-Zero Supercolor Film.

213. David Hockney, *Yellow Guitar, Still Life, L.A., 3rd April 1982*. © 1982 David Hockney. Collage made from Polaroid SX-70 Time-Zero Supercolor Film.

214. Olivia Parker, *Golden Pears*, 1979. Polaroid Polacolor ER 8 × 10 Land Film Type 809.

215. Olivia Parker, *Pomegranates*, 1979. Polaroid Polacolor ER 8 × 10 Land Film Type 809.

216. Olivia Parker, *Lares*, 1984. Polaroid Polacolor ER 8 × 10 Land Film Type 809.

217. Olivia Parker, *The Wolf in the Door*, 1984. Polaroid Polacolor ER 8 × 10 Land Film Type 809.

218–219. Rosamond Purcell, *Landscape Ltd.*, 1984. Polaroid Polacolor ER 20 × 24 Land Film.

220. Rosamond Purcell, *Cebus albifrons*, 1984. Polaroid Polacolor ER 20 × 24 Land Film.

221. Rosamond Purcell, *Monkey/Ear*, 1983. Polaroid Polacolor ER 20 × 24 Land Film.

222. Gwen Akin and Allan Ludwig, *Elk Head Series, #24*, 1987. Courtesy of Susan Harder and Twining Gallery, New York. Platinum palladium print from Polaroid Positive/Negative 4 × 5 Land Film Type 55.

223. Gwen Akin and Allan Ludwig, *Elk Head Series, #18*, 1987. Courtesy of Susan Harder and Twining Gallery, New York. Platinum palladium print from Polaroid Positive/Negative 4 × 5 Land Film Type 55.

225. William Wegman, *Yarn (Chardin)*, 1982. Courtesy of Pace/MacGill Gallery, New York. Polaroid Polacolor ER 20 × 24 Land Film.

226. William Christenberry, *From the Klan Room*, 1978. Polaroid Polacolor 2 8 × 10 Land Film Type 808.

227. William Christenberry, *From the Klan Room*, 1984. Polaroid Black-and-White 20 × 24 Land Film.

228. Barbara Kasten, *Architectural Site 10*, 1986. Courtesy of John Weber Gallery, New York. Polaroid Professional Chrome 4 × 5 Film Type 64T.

229. Barbara Kasten, *Architectural Site 8*, 1986. Courtesy of John Weber Gallery, New York. Polaroid Professional Chrome 4 × 5 Film Type 64T.

230–231. Barbara Kasten, *AP Metaphase 8* (diptych), 1986. Courtesy of John Weber Gallery, New York. Polaroid Polacolor ER 8 × 10 Land Film Type 809.

232. Jan Groover, Untitled, 1986. Polaroid Polacolor ER 4 × 5 Land Film Type 59.

233. Jan Groover, Untitled, 1986. Polaroid Polacolor ER 4 × 5 Land Film Type 59.

234. Jan Groover, Untitled, 1979. Polaroid Polacolor ER 4 × 5 Land Film Type 59.

235. Jan Groover, Untitled, 1979. Polaroid Polacolor ER 4 × 5 Land Film Type 59.

236. Jan Groover, Untitled, 1980. Polaroid Polacolor ER 4 × 5 Land Film Type 59.

237. Jan Groover, Untitled, 1980. Polaroid Polacolor ER 4 × 5 Land Film Type 59.

238. Sheila Metzner, *Mouillé Shapes*, 1986. Fresson print from Polaroid PolaPan CT 35mm Film.

239. Sheila Metzner, *Mouillé Shapes*, 1986. Fresson print from Polaroid PolaPan CT 35mm Film.

240. Grace Knowlton, *Stair Turning*, 1984. Platinum print from Polaroid PolaPan CT 35mm Film.

241. Grace Knowlton, *Adobe Chimney, Cerro Gordo*, 1985. Platinum print from Polaroid PolaPan CT 35mm Film.

242. Victor Schrager, Untitled (Deutsche mark), 1979. Polaroid Polacolor 2 8 × 10 Land Film Type 808.

243. Victor Schrager, Untitled *(The Nude)*, 1978. Collection of Mame Kennedy, New York. Polaroid Polacolor 2 8 × 10 Land Film Type 808.

244. Gyorgy Kepes, Untitled, 1987. International Polaroid Collection. Polaroid Polacolor ER 20 × 24 Land Film.

245. Gyorgy Kepes, Untitled, 1987. International Polaroid Collection. Polaroid Polacolor ER 20 × 24 Land Film.

246. Frank Gillette, Untitled, 1981. International Polaroid Collection. Polaroid Polacolor ER 20 × 24 Land Film.

247. Robert Heinecken, *Pasta Salad (Chopped Olives, Red Pepper, Lettuce, Parsley, Lemon Slices, Grapes, Cherry Tomatoes, Red Wine)*, 1983. Courtesy of the Center for Creative Photography, University of Arizona. Polaroid Polacolor ER 20 × 24 Land Film.

248. Lawrie Brown, *Black Philodendron*, 1984. Polaroid Polacolor ER 4 × 5 Land Film Type 559.

249. Lawrie Brown, *Spotted Croton Plant*, 1985. Polaroid Polacolor ER 4 × 5 Land Film Type 559.